Let Us Python

7th Edition

Yashavant Kanetkar
Aditya Kanetkar

bpb
www.bpbonline.com

Seventh Revised & Updated Edition 2025

FIRST EDITION 2019

ISBN: 978-93-6589-103-4

Distributors:

BPB PUBLICATIONS
20, Ansari Road, Darya Ganj
New Delhi-110002
Ph: 23254990/23254991

DECCAN AGENCIES
4-3-329, Bank Street,
Hyderabad-500195
Ph: 24756967/24756400

MICRO MEDIA
Shop No. 5, Mahendra Chambers,
150 DN Rd. Next to Capital Cinema,
V.T. (C.S.T.) Station, MUMBAI-400 001
Ph: 22078296/22078297

Published by Manish Jain for BPB Publications, 20 Ansari Road, Darya Ganj, New Delhi-110002 and Printed at Akash Press, New Delhi

www.bpbonline.com

Dedicated to

Nalinee & Prabhakar Kanetkar

- Yashavant Kanetkar

Dedicated to Aai

- Aditya Kanetkar

About Yashavant Kanetkar

Through his books and online Quest Video Courses on C, C++, Data Structures, VC++, .NET, etc. Yashavant Kanetkar has created, molded and groomed lacs of IT careers in the last two and half decades. Yashavant's books and online courses have made a significant contribution in creating top-notch IT workforce in India and abroad.

Yashavant's books are globally recognized, and millions of students / professionals have benefited from them. His books have been translated into Hindi, Gujarati, Japanese, Korean and Chinese languages. Many of his books are published in India, USA, Japan, Singapore, Korea and China.

Yashavant is a much sought-after speaker in the IT field and has conducted seminars/workshops at TedEx, IITs, NITs, IIITs and global software companies.

Yashavant has been honored with the prestigious "Distinguished Alumnus Award" by IIT Kanpur for his entrepreneurial, professional and academic excellence. This award was given to top 50 alumni of IIT Kanpur who have made significant contributions towards their profession and betterment of society in the last 50 years.

In recognition of his immense contribution to IT education in India, he has been awarded the "Best .NET Technical Contributor" and "Most Valuable Professional" awards by Microsoft for 5 successive years.

Yashavant holds a BE from VJTI Mumbai and M. Tech. from IIT Kanpur. He can be reached at kanetkar@kicit.com or through http://www.ykanetkar.com.

About Aditya Kanetkar

Aditya Kanetkar is currently working as a Software Engineer at Microsoft India Development Center (IDC), Bengaluru. He has 6 years of experience working in the software development industry. His current passion is anything remotely connected to Python, Machine Learning, Distributed Systems, Cloud Computing, Containers and C#. Formerly, he worked at Microsoft HQ, Redmond, Washington and Oracle HQ, Redwood City, California.

Aditya holds a Bachelor's degree in Computer Science and Engineering from IIT Guwahati and a Master's degree in Computer Science from Georgia Tech, Atlanta.

Preface to Seventh Edition

Programming landscape has changed significantly over the last few years. Python is making inroads into every field that has anything to do with programming. Naturally, Python programming is a skill that one must acquire, the sooner the better.

If you have no programming background and you are learning Python as your first programming language you will find the book very simple to understand. Primary credit of this goes to Python language—it is very simple for the beginner, yet very powerful for the expert who can tap into its power.

If you have some acquaintance with a programming language, you need to get off the ground with Python quickly. To do that you need to understand the similarities/differences in features that you have used in other language(s) and new features that Python offers. In both respects this book should help you immensely. Instead of explaining a feature with verbose text, we have mentioned the key points about it and explained those points with the help of programs.

The most important characteristic of this book is its simplicity—be it the code or the text. You will also notice that very few programming examples in this book are code fragments. We have realized that a program that compiles and runs helps improve one's understanding of a feature a great deal more, than just code snippets.

Exercises are exceptionally useful to complete the reader's understanding of a topic. So, you will find them at the end of each chapter. Please do attempt them. They will really make you battle-ready. If you want solutions to these Exercises, then please refer our book 'Let Us Python Solutions'.

The immense success of first six English, Russian and Chinese editions of 'Let Us Python' has enthused us to pour our best efforts creating this seventh edition. Admittedly, in the previous editions there were a few key places where the topic change was a bit jarring. To address this issue many chapters have been reorganized, split or combined.

To help readers who use Python for learning and practicing Machine Learning, we have added chapters on Numpy, Matplotlib and Pandas libraries too.

In this edition we have also added two brand new chapters on 'Security Programming' and 'Interaction With ChatGPT'. We hope you like the treatment of these important topics.

We have tried to write a Python book that makes reading it as much fun as the language is. Enjoy the book and your journey into the Python world!

Yashavant Kanetkar

Aditya Kanetkar

Brief Contents

Contents

1 Introduction to Python

"Wet your feet..."

Contents

KanNotes

What is Python?

- Python is a high-level programming language created by Guido Van Rossum—fondly known as Benevolent Dictator For Life.
- Python was first released in 1991. Today Python interpreters are available for many Operating Systems including Windows and Linux.
- Python programmers are often called Pythonists or Pythonistas.

Reasons for Popularity

- There are several reasons for Python's popularity. These include:

(a) Free:
  - Python is free to use and distribute and is supported by the community.
  - Python interpreter is available for every major platform.

(b) Software quality:
  - Better than traditional and scripting languages.
  - Readable code, hence reusable and maintainable.
  - Support for advanced reuse mechanisms.

(c) Developer productivity:
  - Much better than statically typed languages.
  - Much smaller code.
  - Less to type, debug and maintain.
  - No lengthy compile and link steps.

(d) Program portability:
  - Python programs run unchanged on most platforms.
  - Python runs on every major platform currently in use.
  - Porting programs to a new platform usually need only cut and paste. This is true even for GUI, DB access, Web programming, OS interfacing, Directory access, etc.

(e) Support libraries:
  - Strong library support from Text pattern matching to networking.
  - Vast collection of third-party libraries.
  - Libraries for Web site construction, Numeric programming, Game development, Machine Learning etc.

(f) Component integration:

- Can invoke C, C++ libraries and Java components.
- Can communicate with frameworks such as COM, .NET.
- Can interact over networks with interfaces like SOAP, XML-RPC, CORBA.
- With appropriate glue code, Python can subclass C++, Java, C#. classes, thereby extending the reach of the program.
- Popularly used for product customization and extension.

(g) Enjoyment:

- Ease of use.
- Built-in toolset.
- Programming becomes pleasure than work.

What sets Python apart?

(a) Powerful:

- Dynamic typing.
- No variable declaration.
- Automatic allocation and Garbage Collection.
- Supports classes, modules and exceptions.
- Permits componentization and reuse.
- Powerful containers - Lists, Dictionaries, Tuples, etc.

(b) Ready-made stuff:

- Support for operations like joining, slicing, sorting, mapping, etc.
- Powerful library.
- Large collection of third-party utilities.

(c) Ease of use:

- Type and run.
- No compile and link steps.
- Interactive programming experience.
- Rapid turnaround.
- Programs are simpler, smaller and more flexible.

Where is Python used?

- Python is used for multiple purposes. These include:

(a) System programming

(b) Building GUI applications

(c) Internet scripting

(d) Component integration

(e) Database programming

(f) Rapid prototyping

(g) Numeric and Scientific programming

(h) Game programming

(i) Robotics programming

Who uses Python today?

- Many organizations use Python for varied purposes. These include:

(a) Google - In web search system

(b) YouTube - Video Sharing service

(c) Bit-torrent - Peer to Peer file sharing system

(d) Intel, HP, Seagate, IBM, Qualcomm - Hardware testing

(e) Pixar, Industrial Light and Magic - Movie animation

(f) JP Morgan, Chase, UBS - Financial market forecasting

(g) NASA, FermiLab - Scientific programming

(h) iRobot - Commercial robot vacuum cleaners

(i) NSA - Cryptographic and Intelligence analysis

(j) IronPort - Email Servers

Programming Paradigms

- Paradigm means organization principle. It is also known as model.
- Programming paradigm/model is a style of building the structure and elements of computer programs.
- There exist many programming models like Functional, Procedural, Object-oriented, Event-driven, etc.
- Many languages facilitate programming in one or more paradigms. For example, Python supports Functional, Procedural, Object-oriented and Event-driven programming models.

- There are situations when Functional programming is the obvious choice, and other situations where Procedural programming is the better choice.
- Paradigms are not meant to be mutually exclusive. A single program may use multiple paradigms.

Functional Programming Model

- Functional programming decomposes a problem into a set of functions. These functions provide the main source of logic in the program.
- Functions take input parameters and produce outputs. Python provides functional programming techniques like lambda, map, reduce and filter. These are discussed in Chapter 15.
- In this model computation is treated as evaluation of mathematical functions. For example, to get factorial value of a number, or n^{th} Fibonacci number we can use the following functions:

```
factorial(n)  = 1                   if n == 0
              = n * factorial(n - 1)   if n > 0

fibo(n) = 0                 if n = 0
        = 1                 if n = 1
        = fibo(n - 2) + fibo(n - 1)     if n > 1
```

- The output value of a function depends only on its arguments, so calling a function with the same value for an argument always produces the same result. As a result, it is a good fit for parallel execution.
- No function can have side effects on other variables (state remains unaltered).
- Functional programming model is often called a 'Declarative' programming paradigm as programming is done with expressions or declarations instead of statements.

Procedural Programming Model

- Procedural programming solves the problem by implementing one statement (a procedure) at a time. Thus, it contains explicit steps that are executed in a specific order.

- It also uses functions, but these are not mathematical functions like the ones used in functional programming. Functional programming focuses on expressions, whereas Procedural programming focuses on statements.
- The statements do not have values and instead modify the state of some conceptual machine.
- Same language expression can result in different values at different times depending on the global state of the executing program. Also, the functions may change a program's state.
- Procedural programming model is often called 'Imperative' programming as it changes state with an explicit sequence of statements.

Object-oriented Programming Model

- This model mimics the real world by creating inside the computer a mini world of objects.
- In a university system, objects can be VC, Professors, Non-teaching staff, students, courses, semesters, examinations, etc.
- Each object has a state (values) and behavior (interface/methods). Objects get state and behavior based on the class from which it created.
- Objects interact with one another by sending messages to each other, i.e., by calling each other's interface methods.

Event-driven Programming Model

- This model is popularly used for programming GUI applications containing elements like windows, check boxes, buttons, combo-boxes, scroll bars, menus, etc.
- When we interact with these elements (like clicking a button or moving the scrollbar or selecting a menu item) events occur and these elements emit messages. There are listener methods which are registered with these GUI elements which react to these events.
- Since there is no guaranteed sequence in which events may occur (based on how we interact with GUI elements), the listeners should be able to handle them in an asynchronous manner.

Exercises

[A] Answer the following:

(a) Mention 5 fields in which Python is popularly used.

(b) Where is event-driven programming popularly used?

(c) Why Python is called portable language?

(d) What is the single most important feature of different programming models discussed in this chapter?

(e) Which of the following is not a feature of Python?

- Static typing
- Dynamic typing
- Run-time error handling through error numbers
- Library support for containers like Lists, Dictionaries, Tuples

(f) Give an example application of each of the following programming models:

- Functional model
- Procedural model
- Object-oriented model
- Event-driven model

[B] State whether the following statements are True or False:

(a) Python is free to use and distribute.

(b) Same Python program can work on different OS - microprocessor combinations.

(c) It is possible to use C++ or Java libraries in a Python program.

(d) In Python type of the variable is decided based on its usage.

(e) Python cannot be used for building GUI applications.

(f) Python supports functional, procedural, object-oriented and event-driven programming models.

(g) GUI applications are based on event-driven programming model.

(h) Functional programming model consists of interaction of multiple objects.

[C] Match the following pairs:

a. Functional programming	1. GUI element-based interaction
b. Event-driven programming	2. Interaction of objects
c. Procedural programming	3. Statements
d. OOP	4. Math-like functions

[D] Fill in the blanks:

(a) Functional programming paradigm is also known as _________ programming model.

(b) Procedural programming paradigm is also known as _________ programming model.

(c) Python was created by _________.

(d) Python programmers are often called _________.

2 Getting Started

"On your mark, set, go..."

Contents

- Python Specification
- Python Installation under Windows
- Python Installation under Linux
- Python Resources
- Third-party Packages
- More Sophisticated Tools
- Compilation Approach in C, C++
- Compilation Approach in Python
- Pros and Cons of Traditional Approach
- Pros and Cons of Modern Approach
- Working with Python
- Python Programming Modes
- Determining Python Version
- Exercises

KanNotes

Python Specification

- Python is a specification for a language that can be implemented in different ways. There are many implementations (often called Python Virtual Machine) of this specification written in different languages.

- Different popular Python implementations are:

  CPython - is the reference implementation, written in C.
  PyPy - Written in a subset of Python language called RPython.
  Jython - Written in Java.
  IronPython - Written in C#.

- All the implementations are compilers as well as interpreters. The compiler converts the Python program into intermediate bytecode. The interpreter then interprets this bytecode.

Python Installation under Windows

- Python has evolved over the years. At the time of writing this edition the latest version for Windows and Linux environments was Python 3.12.6.

- Python is not shipped as part of Windows OS. So, we need to install it separately. For this we need to download the Python installer from www.python.org/downloads/.

- While downloading ensure that you choose the appropriate installer from the following, based on whether you wish to install it on a 32-bit machine or a 64-bit machine:

  64-bit machine: Download Windows x86-64 executable installer
  32-bit machine: Download Windows x86 executable installer

- Once you have chosen and downloaded an installer, execute it by double-clicking on the downloaded file. A dialog shown in Figure 2.1 will appear on the screen.

- In this dialog check the check box 'Add python.exe to PATH' to ensure that Python's executable location will be added to your execution path.

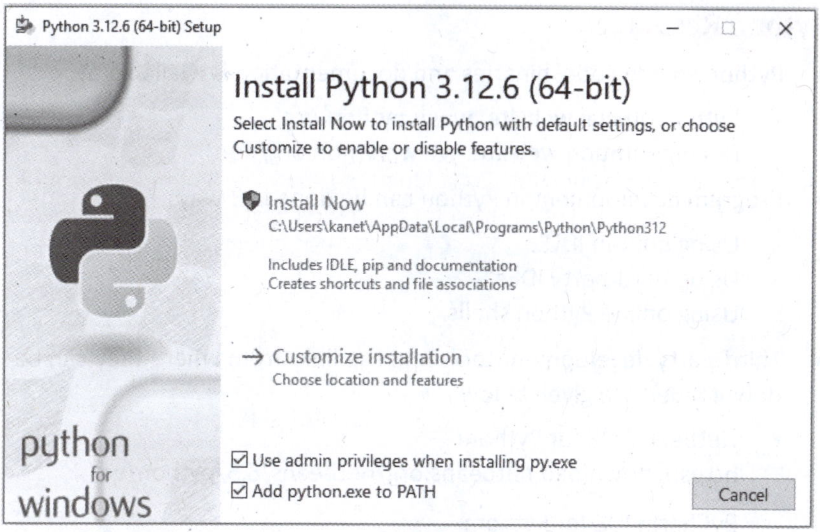

Figure 2.1 Python installation under Windows.

- Click on 'Install Now' and the installation will happen in a few minutes. Python files will get installed in the directory:

  C:\Users\Kanetkar\AppData\Local\Programs\Python\Python312

- In this path 'Kanetkar' will be substituted by your username and 'Python312' by version number of Python installation that you have downloaded and installed.

- If you forget to check the check box, you can add the path mentioned above to PATH variable through Control Panel | System | Environment Variables | Edit. The PATH variable already contains many semicolon-separated values. Append the above path to existing values.

Python Installation under Linux

- Most Linux distributions already contain Python in them. However, the installed Python version may not be the latest one. You can check the version as shown below:

```
$ python3 --version
```

- If you find that the version is not the latest one, then you can install it using the command:

```
$ sudo apt-get install python3.12
```

Python Resources

- Python source code, binaries and documentation is available at:
    - Python official website: www.python.org
    - Documentation website: www.python.org/doc
- Program development in Python can be done in 3 ways:
    - Using built-in IDLE.
    - Using third-party IDEs.
    - Using online Python shells.
- Third-party development tools and the links from where they can be downloaded are given below:
    - NetBeans IDE for Python: https://download.netbeans.org/netbeans/6.5/python/ea/
    - PyCharm IDE for Python: https://www.jetbrains.com/pycharm
    - Visual Studio Code IDE: https://code.visualstudio.com/download
- If you do not wish to install any Python development tool on your machine, then you can use any of the following online Python shells:
    - https://www.python.org/shell/
    - https://ideone.com/
    - https://repl.it/languages/python3

Third-party Packages

- Pythonistas in Python community create packages (libraries) and make them available for use for other programmers. They use PyPI—Python Package Index (www.pypi.org) to distribute their packages. PyPI maintains the list of such third-party Python packages available.
- There are third-party packages available for literally doing everything under the sun. Some packages that are popularly used for creating Data Science applications include:
    - NumPy: Advanced mathematical operations library with support for large multi-dimensional arrays and matrices.
    - SciPy: Scientific computing library for optimization, integration, interpolation, signal processing, image processing, etc.

- Pandas: Library for manipulating numerical tables and time series.
- MatPlotLib: 2D and 3D Data visualization library.
- OpenCV: Open-source Computer Vision library.

- You too can register at PyPI and upload your packages there. You should follow the guidelines given at www.pypi.org to create the package, build it and upload it to the Python Package Index.
- pip is a commonly used tool for installing packages from PyPI. This tool gets installed when you install Python for Windows.

More Sophisticated Tools

- Many tools have come into existence to help Python programmers build and document their Data Science and Artificial Intelligence applications. These include:
  - Jupyter Notebook - It is a very flexible browser-based tool that lets us to interactively work with Python (and many other languages). It lets us put our Python code, output of the code and any kind of visualization or plot etc. in the same document called Notebook. It is a great tool doing modular program development.
  - Google Colab - This tool provides a free Jupyter notebook environment to execute code on Google's cloud servers. As a result, you can leverage the power of Google's hardware.
  - Spyder - This tool provides a **S**cientific **PY**thon **D**evelopment **E**nvi**R**onment with sophisticated testing and debugging features.
- Both Jupyter and Spyder are part of a very popular software distribution called Anaconda. So, once you download and install Anaconda, you get Jupyter and Spyder ready-made.

Compilation Approach in C, C++

- Approach used in compilation and execution method in traditional languages (C, C++) is different as compared to newer languages like (Python, Java, C#).
- These different approaches stem from the goal of achieving speed versus portability (ability of using the same program on multiple platforms).

- A platform is a combination of microprocessor and OS. For example, ARM microprocessor + Android OS, Intel x86 + Windows 10, etc.
- Each microprocessor uses a different instruction set. Each OS performs Input/Output and manages memory in different ways.
- Programs written in C and C++ are converted into machine language using compilers that are targeted for a particular Microprocessor + OS combination.
- The machine language instructions are then executed on a platform for which they are created (refer Figure 2.2).

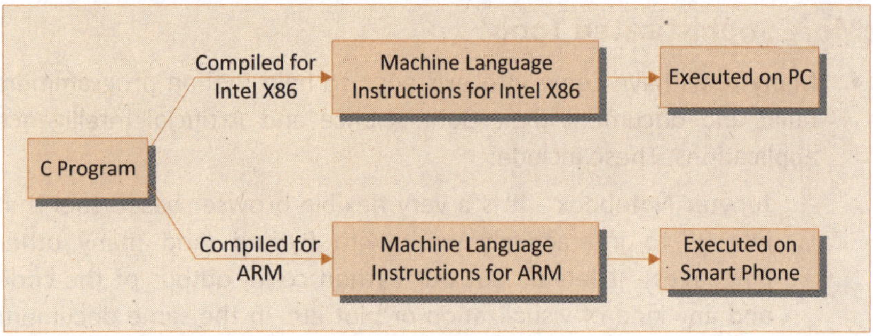

Figure 2.2 Traditional compilation approach.

Compilation Approach in Python

- Modern languages like Python, Java and C# use a different approach for program conversion and execution. Let us understand this approach with reference to Python.
- A Python Virtual Machine (often called PVM or interpreter) is created for each new architecture. This interpreter is installed when we download and install Python.
- A PVM is a software piece that emulates a physical computer. PVM is a stack machine, i.e., it manipulates several stacks to perform its operations (as contrasted with a real register machine, which writes to and reads from specific memory locations).
- Programs written in Python are converted into bytecode instructions by Python compiler. Bytecode instructions remain the same irrespective of the microprocessor + OS combination.
- During execution bytecode instructions are interpreted by the virtual machine (VM) and then executed (refer Figure 2.3).

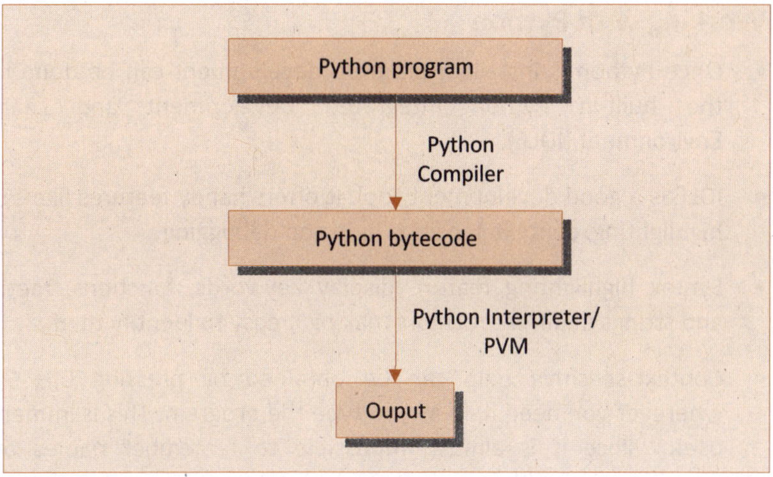

Figure 2.3 Modern compilation approach.

- A major portion of program conversion happens during interpretation stage in Python, it is often considered to be an interpreted language.

Pros and Cons of Traditional Approach

- The traditional approach used by C and C++ has the advantage of producing programs that execute speedily on real machines.
- However, it needs substantial effort to create good compilers for each new platform.
- Also, the executable code created for one platform does not work on another platform. That is why programs created for Windows + x86 do not work on a Linux + ARM platform and vice versa.

Pros and Cons of Modern Approach

- The modern approach used by Python, Java, C# has two distinct advantages:
  - It is much easier to port a VM to a new architecture as compared to writing a conventional compiler for new architecture.
  - The same Python program can work for any architecture for which a PVM is available. That gives Python programs portability.
- The disadvantage of the PVM approach is that it adds an extra layer of software which reduces performance.

Working with Python

- Once Python is installed, program development can be done using the built-in Python Integrated Development and Learning Environment (IDLE).
- IDLE is a good development tool. It offers handy features like syntax highlighting, context-sensitive help and debugging.
- Syntax highlighting feature display keywords, functions, methods and strings in different colors making it easy to identify them.
- Context-sensitive help can be obtained by pressing Ctrl Space wherever you need help as you type the program. This is immensely useful since it is almost impossible to remember names of all functions and methods and their parameters.
- Debugger lets you locate any logical errors that you may have committed in your program by allowing you to trace the flow of execution of the program. This tracing can be done a step at a time by setting up break points and by single stepping through the program. As you do so, IDLE lets you watch the values of different variables as they change during execution. Appendix B shows how to debug a program in IDLE.

Python Programming Modes

- Python can be used in two modes:
    - Interactive mode - used for exploring Python syntax, seeking help and debug short programs.
    - Script mode - used for writing full-fledged Python programs.
- Both modes are supported by IDLE (Python Integrated Development and Learning Environment).
- To use IDLE in Interactive mode:
    - Locate it in Windows by typing IDLE in Windows search bar and hit enter, or double click the IDLE icon.
    - It will open the Python shell window showing >>> Python shell prompt.
    - Execute the following Python code at this prompt.

```
>>> print('Keep calm and bubble on')
```

- It will display the message 'Keep calm and bubble on' followed by the >>> prompt.

- To use IDLE in Script mode:
  - Launch IDLE. In the IDLE shell window from the menu select File | New File. A new window will open. Type the following script in it:

```
print('Those who cannot laugh at themselves...')
print('leave the job to others.')
```

  - Using File | Save save the script under the name 'Test.py'.
  - Execute the script from the Run menu or using F5. The two messages will be printed.

- Instead of IDLE if you decide to use NetBeans or Visual Studio Code for program development then follow the steps given below:
  - Create a new Python project 'Test'.
  - Type the script in Test.py.
  - Execute the script using F6 in NetBeans or Ctrl F5 in Visual Studio Code.
  - On execution it will print the two lines and then you are ready to create another project and another script in it.

Determining Python Version

- Python has evolved over the years. You can determine the version installed on your machine through a simple Python script:

```
import sys
print(sys.version)
```

Exercises

[A] Answer the following questions:

(a) What do the prompts C:\>, $ and >>> signify?

(b) In which two modes can IDLE be used?

(c) What is the purpose of the two programming modes offered by IDLE?

(d) How can third party libraries be used in a Python program?

[B] Match the following pairs:

a. pip	1. Advanced mathematical operations
b. Jupyter	2. Scientific computing
c. Spyder	3. Manipulate numerical tables
d. PyPI	4. Visualization
e. NumPy	5. Computer vision
f. SciPy	6. Package installation tool
g. Pandas	7. Build and document applications
h. MatPlotLib	8. Scientific library
i. OpenCV	9. Python package index

[C] State whether the following statements are True or False:

(a) Python is a specification that can be implemented through languages like Python, C#, Java, etc.

(b) CPython is implementation of Python specification, written in C.

(c) Python program is first compiled into byte code, which is then interpreted.

(d) Most Linux distributions already contain Python.

(e) The Windows system does not contain Python and it needs to be separately installed.

(f) Python programs can be built using IDLE, NetBeans, PyCharm and Visual Studio Code.

(g) Third-party Python packages are distributed using PyPI.

3 Python Basics

"Well begun is half done..."

Contents

KanNotes

Identifiers and Keywords

- Python is a case sensitive language.
- Python identifier is a name used to identify a variable, function, class, module, or other object.
- Rules for creating identifiers:
  - Starts with alphabet or an underscore.
  - Followed by zero or more letters, _ , and digits.
  - keyword cannot be used as identifier.
- All keywords are in lowercase.
- Python has 33 keywords shown in Figure 3.1.

False	continue	from	not
None	def	global	or
True	del	if	pass
and	elif	import	raise
as	else	in	return
assert	except	is	try
break	finally	lambda	while
class	for	nonlocal	with
yield			

Figure 3.1 Python keywords.

- You can print a list of Python keywords through the statements:

```
import keyword            # makes the module 'keyword' available
print(keyword.kwlist)     # syntax modulename.object/function
```

Python Types

- Python supports 3 categories of data types:

  Basic types - int, float, complex, bool, string, bytes
  Container types - list, tuple, set, dict
  User-defined types - class

- Out of these, basic types will be covered in this chapter in detail. Container types will be covered briefly. A separate chapter is dedicated to each container type, where they are covered in detail. User-defined types will not be covered in this chapter. Chapter 18 discusses how to create and use them.

Basic Types

- Examples of different basic types are given below:

```
# int can be expressed in binary, decimal, octal, hexadecimal
# binary starts with 0b/0B, octal with 0o/0O, hex with 0x/0X
0b10111, 156, 0o432, 0x4A3

# float can be expressed in fractional or exponential form
- 314.1528, 3.141528e2, 3.141528E2

# complex contains real and imaginary parts
3 + 2j, 1 + 4J

# bool can take any of the two Boolean values both starting in caps
True, False

# string is an immutable collection of Unicode characters enclosed
# within ' ', " " or """ """.
'Razzmatazz', "Razzmatazz", """Razzmatazz"""

# bytes represent binary data
b'\xa1\xe4\x56'  # represents 3 bytes with hex values a1a456
```

- Type of particular data can be checked using a function called **type( )** as shown below:

```
print(type(35))         # prints <class 'int'>
print(type(3.14))       # prints <class 'float'>
```

Integer and Float Ranges

- **int** can be of any arbitrary size.

```
a = 123
b = 1234567890
c = 123456789012345678901234567890
```

Python has arbitrary precision integers. Hence you can create as big integers as you want. Moreover, arithmetic operations can be performed on integers without worrying about overflow/underflow.

- Floats are represented internally in binary as 64-bit double-precision values, as per the IEEE 754 standard. As per this standard, the maximum value a float can take is approximately 1.8 x 10^{308}. A number greater than this is represented as **inf** (short for infinity).
- Many floats cannot be represented 'exactly' in binary form. So, the internal representation is often an approximation of the actual value.
- The difference between the actual value and the represented value is very small and should not usually cause significant problems.

Variable Type and Assignment

- There is no need to define the type of variable. During execution the type of variable is inferred from the context in which it is being used. Hence Python is called dynamically typed language.

```
a = 25              # type of a is inferred as int
a = 31.4            # type of a is inferred as float
a = 'Hi'            # type of a is inferred as str
```

- Type of a variable can be checked using the built-in function **type( )**.

```
a = 'Jamboree'
print(type(a))      # type will be reported as str
```

- Simple variable assignment:

```
a = 10
pi = 3.14
name = 'Sanjay'
```

- Multiple variable assignment:

```
a = 10 ; pi = 31.4 ; name = 'Sanjay'   # use ; as statement separator
a, pi, name = 10, 3.14, 'Sanjay'
a = b = c = d = 5
```

Arithmetic Operators

- Arithmetic operators: + - * / % // **

```
a = 4 / 2           # performs true division and yields a float 2.0
a = 7 % 2           # % yields remainder 1
```

```
b = 3 ** 4        # ** yields 3 raised to 4 (exponentiation)
c = 4 // 3        # // yields quotient 1 after discarding fractional part
```

- In-place assignment operators offer a good shortcut for arithmetic operations. These include += -= *= /= %= //= **=.

```
a **= 3           # same as a = a ** 3
b %= 10           # same as b = b % 10
```

Operation Nuances

- On performing floor division **a // b**, result is the largest integer which is less than or equal to the quotient. **//** is called floor division operator.

```
print(10 // 3)      # yields 3
print(-10 // 3)     # yields -4
print(10 // -3)     # yields -4
print(-10 // -3)    # yields 3
print(3 // 10)      # yields 0
print(3 // -10)     # yields -1
print(-3 // 10)     # yields -1
print(-3 // -10)    # yields 0
```

In -10 // 3, multiple of 3 which will yield -10 is -3.333, whose floor value is -4.

In 10 // -3, multiple of -3 which will yield 10 is -3.333, whose floor value is -4.

In -10 // -3, multiple of -3 which will yield -10 is 3.333, whose floor value is 3.

- **print( )** is a function which is used for sending output to screen. It can be used in many forms. They are discussed in Chapter 7.

- Operation **a % b** is evaluated as **a - (b * (a // b))**. This can be best understood using the following examples:

```
print(10 % 3)       # yields 1
print(-10 % 3)      # yields 2
print(10 % -3)      # yields -2
print(-10 % -3)     # yields -1
print(3 % 10)       # yields 3
print(3 % -10)      # yields -7
```

```
print(-3 % 10)        # yields 7
print(-3 % -10)       # yields -3
```

Since a % b is evaluated as a - (b * (a // b)),
-10 % 3 is evaluated as -10 - (3 * (-10 // 3)), which yields 2
10 % -3 is evaluated as 10 - (-3 * (10 // -3)), which yields -2
-10 % -3 is evaluated as -10 - (-3 * (-10 // -3)), which yields -1

- Mathematical rule **a / b x c** is same as **a x c / b** holds, but not always.

```
# following expressions give same results
a = 300 / 100 * 250
a = 300 * 250 / 100
```

```
# However, these don't
b = 1e210 / 1e200 * 1e250
b = 1e210 * 1e250 / 1e200      # gives INF
```

- Since True is 1 and False is 0, they can be added.

```
a = True + True         # stores 2
b = True + False        # stores 1
```

Precedence and Associativity

- When multiple operators are used in an arithmetic expression, it is evaluated based on precedence (priority) of the operators used.
- Operators in decreasing order of their priority (PEMDAS):

```
( )                # Parentheses
**                 # Exponentiation
*, /, //, %        # Multiplication, Division
+, -               # Addition, Subtraction
```

- If there is a tie between operators of same precedence, it is settled using associativity of operators.
- Each operator has either left to right associativity or right to left associativity.
- In expression c = a * b / c, * is done before / since arithmetic operators have left to right associativity.

- A complete list of Python operators, their priority and associativity is given in Appendix A.

Conversions

- Mixed mode operations:
  - Operation between **int** and **float** will yield **float**.
  - Operation between **int** and **complex** will yield **complex**.
  - Operation between **float** and **complex** will yield **complex**.

- We can convert one numeric type to another using built-in functions **int( )**, **float( )**, **complex( )** and **bool( )**.

- Type conversions:

```
int(float/numeric string)    # from float/numeric string to int
int(numeric string, base)    # from numeric string to int in base

float(int/numeric string)    # from int/numeric string to float
float(int)                   # from int to float

complex(int/float)  # convert to complex with imaginary part 0
complex(int/float, int/float) # convert to complex

bool(int/float)         # from int/float to True/False (1/0)
str(int/float/bool)     # converts to string
chr(int)                # yields character corresponding to int
```

- **int( )** removes the decimal portion from the quotient, so it always rounds towards zero.

```
int(3.33)       # yields 3
int(-3.33)      # yields -3
```

Built-in Functions

- Python has many built-in functions that are always available in any part of the program. The **print( )** function that we have been using to send output to screen is a built-in function.

- Help about any built-in function is available using **help(function)**.

- Built-in functions that are commonly used with numbers are given below:

```
abs(x)              # returns absolute value of x
pow(x, y)           # returns value of x raised to y
min(x1, x2,...)     # returns smallest argument
```

```
max(x1, x2,...)      # returns largest argument
divmod(x, y)         # returns a pair(x // y, x % y)
round(x [,n])        # returns x rounded to n digits after .
bin(x)               # returns binary equivalent of x
oct(x)               # returns octal equivalent of x
hex(x)               # returns hexadecimal equivalent of x
```

- Following Python program shows how to use some of these built-in functions:

```
a = abs(-3)                  # assigns 3 to a
print(min(10, 20, 30, 40))   # prints 10
print(hex(26))               # prints 1a
```

Built-in Modules

- Apart from built-in functions, Python provides many built-in modules. Each module contains many functions.
- For performing sophisticated mathematical operations, we can use the functions present in built-in modules **math**, **cmath**, **random**, **decimal.**

  math - many useful mathematics functions.
  cmath - functions for performing operations on complex numbers.
  random - functions related to random number generation.
  decimal - functions for performing precise arithmetic operations.

- Mathematical functions in **math** module:

```
pi, e          # values of constants pi and e
sqrt(x)        # square root of x
factorial(x)   # factorial of x
fabs(x)        # absolute value of float x
log(x)         # natural log of x (log to the base e)
log10(x)       # base-10 logarithm of x
exp(x)         # e raised to x
trunc(x)       # truncate to integer
ceil(x)        # smallest integer >= x
floor(x)       # largest integer <= x
modf(x)        # fractional and integer parts of x
```

- **round( )** built-in function can round to a specific number of decimal places, whereas **math** module's library functions **trunc( )**, **ceil( )** and **floor( )** always round to zero decimal places.
- Trigonometric functions in **math** module:

```
degrees(x)     # radians to degrees
radians(x)     # degrees to radians
sin(x)         # sine of x radians
cos(x)         # cosine of x radians
tan(x)         # tan of x radians
sinh(x)        # hyperbolic sine of x
cosh(x)        # hyperbolic cosine of x
tanh(x)        # hyperbolic tan of x
acos(x)        # cos inverse of x, in radians
asin(x)        # sine inverse of x, in radians
atan(x)        # tan inverse of x, in radians
hypot(x, y)    # sqrt(x * x + y * y)
```

- Random number generation functions from **random** module:

```
random( )                  # random number between 0 and 1
randint(start, stop)       # random number in the range
seed( )   # sets current time as seed for random number generation
seed(x)   # sets x as seed for random number generation logic
```

- To use functions defined in a module, we need to import the module using the **import** statement.
- Following Python program shows how to use some of the functions of **math** module and **random** module:

```
import math
import random
print(math.factorial(5))           # prints 120
print(math.degrees(math.pi))       # prints 180.0
print(random.random( ))            # prints 0.8960522546341796
```

- There are many built-in functions and many functions in each built-in module. It is easy to forget the names of the functions. We can get a quick list of them using the following program:

```
import math
print(dir(__builtins__))     # 2 underscores before and after builtins
```

```
print(dir(math))
```

Container Types

- Container types typically refer to multiple values stored together. Examples of different basic types are given below:

  # list is a indexed collection of similar/dissimilar entities
  [10, 20, 30, 20, 30, 40, 50, 10], ['She', 'sold', 10, 'shells"]

  # tuple is an immutable collection
  ('Sanjay', 34, 4500.55), ('Let Us Python', 350, 195.00)

  # set is a collection of unique values
  {10, 20, 30, 40}, {'Sanjay', 34, 45000}

  # dict is a collection of key-value pairs, with unique key enclosed in ' '
  {'ME101' : 'Strength of materials', 'EE101' : 'Electronics'}

- Values in a list and tuple can be accessed using their position in the list or tuple. Values in a set can be accessed using a **for** loop (discussed in Chapter 6). Values in a dictionary can be accessed using a key. This is shown in the following program:

```
lst = [10, 20, 30, 20, 30, 40, 50, 10]
tpl = ('Let Us Python', 350, 195.00)
s = {10, 20, 30, 40}
dct = {'ME101' : 'SOM', 'EE101' : 'Electronics'}
print(lst[0], tpl[2])       # prints 10  195.0
print(dct['ME101'])         # prints SOM
```

Python Type Jargon

- Often the following terms are used while describing Python types:

  Collection - a generic term for container types.

  Iterable - means a collection that can be iterated over using a loop.

  Ordered collection - elements are stored in the same order in which they are inserted. Hence its elements can be accessed using an index, i.e., its position in the collection.

  Unordered collection - elements are not stored in the same order in which they are inserted. So, we cannot predict at which position a particular element is present. So, we cannot access its elements using a position-based index.

Sequence is the generic term for an ordered collection.

Immutable - means unchangeable collection.

Mutable - means changeable collection.

- Let us now see which of these terms apply to types that we have seen so far.

  String - ordered collection, immutable, iterable.
  List - ordered collection, mutable, iterable.
  Tuple - ordered collection, immutable, iterable.
  Set - unordered collection, mutable, iterable.
  Dictionary - unordered collection, mutable, iterable.

Comments and Indentation

- Comments begin with #.

```
# calculate gross salary
gs = bs + da + hra + ca
si = p * n * r / 100     # calculate simple interest
```

- Multi-line comments should be written in a pair of ''' or """.

```
''' Additional program: Calculate bonus to be paid
   URL: https://www.ykanetkar.com
   Author: Yashavant, Date: 18 May 2022 '''
```

- Indentation matters! Do not use it casually. The following code will report an error 'Unexpected indent'.

```
a = 20
    b = 45
```

Multi-lining

- If statements are long, they can be written as multi-lines with each line except the last ending with a \.

```
total = physics + chemistry + maths + \
    english + Marathi + history + \
    geography + civics
```

- Multi-line statements within [ ], { }, or ( ) don't need \.

```
days = [ 'Monday', 'Tuesday', 'Wednesday', Thursday',
         'Friday', 'Saturday', 'Sunday' ]
```

Classes and Objects

- In Python every type is a class. So **int**, **float**, **complex**, **bool**, **str**, **list**, **tuple**, **set**, **dict** are all classes. These are ready-made classes. Python also permits us to create user-defined classes as we would see in Chapter 18.

- An object is created from a class. A class describes two things—the form an object created from it will take and the methods (functions) that can be used to access and manipulate the object.

- From one class multiple objects can be created. When an object is created from a class, it is said that an instance of the class is being created.

- A class has a name, whereas objects are nameless. Since objects do not have names, they are referred to using their addresses in memory.

- All the above statements can be verified through the following program. Refer to Figure 3.2 to understand it better.

```
a = 30
b = 'Good'
print(a, b)                          # prints 3 Good
print(type(a), type(b))              # prints <class 'int'> <class 'str'>
print(id(a), id(b))                  # prints  1356658640  33720000
print(isinstance(a, int), isinstance(b, str))       # prints True True
```

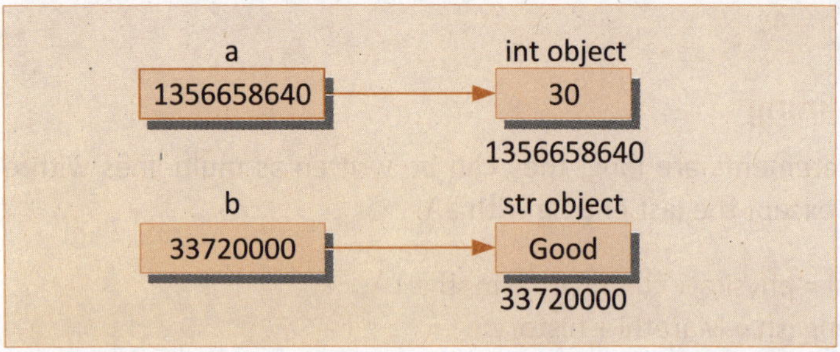

Figure 3.2 Python objects.

- In this program we have created two objects—one from ready-made class **int** and another from ready-made class **str**.
- The object of type **int** contains 30, whereas the object of type **str** contains 'Good'.
- Both objects are nameless. Their addresses in memory are 1356658640 and 33720000 which are stored in **a** and **b**.
- These addresses can be obtained using the built-in function **id( )**. When you execute the program, you may get different addresses.
- Since **a** and **b** contain addresses, they are said to refer to objects present at these addresses. In simpler words they are pointers to objects.
- Types of objects to which **a** and **b** are referring to can be obtained using the built-in function **type( )**.
- Whether **a** refers to an instance of class **int** can be checked using the built-in function **isinstance( )**.

Multiple Objects

- Consider the following program:

```
a = 3
b = 3
print(id(a), id(b))         # prints 1356658640 1356658640
print(a is b)               # prints True
a = 30                      # now a refers to a different object
print(id(a))                # prints 1356659072
```

- Are we creating 2 **int** objects? No. Since the value stored in **int** object is the same, i.e., 3, only 1 **int** object is created. Both **a** and **b** are referring to the same **int** object. That is why **id(a)** and **id(b)** return the same addresses.
- This can also be verified using the **is** operator. It returns True since **a** and **b** both are referring to the same object.
- When we attempt to store a new value in **a**, a new **int** object is created as a different value, 30, is to be stored in it. **a** now starts referring to this new **int** object, whereas **b** continues to refer to **int** object with value 3.

- Instead of saying that **a** is referring to an **int** object containing a value 3, it is often said that **a** is an **int** object, or 3 is assigned to **int** object **a**. Many programmers continue to believe that **a** and **b** are **int** variables, which we now know is not the case.

P</> *Programs*

Problem 3.1

Demonstrate the use of integer types and operators that can be used on them.

Program

```
# use of integer types
print(3 / 4)
print(3 % 4)
print(3 // 4)
print(3 ** 4)

a = 10 ; b = 25 ; c = 15 ; d = 30 ; e = 2 ; f = 3 ; g = 5
w = a + b - c
x = d ** e
y = f % g
print(w, x, y)
h = 99999999999999999
i = 54321
print(h * i)
```

Output

```
0.75
3
0
81
20 900 3
5432099999999999945679
```

Tips

- 3 / 4 does not yield 0.

- Multiple statements in a line should be separated using **;**
- **print(w, x, y)** prints values separated by a space.

Problem 3.2

Demonstrate use of **float**, **complex** and **bool** types and operators that can be used on them.

Program

```
# use of float
i = 3.5
j = 1.2
print(i % j)

# use of complex
a = 1 + 2j
b = 3 *(1 + 2j)
c = a * b
print(a)
print(b)
print(c)
print(a.real)
print(a.imag)
print(a.conjugate( ))

# use of bool
x = True
print(a)
y = 3 > 4
print(x)
print(y)
```

Output

```
1.1
(1+2j)
(3+6j)
(-9+12j)
1.0
2.0
```

```
(1-2j)
(1+2j)
True
False
```

Tips

- % works on floats.
- It is possible to obtain **real** and **imag** part from a complex number.
- On evaluation of a condition, it is replaced by **True** or **False**.

Problem 3.3

Demonstrate how to convert from one number type to another.

Program

```
# convert to int
print(int(3.14))          # from float to int
a = int('485')            # from numeric string to int
b = int('768')            # from numeric string to int
c = a + b
print(c)
print(int('1011', 2))     # convert from binary to decimal int
print(int('341', 8))      # convert from octal to decimal int
print(int('21', 16))      # convert from hex to decimal int

# convert to float
print(float(35))          # from int to float
i = float('4.85')         # from numeric string to float
j = float('7.68')         # from numeric string to float
k = i + j
print(k)

# convert to complex
print(complex(35))         # from int to float
x = complex(4.85, 1.1)  # from numeric string to float
y = complex(7.68, 2.1)  # from numeric string to float
z = x + y
print(z)

# convert to bool
```

```
print(bool(35))
print(bool(1.2))
print(int(True))
print(int(False))
```

Output

```
3
1253
11
225
33
35.0
12.53
(35+0j)
(12.53+3.2j)
True
True
1
0
```

Tips

- It is possible to convert a binary numeric string, octal numeric string or hexadecimal numeric string to equivalent decimal integer. Same cannot be done for a **float**.
- While converting to complex if only one argument is used, imaginary part is considered to be 0.
- Any non-zero number (int or float) is treated as **True**. 0 is treated as **False**.

Problem 3.4

Write a program that makes use of built-in mathematical functions like **abs( )**, **pow( )**, **min( )**, **max( )**, **divmod( )**, **bin( )**, **oct( )**, **hex( )** and **round( )**.

Program

```
# built-in math functions
print(abs(-25))
```

```
print(pow(2, 4))
print(min(10, 20, 30, 40, 50))
print(max(10, 20, 30, 40, 50))
print(divmod(17, 3))
print(bin(64), oct(64), hex(64))
print(round(2.567), round(2.5678, 2))
```

Output

```
25
16
10
50
(5, 2)
0b1000000 0o100 0x40
3 2.57
```

Tips

- **divmod(a, b)** yields a pair **(a // b, a % b)**.
- **bin( ), oct( ), hex( )** return binary, octal and hexadecimal equivalents.
- **round(x)** assumes that rounding-off must be done with 0 places beyond decimal point.

Problem 3.5

Write a program that makes use of functions in the math module.

Program

```
# mathematical functions from math module
import math
x = 1.5357
print(math.pi, math.e)
print(math.sqrt(x))
print(math.factorial(6))
print(math.fabs(x))
print(math.log(x))
print(math.log10(x))
print(math.exp(x))
```

```
print(math.trunc(x))
print(math.floor(x))
print(math.ceil(x))
print(math.trunc(-x))
print(math.floor(-x))
print(math.ceil(-x))
print(math.modf(x))
```

Output

```
3.141592653589793 2.718281828459045
1.2392336341465238
720
1.5357
0.42898630314951025
0.1863063842699079
4.644575595215059
1
1
2
-1
-2
-1
(0.5357000000000001, 1.0)
```

Tips

- **floor( )** rounds down towards negative infinity, **ceil( )** rounds up towards positive infinity, **trunc( )** rounds up or down towards 0.
- **trunc( )** is like **floor( )** for positive numbers.
- **trunc( )** is like **ceil( )** for negative numbers.

Problem 3.6

Write a program that generates float and integer random numbers.

Program

```
# random number operations using random module
import random
```

```
import time
current_time_seconds = int(time.time( ) * 1000)
random.seed(current_time_seconds)
print(random.random( ))
print(random.random( ))
print(random.randint(10, 100))
```

Output

```
0.23796462709189137
0.5442292252959519
57
```

Tips

- It is necessary to import **random** module.
- If we seed the random number generation logic with current time, we get different random numbers on each execution of the program.
- **random.seed( )** with no parameter also seeds the logic with current time.

Problem 3.7

How will you identify which of the following is a string, list, tuple, set or dictionary?

{10, 20, 30.5}
[1, 2, 3.14, 'Nagpur']
{12 : 'Simple', 43 : 'Complicated', 13 : 'Complex'}
"Check it out!"
3 + 2j

Program

```
# determine type of data
print(type({10, 20, 30.5}))
print(type([1, 2, 3.14, 'Nagpur']))
print(type({12 : 'Simple', 43 : 'Complicated', 13 : 'Complex'}))
print(type("Check it out!"))
print(type(3 + 2j))
```

Output

```
<class 'set'>
<class 'list'>
<class 'dict'>
<class 'str'>
<class 'complex'>
```

Tips

- **type( )** is a built-in function which can determine type of any data—built-in, container or user-defined.

Exercises

[A] Answer the following questions:

(a) Write a program that swaps the values of variables **a** and **b**. You are not allowed to use a third variable. You are not allowed to perform arithmetic on **a** and **b**.

(b) Write a program that makes use of trigonometric functions available in math module.

(c) Write a program that generates 5 random numbers in the range 10 to 50. Use a seed value of 6. Make a provision to change this seed value every time you execute the program by associating it with time of execution?

(d) Use **trunc( )**, **floor( )** and **ceil( )** for numbers -2.8, -0.5, 0.2, 1.5 and 2.9 to understand the difference between these functions clearly.

(e) Assume a suitable value for temperature of a city in Fahrenheit degrees. Write a program to convert this temperature into Centigrade degrees and print both temperatures.

(f) Given three sides a, b, and c of a triangle, write a program to obtain and print the values of three angles rounded to the next integer. Use the formulae:

$a^2 = b^2 + c^2 - 2bc \cos A$, $b^2 = a^2 + c^2 - 2ac \cos B$, $c^2 = a^2 + b^2 - 2ab \cos C$

[B] How will you perform the following operations?

(a) Print imaginary part out of 2 + 3j.
(b) Obtain conjugate of 4 + 2j.
(c) Print decimal equivalent of binary '110001110'.
(d) Convert a float value 4.33 into a numeric string.
(e) Obtain integer quotient and remainder while dividing 29 with 5.
(f) Obtain hexadecimal equivalent of decimal 34567.
(g) Round-off 45.6782 to second decimal place.
(h) Obtain 4 from 3.556.
(i) Obtain 17 from 16.7844.
(j) Obtain remainder on dividing 3.45 with 1.22.

[C] Which of the following is invalid variable name and why?

BASICSALARY	_basic	basic-hra	#MEAN
group.	422	pop in 2020	over
timemindovermatter	SINGLE	hELLO	queue.
team'svictory	Plot # 3	2015_DDay	

[D] Evaluate the following expressions:

(a) 2 ** 6 // 8 % 2
(b) 9 ** 2 // 5 - 3
(c) 10 + 6 - 2 % 3 + 7 - 2
(d) 5 % 10 + 10 -23 * 4 // 3
(e) 5 + 5 // 5 - 5 * 5 ** 5 % 5
(f) 7 % 7 + 7 // 7 - 7 * 7

[E] Evaluate the following expressions:

(a) min(2, 6, 8, 5)
(b) bin(46)
(c) round(10.544336, 2)
(d) math.hypot(6, 8)
(e) math.modf(3.1415)

[F] Match the following pairs:

a. complex	1. \
b. Escape special character	2. Container type
c. Tuple	3 Basic type
d. Natural logarithm	4. log( )
e. Common logarithmlog10( )	5. log10( )

4 Strings and Regular Expressions

"Puppeting on strings..."

Contents

- What are Strings?
- Accessing String Elements
- String Properties
- Built-in Functions
- String Methods
- String Conversions
- String Comparisons
- Byte Sequences
- Regular Expressions
- Regex Functionality
- Regex Metacharacters
- Regex Repetition Qualifiers
- Regex Anchors
- Regex Grouping
- Programs
- Exercises

KanNotes

What are Strings?

- Python string is a collection of Unicode characters.
- Python strings can be enclosed in single, double or triple quotes.

  'BlindSpot'
  "BlindSpot"
  ' ' 'BlindSpot' ' '
  """Blindspot"""

- If there are characters like ' " or \ within a string, they can be retained in two ways:

  (a) Escape them by preceding them with a \
  (b) Prepend the string with a 'r' indicating that it is a raw string

```
msg = 'He said, \'Let Us Python.\' '
msg = r'He said, "Let Us Python." '
```

- Multiline strings can be created in 3 ways:
  - All but the last line ends with \
  - Enclosed within """some msg """ or ' ' 'some msg' ' '
  - ('one msg'
    'another msg')

Accessing String Elements

- String elements can be accessed using an index value, starting with 0. Negative index value is allowed. The last character is at index -1. Positive and negative indices are shown in Figure 4.1.

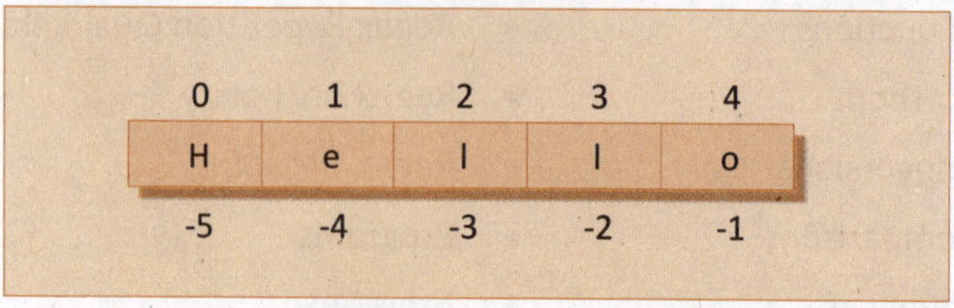

Figure 4.1 Layout of string in memory.

- Examples of positive and negative indexing:

```
msg = 'Hello'
a = msg[0]          # yields H
b = msg[4]          # yields o
c = msg[-0]         # yields H, -0 is same as 0
d = msg[-1]         # yields o
e = msg[-2]         # yields l
f = msg[-5]         # yields H
```

- A sub-string can be sliced out of a string.

  s[start : end] - extract from start to end - 1.
  s[start :] - extract from start to end.
  s[: end] - extract from start to end - 1.
  s[-start :] - extract from -start (included) to end.
  s[: -end] - extract from beginning to -end - 1.

- Using too large an index reports an error but using too large an index while slicing is handled elegantly.

```
msg = 'Rafting'
print(msg[3:100])      # prints elements from 't' up to end of string
print(msg[100])        # error since 100th element doesn't exist
```

String Properties

- Python strings are immutable, they cannot be changed.

```
s = 'Hello'
s[0] = 'M'        # rejected, attempt to mutate string
s = 'Bye'         # s is a variable, it can change
```

- Strings can be concatenated using +.

```
msg3 = ms1 + msg2
```

- Strings can be replicated during printing.

```
print('-' * 50)    # prints 50 dashes
```

- Whether one string is part of another can be found out using **in**.

```
print('e' in 'Hello')       # prints True
print('z' in 'Hello')       # print False
```

```
print('lo' in 'Hello')      # prints True
```

Built-in Functions

- Some built-in functions can be used with a string:

```
msg = 'Surreal'
print(len(msg))          # prints 7 - length of string
print(min(msg))          # prints S - character with min value
print(max(msg))          # prints u - character with max value
```

String Methods

- When we create a string a nameless object of type **str** is created.

```
msg = 'Surreal'
print(type(msg))         # prints <class 'str'>
print(id(msg))           # prints 33720000
```

The address of the nameless **str** object is stored in **msg**. which is returned by the built-in **id( )** function.

- An object of type **str** contains methods using which it can be accessed and modified. These methods can be called using syntax similar to calling a function in a module as shown below:

```
import random
num = random.randint(1, 25)      # syntax  module.function( )
s = 'Hello'
s.upper( )                       # syntax  string.method( )
```

- Different categories of string methods are given below.

  # content test functions
  isalpha( ) - checks if all characters in string are alphabets.
  isdigit( ) - checks if all characters in string are digits.
  isalnum( ) - checks if all characters in string are alphabets or digits.
  islower( ) - checks if all characters in string are lowercase alphabets.
  isupper( ) - checks if all characters in string are uppercase alphabets.
  startswith( ) - checks if string starts with a value.
  endswith( ) - checks if string ends with a value.

  # search and replace
  find( ) - searches for a value, returns its position.
  replace( ) - replace one value with another.

```
# trims whitespace
lstrip( ) - removes whitespace from the left of string including \t.
rstrip( ) - removes whitespace from the right of string including \t.
strip( ) - removes whitespace from left and right

# split and partition
split( ) - split the string at a specified separator string.
partition( ) - partitions string into 3 parts at first occurrence of specified string.

# join - joins string to each element of string1 except last.
s.join(string1)  # joins string s to each element of string1 except last.
```

- The following program shows how to use the string methods:

```
msg = 'Hello'
print(msg.replace('l', 'L'))        # replaces l with L in Hello
print("-".join("Hello"))            # prints H-e-l-l-o
```

String Conversions

- Two types of string conversions are required frequently:
  - Converting the case of characters in string
  - Converting numbers to string and vice versa
- Case conversions can be done using **str** methods:

  upper( ) - converts string to uppercase.
  lower( ) - converts string to lowercase.
  capitalize( ) - converts first character of string to uppercase.
  title( ) - converts first character of each word to uppercase.
  swapcase( ) - swap cases in the string.

```
msg = 'Hello'
print(msg.upper( ))             # prints HELLO
print('Hello'.upper( ))         # prints HELLO
```

- Built-in functions are used for string to number conversions and vice versa:

  str( ) - converts an int, float or complex to string
  int( ) - converts a numeric string to int
  float( ) - converts a numeric string to float
  complex( ) - converts a numeric string to complex

- The built-in function **chr( )** returns a character representing its Unicode value (known as code point). **ord( )** does the reverse.
- The following program shows how to use the conversion functions:

```
age = 25
print('She is ' + str(age) + ' years old')
i = int("34")
f = float("3.14")
c = complex("3+2j")          # "3 + 2j" would be a malformed string
print(ord('A'))              # prints 65
print(chr(65))               # prints A
```

String Comparison

- Two strings can be compared using operators ==, !=, <, >, <=, >=. This is shown in the following program:

```
s1 = "Bombay"
s2 = "bombay"
s3 = "Nagpur"
s4 = "Bombaywala"
s5 = "Bombay"
print(s1 == s2)              # displays False
print(s1 == s5)              # displays True
print(s1 != s3)              # displays True
print(s1 > s5)               # displays False
print(s1 < s2)               # displays True
print(s1 <= s4)              # displays True
```

- String comparison is done in lexicographical order (alphabetical) character by character. Capitals are less than their lowercase counterparts. Result of comparison operation is either True or False.
- Note that there is only one **str** object containing "Bombay", so **s1** and **s5** both contain the same address.

Byte Sequences

- Byte sequences are used to represent binary data. Since 4-bit binary represent one hexadecimal digit, the binary sequence 00000000 00000001 00000001 10000001 in hexadecimal will be 00 01 01 81.

- We can store byte sequence in a variable. When we do so the sequence of bytes is prepended with letter **b**. It is followed by byte value mentioned in hexadecimal sequence of bytes. Since Binary 10000001 in hexadecimal is 81, assignment would look like **a = b'\x81'**.

- The byte sequence can be converted into an **int** using the **from_bytes( )** function as shown below.

```
a = b'\x00\x01\x01\x81'
n1 = int.from_bytes(a, "big")
n2 = int.from_bytes(a, "little")
print(n1)                         # outputs 65921
print(n2)                         # outputs 2164326656
```

- In big-endian form if the byte sequence is ABCD during conversion remains as ABCD. Binary of hexadecimal 00 01 01 81 is 00000000 00000001 00000001 10000001. Decimal equivalent of this binary is 65921.

- In little-endian form if the byte sequence is ABCD during conversion it is reversed to DCBA. So hex and binary sequences would be 81 01 01 00. Its binary form is 10000001 00000001 00000001 00000000. The decimal equivalent of this sequence is 2164326656.

Regular Expressions

- The string methods **find( )** and **index( )** and the membership operator **in** lets us find out whether a string is a substring of another. However, often we need more sophisticated pattern-matching ability. This is facilitated through Regular Expressions (also called REs or regex).

- Regular expressions are often used for validating input. For example, when we fill in a form online, the name, age, email address, mobile number, etc. are matched against acceptable patterns. If the values that we enter conform to these patterns, the input is considered valid.

- For example, a mobile is considered invalid if its length is not 10 and it contains anything else other than digits.

Regex Functionality

- A module called **re** contains many useful functions and methods that help us create and use regular expressions.
- The most commonly used function of **re** module is **search( )**. Its usage is shown below:

```
import re
s = 'Bombaywala'
print(re.search('bay', s))
```

- **re.search( )** scans through the given string, looking for any location where this RE matches. If a match is found, then **re.search( )** returns a **match object**. Otherwise, it returns **None**. In our case since 'bay' is found in 'Bombaywala', so it returns a **match** object.
- The output of the program is **<re.Match object; span = (3, 6), match = 'bay'>**. **span = (3, 6)** indicates the position 'bay' occupies in 'Bombaywala'.

Regex Metacharacters

- A regular expression often contains special characters called metacharacters. These characters are used by Regex matching engine to enhance its search capability.
- Metacharacters used in RE are given below:

```
[]  -  .  ^  \  *  +  ?  {}  |  ()  $
```

- Metacharacters '[ ]' are used to specify a character class, i.e. a set of characters that we wish to match.

```
import re
# match found if first character is h or b followed by owl
print(re.search('[hb]owl', 'howler'))        # returns match
print(re.search('[hb]owl', 'bowler'))        # returns match
print(re.search('[hb]owl', 'cowler'))        # returns None
```

- Metacharacter '-' is used to indicate a range of characters, as in [S-Z] in place of [STUVWXYZ], or [0-9] instead of [0123456789].

```
import re
```

```
# RE for a 6-digit postal index number (PIN)
print(re.search('[0-9][0-9][0-9][0-9][0-9][0-9]', '440010'))  # match
```

- Metacharacter '^' is used to complement a character set.

```
import re
# RE for a string which begins with anything other than a digit
print(re.search('[^0-9]', 'Zebra'))          # returns match
```

- Metacharacter '|' is used to indicate alternation between regular expressions.

```
import re
# RE for a string which starts with alphabet or digit
print(re.search('[a-z|A-Z|0-9]', 'Zebra'))    # returns match
print(re.search('[a-z|A-Z|0-9]', 'zebra'))    # returns match
print(re.search('[a-z|A-Z|0-9]', '9ebra'))    # returns match
```

- Metacharacter '\' is used to escape a metacharacter of its special meaning.

```
import re
# RE for a string in which first character is either an alphabet or $
print(re.search('[a-z\$]', '$25.48'))         # returns match
```

- Metacharacter '\' is also used to introduce a special character class like a set of digits, set of alphabets or set of whitespaces. The meaning of special character class is given below:

  \d - any decimal digit. Same as [0-9]
  \D - any non-digit character. Same as [^0-9]
  \s - any whitespace character. Same as [\t\n\r]
  \S - any non-whitespace character. Same as [^ \t\n\r]
  \w - any alphanumeric character. Same as [a-zA-Z0-9_]
  \W - any non-alphanumeric character. Same as [^a-zA-Z0-9_]

```
import re
print(re.search('\W', '__main__'))             # returns None
print(re.serach([\s,.], ' TRUE '))             # returns match
```

- The '.' metacharacter matches anything except a newline. It is used where you wish to match any character.

```
import re
print(re.search('[A.Z]', 'ANZ'))                  # returns match
print(re.search('[..Z]', 'A3Z'))                  # returns match
```

Regex Repetition Qualifiers

- It is possible to repeat either a portion or a full regex pattern. The metacharacters to do so are '*', '+', '?' and '{ }'.
- **'*'** is used to specify that the character before it can be repeated zero or more times.
- **'+'** is used to specify that the character before it can be repeated one or more times.
- **'?'** is used to specify that the character before it can be repeated zero or one time.
- **'{m}'** specifies that exactly **m** copies of the previous RE should be matched.
- **'{m,n}'** causes the resulting RE to match from **m** to **n** repetitions of the preceding RE.

```
import re
# RE for words connected with 1 or more dashes
print(re.search('\d-+\d', '444--555'))              # returns match
# RE for any number of alphanumeric characters before @gmail.com
print(re.search('\w*@gmail.com', 'abc@gmail.com'))  # match
# RE for a 6 digit pin
print(re.search('[0-9]{6}', '440010'))              # returns match
# RE for 6 alphanumeric characters
print(re.search('[\w]{6}', 'Nagpur'))               # returns match
# RE for 6 to 8 alphanumeric characters
print(re.search('[\w]{6,8}', 'Nagpur10'))           # returns match
```

- Note the special cases of {m, n} qualifier:

  {,n} - m is assumed to be 0.
  {m,} - n is considered to be >= m.
  {,} - is treated as {0,}

Regex Anchors

- Anchors are used to specify the location in the search string where a match must occur.
- Anchor '^' indicates that the match must be found at the beginning of the string, whereas '$' specifies that the match must be anchored at the end of the string.

```
import re
# use of anchor ^
print(re.search('^Ram', 'Ramrod'))              # returns match
print(re.search('^Ram', 'Memory - Ram'))        # returns None
# use of anchor $
print(re.search('pur$', 'Jabalpur'))            # returns match
print(re.search('pur$', 'puri'))                # returns None
```

Regex Grouping

- '( )' are used to represent a subexpression or group.

```
import re
# RE for word containing 'fun' followed by a 'c' or 'd'
print(re.search('(fun[cd])', 'function'))              # returns match

# RE for word containing 1 or more occurrences of 'fun' followed by
# 'C' or 'd'
print(re.search('(fun[cd])+', 'function'))             # returns match

# RE for word containing 'fun' followed by 1 to 3 occurrences of 'c'
followed by 'on'
print(re.search('(fun[c]){1,3}(on)?', 'function'))     # returns match
```

Programs

Problem 4.1

Demonstrate how to create simple and multi-line strings and whether a string can change after creation. Also show the usage of built-in functions **len( )**, **min( )** and **max( )** on a string.

Program

```
# simple strings
msg1 = 'Hoopla'
print(msg1)
# strings with special characters
msg2 = 'He said, \'Let Us Python\'.'
file1 = 'C:\\temp\\newfile'
file2 = r'C:\temp\newfile'   # raw string - prepend r
print(msg2)
print(file1)
print(file2)

# multiline strings
# whitespace at beginning of second line becomes part of string
msg3 = 'What is this life if full of care...\
      We have no time to stand and stare'
# enter at the end of first line becomes part of string
msg4 = """What is this life if full of care...
We have no time to stand and stare"""
# strings are concatenated properly. ( ) necessary
msg5 = ('What is this life if full of care...'
      'We have no time to stand and stare')
print(msg3)
print(msg4)
print(msg5)

# string replication during printing
msg6 = 'MacLearn!!'
print(msg1 * 3)

# immutability of strings
# Utopia cannot change, msg7 can
msg7 = 'Utopia'
msg8 = 'Today!!!'
msg7 = msg7 + msg8    # concatenation using +
print(msg7)

# use of built-in functions on strings
print(len('Hoopla'))
print(min('Hoopla'))
```

```
print(max('Hoopla'))
```

Output

```
Hoopla
He said, 'Let Us Python'.
C:\temp\newfile
C:\temp\newfile
What is this life if full of care...        We have no time to stand and stare
What is this life if full of care...
We have no time to stand and stare
What is this life if full of care...We have no time to stand and stare
HooplaHooplaHoopla
UtopiaToday!!!
6
H
p
```

Tips

- Special characters can be retained in a string by either escaping them or by marking the string as a raw string.
- Strings cannot change, but the variables that store them can.
- **len( )** returns the number of characters present in string. **min( )** and **max( )** return the character with minimum and maximum Unicode value from the string.

Problem 4.2

For a given string 'Bamboozled', write a program to obtain the following output:

```
B a
e d
e d
mboozled
mboozled
mboozled
Bamboo
Bamboo
```

Bamboo
Bamboo
delzoobmaB
Bamboozled
Bmoze
Bbzd
Boe
BamboozledHype!
BambooMonger!

Use multiple ways to get any of the above outputs.

Program

```
s = 'Bamboozled'
# extract B a
print(s[0], s[1])
print(s[-10], s[-9])
# extract e d
print(s[8], s[9])
print(s[-2], s[-1])

# extract mboozled
print(s[2:10])
print(s[2:])
print(s[-8:])

# extract Bamboo
print(s[0:6])
print(s[:6])
print(s[-10:-4])
print(s[:-4])

# reverse Bamboozled
print([::-1])


print(s[0:10:1])
print(s[0:10:2])
print(s[0:10:3])
print(s[0:10:4])

s = s + 'Hype!'
```

```
print(s)
s = s[:6] + 'Monger' + s[-1]
print(s)
```

Tips

- Special characters can be retained in a string by either escaping them or by marking the string as a raw string.
- s[4:8] is same as s[4:8:1], where 1 is the default.
- s[4:8:2] returns a character, then move forward 2 positions, etc.

Problem 4.3

For the following strings find out which are having only alphabets, which are numeric, which are alphanumeric, which are lowercase, which are uppercase. Also find out whether 'And Quiet Flows The Don' begins with 'And' or ends with 'And' :

'NitiAayog'
'And Quiet Flows The Don'
'1234567890'
'Make $1000 a day'

Program

```
s1 = 'NitiAayog'
s2 = 'And Quiet Flows The Don'
s3 = '1234567890'
s4 = 'Make $1000 a day'
print('s1 = ', s1)
print('s2 = ', s2)
print('s3 = ', s3)
print('s4 = ', s4)

# Content test functions
print('check isalpha on s1, s2')
print(s1.isalpha( ))
print(s2.isalpha( ))

print('check isdigit on s3, s4')
print(s3.isdigit( ))
```

```
print(s4.isdigit( ))

print('check isalnum on s1, s2, s3, s4')
print(s1.isalnum( ))
print(s2.isalnum( ))
print(s3.isalnum( ))
print(s4.isalnum( ))

print('check islower on s1, s2')
print(s1.islower( ))
print(s2.islower( ))

print('check isupper on s1, s2')
print(s1.isupper( ))
print(s2.isupper( ))

print('check startswith and endswith on s2')
print(s2.startswith('And'))
print(s2.endswith('And'))
```

Output

```
s1 =  NitiAayog
s2 =  And Quiet Flows The Don
s3 =  1234567890
s4 =  Make $1000 a day
check isalpha on s1, s2
True
False
check isdigit on s3, s4
True
False
check isalnum on s1, s2, s3, s4
True
False
True
False
check islower on s1, s2
False
False
check isupper on s1, s2
```

```
False
False
check startswith and endswith on s2
True
False
```

Problem 4.4

Given the following strings:

'Bring It On'
'   Flanked by spaces on either side   '
'C:\\Users\\Kanetkar\\Documents'

write a program to produce the following output using appropriate string functions.

```
BRING IT ON
bring it on
Bring it on
Bring It On
bRING iT oN
6
9
Bring Him On
Flanked by spaces on either side
    Flanked by spaces on either side
['C:', 'Users', 'Kanetkar', 'Documents']
('C:', '\\', 'Users\\Kanetkar\\Documents')
```

Program

```
s1 = 'Bring It On'
# Conversions
print(s1.upper( ))
print(s1.lower( ))
print(s1.capitalize( ))
print(s1.title( ))
print(s1.swapcase( ))

# search and replace
print(s1.find('I'))
```

```
print(s1.find('On'))
print(s1.replace('It', 'Him'))

# trimming
s2 = '   Flanked by spaces on either side   '
print(s2.lstrip( ))
print(s2.rstrip( ))

# splitting
s3 = 'C:\\Users\\Kanetkar\\Documents'
print(s3.split('\\'))
print(s3.partition('\\'))
```

Problem 4.5

Find all occurrences of 'T' in the string 'The Terrible Tiger Tore The Towel'. Replace all occurrences of 'T' with 't'.

Program

```
s = 'The Terrible Tiger Tore The Towel'
pos = s.find('T', 0)
print(pos, s[pos])
pos = s.find('T', pos + 1)
print(pos, s[pos])
pos = s.find('T', pos + 1)
print(pos, s[pos])
pos = s.find('T', pos + 1)
print(pos, s[pos])
pos = s.find('T', pos + 1)
print(pos, s[pos])
pos = s.find('T', pos + 1)
print(pos, s[pos])
pos = s.find('T', pos + 1)
print(pos)
c = s.count('T')
s = s.replace('T', 't', c)
print(s)
```

Output

```
0 T
4 T
13 T
19 T
24 T
28 T
-1
the terrible tiger tore the towel
```

Tips

- First call to **search( )** returns the position where first 'T' is found. To search subsequent 'T' search is started from **pos + 1**.
- When 'T' is not found **search( )** returns -1.
- **count( )** returns the number of occurrences of 'T' in the string.
- Third parameter in the call to **replace( )** indicates number of replacements to be done.

Exercises

[A] Answer the following questions:

(a) Write a program that generates the following output from the string 'Shenanigan'.

```
S h
a n
enanigan
Shenan
Shenan
Shenan
Shenan
Shenanigan
Seaia
Snin
Saa
ShenaniganType
```

ShenanWabbite

(b) Write a program to convert the following string

'Visit ykanetkar.com for online courses in programming'

into

'Visit Ykanetkar.com For Online Courses In Programming'

(c) Write a program to convert the following string

'Light travels faster than sound. This is why some people appear bright until you hear them speak.'

into

'LIGHT travels faster than SOUND. This is why some people appear bright until you hear them speak.'

(d) What will be the output of the following program?

```
s = 'HumptyDumpty'
print('s = ', s)
print(s.isalpha( ))
print(s.isdigit( ))
print(s.isalnum( ))
print(s.islower( ))
print(s.isupper( ))
print(s.startswith('Hump'))
print(s.endswith('Dump'))
```

(e) What is the purpose of a raw string?

(f) If we wish to work with an individual word in the following string, how will you separate them out:

'The difference between stupidity and genius is that genius has its limits'

(g) Mention two ways to store a string: He said, "Let Us Python".

(h) What will be the output of the following code snippet?

```
print(id('Imaginary'))?
print(type('Imaginary'))?
```

(i) What will be the output of the following code snippet?

```
s3 = 'C:\\Users\\Kanetkar\\Documents'
print(s3.split('\\'))
print(s3.partition('\\'))
```

(j) Strings in Python are iterable, sliceable and immutable. (True/False)

(k) How will you extract ' TraPoete' from the string 'ThreadProperties'?

(l) How will you eliminate spaces on either side of the string '   Flanked by spaces on either side   '?

(m) What will be the output of the following code snippet?

```
s1 = s2 = s3 = "Hello"
print(id(s1), id(s2), id(s3))
```

(n) What will get stored in **ch in** the following code snippet:

```
msg = 'Aeroplane'
ch = msg[-0]
```

[B] Match the following pairs assuming msg = 'Keep yourself warm'

a. msg.partition(' ')	1. 18
b. msg.split(' ')	2. kEEP YOURSELF WARM
c. msg.startswith('Keep')	3. Keep yourself warm
d. msg.endswith('Keep')	4. 3
e. msg.swapcase( )	5. True
f. msg.capitalize( )	6. False
g. msg.count('e')	7. ['Keep', 'yourself', 'warm']
h. len(msg)	8. ('Keep', ' ', 'yourself warm')
i. msg[0]	9. Keep yourself w
j. msg[-1]	10. keep yourself wa
k. msg[1:1:1]	11. K
l. msg[-1:3]	12. empty string
m. msg[:-3]	13. m
n. msg[-3:]	14. arm
o. msg[0:-2]	15. empty string

[C] Give an example string which will return a match for the following regular expressions:

```
\w+
\d{2}
\w{1,}
```

```
\w{2,4}
A*B
\d+?
```

5 Decision Control Instruction

"Indecision cost > Wrong decision cost"

Contents

KanNotes

- So far statements in all our programs got executed sequentially or one after the other.
- Sequence of execution of instructions in a program can be altered using:
  (a) Decision control instruction
  (b) Repetition control instruction

Decision Control Instruction

- Three ways for taking decisions in a program:

```
if condition :
    statement1
    statement2
```

```
if condition :
    statement1
    statement2
else :
    statement3
    statement4
```

```
if condition1 :
    statement1
    statement2
elif condition2 :
    statement3
elif condition3 :
    statement4
else :
    statement5
```

- The colon (:) after **if, else, elif** is compulsory.
- Statements in **if** block, **else**, block, **elif** block must be indented. Indented statements are treated as a block of statements.
- Indentation is used to group statements. Use either 4 spaces or a tab for indentation. Do not mix tabs and spaces. They may appear ok on screen, but would be reported as error.
- In the first form shown above **else** and **elif** are optional.
- In the second form shown above, if condition is True all statements in **if** block get executed. If condition is False then statements in **else** block get executed.
- In the third form shown above, if a condition fails, then condition in the following **elif** block is checked. The **else** block goes to work if all conditions fail.

- **if-else** statements can be nested. Nesting can be as deep as the program logic demands.

Nuances of Conditions

- Condition is built using relation operators <, >, <=, >=, ==, !=.

```
10 < 20                # yields True
'Santosh' < 'Adi'      # yields False, alphabetical order is checked
'gang' < 'God'         # yields False, lowercase is > uppercase
```

- **a = b** is assignment, **a == b** is comparison.

- Ranges or multiple equalities can be checked more naturally.

```
if a < b < c           # checks whether b falls between a and c
if a == b == c         # checks whether all three are equal
if 10 != 20 != 10      # evaluates to True, even though 10 != 10 is False
```

- Any non-zero number (positive, negative, integer, float) is treated as True, and 0 as False.

```
print(bool(3.14))      # prints True
print(bool(25))        # prints True
print(bool(0))         # prints False
```

Logical Operators

- More complex decision making can be made using logical operators **and**, **or** and **not**.

- Conditions can be combined using **and** and **or** as shown below:

  cond1 and cond2 - returns True if both are True, otherwise False
  cond1 or cond2 - returns True if one of them is True, otherwise False

- Strictly speaking, we need not always combine only conditions with **and/or**. We can use any valid expression in place of conditions. Hence when used with expressions we may not get True/False.

- **and** operator evaluates ALL expressions. It returns last expression if all expressions evaluate to True. Otherwise, it returns first value that evaluates to False.

```
a = 40
b = 30
x = 75 and a >= 20 and b < 60 and 35        # assigns 35 to x
```

```
y = -30 and a >= 20 and b < 15 and 35      # assigns False to y
z = -30 and a >= 20 and 0 and 35           # assigns 0 to z
```

- **or** operator evaluates ALL expressions and returns the first value that evaluates to True. Otherwise, it returns the last value that evaluates to False.

```
a = 40
b = 30
x = 75 or a >= 20 or 60        # assigns 75 to x
y = a >= 20 or 75 or 60        # assigns True to y
z = a < 20 or 0 or 35          # assigns 35 to z
```

- Condition's result can be negated using **not**.

```
a = 10
b = 20
not (a <= b)        # yields False. Same as a > b
not (a >= b)        # yields True. Same as a < b
```

- Shortcut for toggling values between 1 and 0:

```
a = int(input('Enter 0 or 1'))
a = int(not a)          # set a to 0 if it is 1, and set it to 1 if it is 0
```

- **a = not b** does not change value of **b**.
- If an operator needs only 1 operand it is known as a Unary operator. If it needs two, then it is a binary operator.

  not - needs only 1 operand, so unary operator

  +, -, <, >, and, or, etc. - need 2 operands, so binary operators

Conditional Expressions

- Python supports one additional decision-making entity called a conditional expression.

  <expr1> if <conditional expression> else <expr2>

  <conditional expression> is evaluated first. If it is true, the expression evaluates to <expr1>. If it is false, the expression evaluates to <expr2>.

- Examples of condition expressions:

```
age = 15
status = 'minor' if age < 18 else 'adult'       # sets minor
sunny = False
print('Let's go to the', 'beach' if sunny else 'room')
humidity = 76.8
setting = 25 if humidity > 75 else 28           # sets 25
```

- Conditional expressions can be nested.

```
# assigns Prim
wt = 55
msg = 'Obese' if wt > 85 else 'Hefty' if wt > 60 else 'Prim'
```

all( ) and any( )

- Instead of using the **and** and **or** logical operators, we can use the built-in functions **all( )** and **any( )** to get the same effect. Their usage is shown in the following program:

```
a, b, c = 10, 20, 30
res = all((a > 5, b > 20, c > 15))
print(res)       # prints False, as second condition is False
res = any((a > 5, b > 20, c > 15))
print(res)       # prints True since one of the conditions is True
```

- Note that **all( )** and **any( )** both receive a single parameter of the type string, list, tuple, set or dictionary. We have passed a tuple of 3 conditions to them. If argument is a dictionary, it is checked whether the keys are true or not.

- **any( )** function returns True if at least one element of its parameter is True. **all( )** function returns True if all elements of its parameter are True.

Receiving Input

- The way **print( )** function is used to output values on screen, **input( )** built-in function can be used to receive input values from keyboard.

- **input( )** function returns a string, i.e. if 23 is entered it returns '23'. So, if we wish to perform arithmetic on the number entered, we need to convert the string into int or float as shown below.

```
name = input('Enter your name: ')
age = int(input('Enter your age: '))
salary = float(input('Enter your salary: '))
print(name, age, salary)
```

pass Statement

- **pass** statement is intended to do nothing on execution. Hence it is often called a no-op instruction.
- If we wish that on execution of a statement nothing should happen, we can achieve this using a **pass** statement. Its utility is shown in Problem 5.6.
- It is often used as a placeholder for unimplemented code in an if, loop, function or class. This is not a good use of **pass**. Instead, you should use ... in its place. If you use **pass**, it might make one believe that you do not intend to do anything in the if/loop/function/class.

Programs

Problem 5.1

While purchasing certain items, a discount of 10% is offered if the quantity purchased is more than 1000. If quantity and price per item are input through the keyboard, write a program to calculate the total expenses.

Program

```
qty = int(input('Enter value of quantity: '))
price = float(input('Enter value of price: '))
if qty > 1000 :
    dis = 10
else :
    dis = 0
totexp = qty * price - qty * price * dis / 100
print('Total expenses = Rs. ' + str(totexp))
```

Output

```
Enter value of quantity: 1200
Enter value of price: 15.50
Total expenses = Rs. 16740.0
```

Tips

- **input( )** returns a string, so it is necessary to convert it into int or float suitably. If we do not do the conversion, **qty > 1000** will throw an error as a string cannot be compared with an int.
- **str( )** should be used to convert **totexp** to string before doing concatenation using +.

Problem 5.2

In a company an employee is paid as under:

If his basic salary is less than Rs. 1500, then HRA = 10% of basic salary and DA = 90% of basic salary. If his salary is either equal to or above Rs. 1500, then HRA = Rs. 500 and DA = 98% of basic salary. If the employee's salary is input through the keyboard write a program to find his gross salary.

Program

```
bs = int(input('Enter value of bs: '))
if bs < 1500 :
    hra = bs * 10 /100
    da = bs * 90 / 100
else:
    hra = 500
    da = bs * 98 / 100
gs = bs + da + hra
print('Gross Salary = Rs. ' + str(gs))
```

Tips

- **if** block and **else** block can contain multiple statements in them, suitably indented.

Problem 5.3

Percentage marks obtained by a student are input through the keyboard. The student gets a division as per the following rules:

Percentage above or equal to 60 - First division
Percentage between 50 and 59 - Second division
Percentage between 40 and 49 - Third division
Percentage less than 40 - Fail

Write a program to calculate the division obtained by the student.

Program

```
per = int(input('Enter value of percentage: '))
if per >= 60 :
    print('First Division')
elif per >= 50 :
    print('Second Division')
elif per >= 40 :
    print('Third Division')
else :
    print('Fail')
```

Output

```
Enter value of percentage: 55
Second Division
```

Problem 5.4

A company insures its drivers in the following cases:

- If the driver is married.
- If the driver is unmarried, male & above 30 years of age.
- If the driver is unmarried, female & above 25 years of age.

In all other cases, the driver is not insured. If the marital status, sex and age of the driver are the inputs, write a program to determine whether the driver should be insured or not.

Program

```
ms = input('Enter marital status: ')
```

```
s = input('Enter sex: ')
age = int(input('Enter age: '))
if ( ms == 'm' ) or ( ms == 'u' and s == 'm' and age > 30 ) \
    or ( ms == 'u' and s == 'f' and age > 25 ) :
    print('Insured')
else :
    print('Not Insured')
```

Output

```
Enter marital status: u
Enter sex: m
Enter age: 23
Not Insured
```

Problem 5.5

Suppose there are four flag variables w, x, y, z. Write a program to check in multiple ways whether one of them is true.

Program

```
# Different ways to test multiple flags
w, x, y, z = 0, 1, 0, 1

if w == 1 or x == 1 or y == 1 or z == 1 :
    print('True')

if w or x or y or z :
    print('True')

if any((w, x, y, z)) :
    print('True')

if 1 in (w, x, y, z) :
    print('True')
```

Output

```
True
```

```
True
True
True
```

Tips

- **any( )** is a built-in function that returns True if at least one of the element of its parameter is True.
- We have to pass a string, list, tuple, set or dictionary to **any( )**.
- There is another similar function called **all( )**, which returns True if all elements of its parameter are True. This function too should be passed a string, list, tuple, set or dictionary.

Problem 5.6

Given a number n we wish to do the following:

If n is positive - print n * n, set a flag to true
If n is negative - print n * n * n, set a flag to true
if n is 0 - do nothing

Is the code given below correct for this logic?

```
n = int(input('Enter a number: '))
if n > 0 :
    flag = True
    print(n * n)
elif n < 0 :
    flag = True
    print(n * n * n)
```

Answer

- This is misleading code. Later, anybody looking at this code may feel that **flag = True** should be written outside **if** and **else**.
- Better code will be as follows:

```
n = int(input('Enter a number: '))
if n > 0 :
    flag = True
    print(n * n)
elif n < 0 :
    flag = True
    print(n * n * n)
```

```
else :
    pass      # does nothing on execution
```

Exercises

[A] Answer the following questions:

(a) Write conditional expressions for

- If a < 10 b = 20, else b = 30
- Print 'Morning' if time < 12, otherwise print 'Afternoon'
- If marks >= 70, set remarks to True, otherwise False

(b) Rewrite the following code snippet in 1 line:

```
x = 3
y = 3.0
if x == y :
    print('x and y are equal')
else :
    print('x and y are not equal')
```

(c) What happens when a **pass** statement is executed?

[B] What will be the output of the following programs?

(a)
```
i, j, k = 4, -1, 0
w = i or j or k
x = i and j and k
y = i or j and k
z = i and j or k
print(w, x, y, z)
```

(b)
```
a = 10
a = not not a
print(a)
```

(c)
```
x, y, z = 20, 40, 45
if x > y and x > z :
    print('biggest = ' + str(x))
elif y > x and y > z :
    print('biggest = ' + str(y))
elif z > x and z > y :
    print('biggest = ' + str(z))
```

(d)
```
num = 30
k = 100 if num <= 10 else 500
print(k)
```

(e)
```
a = 10
b = 60
if a and b > 20 :
    print('Hello')
else :
    print('Hi')
```

(f)
```
a = 10
b = 60
if a > 20 and b > 20 :
    print('Hello')
else :
    print('Hi')
```

(g)
```
a = 10
if a = 30 or 40 or 60 :
    print('Hello')
else :
    print('Hi')
```

(h)
```
a = 10
if a = 30 or a == 40 or a == 60 :
    print('Hello')
else :
    print('Hi')
```

(i)
```
a = 10
if a in (30, 40, 50) :
    print('Hello')
else :
    print('Hi')
```

[C] Point out the errors, if any, in the following programs:

(a)
```
a = 12.25
b = 12.52
if a = b :
    print('a and b are equal')
```

(b)
```
if ord('X') < ord('x')
    print('Unicode value of X is smaller than that of x')
```

(c)
```
x = 10
if x >= 2 then
    print('x')
```

(d)
```
x = 10 ; y = 15
if x % 2 = y % 3
    print('Carpathians\n')
```

(e)
```
x, y = 30, 40
if x == y :
    print('x is equal to y')
elseif x > y :
    print('x is greater than y')
elseif x < y :
    print('x is less than y')
```

[D] If a = 10, b = 12, c = 0, find the values of the following expressions:

```
a != 6 and b > 5
a == 9 or b < 3
not ( a < 10 )
not ( a > 5 and c )
5 and c != 8 or !c
```

[E] Attempt the following questions:

(a) Any integer is input through the keyboard. Write a program to find out whether it is an odd number or even number.

(b) Any year is input through the keyboard. Write a program to determine whether the year is a leap year or not.

(c) If ages of Ram, Shyam and Ajay are input through the keyboard, write a program to determine the youngest of the three.

(d) Write a program to check whether a triangle is valid or not, when the three angles of the triangle are entered through the keyboard. A triangle is valid if the sum of all the three angles is equal to 180 degrees.

(e) Write a program to find the absolute value of a number entered through the keyboard.

(f) Given the length and breadth of a rectangle, write a program to find whether the area of the rectangle is greater than its perimeter. For example, the area of the rectangle with length = 5 and breadth = 4 is greater than its perimeter.

(g) Given three points **(x1, y1)**, **(x2, y2)** and **(x3, y3)**, write a program to check if all the three points fall on one straight line.

(h) Given the coordinates **(x, y)** of the center of a circle and its radius, write a program that will determine whether a point lies inside the circle, on the circle or outside the circle. (Hint: Use **sqrt( )** function)

(i) Given a point **(x, y)**, write a program to find out if it lies on the X-axis, Y-axis, on the origin or in one of the four quadrants.

(j) A year is entered through the keyboard, write a program to determine whether the year is leap or not. Use logical operators **and** and **or**.

(k) If the three sides of a triangle are entered through the keyboard, write a program to check whether the triangle is valid or not. The triangle is valid if the sum of two sides is greater than the largest of the three sides.

(l) If the three sides of a triangle are entered through the keyboard, write a program to check whether the triangle is isosceles, equilateral, scalene or right-angled triangle.

6 Repetition Control Instruction

"Merry go round..."

Contents

- Repetition Control Instruction
- Usage of *while* Loop
- Usage of *for* Loop
- *break* and *continue*
- Else Block of a Loop
- Programs
- Exercises

KanNotes

Repetition Control Instruction

- It helps us a repeat a set of statements in a program. There are two types of repetition control instructions:

  (a) while
  (b) for

  Unlike many other languages there is no do-while loop in Python.

- **while** is used to repeatedly execute instructions as long as condition is true. It has two forms:

while condition :
    statement1
    statement2
	while condition :
	    statement1
	    statement2
	else :
	    statement3
	    statement4

  - **else** block is optional. If present, it is executed when **condition** fails.
  - If the **while** loop is terminated abruptly using a **break** statement, then the **else** block is not executed.

- **for** is used to iterate over elements of a sequence such as string, tuple or list. It has two forms:

for var in list :
    statement1
    statement2
	for var in list :
	    statement1
	    statement2
	else :
	    statement3
	    statement4

  - During each iteration **var** is assigned the next value from the list.
  - In place of a list a string, tuple, set or dictionary can also be used.
  - **else** block is optional. If present, it is executed if loop is not terminated abruptly using **break**.

Usage of *while* loop

- A **while** loop can be used in the following three situations:
  - Repeat a set of statements till a condition remains True.

- Repeat a set of statements a finite number of times.
- Iterate through a string, list and tuple.

- When we use **while** loop to repeat a set of statements till a condition remains True, it means that when we do not know beforehand how many times the statements are to be executed.

```
num = int(input('Enter a number: '))
while num != 5 :
    print(num, num * num)
    num = int(input('Enter a number: '))
```

The loop terminates when 5 is entered as input.

- We can use a **while** loop to repeat a set of statements a finite number of times.

```
count = 0
while count < 10 :
   print(count, count * count, count * count * count)
   count += 1
```

- A **while** loop can also be used to iterate through a string, a list or a tuple using an index value as shown in the following program:

```
s = 'Mumbai'
lst = ['desert', 'dessert', 'to', 'too', 'lose', 'loose']
tpl = (10, 20, 30, -20, -10)
i = 0
while i < len(lst) :
   print(i, s[i], lst[i], tpl[i])
   i += 1
```

Since items in a set or a dictionary cannot be accessed using an index value, it is better to use a **for** loop to access their elements.

- Of the three usages of while loop shown above, the most popular is the first usage—repeat statements an unknown number of times. The other two situations are usually handled using a **for** loop.

Usage of *for* loop

- A **for** loop can be used in the following two situations:
  - Repeat a set of statements a finite number of times.
  - Iterate through a string, list, tuple, set or dictionary.

- To repeat a set of statements a finite number of times a built-in function **range( )** is used.
- **range( )** function generates a sequence of integers.
  range(10) - generates numbers from 0 to 9.
  range(10, 20) - generates numbers from 10 to 19.
  range(10, 20, 2) - generates numbers from 10 to 19 in steps of 2.
  range(20, 10, -3) - generates numbers from 20 to 9 in steps of -3.

  Note that **range( )** cannot generate a sequence of **floats**.
- In general,

  range(start, stop, step)

  produces a sequence of integers from start (inclusive) to stop (exclusive) by step.
- The list of numbers generated using **range( )** can be iterated through using a **for** loop.

```
for i in range(1, 10, 2) :
    print(i, i * i, i * i * i)
```

- A **for** loop is very popularly used to iterate through a string, list, tuple, set or dictionary, as shown below.

```
for char in 'Leopard' :
    print(char)
for animal in ['Cat', 'Dog', 'Tiger', 'Lion', 'Leopard'] :
    print(animal)
for flower in ('Rose', 'Lily', 'Jasmine') :
    print(flower)
for num in {10, 20, 30, -10, -25} :
    print(num)
for key in {'A101' : 'Rajesh', 'A111' : 'Sunil', 'A112' : 'Rakesh'} :
    print(key)
```

In the first **for** loop in each iteration of the loop **char** is assigned the next value from the string.

Similarly, in the second, third and fourth **for** loop, in each iteration of the loop **animal/flower/num** is assigned the next value form the list/tuple/set.

Note that in the last for loop we are printing only the keys in the dictionary. Printing values, or printing both keys and values are covered in Chapter 11.

- If while iterating through a collection using a **for** loop if we wish to also get an index of the item we should use the built-in **enumerate( )** function as shown below:

```
lst = ['desert', 'dessert', 'to', 'too', 'lose', 'loose']
for i, ele in enumerate(lst) :
    print(i, ele)
```

break and *continue*

- **break** and **continue** statements can be used with **while** and **for**.
- **break** statement terminates the loop without executing the **else** block.
- **continue** statement skips the rest of the statements in the block and continues with the next iteration of the loop.

Else Block of a Loop

- **else** block of a **while** loop should be used in situations where you wish to execute some statements if the loop is terminated normally and not if it is terminated abruptly.
- Such a situation arises if we are to determine whether a number is prime or not.

```
num = int(input('Enter an integer: '))
i = 2
while i <= num - 1 :
    if num % i == 0 :
        print(num, 'is not a prime number')
        break
    i += 1
else :
    print(num, 'is a prime number')
```

Note the indentation of **else**. **else** is working for the **while** and not for **if**.

- In the following example **else** block will not go to work as the list contains 3, a non-multiple of 10, on encountering which we terminate the loop.

```
for ele in [10, 20, 30, 3, 40, 50] :
    if ele % 10 != 0 :
        print(ele, 'is a not a multiple of 10')
        break
else :
    print('all numbers in list are multiples of 10')
```

P</> Programs

Problem 6.1

Write a program that receives 3 sets of values of p, n and r and calculates simple interest for each.

Program

```
i = 1
while i <= 3 :
    p = float(input('Enter value of p: '))
    n = int(input('Enter value of n: '))
    r = float(input('Enter value of r: '))
    si = p * n * r / 100
    print('Simple interest = Rs. ' + str (si))
    i = i + 1
```

Output

```
Enter value of p: 1000
Enter value of n: 3
Enter value of r: 15.5
Simple interest = Rs. 465.0
Enter value of p: 2000
Enter value of n: 5
Enter value of r: 16.5
Simple interest = Rs. 1650.0
Enter value of p: 3000
```

```
Enter value of n: 2
Enter value of r: 10.45
Simple interest = Rs. 626.9999999999999
```

Problem 6.2

Write a program that prints numbers from 1 to 10 using an infinite loop. All numbers should get printed in the same line.

Program

```
i = 1
while 1 :
    print(i, end = ' ')
    i += 1
    if i > 10 :
        break
```

Output

1 2 3 4 5 6 7 8 9 10

Tips

- **while 1** creates an infinite loop, as 1 is non-zero, hence true. Replacing 1 with any non-zero number will create an infinite loop.
- Another way of creating an infinite loop is **while True**.
- **end = ' '** in **print( )** prints a space after printing **i** in each iteration. Default value of **end** is newline ('\n').

Problem 6.3

Write a program that prints all unique combinations of 1, 2 and 3.

Program

```
i = 1
while i <= 3 :
    j = 1
    while j <= 3 :
        k = 1
```

```
        while k <= 3 :
            if i == j or j == k or k == i :
                k += 1
                continue
            else :
                print(i, j, k)
            k += 1
        j += 1
    i += 1
```

Output

```
1 2 3
1 3 2
2 1 3
2 3 1
3 1 2
3 2 1
```

Problem 6.4

Write a program that obtains decimal value of a binary numeric string. For example, the decimal value of '1111' is 15.

Program

```
b = '1111'
i = 0
while b :
    i = i * 2 + (ord(b[0]) - ord('0'))
    b = b[1:]
print('Decimal value = ' + str(i))
```

Output

```
Decimal value = 15
```

Tips

- **ord(1)** is 49, whereas **ord('0')** is 0.
- **b = b[1:]** strips the first character in **b**.

Problem 6.5

Write a program that generates the following output using a **for** loop:

A,B,C,D,E,F,G,H,I,J,K,L,M,N,O,P,Q,R,S,T,U,V,W,X,Y,Z,
z,y,x,w,v,u,t,s,r,q,p,o,n,m,l,k,j,i,h,g,f,e,d,c,b,a,

Program

```
for alpha in range(65, 91) :
    print(chr(alpha), end=',')
print( )
for alpha in range(122, 96, -1) :
    print(chr(alpha), end=',')
```

Tips

- Unicode values of alphabets A-Z are 65-90. Unicode values of alphabets a-z are 97-122.
- Each output of print statement ends with a comma.
- Empty **print( )** statement positions the cursor at the beginning of the next line.

Exercises

[A] Answer the following questions:

(a) When does the **else** block of a **while** loop go to work?

(b) Can **range( )** function be used to generate numbers from 0.1 to 1.0 in steps of 0.1?

(c) Can a **while** loop be nested within a **for** loop and vice versa?

(d) Can a **while/for** loop be used in an **if/else** and vice versa?

(e) Can a do-while loop be used to repeat a set of statements?

(f) How will you write an equivalent **for** loop for the following?

```
count = 1
while count <= 10 :
    print(count)
    count = count + 1
```

(g) What will be the output of the following code snippet?

```
for index in range(20, 10,-3) :
    print(index, end = ' ')
```

(h) Why should **break** and **continue** be always used with an **if** embedded in a **while** or **for** loop?

[B] Point out the errors, if any, in the following programs:

(a)
```
j = 1
while j <= 10 :
    print(j)
    j++
```

(b)
```
while true :
    print('Infinite loop')
```

(c)
```
lst = [10, 20, 30, 40, 50]
for count = 1 to 5 :
    print(lst[ i ])
```

(d)
```
i = 15
not while i < 10 :
    print(i)
    i -= 1
```

(e)
```
# Print alphabets from A to Z
for alpha in range(65, 91) :
    print(ord(alpha), end=' ')
```

(f)
```
for i in range(0.1, 1.0, 0.25) :
    print(i)
```

(g)
```
i = 1
while i <= 10 :
    j = 1
    while j <= 5 :
        print(i, j )
        j+= 1
        break
    print(i, j)
    i += 1
```

[C] Match the following pairs for the values each **range( )** function will generate.

a. range(5)	1. 1, 2, 3, 4
b. range(1, 10, 3)	2. 0, 1, 2, 3, 4
c. range(10, 1, -2)	3. Nothing
d. range(1, 5)	4. 10, 8, 6, 4, 2
e. range(-2)	5. 1, 4, 7

[D] Attempt the following questions:

(a) Write a program to print first 25 odd numbers using **range( )**.

(b) Rewrite the following program using for loop.

```
lst = ['desert', 'dessert', 'to', 'too', 'lose', 'loose']
s = 'Mumbai'
i = 0
while i < len(lst) :
    if i > 3 :
        break
    else :
        print(i, lst[i], s[i])
        i += 1
```

(c) Write a program to count the number of alphabets and number of digits in the string 'Nagpur-440010'

(d) A five-digit number is entered through the keyboard. Write a program to obtain the reversed number and to determine whether the original and reversed numbers are equal or not.

(e) Write a program to find the factorial value of any number entered through the keyboard.

(f) Write a program to print out all Armstrong numbers between 1 and 500. If sum of cubes of each digit of the number is equal to the number itself, then the number is called an Armstrong number. For example, 153 = (1 * 1 * 1) + (5 * 5 * 5) + (3 * 3 * 3).

(g) Write a program to print all prime numbers from 1 to 300.

(h) Write a program to print the multiplication table of the number entered by the user. The table should be displayed in the following form:

```
29 * 1 = 29
29 * 2 = 58
```

...

(i) When interest compounds **q** times per year at an annual rate of **r** % for **n** years, the principal **p** compounds to an amount **a** as per the following formula:

$$a = p (1 + r / q)^{nq}$$

Write a program to read 10 sets of **p, r, n** & **q** and calculate the corresponding **a**s.

(j) Write a program to generate all Pythagorean Triplets with side lengths less than or equal to 30.

(k) The population of a town today is 100000. The population has increased steadily at the rate of 10 % per year for the last 10 years. Write a program to determine the population at the end of each year in the last decade.

(l) Ramanujan number is the smallest number that can be expressed as sum of two cubes in two different ways. Write a program to print all such numbers up to a reasonable limit.

(m) Write a program to print 24 hours of day with suitable suffixes like AM, PM, Noon and Midnight.

7 Console Input/Output

"Input from keyboard, output to screen..."

Contents

KanNotes

- Console Input/Output means input from keyboard and output to screen.

Console Input

- Console input can be received using the built-in **input( )** function.
- General form of **input( )** function is

  s = input('prompt')

  prompt is a string that is displayed on the screen, soliciting a value. **input( )** returns a string. If 123 is entered as input, '123' is returned.
- **input( )** can be used to receive, 1, or more values.

```
# receive full name
name = input('Enter full name')
# separate first name, middle name and surname
fname, mname, sname = input('Enter full name: ').split( )
```

  split( ) function will split the entered fullname with space as a delimiter. The split values will then be assigned to **fname**, **mname**, **lname**.

- If we are to receive multiple **int** values, we can receive them as strings and then convert them to **int**s.

```
n1, n2, n3 = input('Enter three values: ').split( )
n1, n2, n3 = int(n1), int(n2), int(n3)
print(n1 + 10, n2 + 20, n3 + 30)
```

- The same thing can be done using in a more compact manner using a feature called list comprehension. It applies **int( )** function to every element of the list returned by the **split( )** function.

```
n1, n2, n3 = [int(n) for n in input('Enter three values: ').split( )]
print(n1 + 10, n2 + 20, n3 + 30)
```

  The expression enclosed within [ ] is called list comprehension. It is discussed in detail in Chapter 12.

- **input( )** can be used to receive arbitrary number of values.

```
numbers = [int(x) for x in input('Enter values: ').split( )]
for n in numbers :
    print(n + 10)
```

- **input( )** can be used to receive different types of values at a time.

```
data = input('Enter name, age, salary: ').split( )
name = data[0]
age = int(data[1])
salary = float(data[2])
```

Console Output

- Built-in function **print( )** is used to send output to screen.
- **print( )** function has this form:

```
print(objects, sep = '  ', end = '\n', file = sys.stdout, flush = False)
```

This means that by default objects will be printed on screen (sys.stdout), separated by space (sep = ' ') and last printed object will be followed by a newline (end = '\n'). **flush = False** indicates that output stream will not be flushed.

- Python has a facility to call functions and pass keyword-based values as arguments. So while calling **print( )** we can pass specific values for **sep** and **end**. In this case, default values will not be used; instead, the values that we pass will be used.

```
print(a, b, c, sep = ',', end = '!')  # prints ',' after each value, ! at end
print(x, y, sep = '...', end = '#')   # prints '...' after each value, # at end
```

Formatted Printing

- There are 4 ways to control the formatting of output:
  (a) Using formatted string literals - easiest
  (b) Using the **format( )** method - older
  (c) C **printf( )** style - legacy
  (d) Using slicing and concatenation operation - difficult

  Today (a) is most dominantly used method followed by (b).

- Using formatted string literals (often called fstrings):

```
r, l, b = 1.5678, 10.5, 12.66
print(f'radius = {r}')
print(f'length = {l} breadth = {b} radius = {r}')

name = 'Sushant Ajay Raje'
for n in name.split( ) :
    print(f'{n:10}')              # print in 10 columns
```

- Using **format( )** method of string object:

```
r, l, b = 1.5678, 10.5, 12.66
name, age, salary = 'Rakshita', 30, 53000.55

# print in order by position of variables using empty {}
print('radius = {} length = {} breadth ={}'.format(r, l, b))
print('name = {} age = {} salary = {}'.format(name, age, salary))

# print in any desired order
print('breadth = {2} length = {1} radius ={0}'.format(r, l, b))
print('age = {1} salary = {2} name = {0}'.format(name, age, salary))

# print name in 15 columns, salary in 10 columns
print('name = {0:15} salary = {1:10}'.format(name, salary))

# print radius in 10 columns, with 2 digits after decimal point
print('radius = {0:10.2f}'.format(r))
```

On execution, the above code snippet will produce the following output:

```
radius = 1.5678 length = 10.5 breadth =12.66
name = Rakshita age = 30 salary = 53000.55
breadth = 12.66 length = 10.5 radius =1.5678
age = 30 salary = 53000.55 name = Rakshita
name = Rakshita        salary =   53000.55
radius =       1.57
```

P</> *Programs*

Problem 7.1

Write a program to receive radius of a circle, and length and breadth of a rectangle in one call to **input( )**. Calculate and print the circumference of circle and perimeter of rectangle.

Program

```
r, l, b = input('Enter radius, length and breadth: ').split( )
radius = int(r)
length = int(l)
breadth = int(b)
circumference = 2 * 3.14 * radius
perimeter = 2 * (length + breadth)
print(circumference)
print(perimeter)
```

Output

```
Enter radius, length and breadth: 3 4 5
18.84
18
```

Tips

- **input( )** returns a string, so it is necessary to convert it into int or float suitably, before performing arithmetic operations.

Problem 7.2

Write a program to receive 3 integers using one call to **input( )**. The three integers signify starting value, ending value and step value for a range. The program should use these values to print the number, its square and its cube, all properly right-aligned. Also output the same values left-aligned.

Program

```
start, end, step = input('Enter start, end, step values: ').split( )
# right aligned printing
for n in range(int(start), int(end), int(step)) :
    print(f'{n:>5}{n**2:>7}{n**3:>8}')
print( )

# left aligned printing
for n in range(int(start), int(end), int(step)) :
    print('{0:<5}{1:<7}{2:<8}'.format(n, n ** 2, n ** 3))
```

Output

```
Enter start, end, step values: 1 10 2
    1      1       1
    3      9      27
    5     25     125
    7     49     343
    9     81     729

1    1      1
3    9      27
5    25     125
7    49     343
9    81     729
```

Tips

- **{n:>5}** will print **n** right-justified within 5 columns. Use < to left-justify.
- **{0:<5}** will left-justify 0th parameter in the list within 5 columns. Use > to right-justify.

Problem 7.3

Write a program to maintain names and cell numbers of 4 persons and then print them systematically in a tabular form.

Program

```
contacts = {
              'Dilip' : 9823077892, 'Shekhar' : 6784512345,
              'Vivek' : 9823011245, 'Riddhi' : 9766556779
          }
for name, cellno in contacts.items( ) :
    print(f'{name:15} : {cellno:10d}')
```

Output

```
Dilip          : 9823077892
Shekhar        : 6784512345
Vivek          : 9823011245
Riddhi         : 9766556779
```

Problem 7.4

Suppose there are 5 variables in a program—**max**, **min**, **mean**, **sd** and **var**, having some suitable values. Write a program to print these variables properly aligned using multiple fstrings, but one call to **print( )**.

Program

```
min, max = 25, 75
mean = 35
sd = 0.56
var  = 0.9
print(
        f'\n{"Max Value:":<15}{max:>10}',
        f'\n{"Min Value:":<15}{min:>10}',
        f'\n{"Mean:":<15}{mean:>10}',
        f'\n{"Std Dev:":<15}{sd:>10}',
        f'\n{"Variance:":<15}{var:>10}' )
```

Output

```
Max Value:             75
Min Value:             25
Mean:                  35
```

```
Std Deviation:  0.56
Variance:        0.9
```

Problem 7.5

Write a program that prints square root and cube root of numbers from 1 to 10, up to 3 decimal places. Ensure that the output is displayed in separate lines, with number center-justified and square and cube roots, right-justified.

Program

```
import math
for n in range(1, 10) :
    s = round(math.sqrt(n), 3)
    c = round(math.pow(n,1/3), 3)
    print(f'{n:^5}{s:10}{c:10}')
```

Output

```
  1       1.0       1.0
  2     1.414      1.26
  3     1.732     1.442
  4       2.0     1.587
  5     2.236      1.71
  6     2.449     1.817
  7     2.646     1.913
  8     2.828       2.0
  9       3.0      2.08
```

Exercises

[A] Attempt the following questions:

(a) How will you make the following code more compact?

```
print('Enter ages of 3 persons')
age1 = input( )
age2 = input( )
age3 = input( )
```

(b) How will you print "Rendezvous" in a line and retain the cursor in the same line in which the output has been printed?

(c) What will be the output of the following code snippet?

```
l, b = 1.5678, 10.5
print('length = {l} breadth = {b}')
```

(d) In the following statement what do > 5, > 7 and > 8 signify?

```
print(f'{n:>5}{n**2:>7}{n**3:>8}')
```

(e) What will be the output of the following code segment?

```
name = 'Sanjay'
cellno = 9823017892
print(f'{name:15} : {cellno:10}')
```

(f) How will you print the output of the following code segment using fstring?

```
x, y, z =10, 20, 40
print('{0:<5}{1:<7}{2:<8}'.format(x, y, z))
```

(g) How will you receive arbitrary number of floats from keyboard?

(h) What changes should be made in

```
print(f'{'\nx = ':4}{x:>10}{'\ny = ':4}{y:>10}')
```

to produce the output given below:

```
x =      14.99
y =     114.39
```

(i) How will you receive a boolean value as input?

(j) How will you receive a complex number as input?

(k) How will you display **price** in 10 columns with 4 places beyond decimal points? Assume value of price to be 1.5567894.

(l) Write a program to receive an arbitrary number of floats using one **input( )** statement. Calculate the average of floats received.

(m) Write a program to receive the following using one **input( )** statement.

Name of the person
Years of service

Diwali bonus received

Calculate and print the agreement deduction as per the following formula:

deduction = 2 * years of service + bonus * 5.5 / 100

(n) Which import statement should be added to use the built-in functions **input( )** and **print( )**?

(o) Is the following statement correct?

print('Result = ' + 4 > 3)

(p) Write a program to print the following values

a = 12.34, b = 234.39, c = 444.34, d = 1.23, e = 34.67

as shown below:

```
a =    12.34
b =   234.39
c =   444.34
d =     1.23
e =    34.67
```

[B] Match the following pairs:

a. Default value of sep in print( )	1. ' '
b. Default value of end in print( )	2. Using fstring
c. Easiest way to print output	3. Right justify num in 5 columns
d. Return type of split( )	4. Left justify num in 5 columns
e. print('{num:>5}')	5. list
f. print('{num:<5}')	6. \n

8 Lists

"Bringing order to chaos..."

Contents

- What are Lists?
- Accessing List Elements
- Looping in Lists
- Basic List Operations
- Using Built-in Functions on Lists
- List Methods
- Sorting and Reversing
- List Varieties
- Stack Data Structure
- Queue Data structure
- Programs
- Exercises

KanNotes

What are Lists?

- Container is an entity which contains multiple data items. It is also known as a collection or a compound data type.
- Python has the following container data types:

  Lists Tuples
  Sets Dictionaries

- A list can grow or shrink during execution of the program. Hence it is also known as a dynamic array. Because of this nature of lists they are commonly used for handling variable length data.
- A list is defined by writing comma-separated elements within [ ].

```
num = [10, 25, 30, 40, 100]
names = ['Sanjay', 'Anil', 'Radha', 'Suparna']
```

- List can contain dissimilar types, though usually they are a collection of similar types. For example:

```
animal = ['Zebra', 155.55, 110]
```

- Items in a list can be repeated, i.e., a list may contain duplicate items. Like printing, * can be used to repeat an element multiple time. An empty list is also feasible.

```
ages = [25, 26, 25, 27, 26]     # duplicates allowed
num = [10] * 5                  # stores [10, 10, 10, 10, 10]
lst = [ ]                       # empty list, valid
```

Accessing List Elements

- Entire list can be printed by just using the name of the list.

```
l = ['Able', 'was', 'I', 'ere', 'I', 'saw', 'elbA']
print(l)
```

- Like strings, individual elements in a list can be accessed using indices. Hence, they are also known as sequence types. The index value starts from 0.

```
print(animals[1], ages[3])
```

- Like strings, lists can be sliced.

```
print(animals[1:3])
print(ages[3:])
```

Looping in Lists

- If we wish to process each item in the list, we should be able to iterate through the list. This can be done using a **while** or **for** loop.

```
animals = ['Zebra', 'Tiger', 'Lion', 'Jackal', 'Kangaroo']
# using while loop
i = 0
while i < len(animals) :
    print(animals[i])
    i += 1
# using more convenient for loop
for a in animals :
    print(a)
```

- While iterating through a list using a **for** loop, if we wish to keep track of index of the element that **a** is referring to, we can do so using the built-in **enumerate( )** function.

```
animals = ['Zebra', 'Tiger', 'Lion', 'Jackal', 'Kangaroo']
for index, a in enumerate(animals) :
    print(index, a)
```

Basic List Operations

- Mutability - Unlike strings, lists are mutable (changeable). So, lists can be updated as shown below:

```
animals = ['Zebra', 'Tiger', 'Lion', 'Jackal', 'Kangaroo']
ages = [25, 26, 25, 27, 26, 28, 25]
animals[2] ='Rhinoceros'
ages[5] = 31
ages[2:5] = [24, 25, 32]     # sets items 2 to 4 with values 24, 25, 32
ages[2:5] = [ ]              # delete items 2 to 4
```

- Concatenation - One list can be concatenated (appended) at the end of another as shown below:

```
lst = [12, 15, 13, 23, 22, 16, 17]
lst = lst + [33, 44, 55]
print(lst)              # prints [12, 15, 13, 23, 22, 16, 17, 33, 44, 55]
```

- Merging - Two lists can be merged to create a new list.

```
s = [10, 20, 30]
t = [100, 200, 300]
z = s + t
print(z)                # prints [10, 20, 30, 100, 200, 300]
```

- Conversion - A string/tuple/set can be converted into a list using the **list( )** conversion function.

```
l = list('Africa')      # converts the string to a list ['A', 'f', 'r', 'i', 'c', 'a']
```

- Aliasing - On assigning one list to another, both refer to the same list. Changing one changes the other. This assignment is often known as shallow copy or aliasing.

```
lst1 = [10, 20, 30, 40, 50]
lst2 = lst1             # doesn't copy list. lst2 refers to same list as lst1
print(lst1)             # prints [10, 20, 30, 40, 50]
print(lst2)             # prints [10, 20, 30, 40, 50]
lst1[0] = 100
print(lst1[0], lst2[0])   # prints 100 100
```

- Cloning - This involves copying contents of one list into another. After copying both refer to different lists, though both contain the same values. Changing one list does not change another. This operation is often known as deep copy.

```
lst1 = [10, 20, 30, 40, 50]
lst2 = [ ]                  # empty list
lst2 = lst2 + lst1          # lst1, lst2 refer to different lists
print(lst1)                 # prints [10, 20, 30, 40, 50]
print(lst2)                 # prints [10, 20, 30, 40, 50]
lst1[0] = 100
print(lst1[0], lst2[0])     # prints 100, 10
```

- Searching - An element can be searched in a list using the **in** membership operator as shown below:

```
lst = ['a', 'e', 'i', 'o', 'u']
res = 'a' in lst            # return True since 'a' is present in list
res = 'z' not in lst        # return True since 'z' is absent in list
```

- Identity - Whether the two variables are referring to the same list can be checked using the **is** identity operator as shown below:

```
lst1 = [10, 20, 30, 40, 50]
lst2 = [10, 20, 30, 40, 50]
lst3 = lst1
print(lst1 is lst2)        # prints False
print(lst1 is lst3)        # prints True
print(lst1 is not lst2)    # prints True
```

Note the difference for basic types like **int** or **str**:

```
num1 = 10
num2 = 10
s1 = 'Hi'
s2 = 'Hi'
print(num1 is num2)    # prints True
print(s1 is s2)        # prints True
```

- Comparison - It is possible to compare the contents of two lists. Comparison is done item by item till there is a mismatch. In the following code it would be decided that **a** is less than **b** when 3 and 5 are compared.

```
a = [1, 2, 3, 4]
b = [1, 2, 5]
print(a < b)           # prints True
```

- Emptiness - We can check if a list is empty using **not** operator.

```
lst = [ ]
if not lst :           # lst returns False
    print('Empty list')
```

Alternately, we can convert a list to a **bool** and check the result.

```
lst = [ ]
print(bool(lst))        # prints False
```

- Also note that the following values are considered to be False:

  None
  Number equivalent to zero: 0, 0.0, 0j
  Empty string, list and tuple: ' ', "", [ ], ( )
  Empty set and dictionary: { }

Using Built-in Functions on Lists

- Many built-in functions can be used with lists.

```
len(lst)          # return number of items in the list
max(lst)          # return maximum element in the list
min(lst)          # return minimum element in the list
sum(lst)          # return sum of all elements in the list
any(lst)          # return True if any element of lst is True
all(lst)          # return True if all elements of lst are True
del( )            # deletes element or slice or entire list
sorted(lst)       # return sorted list, lst remains unchanged
reversed(lst)     # used for reversing lst
```

Except for the last 3, other functions are self-explanatory. **sorted( )** and **reversed( )** are discussed in section after next. **del( )** function's usage is shown below:

```
lst = [10, 20, 30, 40, 50]
lst = del(lst[3])     # delete 3rd item in the list
del(lst[2:5])         # delete items 2 to 4 from the list
del(lst[:])           # delete entire list
lst = [ ]             # another way to delete an entire list
```

- If multiple variables are referring to same list, then deleting one does not delete the others.

```
lst1 = [10, 20, 30, 40, 50]
lst3 = lst2 = lst1    # all refer to same list
lst1 = [ ]            # lst1 refers to empty list; lst2, lst3 to original list
print(lst2)           # prints [10, 20, 30, 40, 50]
print(lst3)           # prints [10, 20, 30, 40, 50]
```

- If multiple variables refer to the same list and we wish to delete all, we can do so as shown below:

```
lst2[:] = [ ]               # list is emptied by deleting all items
print(lst2)                 # prints [ ]
print(lst3)                 # prints [ ]
```

List Methods

- Any list is an object of type **list**. Its methods can be accessed using the syntax **lst.method( )**. Usage of some of the commonly used methods is shown below:

```
lst = [12, 15, 13, 23, 22, 16, 17]  # create list
lst.append(22)              # add new item at end
lst.remove(13)              # delete item 13 from list
lst.remove(30)              # reports valueError as 30 is absent in lst
lst.pop( )                  # removes last item in list
lst.pop(3)                  # removes 3rd item in the list
lst.insert(3, 21)           # insert 21 at 3rd position
lst.count(23)               # return no. of times 23 appears in lst
idx = lst.index(22)         # return index of item 22
idx = lst.index(50)         # reports valueError as 50 is absent in lst
```

Sorting and Reversing

- Usage of list methods for reversing a list and for sorting is shown below:

```
lst = [10, 2, 0, 50, 4]
lst.reverse( )
print(lst)                       # prints [4, 50, 0, 2, 10]
lst.sort( )
print(lst)                       # prints [0, 2, 4, 10, 50]
lst.sort(reverse = True)         # sort items in reverse order
print(lst)                       # prints [50, 10, 4, 2, 0]
```

Note that **reverse( )** and **sort( )** do not return a list. Both manipulate the list in place.

- Usage of built-in functions for reversing a list and for sorting is shown below:

```
lst = [10, 2, 0, 50, 4]
print(sorted(lst))                    # prints [0, 2, 4, 10, 50]
print(sorted(lst, reverse = True))    # prints [50, 10, 4, 2, 0]
print(list(reversed(lst)))            # prints [4, 50, 0, 2, 10]
```

Note that **sorted( )** function returns a new sorted list and keeps the original list unchanged. Also, **reversed( )** function returns a **list_reverseiterator** object which has to converted into a list using **list( )** to get a reversed list.

- Reversal is also possible using a slicing operation as shown below:

```
lst = [10, 2, 0, 50, 4]
print(lst[::-1])                      # prints [4, 50, 0, 2, 10]
```

List Varieties

- It is possible to create a list of lists (nested lists).

```
a = [1, 3, 5, 7, 9]
b = [2, 4, 6, 8, 10]
c = [a, b]
print(c[0][0], c[1][2])   # 0th element of 0th list, 2nd ele. of 1st list
```

- A list may be embedded in another list.

```
x = [1, 2, 3, 4]
y = [10, 20, x, 30]
print(y)                  # outputs [10, 20, [1, 2, 3, 4], 30]
```

- It is possible to unpack a string or list within a list using the * operator.

```
s = 'Hello'
l = [*s]
print(l)                  # outputs ['H', 'e', 'l', 'l', 'o']

x = [1, 2, 3, 4]
y = [10, 20, *x, 30]
print(y)                  # outputs [10, 20, 1, 2, 3, 4, 30]
```

Stack Data Structure

- A data structure refers to an arrangement of data in memory. Popular data structures are stack, queue, tree, graph and map.
- Stack is a last in first out (LIFO) list, i.e., last element that is added to the list is the first element that is removed from it.
- Adding an element to a stack is called push operation and removing an element from it is called pop operation. Both these operations are carried out at the rear end of the list.
- Push and pop operations can be carried out using the **append( )** and **pop( )** methods of list object. This is demonstrated in Program 8.3.

Queue Data Structure

- Queue is a first in first out (FIFO) list, i.e., the first element that is added to the list is the first element that is removed from it.
- Lists are not efficient for implementation of queue data structure.
- With lists removal of items from beginning is not efficient, since it involves shifting of rest of the elements by 1 position after deletion.
- Hence for fast additions and deletions, **deque** class of **collections** module is preferred.
- Deque stands for double ended queue. Addition and deletion in a deque can take place at both ends.
- Usage of **deque** class to implement a queue data structure is demonstrated in Program 8.4.

P</> Programs

Problem 8.1

Perform the following operations on a list of names.

- Create a list of 5 names - 'Anil', 'Amol', 'Aditya', 'Avi', 'Alka'
- Insert a name 'Anuj' before 'Aditya'
- Append a name 'Zulu'
- Delete 'Avi' from the list
- Replace 'Anil' with 'AnilKumar'

- Sort all the names in the list
- Print reversed sorted list

Program

```
# Create a list of 5 names
names = ['Anil', 'Amol', 'Aditya', 'Avi', 'Alka']
print(names)

# insert a name 'Anuj' before 'Aditya'
names.insert(2,'Anuj')
print(names)

# append a name 'Zulu'
names.append('Zulu')
print(names)
# delete 'Avi' from the list
names.remove('Avi')
print(names)

# replace 'Anil' with 'AnilKumar'
i=names.index('Anil')
names[i] = 'AnilKumar'
print(names)

# sort all the names in the list
names.sort( )
print(names)

# print reversed sorted list
names.reverse( )
print(names)
```

Output

```
['Anil', 'Amol', 'Aditya', 'Avi', 'Alka']
['Anil', 'Amol', 'Anuj', 'Aditya', 'Avi', 'Alka']
['Anil', 'Amol', 'Anuj', 'Aditya', 'Avi', 'Alka', 'Zulu']
['Anil', 'Amol', 'Anuj', 'Aditya', 'Alka', 'Zulu']
['AnilKumar', 'Amol', 'Anuj', 'Aditya', 'Alka', 'Zulu']
['Aditya', 'Alka', 'Amol', 'AnilKumar', 'Anuj', 'Zulu']
```

```
['Zulu', 'Anuj', 'AnilKumar', 'Amol', 'Alka', 'Aditya']
```

Problem 8.2

Perform the following operations on a list of numbers.

- Create a list of 5 odd numbers
- Create a list of 5 even numbers
- Combine the two lists
- Add prime numbers 11, 17, 29 at the beginning of the combined list
- Report how many elements are present in the list
- Replace last 3 numbers in the list with 100, 200, 300
- Delete all the numbers in the list
- Delete the list

Program

```
# create a list of 5 odd numbers
a = [1, 3, 5, 7, 9]
print(a)

# create a list of 5 even numbers
b = [2, 4, 6, 8, 10]
print(b)
# combine the two lists
a = a + b
print(a)

# add prime numbers 11, 17, 29 at the beginning of the combined list
a = [11, 17, 29] + a
print(a)

# report how many elements are present in the list
num = len(a)
print(num)

# replace last 3 numbers in the list with 100, 200, 300
a[num-3:num] = [100, 200, 300]
print(a)

# delete all the numbers in the list
a[:] = [ ]
```

```
print(a)

# delete the list
del a
```

Output

```
[1, 3, 5, 7, 9]
[2, 4, 6, 8, 10]
[1, 3, 5, 7, 9, 2, 4, 6, 8, 10]
[11, 17, 29, 1, 3, 5, 7, 9, 2, 4, 6, 8, 10]
13
[11, 17, 29, 1, 3, 5, 7, 9, 2, 4, 100, 200, 300]
[]
```

Problem 8.3

Write a program to implement a Stack data structure. Stack is a Last In First Out (LIFO) list in which addition and deletion takes place at the same end.

Program

```
# stack - LIFO list
s = [ ] # empty stack
# push elements on stack
s.append(10)
s.append(20)
s.append(30)
s.append(40)
s.append(50)
print(s)

# pop elements from stack
print(s.pop( ))
print(s.pop( ))
print(s.pop( ))
print(s)
```

Output

```
[10, 20, 30, 40, 50]
50
40
30
[10, 20]
```

Problem 8.4

Write a program to implement a Queue data structure. Queue is a First In First Out (FIFO) list, in which addition takes place at the rear end of the queue and deletion takes place at the front end of the queue.

Program

```
import collections
q = collections.deque( )

q.append('Suhana')
q.append('Shabana')
q.append('Shakila')
q.append('Shakira')
q.append('Sameera')
print(q)

print(q.popleft( ))
print(q.popleft( ))
print(q.popleft( ))
print(q)
```

Output

```
deque(['Suhana', 'Shabana', 'Shakila', 'Shakira', 'Sameera'])
Suhana
Shabana
Shakila
deque(['Shakira', 'Sameera'])
```

Problem 8.5

Write a program to generate and store in a list 20 random numbers in the range 10 to 100. From this list delete all those entries which have value between 20 and 50. Print the remaining list.

Program

```
import random

a = [ ]
i = 1
while i <= 15 :
    num = random.randint(10,100)
    a.append(num)
    i += 1

print(a)

for num in a :
    if num > 20 and num < 50 :
        a.remove(num)

print(a)
```

Output

```
[64, 10, 13, 25, 16, 39, 80, 100, 45, 33, 30, 22, 59, 73, 83]
[64, 10, 13, 16, 80, 100, 33, 22, 59, 73, 83]
```

Problem 8.6

Write a program to add two 3 x 4 matrices.

Program

```
mat1 = [[1, 2, 3, 4], [5, 6, 7, 8], [9, 10, 11, 12]]
mat2 = [[1, 2, 3, 4], [5, 6, 7, 8], [9, 10, 11, 12]]
mat3 = [[0, 0, 0, 0], [0, 0, 0, 0], [0, 0, 0, 0]]

# iterate through rows
```

```
for i in range(len(mat1)) :
    # iterate through columns
    for j in range(len(mat1[0])) :
        mat3[i][j] = mat1[i][j] + mat2[i][j]

print(mat3)
```

Output

```
[[2, 4, 6, 8], [10, 12, 14, 16], [18, 20, 22, 24]]
```

Exercises

[A] What will be the output of the following programs?

(a)
```
msg = list('www.kicit.com')
ch = msg[-1]
print(ch)
```

(b)
```
msg = list('kanlabs.teachable.com')
s = msg[4:6]
print(s)
```

(c)
```
msg = 'Online Courses - KanLabs'
s = list(msg[:3])
print(s)
```

(d)
```
msg = 'Rahate Colony'
s = list(msg[-5:-2])
print(s)
```

(e)
```
s = list('KanLabs')
t = s[::-1]
print(t)
```

(f)
```
num1 = [10, 20, 30, 40, 50]
num2 = num1
print(id(num1))
print(type(num2))
print(isinstance(num1, list))
print(num1 is num2)
```

(g)
```
num = [10, 20, 30, 40, 50]
```

```
num[2:4] = [ ]
print(num)
```

(h)
```
num1 = [10, 20, 30, 40, 50]
num2 = [60, 70, 80]
num1.append(num2)
print(num1)
```

(i)
```
lst = [10, 25, 4, 12, 3, 8]
sorted(lst)
print(lst)
```

(j)
```
a = [1, 2, 3, 4]
b = [1, 2, 5]
print(a < b)
```

[B] Attempt the following questions:

(a) Which of the following is a valid List?

['List'] {"List"} ("List") "List"

(b) What will happen on execution of the following code snippet?

```
s = list('Hello')
s[1] = 'M'
```

(c) The following code snippet deletes elements 30 and 40 from the list:

```
num = [10, 20, 30, 40, 50]
del(num[2:4])
```

In which other way can the same effect be obtained?

(d) Which of the following is an INCORRECT list?

```
a = [0, 1, 2, 3, [10, 20, 30]]
a = [10, 'Suraj', 34555.50]
a = [[10, 20, 30], [40, 50, 60]]
```

(e) From the list given below

```
num1 = [10, 20, 30, 40, 50]
```

How will you create the list **num2** containing:

['A', 'B', 'C', 10, 20, 30, 40, 50, 'Y', 'Z']

(f) Given a list

lst = [10, 25, 4, 12, 3, 8]

How will you sort it in descending order?

(g) Given a list

lst = [10, 25, 4, 12, 3, 8]

How will you check whether 30 is present in the list or not?

(h) Given a list

lst = [10, 25, 4, 12, 3, 8]

How will you insert 30 between 25 and 4?

(i) Given a string

s = 'Hello'

How will you obtain a list ['H', 'e', 'l', 'l', 'o'] from it?

[C] Answer the following questions:

(a) Write a program to create a list of 5 odd integers. Replace the third element with a list of 4 even integers. Flatten, sort and print the list.

(b) Suppose a list contains 20 integers generated randomly. Receive a number from the keyboard and report position of all occurrences of this number in the list.

(c) Suppose a list has 20 numbers. Write a program that removes all duplicates from this list.

(d) Suppose a list contains positive and negative numbers. Write a program to create two lists—one containing positive numbers and another containing negative numbers.

(e) Suppose a list contains 5 strings. Write a program to convert all these strings to uppercase.

(f) Write a program that converts a list of temperatures in Fahrenheit degrees to equivalent Celsius degrees.

(g) Write a program to obtain a median value of a list of numbers, without disturbing the order of the numbers in the list.

(h) A list contains only positive and negative integers. Write a program to obtain the number of negative numbers present in the list.

(i) Suppose a list contains several words. Write a program to create another list that contains the first character of each word present in the first list.

(j) A list contains 10 numbers. Write a program to eliminate all duplicates from the list.

(k) Write a program to find the mean, median and mode of a list of 10 numbers.

9 Tuples

"Ordered, heterogenous, immutable...."

Contents

- What are Tuples?
- Accessing Tuple Elements
- Looping in Tuples
- Basic Tuple Operations
- Using Built-in Functions on Tuples
- Tuple Methods
- Tuple Varieties
- Programs
- Exercises

KanNotes

What are Tuples?

- Though a list can store dissimilar data, it is commonly used for storing similar data.

- Though a tuple can store similar data it is commonly used for storing dissimilar data. The tuple data is enclosed within ( ) as shown below.

```
a = ( )                      # empty tuple
b = (10,)                    # tuple with one item. , after 10 is necessary
c = ('Sanjay', 25, 34555.50)      # tuple with dissimilar items
d = (10, 20, 30, 40)              # tuple with similar items
```

  While creating the tuple **b**, if we do not use the comma after 10, **b** is treated to be of type **int**.

- While initializing a tuple, we may drop ( ).

```
c = 'Sanjay', 25, 34555.50       # tuple with multiple items
print(type(c))                   # c is of the type tuple
```

- Items in a tuple can be repeated, i.e., tuple may contain duplicate items. Like list, tuple elements can be repeated using a *.

```
tpl1 = (10,) * 5                 # stores (10, 10, 10, 10, 10)
tpl2 = (10) * 5                  # stores (50)
```

Accessing Tuple Elements

- Entire tuple can be printed by just using the name of the tuple.

```
tpl = ('Sanjay', 25, 34555.50)
print(tpl)
```

- Tuple is an ordered collection. So, order of insertion of elements in a tuple is same as the order of access. So, like a string and list, tuple items too can be accessed using indices, starting with 0.

```
msg = ('Handle', 'Exceptions', 'Like', 'a', 'boss')
print(msg[1], msg[3])
```

- Like strings and lists, tuples too can be sliced to yield smaller tuples.

```
emp = ('Sanjay', 23, 23000, 1760, 2040)
print(emp[1:3])         # prints (23, 23000)
print(emp[3:])          # prints  (1760, 2040)
print(emp[:3])          # prints ('Sanjay', 23, 23000)
```

Looping in Tuples

- If we wish to process each item in a tuple, we should be able to iterate through it. This can be done using a while loop or **for** loop.

```
tpl = (10, 20, 30, 40, 50)
i = 0
while i < len(tpl) :
    print(tpl[i])
    i += 1
for n in tpl :
    print(n)
```

- While iterating through a tuple using a **for** loop, if we wish to keep track of index of the element that is being currently processed, we can do so using the built-in **enumerate( )** function.

```
tpl = (10, 20, 30, 40, 50)
for index, n in enumerate(tpl) :
    print(index, n)
```

Basic Tuple Operations

- Mutability - Unlike a list, a tuple is immutable, i.e., it cannot be modified.

```
msg = ('Fall', 'In', 'Line')
msg[0] ='FALL'                      # error
msg[1:3] = ('Above', 'Mark')        # error
```

- Since a tuple is immutable operations like append, remove and insert do not work with a tuple.

- Though a tuple itself is immutable, it can contain mutable objects like lists.

```
# mutable lists, immutable string—all can belong to tuple
s = ([1, 2, 3, 4], [4, 5], 'Ocelot')
```

- If a tuple contains a list, the list can be modified since list is a mutable object.

```
s = ([1, 2, 3, 4], [10, 20], 'Oynx')
s[1][1] = 45          # changes first item of first list, i.e. 20
print(s)              # prints ([1, 2, 3, 4], [4, 45], 'Oynx')

# one more way to change first item of first list
p = s[1]
p[1] = 100
print(s)              # prints ([1, 2, 3, 4], [4, 100], 'Oynx')
```

- The other basic operations that are done on a tuple are very similar to the ones done on a list. These operations are discussed in Chapter 8. You may try the following operations on tuples as an exercise:

  Concatenation
  Merging
  Conversion
  Aliasing
  Cloning
  Searching
  Identity
  Comparison
  Emptiness

Using Built-in Functions on Tuples

- Many built-in functions can be used with tuples.

```
t = (12, 15, 13, 23, 22, 16, 17)  # create tuple
len(t)            # return number of items in tuple t
max(t)            # return maximum element in tuple t
min(t)            # return minimum element in tuple t
sum(t)            # return sum of all elements in tuple t
any(t)            # return True if any element of tpl is True
all(t)            # return True if all elements of tpl are True
sorted(t)         # return sorted list (not sorted tuple)
reversed(t)       # used for reversing t
```

Tuple Methods

- Any tuple is an object of type **tuple**. Its methods can be accessed using the syntax **tpl.method( )**. Usage of two methods is shown below:

```
tpl = (12, 15, 13, 23, 22)    # create tuple
print(tpl.count(23))          # return no. of times 23 appears in tpl
print(tpl.index(22))          # return index of item 22
print(tpl.index(50))          # reports valueError as 50 is absent in tpl
```

Tuple Varieties

- It is possible to create a tuple of tuples.

```
a = (1, 3, 5, 7, 9)
b = (2, 4, 6, 8, 10)
c = (a, b)
print(c[0][0], c[1][2]) # 0th element of 0th tuple, 2nd ele of 1st tuple
```

```
records = (
            ('Priyanka', 24, 3455.50), ('Shailesh', 25, 4555.50),
            ('Subhash', 25, 4505.50), ('Sugandh', 27, 4455.55)
          )
print(records[0][0], records[0][1], records[0][2])
print(records[1][0], records[1][1], records[1][2])
for n, a, s in records :
    print(n, a, s)
```

- A tuple may be embedded in another tuple.

```
x = (1, 2, 3, 4)
y = (10, 20, x, 30)
print(y)                 # outputs (10, 20, (1, 2, 3, 4), 30)
```

- It is possible to unpack a tuple within a tuple using the *operator.

```
x = (1, 2, 3, 4)
y = (10, 20, *x, 30)
print(y)                 # outputs (10, 20, 1, 2, 3, 4, 30)
```

- It is possible to create a list of tuples, or a tuple of lists.

```
lst = [('Priyanka', 24, 3455.50), ('Shailesh', 25, 4555.50)]
tpl = (['Priyanka', 24, 3455.50], ['Shailesh', 25, 4555.50])
```

- If we wish to sort a list of tuples or tuple of lists, it can be done as follows:

```
import operator
# each embedded tuple/list contains name, age, salary
lst = [('Shailesh', 24, 3455.50), ('Priyanka', 25, 4555.50)]
tpl = (['Shailesh', 24, 3455.50], ['Priyanka', 25, 4555.50])
print(sorted(lst))
print(sorted(tpl))
print(sorted(lst, key = operator.itemgetter(2)))
print(sorted(tpl, key = operator.itemgetter(2)))
```

- By default, **sorted( )** sorts by first item in list/tuple, i.e. name.
- If we wish to sort by salary, we need to use the **itemgetter( )** function of **operator** module.
- The **key** parameter of **sorted( )** requires a key function (to be applied to objects to be sorted) rather than a single key value.
- **operator.itemgetter(2)** will give us a function that fetches salary from a list/tuple.
- In general, **operator.itemgetter(n)** constructs a function that takes a list/tuple as input, and fetches the nth element out of it.

P</> Programs

Problem 8.1

Pass a tuple to the **divmod( )** function and obtain the quotient and the remainder.

Program

```
result = divmod(17,3)
print(result)
t = (17, 3)
result = divmod(*t)
```

```
print(result)
```

Output

```
(5, 2)
(5, 2)
```

Tips

- If we pass **t** to **divmod( )** an error is reported. We have to unpack the tuple into two distinct values and then pass them to **divmod( )**.
- **divmod( )** returns a tuple consisting of quotient and remainder.

Problem 8.2

Write a Python program to perform the following operations:

- Pack first 10 multiples of 10 into a tuple
- Unpack the tuple into 10 variables, each holding 1 value
- Unpack the tuple such that first value gets stored in variable x, last value in y and all values in between into disposable variables _
- Unpack the tuple such that first value gets stored in variable i, last value in j and all values in between into a single disposable variable _

Program

```
tpl = (10, 20, 30, 40, 50, 60, 70, 8, 90, 100)
a, b, c, d, e, f, g, h, i, j = tpl
print(tpl)
print(a, b, c, d, e, f, g, h, i, j)
x, _, _, _, _, _, _, _, _, y = tpl
print(x, y, _)
i, *_, j = tpl
print(i, j, _)
```

Output

```
(10, 20, 30, 40, 50, 60, 70, 8, 90, 100)
10 20 30 40 50 60 70 8 90 100
10 100 90
10 100 [20, 30, 40, 50, 60, 70, 8, 90]
```

Tips

- Disposable variable _ is usally used when you do not wish to use the variable further, and is being used only as a place-holder.

Problem 8.3

A list contains names of boys and girls as its elements. Boys' names are stored as tuples. Write a Python program to find out number of boys and girls in the list.

Program

```
lst = ['Shubha', 'Nisha', 'Sudha', ('Suresh',), ('Rajesh',), 'Radha']
boys = 0
girls = 0
for ele in lst:
    if isinstance(ele, tuple):
        boys += 1
    else :
        girls += 1
print('Boys = ', boys, 'Girls = ', girls)
```

Output

```
Boys =  2 Girls =  4
```

Tips

- **isinstance( )** functions checks whether **ele** is an instance of tuple type.
- Note that since the tuples contain a single element, it is followed by a comma.

Problem 8.4

A list contains tuples containing roll number, names and age of student. Write a Python program to gather all the names from this list into another list.

Program

```
lst = [('A101', 'Shubha', 23), ('A104', 'Nisha', 25), ('A111', 'Sudha', 24)]
nlst = [ ]
for ele in lst:
    nlst = nlst + [ele[1]]

print(nlst)
```

Output

```
['Shubha', 'Nisha', 'Sudha']
```

Tips

- **nlst** is an empty to begin with. During each iteration name is extracted from the tuple using **ele[1**] and added to the current list of names in **nlst**.

Problem 8.5

Given the following tuple

('F', 'l', 'a', 'b', 'b', 'e', 'r', 'g', 'a', 's', 't', 'e', 'd')

Write a Python program to carry out the following operations:

- Add an ! at the end of the tuple
- Convert a tuple to a string
- Extract ('b', 'b') from the tuple
- Find out number of occurrences of 'e' in the tuple
- Check whether 'r' exists in the tuple
- Convert the tuple to a list
- Delete characters 'b, 'b', 'e', 'r' from the tuple

Program

```
tpl = ('F', 'l', 'a', 'b', 'b', 'e', 'r', 'g', 'a', 's', 't', 'e', 'd')

# addition of ! is not possible as tuple is an immutable
# so to add ! we need to create a new tuple and then make tpl refer to it
tpl = tpl + ('!',)
print(tpl)
```

```
# convert tuple to string
s = ''.join(tpl)
print(s)

# extract ('b', 'b') from the tuple
t = tpl[3:5]
print(t)

# count number of 'e' in the tuple
count = tpl.count('e')
print('count = ', count)

# check whether 'r' exists in the tuple
print('r' in tpl)

# Convert the tuple to a list
lst = list(tpl)
print(lst)

# tuples are immutable, so we cannot remove elements from it
# we need to split the tuple, eliminate the unwanted element and then
merge the tuples
tpl = tpl[:3] + tpl[7:]
print(tpl)
```

Output

```
('F', 'l', 'a', 'b', 'b', 'e', 'r', 'g', 'a', 's', 't', 'e', 'd', '!')
Flabbergasted!
('b', 'b')
count =  2
True
['F', 'l', 'a', 'b', 'b', 'e', 'r', 'g', 'a', 's', 't', 'e', 'd', '!']
('F', 'l', 'a', 'g', 'a', 's', 't', 'e', 'd', '!')
```

Exercises

[A] Which of the following properties apply to string, list and tuple?

- Iterable
- Sliceable
- Indexable
- Immutable
- Sequence
- Can be empty
- Sorted collection
- Ordered collection
- Unordered collection
- Elements can be accessed using their position in the collection

[B] Which of the following operations can be performed on string, list and tuple?

- a = b + c
- a += b
- Appending a new element at the end
- Deletion of an element at the 0th position
- Modification of last element
- In place reversal

[C] Answer the following questions:

(a) Is this a valid tuple?

```
tpl = ('Square')
```

(b) What will be the output of the following code snippet?

```
num1 = num2 = (10, 20, 30, 40, 50)
print(id(num1), type(num2))
print(isinstance(num1, tuple))
print(num1 is num2)
print(num1 is not num2)
print(20 in num1)
print(30 not in num2)
```

(c) Suppose a date is represented as a tuple (d, m, y). Write a program to create two date tuples and find the number of days between the two dates.

(d) Create a list of tuples. Each tuple should contain an item and its price in float. Write a program to sort the tuples in descending order by price. Hint: Use **operator.itemgetter( )**.

(e) Store the data about shares held by a user as tuples containing the following information about shares:

Share name
Date of purchase
Cost price
Number of shares
Selling price

Write a program to determine:

- Total cost of the portfolio.
- Total amount gained or lost.
- Percentage profit made or loss incurred.

(f) Write a program to remove empty tuple from a list of tuples.

(g) Write a program to create following 3 lists:

- a list of names
- a list of roll numbers
- a list of marks

Generate and print a list of tuples containing name, roll number and marks from the 3 lists. From this list generate 3 tuples—one containing all names, another containing all roll numbers and third containing all marks.

[D] Match the following pairs:

a. tpl1 = ('A',)	1. tuple of length 6
b. tpl1 = ('A')	2. tuple of lists
c. t = tpl[::-1]	3. Tuple
d. ('A', 'B', 'C', 'D')	4. list of tuples
e. [(1, 2), (2, 3), (4, 5)]	5. String
f. tpl = tuple(range(2, 5))	6. Sorts tuple
g. ([1, 2], [3, 4], [5, 6])	7. (2, 3, 4)
h. t = tuple('Ajooba')	8. tuple of strings
i. [*a, *b, *c]	9. Unpacking of tuples in a list
j. (*a, *b, *c)	10. Unpacking of lists in a tuple

10 Sets

"Chic and unique...."

Contents

- What are Sets?
- Accessing Set Elements
- Looping in Sets
- Basic Set Operations
- Using Built-in Functions on Sets
- Set Methods
- Mathematical Set Operations
- Updating Set Operations
- Set Varieties
- Programs
- Exercises

KanNotes

What are Sets?

- Sets are like lists, with an exception that they do not contain duplicate entries.

```
a = set( )                          # empty set, use ( ) instead of { }
b = {20}                            # set with one item
c = {'Sanjay', 25, 34555.50}        # set with multiple items
d = {10, 10, 10, 10}                # only one 10 gets stored
```

- While storing an element in a set, its hash value is computed using a hashing technique to determine where it should be stored in the set.
- Since hash value of an element will always be same, no matter in which order we insert the elements in a set, they get stored in the same order.

```
s = {12, 23, 45, 16, 52}
t = {16, 52, 12, 23, 45}
u = {52, 12, 16, 45, 23}
print(s)                            # prints {12, 45, 16, 52, 23}
print(t)                            # prints {12, 45, 16, 52, 23}
print(u)                            # prints {12, 45, 16, 52, 23}
```

- It is possible to create a set of strings and tuples, but not a set of lists.

```
s1 = {'Morning', 'Evening'}                 # works
s2 = {(12, 23), (15, 25), (17, 34)}         # works
s3 = {[12, 23], [15, 25], [17, 34]}         # error
```

  Since strings and tuples are immutable, their hash value always remains the same. Hence a set of strings or tuples is permitted. However, a list may change, so its hash value may change, hence a set of lists is not permitted.

- Sets are commonly used for eliminating duplicate entries and membership testing.

Accessing Set Elements

- Entire set can be printed by just using the name of the set. Set is an unordered collection. Hence the order of insertion is not same as the order of access.

```
s = {15, 25, 35, 45, 55}
print(s)                      # prints {35, 45, 15, 55, 25}
```

- Being an unordered collection, items in a set cannot be accessed using indices.

- Sets cannot be sliced using [ ].

Looping in Sets

- Like strings, lists and tuples, sets too can be iterated over using a **for** loop.

```
s = {12, 15, 13, 23, 22, 16, 17}
for ele in s :
    print(ele)
```

- Note that unlike a string, list or tuple, a **while** loop should not be used to access the set elements. This is because we cannot access a set element using an index, as in **s[i]**.

- Built-in function **enumerate( )** can be used with a set. The enumeration is done on access order, not insertion order.

Basic Set Operations

- Sets like lists are mutable. Their contents can be changed.

```
s = {'gate', 'fate', 'late'}
s.add('rate')                 # adds one more element to set s
```

- If we want an immutable set, we should use a **frozenset**.

```
s = frozenset({'gate', 'fate', 'late'})
s.add('rate')  # error
```

- Given below are the operations that work on lists and tuples. These operations are discussed in detail in Chapter 8. Try these operations on sets too.

Concatenation - does not work
Merging - does not work
Conversion - works
Aliasing - works
Cloning - works
Searching - works
Identity - works
Comparison - works
Emptiness - works

- Two sets cannot be concatenated using +.
- Two sets cannot be merged using the form **z = s + t**.
- While converting a set using **set( )**, repetitions are eliminated.

```
lst = [10, 20, 10, 30, 40, 50, 30]
s = set(lst)        # will create set containing 10, 20, 30, 40, 50
```

Using Built-in Functions on Sets

- Many built-in functions can be used with sets.

```
s = {10, 20, 30, 40, 50}
len(s)          # return number of items in set s
max(s)          # return maximum element in set s
min(s)          # return minimum element in set s
sorted(s)       # return sorted list (not sorted set)
sum(s)          # return sum of all elements in set s
any(t)          # return True if any element of s is True
all(t)          # return True if all elements of s are True
```

Note that **reversed( )** built-in function doesn't work on sets.

Set Methods

- Any set is an object of type **set**. Its methods can be accessed using the syntax **s.method( )**. Usage of commonly used set methods is shown below:

```
s = {12, 15, 13, 23, 22, 16, 17}
t = {'A', 'B', 'C'}
u = set ( )          # empty set
s.add('Hello')       # adds 'Hello' to s
s.update(t)          # adds elements of t to s
```

```
u = s.copy( )          # performs deep copy (cloning)
s.remove(15)           # deletes 15 from s
s.remove(101)          # would raise error, as 101 is not a member of s
s.discard(12)          # removes 12 from s
s.discard(101)         # won't raise an error, though 101 is not in s
s.clear( )             # removes all elements
```

- The following methods can be used on 2 sets to check the relationship between them:

```
s = {12, 15, 13, 23, 22, 16, 17}
t = {13, 15, 22}
print(s.issuperset(t))    # prints True
print(s.issubset(t))      # prints False
print(s.isdisjoint(t))    # prints False
```

Since all elements of **t** are present in **s**, **s** is a superset of **t** and **t** is subset of **s**. If the intersection of two sets is null, the sets are called disjoint sets.

Mathematical Set Operations

- Following union, intersection and difference operations can be carried out on sets:

```
# sets
engineers = {'Vijay', 'Sanjay', 'Ajay', 'Sujay', 'Dinesh'}
managers = {'Aditya', 'Sanjay'}

# union - all people in both categories
print(engineers | managers)

# intersection - who are engineers and managers
print(engineers & managers)

# difference - engineers who are not managers
print(engineers - managers)

# difference - managers who are not engineers
print(managers - engineers)

# symmetric difference - managers who are not engineers
# and engineers who are not managers
print(managers ^ engineers)

a = {1, 2, 3, 4, 5}
```

```
b = {2, 4, 5}
print(a >= b)    # prints True as a is superset of b
print(a <= b)    # prints False as a is not a subset of b
```

Updating Set Operations

- Mathematical set operations can be extended to update an existing set.

```
a |= b       # update a with the result of a | b
a &= b       # update a with the result of a & b
a -= b       # update a with the result of a - b
a ^= b       # update a with the result of a ^ b
```

Set Varieties

- Unlike a list and tuple, a set cannot contain a set embedded in it.

```
s = {'gate', 'fate', {10, 20, 30}, 'late'}    # error, nested sets
```

- It is possible to unpack a set using the *operator.

```
x = {1, 2, 3, 4}
print(*x)        # outputs 1, 2, 3, 4
```

P</> Programs

Problem 10.1

What will be the output of the following program?

```
a = {10, 20, 30, 40, 50, 60, 70}
b = {33, 44, 51, 10, 20,50, 30, 33}
print(a | b)
print(a & b)
print(a - b)
print(b - a)
print(a ^ b)
print(a >= b)
print(a <= b)
```

Output

```
{33, 70, 40, 10, 44, 50, 51, 20, 60, 30}
{10, 50, 20, 30}
{40, 60, 70}
{33, 51, 44}
{33, 70, 40, 44, 51, 60}
False
False
```

Problem 10.2

What will be the output of the following program?

```
a = {1, 2, 3, 4, 5, 6, 7}
b = {1, 2, 3, 4, 5, 6, 7}
c = {1, 2, 3, 4, 5, 6, 7}
d = {1, 2, 3, 4, 5, 6, 7}
e = {3, 4, 1, 0, 2, 5, 8, 9}
a |= e
print(a)
b &= e
print(b)
c -= e
print(c)
d ^= e
print(d)
```

Output

```
{0, 1, 2, 3, 4, 5, 6, 7, 8, 9}
{1, 2, 3, 4, 5}
{6, 7}
{0, 6, 7, 8, 9}
```

Problem 10.3

Write a program to carry out the following operations on the given set

s = {10, 2, -3, 4, 5, 88}

- number of items in set s
- maximum element in set s
- minimum element in set s

- sum of all elements in set s
- obtain a new sorted set from s, set s remaining unchanged
- report whether 100 is an element of set s
- report whether -3 is an element of set s

Program

```
s = {10, 2, -3, 4, 5, 88}
print(len(s))
print(max(s))
print(min(s))
print(sum(s))
t = sorted(s)
print(t)
print(100 in s)
print(-3 not in s)
```

Output

```
6
88
-3
106
[-3, 2, 4, 5, 10, 88]
False
False
```

Problem 10.4

What will be the output of the following program?

Program

```
l = [10, 20, 30, 40, 50]
t = ('Sundeep', 25, 79.58)
s = 'set theory'
s1 = set(l)
s2 = set(t)
s3 = set(s)
print(s1)
print(s2)
print(s3)
```

Output

```
{40, 10, 50, 20, 30}
{25, 79.58, 'Sundeep'}
{'h', 's', 't', 'y', ' ', 'r', 'e', 'o'}
```

Exercises

[A] What will be the output of the following programs:

(a)
```
s = {1, 2, 3, 7, 6, 4}
s.discard(10)
s.remove(10)
print(s)
```

(b)
```
s1 = {10, 20, 30, 40, 50}
s2 = {10, 20, 30, 40, 50}
print(id(s1), id(s2))
```

(c)
```
s1 = {10, 20, 30, 40, 50}
s2 = {10, 20, 30, 40, 50}
s3 = {*s1, *s2}
print(s3)
```

(d)
```
s = set('KanLabs')
t = s[::-1]
print(t)
```

(e)
```
num = {10, 20, {30, 40}, 50}
print(num)
```

(f)
```
s = {'Tiger', 'Lion', 'Jackal'}
del(s)
print(s)
```

(g)
```
fruits = {'Kiwi', 'Jack Fruit', 'Lichi'}
fruits.clear( )
print(fruits)
```

(h)
```
s = {10, 25, 4, 12, 3, 8}
sorted(lst)
print(lst)
```

(i)
```
s = { }
t = {1, 4, 5, 2, 3}
```

```
print(type(s), type(t))
```

[B] Answer the following questions:

(a) A set contains names which begin either with A or with B. Write a program to separate out the names into two sets, one containing names beginning with A and another containing names beginning with B.

(b) Create an empty set. Write a program that adds five new names to this set, modifies one existing name and deletes two names existing in it.

(c) What is the difference between the two set functions—**discard( )** and **remove( )**.

(d) Write a program to create a set containing 10 randomly generated numbers in the range 15 to 45. Count how many of these numbers are less than 30. Delete all numbers which are greater than 35.

(e) What do the following set operators do?

|, &, ^, ~

(f) What do the following set operators do?

|=, &=, ^=, -=

(g) How will you remove all duplicate elements present in a string, a list and a tuple?

(h) Which operator is used for determining whether a set is a subset of another set?

(i) What will be the output of the following program?

```
s = {'Mango', 'Banana', 'Guava', 'Kiwi'}
s.clear( )
print(s)
del(s)
print(s)
```

(j) Which of the following is the correct way to create an empty set?

```
s1 = set( )
s2 = { }
```

What are the types of **s1** and **s2**? How will you confirm the type?

11 Dictionaries

"Versatility, thy name is dictionary..."

Contents

- What are Dictionaries?
- Accessing Dictionary Elements
- Looping in Dictionaries
- Basic Dictionary Operations
- Using Built-in Functions on Dictionaries
- Dictionary Methods
- Dictionary Varieties
- Programs
- Exercises

KanNotes

What are Dictionaries?

- A Dictionary is a collection of key-value pairs.
- Dictionaries are also known as maps or associative arrays.
- A dictionary contains comma-separated key : value pairs enclosed within { }.

```
d1 = { }        # empty dictionary
d2 = {'A101' : 'Amol', 'A102' : 'Anil', 'B103' : 'Ravi'}
```

  Here, 'A101', 'A102', 'B103' are keys, whereas, 'Amol', 'Anil', 'Ravi' are values.

- Different keys may have the same values.

```
d = {10 : 'A', 20 : 'A', 30 : 'Z'}     # ok
```

- Keys must be unique. If keys are same, but values are different, latest key value pair gets stored.

```
d = {10 : 'A', 20 : 'B', 10 : 'Z'}     # will store {10 : 'Z', 20 : 'B'}
```

- If key value pairs are repeated, then only one pair gets stored.

```
d = {10 : 'A', 20 : 'B', 10 : 'A'}     # will store {10 : 'A', 20 : 'B'}
```

Accessing Dictionary Elements

- Entire dictionary can be printed by just using the name of the dictionary.

```
d = {'A101' : 'Amol', 'A102' : 'Anil', 'B103' : 'Ravi'}
print(d)
```

- Unlike sets, dictionaries preserve insertion order. However, elements are not accessed using the position but using the key.

```
d = {'A101' : 'Dinesh', 'A102' : 'Shrikant', 'B103' : 'Sudhir'}
print(d['A102'])     # prints value for key 'A102'
```

Thus, elements are not position indexed, but key indexed.

- Dictionaries cannot be sliced using [ ].

Looping in Dictionaries

- Like strings, lists, tuples and sets, dictionaries too can be iterated over using a **for** loop. There are three ways to do so:

```
courses = {'DAA' : 'CS', 'AOA' : 'ME', 'SVY' : 'CE' }

# iterate over key-value pairs
for k, v in courses.items( ) :
    print(k, v)

# iterate over keys
for k in courses.keys( ) :
    print(k)

# iterate over keys - shorter way
for k in courses :
    print(k)

# iterate over values
for v in courses.values( ) :
    print(v)
```

- While iterating through a dictionary using a for loop, if we wish to keep track of index of the key-value pairs that is being referred to, we can do so using the built-in **enumerate( )** function.

```
courses = {'DAA' : 'CS', 'AOA' : 'ME', 'SVY' : 'CE' }
for i, (k, v) in enumerate(courses.items( )) :
    print(i,k)
```

Note that ( ) around **k, v** are necessary.

Basic Dictionary Operations

- Dictionaries are mutable. So, we can perform add/delete/modify operations on a dictionary.

```
courses = {'CS101' : 'CPP', 'CS102' : 'DS', 'CS201' : 'OOP',
           'CS226' : 'DAA', 'CS601' : 'Crypt', 'CS442' : 'Web'}
# add, modify, delete
courses['CS444'] = 'Web Services'        # add new key-value pair
```

```
courses['CS201'] = 'OOP Using java'   # modify value for a key
del(courses['CS102'])                 # delete a key-value pair
del(courses)                          # delete dictionary object
```

- Note that any new addition will take place at the end of the existing dictionary, since dictionary preserves the insertion order.
- Dictionary keys cannot be changed in place.
- Given below are the operations that work on lists and tuples. These operations are discussed in detail in Chapter 8. Try these operations on dictionaries as an exercise.

  Concatenation - does not work
  Merging - does not work
  Conversion - works
  Aliasing - works
  Cloning - works
  Searching - works
  Identity - works
  Comparison - does not work
  Emptiness - works

- Two dictionaries cannot be concatenated using +.
- Two dictionaries cannot be merged using the form **z = s + t**.
- Two dictionary objects cannot be compared using <, >.

Using Built-in Functions on Dictionaries

- Many built-in functions can be used with dictionaries.

```
d = {'CS101' : 'CPP', 'CS102' : 'DS', 'CS201' : 'OOP'}
len(d)          # return number of key-value pairs
max(d)          # return maximum key in dictionary d
min(d)          # return minimum key in dictionary d
sorted(d)       # return sorted list of keys
sum(d)          # return sum of all keys if keys are numbers
any(d)          # return True if any key of dictionary d is True
all(d)          # return True if all keys of dictionary d are True
reversed(d)     # can be used for reversing dict/keys/values
```

- Use of reversed function to reverse a dictionary by keys is shown below:

```
courses = {'CS101' : 'CPP', 'CS102' : 'DS', 'CS201' : 'OOP'}
for k, v in reversed(courses.items( )) :
    print(k, v)
```

Dictionary Methods

- There are many dictionary methods. Many of the operations performed by them can also be performed using built-in functions. The useful dictionary methods are shown below:

```
c = {'CS101' : 'CPP', 'CS102' : 'DS', 'CS201' : 'OOP'}
d = {'ME126' : 'HPE', 'ME102' : 'TOM', 'ME234' : 'AEM'}

print(c.get('CS102', 'Absent'))      # prints DS
print(c.get('EE102', 'Absent'))      # prints Absent
print(c['EE102'])                    # raises keyerror

c.update(d)                          # updates c with items in d
print(c.popitem( ))         # removes and returns item in LIFO order
print(c.pop('CS102'))       # removes key and returns its value
c.clear( )                  # clears all dictionary entries
```

Note that while updating a dictionary if keys are same, values are overwritten.

popitem( ) is useful in destructively iterate through a dictionary.

Dictionary Varieties

- Keys in a dictionary must be unique and immutable. Numbers, strings or tuples can be used as keys. If tuple is used as a key, it should not contain any mutable element like list.

```
d = {(1, 5) : 'ME126', (3, 2)  : 'ME102', (5, 4) : 'ME234'}
```

- Dictionaries can be nested.

```
contacts = {
            'Anil': {'DOB' : '17/11/98', 'Favorite' : 'Igloo'},
            'Amol': {'DOB' : '14/10/99', 'Favorite' : 'Tundra'},
            'Ravi': {'DOB' : '19/11/97', 'Favorite' : 'Artic'}
    }
```

- Two dictionaries can be merged to create a third dictionary by unpacking the two dictionaries using **. If we use * only keys will be unpacked.

```
animals = {'Tiger' : 141, 'Lion' : 152, 'Leopard' : 110}
birds = {'Eagle' : 38, 'Crow': 3, 'Parrot' : 2}
```

```
combined = {** animals, ** birds}
```

- A dictionary containing different keys but same values can be created using a **fromkeys( )** function as shown below:

```
lst = [12, 13, 14, 15, 16]
d = dict.fromkeys(lst, 25)  # keys - list items, all values set to 25
```

P</> Programs

Problem 11.1

Create a dictionary called **students** containing names and ages. Copy the dictionary into **stud**. Empty the **students** dictionary, as **stud** continues to hold the data.

Program

```
students = {'Anil' : 23, 'Sanjay' : 28, 'Ajay' : 25}
stud = students     # shallow copy, stud starts referring to same dictionary
students = { }      # students now refers to an empty dictionary
print(stud)
```

Output

```
{'Anil': 23, 'Sanjay': 28, 'Ajay': 25}
```

Tips

- By making a shallow copy, a new dictionary is not created. **stud** just starts referring (pointing) to the same data to which **students** was referring (pointing).
- Had we used **students.clear( )** it would have cleared all the data, so **students** and **stud** both would have referred to an empty dictionary.

Problem 11.2

Create a list of cricketers. Use this list to create a dictionary in which the list values become keys of the dictionary. Set the values of all keys to 50 in the dictionary created.

Program

```
lst = ['Sunil', 'Sachin', 'Rahul', 'Kapil', 'Sunil', 'Rahul']
d = dict.fromkeys(lst, 50)
print(len(lst))
print(len(d))
print(d)
```

Output

```
6
4
{'Sunil': 50, 'Sachin': 50, 'Rahul': 50, 'Kapil': 50}
```

Tips

- The list may contain duplicate items, whereas a dictionary always contains unique keys. Hence when the dictionary is created from list, duplicates are eliminated, as seen in the output.

Problem 11.3

Write a program to sort a dictionary in ascending/descending order by key and ascending/descending order by value.

Program

```
import operator
d = {'Oil' : 230, 'Clip' : 150, 'Stud' : 175, 'Nut' : 35}
print('Original dictionary : ', d)

# sorting by key
d1 = sorted(d.items( ))
print('Asc. order by key : ', d1)
d2 = sorted(d.items( ), reverse = True)
print('Des. order by key : ', d2)

# sorting by value
d1 = sorted(d.items( ), key = operator.itemgetter(1))
print('Asc. order by value : ', d1)
d2 = sorted(d.items( ), key = operator.itemgetter(1), reverse = True)
```

```
print('Des. order by value : ', d2)
```

Output

```
Original dictionary : {'Oil': 230, 'Clip': 150, 'Stud': 175, 'Nut': 35}
Asc. order by key : [('Clip', 150), ('Nut', 35), ('Oil', 230), ('Stud', 175)]
Des. order by key : [('Stud', 175), ('Oil', 230), ('Nut', 35), ('Clip', 150)]
Asc. order by value : [('Nut', 35), ('Clip', 150), ('Stud', 175), ('Oil', 230)]
Des. order by value : [('Oil', 230), ('Stud', 175), ('Clip', 150), ('Nut', 35)]
```

Tips

- By default, items in a dictionary would be sorted as per the key.
- To sort by values we need to use **operator.itemgetter(1)**.
- The **key** parameter of **sorted( )** requires a key function (to be applied to be objects to be sorted) rather than a single key value.
- **operator.itemgetter(1)** gives a function that grabs the first item from a list-like object.
- In general, **operator.itemgetter(n)** constructs a callable that assumes an iterable object (e.g. list, tuple, set) as input, and fetches the nth element out of it.

Problem 11.4

Write a program to create three dictionaries and concatenate them to create a fourth dictionary.

Program

```
d1 = {'Mango' : 30, 'Guava': 20}
d2 = {'Apple' : 70, 'Pineapple' : 50}
d3 = {'Kiwi' : 90, 'Banana' : 35}
d4 = { }
for d in (d1, d2, d3) :
    d4.update(d)
print(d4)

# one more way
d5 = {**d1, **d2, **d3}
```

```
print(d5)

# will unpack only the keys into the list
d6 = list({*d1, *d2, *d3})
print(d6)
```

Output

```
{'Mango': 30, 'Guava': 20, 'Apple': 70, 'Pineapple': 50, 'Kiwi': 90,
'Banana': 35}
{'Mango': 30, 'Guava': 20, 'Apple': 70, 'Pineapple': 50, 'Kiwi': 90,
'Banana': 35}
[Apple', 'Guava', 'Kiwi', 'Mango', 'Banana', 'Pineapple']
```

Tips

- From the output it can be observed that the dictionaries are merged in the order listed in the expression.
- Note that list of keys is constructed from a dictionary they are not stored in the order listed in the expression.

Problem 11.5

Write a program to check whether a dictionary is empty or not.

Program

```
d1 = {'Anil' : 45, 'Amol' : 32}
if bool(d1) :
    print('Dictionary is not empty')
d2 = { }
if not bool(d2) :
    print('Dictionary is empty')
```

Output

```
Dictionary is not empty
Dictionary is empty
```

Problem 11.6

Suppose there are two dictionaries called **boys** and **girls** containing names as keys and ages as values. Write a program to merge the two dictionaries into a third dictionary.

Program

```
boys = {'Nilesh' : 41, 'Soumitra' : 42, 'Nadeem' : 47}
girls = {'Rasika' : 38, 'Rajashree': 43, 'Rasika' : 45}
combined = {**boys, **girls}
print(combined)
combined = {**girls, **boys}
print(combined)
```

Output

```
{'Nilesh': 41, 'Soumitra': 42, 'Nadeem': 47, 'Rasika': 45, 'Rajashree': 43}
{'Rasika': 45, 'Rajashree': 43, 'Nilesh': 41, 'Soumitra': 42, 'Nadeem': 47}
```

Tips

- From the output it can be observed that the dictionaries are merged in the order listed in the expression.
- As the merging takes place, duplicates get overwritten from left to right. So Rasika : 38 got overwritten with Rasika : 45.

Problem 11.7

For the following dictionary, write a program to report the maximum and minimum salary.

Program

```
d = {
        'anuj' : {'salary' : 10000, 'age' : 20, 'height' : 6},
        'aditya' : {'salary' : 6000, 'age'  : 26, 'height' : 5.6},
        'rahul' :  {'salary' : 7000, 'age'  : 26, 'height' : 5.9}
    }
lst = [ ]
for v in d.values( ) :
```

```
    lst.append(v['salary'])
print(max(lst))
print(min(lst))
```

Output

```
10000
6000
```

Problem 11.8

Suppose a dictionary contains roll numbers and names of students. Write a program to receive the roll number, extract the name corresponding to the roll number and display a message congratulating the student by his name. If the roll number does not exist in the dictionary, the message should be 'Congratulations Student!'.

Program

```
students = {554 : 'Ajay', 350: 'Ramesh', 395: 'Rakesh'}
rollno = int(input('Enter roll number: '))
name = students.get(rollno, 'Student')
print(f'Congratulations {name}!')
rollno = int(input('Enter roll number: '))
name = students.get(rollno, 'Student')
print(f'Congratulations {name}!')
```

Output

```
Enter roll number: 350
Congratulations Ramesh!
Enter roll number: 450
Congratulations Student!
```

Exercises

[A] State whether the following statements are True or False:

(a) Dictionary elements can be accessed using position-based index.

(b) Dictionaries are immutable.

(c) Insertion order is preserved by a dictionary.

(d) The very first key - value pair in a dictionary **d** can be accessed using the expression **d[0]**.

(e) **courses.clear( )** will delete the dictionary object called **courses**.

(f) It is possible to nest dictionaries.

(g) It is possible to hold multiple values against a key in a dictionary.

[B] Attempt the following questions:

(a) Write a program that reads a string from the keyboard and creates dictionary containing frequency of each character occurring in the string. Also print these occurrences in the form of a histogram.

(b) Create a dictionary containing names of students and marks obtained by them in three subjects. Write a program to replace the marks in three subjects with the total in three subjects, and average marks. Also report the topper of the class.

(c) Given the following dictionary:

```
portfolio = {
        'accounts' :  ['SBI', 'IOB'],
        'shares' : '  [HDFC, 'ICICI', 'TM', 'TCS'],
        'ornaments' : ['10 gm gold', '1 kg silver']
    }
```

Write a program to perform the following operations:

- Add a key to portfolio called 'MF' with values 'Reliance' and 'ABSL'.
- Set the value of 'accounts' to a list containing 'Axis' and 'BOB'.
- Sort the items in the list stored under the 'shares' key.
- Delete the list stored under 'ornaments' key.

(d) Create two dictionaries—one containing grocery items and their prices and another containing grocery items and quantity purchased. By using the values from these two dictionaries compute the total bill.

(e) Which functions will you use to fetch all keys, all values and key value pairs from a given dictionary?

(f) Create a dictionary of 10 usernames and passwords. Receive the username and password from keyboard and search for them in the dictionary. Print appropriate message on the screen based on whether a match is found or not.

(g) Given the following dictionary

```
marks = {
                 'Subu' : {'Maths' : 88, 'Eng' : 60, 'SSt' : 95},
                 'Amol' : {'Maths' : 78, 'Eng' : 68, 'SSt' : 89},
                 'Raka' : {'Maths' : 56, 'Eng' : 66, 'SSt' : 77}
        }
```

Write a program to perform the following operations:

- Print marks obtained by Amol in English.
- Set marks obtained by Raka in Maths to 77.
- Sort the dictionary by name.

(h) Create a dictionary which stores the following data:

Interface	**IP Address**	**status**
eth0	1.1.1.1	up
eth1	2.2.2.2	up
wlan0	3.3.3.3	down
wlan1	4.4.4.4	up

Write a program to perform the following operations:

- Find the status of the given interface.
- Find the interface and IP of all interfaces which are up.
- Find the total number of interfaces.
- Add two new entries to the dictionary.

(i) Suppose a dictionary contains 5 key-value pairs of name and marks. Write a program to print them from last pair to first pair. Keep deleting every pair printed, such that the end of printing the dictionary falls empty.

[C] Answer the following questions:

(a) What will be the output of the following code snippet?

```
d = {'Milk' : 1, 'Soap' : 2, 'Towel' : 3, 'Shampoo' : 4, 'Milk' : 7}
print(d[0], d[1], d[2])
```

(b) Which of the following statements are CORRECT?

i. A dictionary will always contain unique keys.
ii. Each key in a dictionary may have multiple values.
iii. If same key is assigned a different value, latest value will prevail.

(c) How will you create an empty list, empty tuple, empty set and empty dictionary?

(d) How will you create a list, tuple, set and dictionary, each containing one element?

(e) Given the following dictionary:

```
d = {'d1' : {'Fruitname' : 'Mango', 'Season' : 'Summer'},
     'd2' : {'Fruitname' : 'Orange', 'Season' : 'Winter'}}
```

How will you access and print Mango and Winter?

(f) In the following table check the box if a property is enjoyed by the data types mentioned in columns?

Property	str	list	tuple	set	dict
Object					
Collection					
Mutable					
Ordered					
Indexed by position					
Indexed by key					
Iterable					
Slicing allowed					
Nesting allowed					
Homogeneous elements					
Heterogeneous elements					

(g) What is the most common usage of the data types mentioned below?

str
list
tuple
set
dict

12 Comprehensions

"Add punch to your thought..."

Contents

- What are Comprehensions?
- List Comprehension
- Set Comprehension
- Dictionary Comprehension
- Programs
- Exercises

KanNotes

What are Comprehensions?

- Comprehensions offer an easy and compact way of creating lists, sets and dictionaries.
- A comprehension works by looping or iterating over items and assigning them to a container like list, set or dictionary.
- This container cannot be a tuple as tuple being immutable is unable to receive assignments.

List Comprehension

- List comprehension consists of brackets containing an expression followed by a **for** clause, and zero or more **for** or **if** clauses.
- So general form of a list comprehension is

  lst = [expression for var in sequence [optional for and/or if]]

- Examples of list comprehension:

```
# generate 20 random numbers in the range 10 to 100
a = [random.randint(10, 100) for n in range(20)]

# generate square and cube of all numbers between 0 and 10
a = [( x, x**2, x**3) for x in range(10)]

# convert a list of strings to a list of integers
a = [int(x) for x in ['10', '20', '30', '40']
```

- Examples of use of **if** in list comprehension:

```
# generate a list of even numbers in the range 10 to 30
a = [n for n in range(10, 30) if n % 2 == 0]

# from a list delete all numbers having a value between 20 and 50
a = [num for num in a if num < 20 or num > 50]
```

- Example of use of **if-else** in list comprehension:

```
# when if-else both are used, place them before for
# replace a vowel in a string with !
a = ['!' if alphabet in 'aeiou' else alphabet for alphabet in 'Technical' ]
```

- Example of use of multiple **for**s and if in list comprehension:

```
# flatten a list of lists
arr = [[1,2,3,4], [5,6,7,8], [10, 11, 12, 13]]
b = [n for ele in arr for n in ele]            # one way

# * can be used to unpack a list
c = [*arr[0], *arr[1], *arr[2]]                # one more way
```

- Note the difference between nested **for** in a list comprehension and a nested comprehension:

```
# produces [4, 5, 6, 5, 6, 7, 6, 7, 8]. Uses nested for
lst = [a + b for a in [1, 2, 3] for b in [3, 4, 5]]

# produces [[4, 5, 6], [5, 6, 7], [6, 7, 8]]. Uses nested comprehension
lst = [[a + b for a in [1, 2, 3]] for b in [3, 4, 5]]
```

Think of first **for** as outer loop and second **for** as inner loop.

- Example of use of multiple **for**s and **if** in list comprehension:

```
# generate all unique combinations of 1, 2 and 3
a = [(i, j, k) for i in [1,2,3] for j in [1,2,3] for k in [1, 2, 3] if i != j \
        and j !=k and k != i]
```

Set Comprehension

- Like list comprehensions, set comprehensions offer an easy way of creating sets. It consists of braces containing an expression followed by a **for** clause, and zero or more **for** or **if** clauses.
- So general form of a set comprehension is

  s = {expression for var in sequence [optional for and/or if]}
- Examples of set comprehension:

```
# generate a set containing square of all numbers between 0 and 10
a = {x**2 for x in range(10)}

# from a set delete all numbers between 20 and 50
a = {num for num in a if num < 20 or num > 50}
```

Dictionary Comprehension

- General form of a dictionary comprehension is as follows:

  dict_var = {key:value for (key, value) in dictonary.items( )}
- Examples of dictionary comprehension:

```
d = {'a': 1, 'b': 2, 'c': 3, 'd': 4}

# obtain dictionary with each value cubed
d1 = {k : v ** 3 for (k, v) in d.items( )}
print(d1)          # prints {'a': 1, 'b': 8, 'c': 27, 'd': 64}

# obtain dictionary with each value cubed if value > 3
d2 = {k : v ** 3 for (k, v) in d.items( ) if v > 3}
print(d2)          # prints {'d': 64}

# Identify odd and even entries in the dictionary
d3 = {k : ('Even' if v % 2 == 0 else 'Odd') for (k, v) in d.items( )}
print(d3)          # prints {'a': 'Odd', 'b': 'Even', 'c': 'Odd', 'd': 'Even'}
```

P</> Programs

Problem 12.1

Using list comprehension, write a program to generate a list of numbers in the range 2 to 50 that are divisible by 2 and 4.

Program

```
lst = [num for num in range(2,51) if num % 2 == 0 and num % 4 == 0]
print(lst)
```

Output

```
[4, 8, 12, 16, 20, 24, 28, 32, 36, 40, 44, 48]
```

Problem 12.2

Write a program to flatten the following list using list comprehension:

mat = [[1, 2, 3, 4], [5, 6, 7, 8], [9, 10, 11, 12]]

Program

```
mat = [[1, 2, 3, 4], [5, 6, 7, 8], [9, 10, 11, 12]]
a = [num for lst in mat for num in lst]
print(a)
```

Output

```
[1, 2, 3, 4, 5, 6, 7, 8, 9, 10, 11, 12]
```

Problem 12.3

Write a program to create a set containing some randomly generated numbers in the range 15 to 45. Count how many of these numbers are less than 30. Delete all numbers which are less than 30.

Program

```
import random
r = {int(15 + 30 * random.random( )) for num in range(10)}
print(r)
count = len({num for num in r if num < 30})
print(count)
s = {num for num in r if num < 30}
r = r - s
print(r)
```

Output

```
{32, 35, 36, 38, 41, 43, 21, 23, 25, 26}
4
{32, 35, 36, 38, 41, 43}
```

Tips

- Deletion of elements cannot be done while iterating the set. Hence a separate set **s** containing elements below 30 is first created and then **r = r - s** is done to delete set s elements from set r.

Problem 12.4

Write a program using list comprehension to eliminate empty tuples from a list of tuples.

Program

```
lst = [( ), ( ), (10), (10, 20), ('',), (10, 20, 30), (40, 50), ( ), (45)]
lst = [tpl for tpl in lst if tpl]
print(lst)
```

Output

```
[10, (10, 20), ('',), (10, 20, 30), (40, 50), 45]
```

Tips

- **if tpl** returns **True** if the tuple is not empty.

Problem 12.5

Given a string, split it on whitespace, capitalize each element of the resulting list and join them back into a string. Your implementation should use list comprehension.

Program

```
s1 = 'dreams may change, but friends are forever'
s2 = [' '.join(w.capitalize( ) for w in s1.split( ))]
s3 = s2[0]
print(s3)
```

Output

```
'Dreams May Change, But Friends Are Forever'
```

Tips

- To rebuild the list from capitalized elements, start with an empty string.

Problem 12.6

From a dictionary with string keys create a new dictionary with the vowels removed from the keys.

Program

```
words = { 'Tub' : 1, 'Toothbrush' : 2, 'Towel' : 3, 'Nailcutter' : 4}
d = {''.join(alpha for alpha in k if alpha not in 'aeiou'): v for (k, v) in
        words.items( )}
print(d)
```

Output

```
{'Tb': 1, 'Tthbrsh': 2, 'Twl': 3, 'Nlcttr': 4}
```

Tips

- We have used a list comprehension nested inside a dictionary comprehension.
- The list comprehension builds a new key starting with an empty string, adding only those characters from the key which are not vowels.
- The list comprehension is fed with keys by dictionary comprehension.

Problem 12.7

Write a program to add two 3 x 4 matrices using

(a) lists
(b) list comprehension

Program

```
mat1 = [[1, 2, 3, 4], [5, 6, 7, 8], [9, 10, 11, 12]]
mat2 = [[1, 2, 3, 4], [5, 6, 7, 8], [9, 10, 11, 12]]
mat3 = [[0, 0, 0, 0], [0, 0, 0, 0], [0, 0, 0, 0]]

# iterate through rows
for i in range(len(mat1)) :
```

```
    # iterate through columns
    for j in range(len(mat1[0])) :
        mat3[i][j] = mat1[i][j] + mat2[i][j]
print(mat3)
mat3 = [[mat1[i][j] + mat2[i][j] for j in range(len(mat1[0]))]
            for i in range(len(mat1))]
print(mat3)
```

Output

```
[[2, 4, 6, 8], [10, 12, 14, 16], [18, 20, 22, 24]]
[[2, 4, 6, 8], [10, 12, 14, 16], [18, 20, 22, 24]]
```

Tips

- Nested list comprehension is evaluated in the context of the **for** that follows it.

Problem 12.8

Suppose a dictionary contains following information for 5 employees:

```
emp = {
        'A101' : {'name' : 'Ashish', 'age' : 30, 'salary' : 21000},
        'B102' : {'name' : 'Dinesh', 'age' : 25, 'salary' : 12200},
        'A103' : {'name' : 'Ramesh', 'age' : 28, 'salary' : 11000},
        'D104' : {'name' : 'Akheel', 'age' : 30, 'salary' : 18000},
        'A105' : {'name' : 'Akaash', 'age' : 32, 'salary' : 20000}
    }
```

Using dictionary comprehensions, write a program to create:

- Dictionary of all those codes and values, where codes start with 'A'.
- Dictionary of all codes and names.
- Dictionary of all codes and ages.
- Dictionary of all codes and ages, where age is more than 30.
- Dictionary of all codes and names, where names start with 'A'.
- Dictionary of all codes and salaries, where salary is in the range 13000 to 20000.

Program

```
emp = {
        'A101' : {'name' : 'Ashish', 'age' : 30, 'salary' : 21000},
        'B102' : {'name' : 'Dinesh', 'age' : 25, 'salary' : 12200},
        'A103' : {'name' : 'Ramesh', 'age' : 28, 'salary' : 11000},
        'D104' : {'name' : 'Akheel', 'age' : 30, 'salary' : 18000},
    }
d1 = {k : v for (k, v) in emp.items( ) if k.startswith('A')}
d2 = {k : v['name'] for (k, v) in emp.items( )}
d3 = {k : v['age'] for (k, v) in emp.items( )}
d4 = {k : v['age'] for (k, v) in emp.items( ) if v['age'] > 30}
d5 = {k : v['name'] for (k, v) in emp.items( ) if v['name'].startswith('A')}
d6 = {k : v['salary'] for (k, v) in emp.items( ) if v['salary'] > 13000 and
v['salary'] <= 20000}
print(d1)
print(d2)
print(d3)
print(d4)
print(d5)
print(d6)
```

Output

```
{'A101': {'name': 'Ashish', 'age': 30, 'salary': 21000}, 'A103': {'name':
'Ramesh', 'age': 28, 'salary': 11000}}
{'A101': 'Ashish', 'B102': 'Dinesh', 'A103': 'Ramesh', 'D104': 'Akheel'}
{'A101': 30, 'B102': 25, 'A103': 28, 'D104': 30}
{}
{'A101': 'Ashish', 'D104': 'Akheel'}
{'D104': 18000}
```

Tips

- Note that the data has been organized in nested directories.
- To access 'Ashish' we need to use the syntax **emp['A101']['name']**
- To access 32 we need to use the syntax **emp['A105']['age']**

Exercises

[A] State whether the following statements are True or False:

(a) Tuple comprehension offers a fast and compact way to generate a tuple.

(b) List comprehension and dictionary comprehension can be nested.

(c) A list being used in a list comprehension cannot be modified when it is being iterated.

(d) Sets being immutable cannot be used in comprehension.

(e) Comprehension can be used create a list, set or a dictionary.

[B] Answer the following questions:

(a) Write a program that generates a list of integer coordinates for all points in the first quadrant from (1, 1) to (5, 5). Use list comprehension.

(b) Using list comprehension, write a program to create a list by multiplying each element in the list by 10.

(c) Write a program to generate first 20 Fibonacci numbers using list comprehension.

(d) Write a program to generate two lists using list comprehension. One list should contain first 20 odd numbers, and another should contain first 20 even numbers.

(e) Suppose a list contains positive and negative numbers. Write a program to create two lists—one containing positive numbers and another containing negative numbers.

(f) Suppose a list contains 5 strings. Write a program to convert all these strings to uppercase.

(g) Write a program that converts a list of temperatures in Fahrenheit degrees to equivalent Celsius degrees using list comprehension.

(h) Write a program to generate a 2D matrix of size 4 x 5 containing random multiples of 4 in the range 40 to 160.

(i) Write a program that converts words present in a list into uppercase and stores them in a set.

[C] Attempt the following questions:

(a) Consider the following code snippet:

```
s = set([int(n) for n in input('Enter values: ').split( )])
print(s)
```

What will be the output of the above code snippet if input provided to it is 1 2 3 4 5 6 7 2 4 5 0?

(b) How will you convert the following code into a list comprehension?

```
a = [ ]
for n in range(10, 30) :
    if n % 2 == 0 :
        a.append(n)
```

(c) How will you convert the following code into a set comprehension?

```
a = set( )
for n in range(21, 40) :
    if n % 2 == 0 :
        a.add(n)
print(a)
```

(d) What will be the output of the following code snippet?

```
s = [a + b for a in ['They ', 'We '] for b in ['are gone!', 'have come!']]
print(s)
```

(e) From the sentence

sent = 'Pack my box with five dozen liquor jugs'

how will you generate a set given below?

{'liquor', 'jugs', 'with', 'five', 'dozen', 'Pack'}

(f) Which of the following the correct form of dictionary comprehension?

i. dict_var = {key : value for (key, value) in dictonary.items( )}
ii. dict_var = {key : value for (key, value) in dictonary}
iii. dict_var = {key : value for (key, value) in dictonary.keys( )}

(g) Using comprehension how will you convert

{'a' : 1, 'b' : 2, 'c' : 3, 'd' : 4, 'e' : 5}

into

{'A' : 100, 'B' : 200, 'C' : 300, 'D' : 400, 'E' : 500}?

(h) What will be the output of the following code snippet?

```
lst = [2, 7, 8, 6, 5, 5, 4, 4, 8]
s = {True if n % 2 == 0 else False for n in lst}
print(s)
```

(i) How will you convert

d = {'AMOL' : 20, 'ANIL' : 12, 'SUNIL' : 13, 'RAMESH' : 10}

into

{'Amol' : 400, 'Anil' : 144, 'Sunil' : 169, 'Ramesh' : 100}

(j) How will you convert the words present in a list given below into uppercase and store them in a set?

lst = ['Amol', 'Vijay', 'Vinay', 'Rahul', 'Sandeep']

13 Functions

"Think modular, think of functions..."

Contents

KanNotes

What are Functions?

- Python function is a block of code that performs a specific and well-defined task.
- Two main advantages of function are:
  (a) They help us divide our program into multiple tasks. For each task we can define a function. This makes the code modular.
  (b) Functions provide a reuse mechanism. The same function can be called any number of times.
- There are two types of Python functions:
  (a) Built-in functions - Ex. **len( )**, **sorted( )**, **min( )**, **max( )**, etc.
  (b) User-defined functions
- Given below is an example of user-defined function. Note that the body of the function must be indented suitably.

```
# function definition
def fun( ) :
    print('My opinions may have changed')
    print('But not the fact that I am right')
```

- A function can be called any number of times.

```
fun( )          # first call
fun( )          # second call
```

- When a function is called, control is transferred to the function, its statements are executed, and control is returned to place from where the call originated.
- Python convention for function names:
  - Always use lowercase characters
  - Connect multiple words using _
    Example: cal_si( ), split_data( ), etc.
- A function can be redefined. While calling the function its latest definition will be called.

- Function definitions can be nested. When we do so, the inner function is able to access the variables of outer function. The outer function must be called for the inner function to execute.

```
def fun1( ) :
    print('Reached fun1')
    def fun2( ) :                # nested definition
        print('Inner avatar')
    print('Outer avatar')
    fun2( )

fun1( )                          # ok
fun2( )                          # cannot call inner function from here
print(type(fun1))                # nested call
```

- Suppose we wish to develop a function **myrandom( )** to generate random numbers. While executing this function we wish to check whether a number is a prime number or not. We can do so by defining a function **isprime( )**. But we do not want want **isprime( )** to be callable from outside **myrandom( )**. In a way we wish to protect it. In such a case we can define **isprime( )** as an inner function.

- Another use of inner functions is in creating decorators. This usage is discussed in Chapter 25.

Communication with Functions

- Communication with functions is done using parameters/arguments passed to it and the value(s) returned from it.

- The way to pass values to a function and return value from it is shown below:

```
def cal_sum(x, y, z) :
    return x + y + z

# pass 10, 20, 30 to cal_sum( ), collect value returned by it
s1 = cal_sum(10, 20, 30)
# pass a, b, c to cal_sum( ), collect value returned by it
a, b, c = 1, 2, 3
s2 = cal_sum(a, b, c)
```

- **return** statement returns control and value from a function. **return** without an expression returns **None**.
- To return multiple values from a function we can put them into a list/tuple/set/dictionary and then return it.
- Suppose we pass arguments **a**, **b**, **c** to a function and collect them in **x**, **y**, **z**. Changing **x**, **y**, **z** in the function body, does not change **a**, **b**, **c**. Thus, a function is always called by value.
- A function can return different types through different return statements.
- A function that reaches the end of execution without a **return** statement will always return **None**.

Types of Arguments

- Arguments in a Python function can be of 4 types:

  (a) Positional arguments
  (b) Keyword arguments
  (c) Variable-length positional arguments
  (d) Variable-length keyword arguments

  Positional and keyword arguments are often called 'required' arguments, whereas variable-length arguments are called 'optional' arguments.

- Positional arguments must be passed in correct positional order. For example, if a function expects an int, float and string to be passed to it, then while calling this function the arguments must be passed in the same order.

```
def fun(i, j, k) :
    print(i + j)
    print(k.upper( ))

fun(10, 3.14, 'Rigmarole')      # correct call
fun('Rigmarole', 3.14, 10)      # error, incorrect order
```

  While passing positional arguments, the number of arguments passed must match with number of arguments received.

- Keyword arguments can be passed out of order. Python interpreter uses keywords (variable names) to match the values passed with the arguments used in the function definition.

```
def print_it(i, a, str) :
    print(i, a, str)

print_it(a = 3.14, i = 10, str = 'Sicilian')        # keyword, ok
print_it(str = 'Sicilian', a = 3.14, i = 10)        # keyword, ok
print_it(str = 'Sicilian', i = 10, a = 3.14)        # keyword, ok
print_it(s = 'Sicilian', j = 10, a = 3.14)          # error, keyword name
```

An error is reported in the last call since the variable names in the call and the definition do not match.

- In a call we can use positional as well as keyword arguments. If we do so, the positional arguments must precede keyword arguments.

```
def print_it(i, a, str) :
    print(i, a, str)

print_it(10, a = 3.14, str = 'Ngp')    # ok
print_it(10, str = 'Ngp', a = 3.14)    # ok
print_it(str = 'Ngp', 10, a = 3.14)    # error, positional after keyword
print_it(str = 'Ngp', a = 3.14, 10)    # error, positional after keyword
```

- Sometimes the number of positional arguments to be passed to a function is not certain. In such cases, variable-length positional arguments can be received using ***args**.

```
def print_it(*args) :
    print( )
    for var in args :
        print(var, end = ' ')

print_it(10)                                    # 1 arg, ok
print_it(10, 3.14)                              # 2 args, ok
print_it(10, 3.14,'Sicilian')                   # 3 args, ok
print_it(10, 3.14, 'Sicilian', 'Punekar')       # 4 args, ok
```

args used in definition of **print_it( )** is a tuple. * indicates that it will hold all the arguments passed to **print_it( )**. The tuple can be iterated through using a **for** loop.

- Sometimes the number of keyword arguments to be passed to a function is not certain. In such cases, variable-length keyword arguments can be received using ****kwargs**.

```
def print_it(**kwargs) :
    print( )
    for name, value in kwargs.items( ) :
        print(name, value, end = ' ')

print_it(a = 10)                                  # keyword, ok
print_it(a = 10, b = 3.14)                        # keyword, ok
print_it(a = 10, b = 3.14, s = 'Sicilian')        # keyword, ok
dct = {'Student' : 'Ajay', 'Age' : 23}
print_it(**dct)                                   # ok
```

  kwargs used in definition of **print_it( )** is a dictionary containing variable names as keys and their values as values. ** indicates that it will hold all the arguments passed to **print_it( )**.

- We can use any other names in place of **args** and **kwargs**. We cannot use more than one **args** and more than one **kwargs** while defining a function.

- If a function is to receive required as well as optional arguments then they must occur in following order:
  - positional arguments
  - variable-length positional arguments
  - keyword arguments
  - variable-length keyword arguments

```
def print_it(i, j, *args, x, y, **kwargs) :
    print( )
    print(i, j, end = ' ')
    for var in args :
        print(var, end = ' ')
    print(x, y, end = ' ')
    for name, value in kwargs.items( ) :
        print(name, value, end = ' ')

# nothing goes to args, kwargs
print_it(10, 20, x = 30, y = 40)

# 100, 200 go to args, nothing goes to kwargs
```

```
print_it(10, 20, 100, 200, x = 30, y = 40)

# 100, 200 go to args, nothing goes to kwargs
print_it(10, 20, 100, 200, y = 40, x = 30)

# 100, 200 go to args. 'a' : 5, ' b' : 6, 'c' : 7 go to kwargs
print_it(10, 20, 100, 200, x = 30, y = 40, a = 5, b = 6, c = 7)

# error, 30 40 go to args, nothing left for required arguments x, y
print_it(10, 20, 30, 40)
```

- While defining a function default value can be given to arguments. Default value will be used if we do not pass the value for that argument during the call.

```
def fun(a, b = 100, c = 3.14) :
    return a + b + c

w = fun(10)              # passes 10 to a, b is taken as 100, c as 3.14
x = fun(20, 50)          # passes 20, 50 to a, b. c is taken as 3.14
y = fun(30, 60, 6.28)    # passes 30, 60, 6.28 to a, b, c
z = fun(1, c = 3, b = 5) # passes 1 to a, 5 to b, 3 to c
```

- Note that while defining a function, default arguments must follow non-default arguments.

Unpacking Arguments

- Suppose a function is expecting positional arguments and the arguments to be passed are in a list, tuple or set. In such a case we need to unpack the list/tuple/set using * operator before passing it to the function.

```
def print_it(a, b, c, d, e) :
    print(a, b, c, d, e)

lst = [10, 20, 30, 40, 50]
tpl = ('A', 'B', 'C', 'D', 'E')
s = {1, 2, 3, 4, 5}
print_it(*lst)
print_it(*tpl)
print_it(*s)
```

- Suppose a function is expecting keyword arguments and the arguments to be passed are in a dictionary. In such a case we need to unpack the dictionary using ** operator before passing it to the function.

```
def print_it(name = 'Sanjay', marks = 75) :
    print(name, marks)

d = {'name' : 'Anil', 'marks' : 50}
print_it(*d)
print_it(**d)
```

The first call to **print_it( )** passes keys to it, whereas, the second call passes values.

P</> Programs

Problem 13.1

Write a program to receive three integers from keyboard and get their sum and product calculated through a user-defined function **cal_sum_prod( )**.

Program

```
def cal_sum_prod(x, y, z) :
    ss = x + y + z
    pp = x * y * z
    return ss, pp                    # or return(ss, pp)

a = int(input('Enter a: '))
b = int(input('Enter b: '))
c = int(input('Enter c: '))
s, p = cal_sum_prod(a, b, c)
print(s, p)
```

Output

```
Enter a: 10
Enter b: 20
Enter c: 30
```

```
60 6000
```

Tips

- Multiple values can be returned from a function as a tuple.

Problem 13.2

Pangram is a sentence that uses every letter of the alphabet. Write a program that checks whether a given string is pangram or not, through a user-defined function **ispangram( )**.

Program

```
def ispangram(s) :
    alphaset = set('abcdefghijklmnopqrstuvwxyz')
    return alphaset <= set(s.lower( ))
print(ispangram('The quick brown fox jumps over the lazy dog'))
print(ispangram('Crazy Fredrick bought many very exquisite opal
jewels'))
```

Output

```
True
True
```

Tips

- **set( )** converts the string into a set of characters present in the string.
- <= checks whether **alphaset** is a subset of the given string.

Problem 13.3

Write a Python program that accepts a hyphen-separated sequence of words as input and calls a function **convert( )** which converts it into a hyphen-separated sequence after sorting them alphabetically. For example, if the input string is

'here-come-the-dots-followed-by-dashes'

then, the converted string should be

'by-come-dashes-dots-followed-here-the'

Program

```
def convert(s1) :
    items = [s for s in s1.split('-')]
    items.sort( )
    s2 = '-'.join(items)
    return s2
s = 'here-come-the-dots-followed-by-dashes'
t = convert(s)
print(t)
```

Output

```
by-come-dashes-dots-followed-here-the
```

Tips

- We have used list comprehension to create a list of words present in the string **s1**.
- The **join( )** method returns a string concatenated with the elements of an iterable. In our case the iterable is the list called **items**.

Problem 13.4

Write a Python function to create and return a list containing tuples of the form (x, x^2, x^3) for all x between 1 and 20 (both included).

Program

```
def generate_list( ):
    lst = list( )              # or lst = [ ]
    for i in range(1, 11):
        lst.append((i, i ** 2, i ** 3))

    return lst
l = generate_list( )
print(l)
```

Output

```
[(1, 1, 1), (2, 4, 8), (3, 9, 27), (4, 16, 64), (5, 25, 125), (6, 36, 216),
(7, 49, 343), (8, 64, 512), (9, 81, 729), (10, 100, 1000)]
```

Tips

- **range(1, 11)** produces a list of numbers from 1 to 10.
- **append( )** adds a new tuple to the list in each iteration.

Problem 13.5

A palindrome is a word or phrase which reads the same in both directions. Given below are some palindromic strings:

deed
level
Malayalam
Rats live on no evil star
Murder for a jar of red rum

Write a program that defines a function **ispalindrome( )** which checks whether a given string is a palindrome or not. Ignore spaces and case mismatches while checking for palindrome.

Program

```
def ispalindrome(s):
    t = s.lower( )
    left = 0
    right = len(t) - 1

    while right >= left :
        if t[left] == ' ' :
            left += 1
        if t[right] == ' ' :
            right -= 1
        if t[left] != t[right]:
            return False
        left += 1
        right -= 1
    return True
```

```
print(ispalindrome('Malayalam'))
print(ispalindrome('Rats live on no evil star'))
print(ispalindrome('Murder for a jar of red rum'))
```

Output

```
True
True
True
```

Tips

- Since strings are immutable the string converted to lowercase has to be collected in another string **t**.

Problem 13.6

Write a program that defines a function **convert( )** that receives a string containing a sequence of whitespace separated words and returns a string after removing all duplicate words and sorting them alphanumerically.

For example, if the string passed to **convert( )** is

s = 'Sakhi was a singer because her mother was a singer, and Sakhi\'s mother was a singer because her father was a singer'

then the output should be:

```
Sakhi Sakhi's a and because father her mother singer singer, was
```

Program

```
def convert(s) :
    words = [word for word in s.split(' ')]
    return ' '.join(sorted(list(set(words))))

s = 'I felt happy because I saw the others were happy and because I
knew I should feel happy, but I wasn\'t really happy'
t = convert(s)
print(t)
```

```
s = 'Sakhi was a singer because her mother was a singer, and Sakhi\'s mother was a singer because her father was a singer'
t = convert(s)
print(t)
```

Output

```
I and because but feel felt happy happy, knew others really saw should the wasn't were
Sakhi Sakhi's a and because father her mother singer singer, was
```

Tips

- **set( )** removes duplicate data automatically.
- **list( )** converts the set into a list.
- **sorted( )** sorts the list data and returns sorted list.
- Sorted data list is converted to a string using a **str** method **join( )**, appending a space at the end of each word, except the last.

Problem 13.7

Write a program that defines a function **count_alphabets_digits( )** that accepts a string and calculates the number of alphabets and digits in it. It should return these values as a dictionary. Call this function for some sample strings.

Program

```
def count_alphabets_digits(s) :
    d={'Digits' : 0, 'Alphabets' : 0}
    for ch in s:
        if ch.isalpha( ) :
            d['Alphabets'] += 1
        elif ch.isdigit( ) :
            d['Digits'] += 1
        else :
            pass
    return(d)

d = count_alphabets_digits('James Bond 007')
```

```
print(d)
d = count_alphabets_digits('Kholi Number 420')
print(d)
```

Output

```
{'Digits': 3, 'Alphabets': 9}
{'Digits': 3, 'Alphabets': 11}
```

Tips

- **pass** does not do anything on execution.

Problem 13.8

Write a program that defines a function called **frequency( )** which computes the frequency of words present in a string passed to it. The frequencies should be returned in sorted order by words in the string.

Program

```
def frequency(s) :
    freq = { }
    for word in s.split( ) :
        freq[word] = freq.get(word, 0) + 1
    return freq

sentence = 'It is true for all that that that that \
that that that refers to is not the same that \
that that that refers to'
d = frequency(sentence)
words = sorted(d)

for w in words:
  print ('%s:%d' % (w, d[w]))
```

Output

```
It:1
all:1
for:1
```

```
is:2
not:1
refers:2
same:1
that:11
the:1
to:2
true:1
```

Tips

- We did not use **freq[word] = freq[word] + 1** because we have not initialized all word counts for each unique word to 0 to begin with.
- When we use **freq.get(word, 0)**, **get( )** searches the word. If it is not found, the second parameter, i.e., 0 will be returned. Thus, for the first call for each unique word, the word count is properly initialized to 0.
- **sorted( )** returns a sorted list of key values in the dictionary.
- **w, d[w]** yields the word and its frequency count stored in the dictionary **d**.

Problem 13.9

Write a program that defines two functions called **create_sent1( )** and **create_sent2( )**. Both receive the following 3 lists:

```
subjects = ['He', 'She']
verbs = ['loves', 'hates']
objects = ['TV Serials','Netflix']
```

Both functions should form sentences by picking elements from these lists and return them. Use **for** loops in **create_sent1( )** and list comprehension in **create_sent2( )**.

Program

```
def create_sent1(sub, ver, obj) :
    lst = [ ]
    for i in range(len(sub)) :
        for j in range(len(ver)) :
```

```
            for k in range(len(obj)) :
                sent = sub[i] + ' ' + ver[j] + ' ' + obj[k]
                lst.append(sent)
    return lst

def create_sent2(sub, ver, obj) :
    return [(s + ' ' + v + ' ' + o) for s in sub for v in ver for o in obj]

subjects = ['He', 'She']
verbs = ['loves', 'hates']
objects = ['TV Serials','Netflix']

lst1 = create_sent1( subjects, verbs, objects)
for l in lst1 :
    print(l)
print( )
lst2 = create_sent2( subjects, verbs, objects)
for l in lst2 :
    print(l)
```

Output

```
He loves TV Serials
He loves Netflix
He hates TV Serials
He hates Netflix
She loves TV Serials
She loves Netflix
She hates TV Serials
She hates Netflix

He loves TV Serials
He loves Netflix
He hates TV Serials
He hates Netflix
She loves TV Serials
She loves Netflix
She hates TV Serials
She hates Netflix
```

Exercises

[A] Answer the following questions:

(a) Write a program that defines a function **count_lower_upper( )** that accepts a string and calculates the number of uppercase and lowercase alphabets in it. It should return these values as a dictionary. Call this function for some sample strings.

(b) Write a program that defines a function **compute( )** that calculates the value of n + nn + nnn + nnnn, where n is digit received by the function. Test the function for digits 4 and 7.

(c) Write a program that defines a function **create_array( )** to create and return a 3D array whose dimensions are passed to the function. Also initialize each element of this array to a value passed to the function.

(d) Write a program that defines a function **create_list( )** to create and return a list which is an intersection of two lists passed to it.

(e) Write a program that defines a function **sanitize_list( )** to remove all duplicate entries from the list that it receives.

(f) Which of the calls to **print_it( )** in the following program will report errors?

```
def print_it(i, a, s, *args) :
    print( )
    print(i, a, s, end = ' ')
    for var in args :
        print(var, end = ' ')

print_it(10, 3.14)
print_it(20, s = 'Hi', a = 6.28)
print_it(a = 6.28, s = 'Hello', i = 30)
print_it(40, 2.35, 'Nag', 'Mum', 10)
```

(g) Which of the calls to **fun( )** in the following program will report errors?

```
def fun(a, *args, s = '!') :
    print(a, s)
    for i in args :
```

```
        print(i, s)

fun(10)
fun(10, 20)
fun(10, 20, 30)
fun(10, 20, 30, 40, s = '+')
```

[B] Attempt the following questions:

(a) What is being passed to function **fun( )** in the following code?

```
int a = 20
lst = [10, 20, 30, 40, 50]
fun(a, lst)
```

(b) Which of the following are valid **return** statements?

```
return (a, b, c)
return a + b + c
return a, b, c
```

(c) What will be the output of the following program?

```
def fun( ) :
    print('First avatar')
fun( )
def fun( ) :
    print('New avatar')
fun( )
```

(d) How will you define a function containing three **return** statements, each returning a different type of value?

(e) Can function definitions be nested? If yes, why would you want to do so?

(f) How will you call **print_it( )** to print elements of **tpl**?

```
def print_it(a, b, c, d, e) :
    print(a, b, c, d, e)
tpl = ('A', 'B', 'C', 'D', 'E')
```

14 Recursion

"To iterate is human, to recurse divine..."

Contents

KanNotes

Repetitions

- There are two ways to repeat a set of statements in a function:
  - By using **while** or **for** loop
  - By calling the function from within itself
- The first method is known as iteration, whereas the second is known as recursion.
- The functions that use iteration are called iterative functions and those that use recursion are called recursive functions.

Recursive Function

- A Python function can be called from within its body. When we do so it is called a recursive function.

```
def fun( ) :
    # some statements
    fun( )    # recursive call
```

- Recursive call keeps calling the function again and again, leading to an infinite loop.
- A provision must be made to get outside this infinite recursive loop. This is done by making the recursive call either in if block or in else block as shown below:

```
def fun( ) :
    if condition :
        # some statements
    else
        fun( )    # recursive call
```

```
def fun( ) :
    if condition :
        fun( )
    else
        # some statements
```

- The case when a recursive call is made is called the recursive case, whereas the other case is called the base case.
- If recursive call is made in if block (recursive case), else block should contain the base case logic. If recursive call is made in else block (recursive case), if block should contain the base case logic.

When to use Recursion

- Recursion is useful in 2 scenarios:
  - When a problem can be solved by breaking it down into similar sub-problems.
  - When a problem requires an unknown number of loops.

- Examples of problem as similar sub-problems:
  - Finding factorial value of a number
  - Finding sum of digits of an integer
  - Finding a binary equivalent of a number

- Examples of unknown number of nested loops:
  - Finding all combinations of 1 to n, where n is received as input
  - Traversing a binary tree data structure
  - Traversing a graph data structure

- In this book we would cover both sets of problems that can be solved using recursion.

Problem as Similar Sub-problems

- In a problem that can be solved by breaking it down into similar sub-problems the computation of a function is described in terms of the function itself.

- For example, suppose we wish to calculate factorial value of **n**. Then

  n! = n * (n - 1) * (n - 2) * (n - 3) * ... * 2 * 1

  We can write this as:

  n! = 1 if n = 0
  = n * (n -1)! if n > 0

- In terms of function this can be written as:

  factorial(n) = 1 if n = 0 (base case)
  = n * factorial(n - 1) if n > 0 (recursive case)

- If we are to obtain sum of digits of an integer **n**, then the recursive function can be written as

  sumdig(n) = 0 if n = 0 (base case)
  = n % 10 + sumdig(n / 10) if n > 0 (recursive case)

- The following tips will help you understand recursive functions better:
  - A fresh set of variables are born during each function call—normal call as well as recursive call.
  - Variables created in a function die when control returns from a function.
  - Recursive function may or may not have a return statement.
  - Typically, during execution of a recursive function many recursive calls happen, so several sets of variables get created. This increases the space requirement of the function.
  - Recursive functions are inherently slow since passing value(s) and control to a function and returning value(s) and control will slow down the execution of the function.
  - Recursive calls terminate when the base case condition is satisfied.

Recursive Factorial Function

- A simple program that calculates factorial of a given number using a recursive function is given below, followed by a brief explanation of its working.

```
def refact(n) :
    if n == 0 :
        return 1
    else :
        p = n * refact(n - 1)
    return p

num = int(input('Enter any number: '))
fact = refact(num)
print('Factorial value = ', fact)
```

- Suppose 2 is supplied as input, we should get the output as 2, since 2! evaluates to 2.
- It becomes easier to follow the working of a recursive function if we make copies of the function on paper and then perform a dry run of the program to follow the control flow. In reality, multiple copies of function are not created in memory.

- Trace the control flow of the recursive factorial function in Figure 14.1. Assume that we are trying to find factorial value of 2. The solid arrows indicate the call to the function, whereas dashed arrows indicate return from the function.
- Note that **return 1** goes to work only during the last call. All other calls return via **return p**.

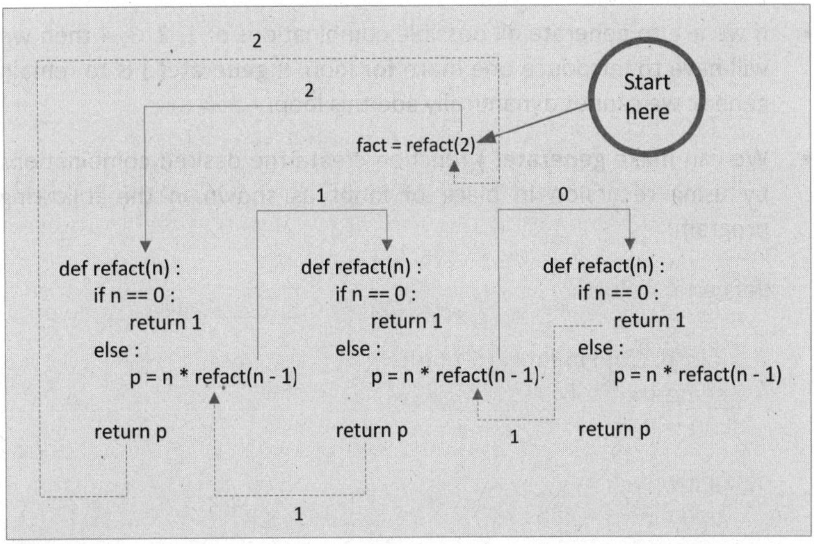

Figure 14.1

Problem with Unknown Loops

- If we are to define a function which generates and returns a list of lists containing all possible combinations of numbers 1, 2 and 3 we can do so through the following program:

```
def generate(n) :
    lol = [[ ] for i in range(n ** n)]
    pos = 0
    for i in range(1, n + 1) :
        for j in range(1, n + 1) :
            for k in range(1, n + 1) :
                t = [i, j, k]
                lol[pos] = t
                pos += 1
    return lol
```

```
l = generate(3)
print(l)
```

Since we can generate 27 combinations out of 1, 2, 3 ([1, 1, 1], [1, 1, 2], ... [3, 3, 3]), list of lists **lol** is set up with 27 empty lists. Then through 3 **for** loops we have generated each sub-list and inserted it in **lol**.

- If we are to generate all possible combinations of 1, 2, 3, 4 then we will have to introduce one more **for** loop. If **generate( )** is to remain generic we cannot dynamically add this loop.
- We can make **generate( )** function create the desired combinations by using recursion in place of loops as shown in the following program:

```
def generate(n) :
    t = [ ]
    lol = [[ ] for i in range(n ** n)]
    helper(n, t, lol)
    return(lol)

def helper(n, t, lol) :
    global j
    if len(t) == n :
        lol[ j ] = lol[ j ] + t
        j += 1
        return
    for i in range(1, n + 1) :
        t.append(i)
        helper(n, t, lol);
        t.pop( )

j = 0
l = generate(3)
print(l)
```

In addition to **generate( )** we have defined the **helper( )** function since we wish to build each sub-list incrementally and **generate( )** receives only **n**.

After generating a sub-list like [1, 1, 1], **list** method **pop( )** has been called to remove the last 1 from this sub-list and create the next sub-list [1, 1, 2].

Types of Recursion

- Two types of recursions can exist:

  (a) Head recursion
  (b) Tail recursion

- Head recursion - In this type of recursion the recursive call is made before other processing in the function.

```
def headprint(n) :
    if n == 0 :
        return
    else :
        headprint(n - 1)
        print(n)

headprint(10)
```

  Here firstly the recursive calls happen and then the printing takes place. Hence last value of **n,** i.e., 1 gets printed first. So, numbers get printed in order 1 to 10.

- Tail recursion - In this type of recursion processing is done before the recursive call. The tail recursion is similar to a loop—the function executes all the statements before making the recursive call.

```
def tailprint(n) :
    if n == 11 :
        return
    else :
        print(n)
        tailprint(n + 1)

tailprint(1)
```

  Here firstly printing takes place and then the recursive call is made. Hence the first value of **n,** i.e., 1 gets printed first and then the recursive call is done. So once again numbers get printed in order 1 to 10.

Recursion Limit

- In head recursion we do not get the result of our calculation until we have returned from every recursive call. So, the state (local variables) must be saved before making the next recursive call. This results in consumption of more memory. Too many recursive calls may result into an error.
- Default recursion limit in Python is usually set to a small value (approximately, 10 ** 4). So, if we provide a large input to the recursive function, a **RecursionError** will be raised.
- The **setrecursionlimit( )** function in **sys** module permits us to set the recursion limit. Once set to 10^6, large inputs can be handled without any errors.

Iteration to Recursion

- Given below are the steps that should be followed if we are to convert an iterative function to a recursive function:
    - Use the local variables in the iterative function as parameters of the recursive function.
    - Identify the main loop in the iterative function. This loop typically modifies one or more variables and returns some final value(s).
    - Write the condition in the loop as the base case and the body of the loop as the recursive case.
    - Run to check whether recursive function achieves the desired result.
    - Remove any unnecessary variables and improve the structure of the recursive function.

Programs

Problem 14.1

If a positive integer is entered through the keyboard, write a recursive function to obtain the prime factors of the number.

Program

```
def factorize(n, i) :
    if i <= n :
        if n % i == 0 :
            print( i, end =', ' )
            n = n // i
        else :
            i += 1
    factorize(n, i)

num = int(input('Enter a number: '))
print('Prime factors are:')
factorize(num, 2)
```

Output

```
Enter a number: 50
Prime factors are:
2, 5, 5,

Enter a number: 24
Prime factors are:
2, 2, 2, 3,
```

Tips

- In **factorize( )** we keep checking, starting with 2, whether **i** is a factor of **n** (means, can **i** divide **n** exactly). If so, we print that factor, reduce **n** and again call **factorize( )** recursively. If not, we call **factorize( )** to check whether **i + 1** is a factor of **n**.

Problem 14.2

A positive integer is entered through the keyboard, write a recursive function to calculate sum of digits of the 5-digit number.

Program

```
def rsum(num) :
    if num != 0 :
        digit = num % 10
```

```
        num = int(num / 10)
        sum = digit + rsum(num)
    else :
        return 0
    return sum

n = int(input('Enter number: '))
rs = rsum(n)
print('Sum of digits = ', rs)
```

Output

```
Enter number:
345
Sum of digits = 12
```

Tips

- In the **rsum( )** function, we extract the last digit, reduce the number and call **rsum( )** with reduced value of **num**. Thus if the number entered is 3256, the call becomes **sum = 6 + rsum(325)**.
- During each call additions are kept pending, for example the addition to 6 is kept pending as the program calls **rsum(325)** to obtain sum of digits of 325.
- The recursive calls end when **n** falls to 0, whereupon the function returns a 0, because sum of digits of 0 is 0. The 0 is returned to the previous pending call, i.e., **sum = 3 + rsum (0)**. Now **sum = 3 + 0** is completed and the control reaches **return s**. Now the value of **sum**, i.e., 3 is returned to the previous call made during the pending addition **2 + rsum (3)**. This way all pending calls are completed and finally the sum of 3256 is returned.
- In short, **return 0** goes to work only once (during the last call to **rsum( )**), whereas, for all previous calls **return sum** goes to work.

Problem 14.3

Paper of size A0 has dimensions 1189 mm x 841 mm. Each subsequent size A(n) is defined as A(n-1) cut in half, parallel to its shorter sides. Write a program to calculate and print paper sizes A0, A1, A2, ... A8 using recursion.

Program

```
def papersizes(i, n, l, b) :
    if n != 0 :
        print(f'A{i}: L = {int(l)} B = {int(b)}')
        newb = l / 2
        newl = b
        n -= 1
        i += 1
        papersizes(i, n, newl, newb)

papersizes(0, 7, 1189, 841)
```

Output

```
A0: L = 1189 B = 841
A1: L = 841 B = 594
A2: L = 594 B = 420
A3: L = 420 B = 297
A4: L = 297 B = 210
A5: L = 210 B = 148
A6: L = 148 B = 105
```

Tips

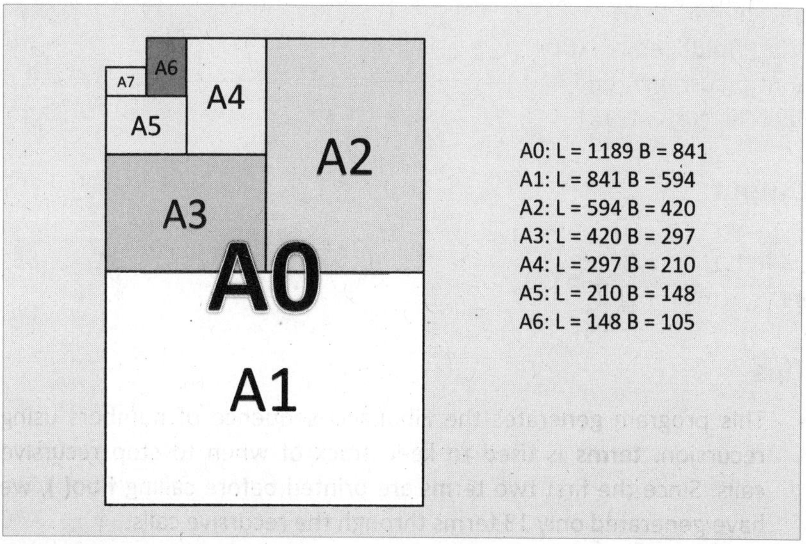

Figure 14.2

- Figure 14.2 shows different paper sizes are obtained. In function **papersizes( )**, **i** is used to obtain the digit in A0, A1, A2, etc., whereas **n** is used to keep track of number of times the function should be called. The moment **n** falls to 0, the recursive calls are stopped. Alternately, we could have dropped **n** and stopped recursive calls when **i** reaches 7.

Problem 14.4

Write a recursive function to obtain the first 15 numbers of a Fibonacci sequence. In a Fibonacci sequence the sum of two successive terms gives the third term. First few terms of the Fibonacci sequence:

1 1 2 3 5 8 13 21 34 55 89....

Program

```
def fibo(old, current, terms) :
    if terms >= 1 :
        new = old + current
        print( f'{new}', end = '\t')
        terms = terms - 1
        fibo(current, new, terms)

old = 1
current = 1
print(f'{old}', end = '\t')
print(f'{current}', end = '\t')
fibo(old, current, 13)
```

Output

```
1	1	2	3	5	8	13	21	34	55
89	144	233	377	610
```

Tips

- This program generates the Fibonacci sequence of numbers using recursion. **terms** is used to keep track of when to stop recursive calls. Since the first two terms are printed before calling **fibo( )**, we have generated only 13 terms through the recursive calls.

Problem 14.5

A positive integer is entered through the keyboard; write a function to find the binary equivalent of this number using recursion.

Program

```
import sys

def dec_to_binary(n) :
    r = n % 2
    n = int(n / 2)
    if n != 0 :
        dec_to_binary(n)
    print(r, end = '')

sys.setrecursionlimit(10 ** 6)
num = int(input('Enter the number: '))
print('The binary equivalent is:')
dec_to_binary(num)
```

Output

```
Enter the number: 32
The binary equivalent is:
100000

Enter the number: 45
The binary equivalent is:
101101
```

Tips

- To obtain a binary equivalent of a number, we must keep dividing the dividend till it does not become 0. Finally, the remainders obtained during each successive division must be written in reverse order to get the binary equivalent.
- Since the remainders are to be written in the reverse order, we start printing only when **n** falls to 0, otherwise we make a call to **dec_to_binary( )** with a reduced dividend value.

Problem 14.6

Write a recursive function to obtain the running sum of first 25 natural numbers.

Program

```
def runningSum(n) :
    if n == 0 :
        return 0
    else :
        s = n + runningSum(n - 1)
        return(s)
max = int(input('Enter the positive largest number for running sum: '))
if max > 0 :
    sum = runningSum(max)
    print(f'Running Sum: {sum}')
else :
    print('Entered number is negative')
```

Output

```
Enter the positive largest number for running sum: 25
Running Sum: 325
```

Tips

- We calculate the running sum as we calculate the factorial value, starting from **n** and then go on reducing it moving towards 0. We stopped on reaching 0.

Exercises

[A] State whether the following statements are True or False:

(a) A recursive function is the one that calls another execution instance of the same function.

(b) If a recursive function uses three variables **a**, **b** and **c**, then the same set of variables are used during each recursive call.

(c) Multiple copies of the recursive function are created in memory.

(d) A recursive function must contain at least 1 **return** statement.

(e) Every iteration done using a **while** or **for** loop can be replaced with recursion.

(f) Logics expressible in the form of themselves are good candidates for writing recursive functions.

(g) Tail recursion is similar to a loop.

(h) Infinite recursion can occur if the base case is not properly defined.

(i) A recursive function is easy to write, understand and maintain as compared to a one that uses a loop.

[B] Answer the following questions:

(a) Write a program that calculates the sum of first 5 natural numbers using tail recursion. Rewrite the function to obtain the sum using head recursion.

(b) There are three pegs labeled A, B and C. Four disks are placed on peg A. The bottom-most disk is largest, and disks go on decreasing in size with the topmost disk being smallest. The objective of the game is to move the disks from peg A to peg C, using peg B as an auxiliary peg. The rules of the game are as follows:

- Only one disk may be moved at a time, and it must be the top disk on one of the pegs.
- A larger disk should never be placed on the top of a smaller disk.

Write a program to print out the sequence in which the disks should be moved such that all disks on peg A are finally transferred to peg C.

(c) A string is entered through the keyboard. Write a recursive function that counts the number of vowels in this string.

(d) A string is entered through the keyboard. Write a recursive function that removes any tabs present in this string.

(e) A string is entered through the keyboard. Write a recursive function that checks whether the string is a palindrome or not.

(f) Two numbers are received through the keyboard into variables **a** and **b**. Write a recursive function that calculates the value of $\mathbf{a^b}$.

(g) Write a recursive function that reverses the list of numbers that it receives.

(h) A list contains some negative and some positive numbers. Write a recursive function that sanitizes the list by replacing all negative numbers with 0.

(i) Write a recursive function to obtain average of all numbers present in a given list.

(j) Write a recursive function to obtain length of a given string.

(k) Write a recursive function that receives a number as input and returns the square of the number. Use the mathematical identity $(n - 1)^2 = n^2 - 2n + 1$.

[C] What will be the output of the following programs?

(a)
```
def fun(x, y) :
    if x == 0 :
        return y
    else :
        return fun(x - 1, x * y)
print(fun(4, 2))
```

(b)
```
def fun(num) :
    if num > 100 :
        return num - 10
    return fun(fun(num + 11))
print(fun(75))
```

(c)
```
def fun(num) :
    if num == 0 :
        print("False")
    if num == 1 :
        print("True")
    if num % 2 == 0 :
        fun(num / 2)
fun(256)
```

15 Functional Programming

"Map it, reduce it, filter it......"

Contents

KanNotes

Functional Programming

- In functional programming a problem is treated as evaluation of one or more functions.
- Hence a given problem is decomposed into a set of functions. These functions provide the main source of logic in the program.

Functions as First-Class Values

- Python facilitates functional programming by treating functions as 'first-class' data values. This means that:
  - Functions can be assigned to variables and then called using these variables.
  - Functions can be passed as arguments to function and returned from function.
  - Functions can be built at execution time, the way lists, tuples, etc. can be.
- Example of assigning a function to a variable and calling the function using the variable:

```
def func( ) :
    print('Hello')
def sum(x, y) :
    print(x + y)
f = func            # assignment of function to a variable
f( )                # call to func( )
g = sum             # assignment of function to a variable
g(10, 20)           # call to sum( )
```

- Example of passing a function as argument to a function:

```
def sum(x, y, f) :
    print(x + y)
    f( )            # calls func( )
def func( ) :
    print('Hello')
f = func            # assignment of function to a variable
```

```
sum(10, 20, f)        # pass function as argument to a function
```

- Example of building function at execution time is discussed in the next section on lambda functions.

Lambda Functions

- Normal functions have names. They are defined using the **def** keyword.
- Lambda functions do not have names. They are defined by using the **lambda** keyword and are built at execution time.
- Lambda functions are commonly used for short functions that are convenient to define at the point where they are called.
- Lambda functions are also called anonymous functions or inline functions.
- A lambda function can take any number of arguments but can return only one value. Its syntax is:

  lambda arguments : expression

  : separates the parameters to be passed to the lambda function and the function body. The result of running the function body is returned implicitly.

- A few examples of lambda functions:

```
# function that receives an argument and returns its cube
lambda  n : n * n * n

# function that receives 3 arguments and return their average
lambda x, y, z : (x + y + z) / 3

# function that receives a string, strips any whitespace and returns
# the uppercase version of the string
lambda s : s.trim( ).upper( )
```

- Lambda functions are often used as an argument to other functions. For example, the above lambdas can be passed to **print( )** function to print the value that they return.

```
print((lambda  n : n * n * n)(3))                     # prints 27
print((lambda  x, y, z : (x + y + z) / 3)(10, 20, 30))      # prints 20.0
```

```
print((lambda s : s.lstrip( ).rstrip( ).upper( ))('   Ngp   ')) # prints NGP
```

- The lambda can also be assigned to a variable and then invoked.

```
p = lambda n : n * n * n
q = lambda x, y, z : (x + y + z) / 3
r = lambda s : s.lstrip( ).rstrip( ).upper( )
print(p(3))                          # calls first lambda function
print(q(10, 20, 30))                 # calls second lambda function
print(r('   Nagpur   '))             # calls third lambda function
```

- Container types can also be passed to a lambda function. For example, a lambda function that calculates average of numbers in a list can be passed to **print( )** function:

```
lst1 = [1, 2, 3, 4, 5]
lst2 = [10, 20, 30, 40, 50]
print((lambda l : sum(l) / len(l)) (lst1))
print((lambda l : sum(l) / len(l)) (lst2))
```

Here instead of assigning a lambda function to a variable and then passing the variable to **print( )**, we have passed the lambda function itself to **print( )**.

Higher Order Functions

- A higher order function is a function that can receive other functions as arguments or return them.

- For example, we can pass a lambda function to the built-in **sorted( )** function to sort a dictionary by values.

```
d = {'Oil' : 230, 'Clip' : 150, 'Stud' : 175, 'Nut' : 35}
# lambda takes a dictionary item and returns a value
d1 = sorted(d.items( ), key = lambda kv : kv[1])
print(d1)  # prints [('Nut', 35), ('Clip', 150), ('Stud', 175), ('Oil', 230)]
```

The **sorted( )** function uses a parameter **key**. It specifies a function of one argument that is used to extract a comparison for each element in the first argument of **sorted( )**. The default value of key is **None**, indicating that the elements in the first argument are to be compared directly.

- To facilitate functional programming Python provides 3 higher order functions—**map( )**, **filter( )** and **reduce( )**. Before we see how to use these functions, we need to understand the map, filter and reduce operations.

Map, Filter, Reduce

- A map operation applies a function to each element in the sequence like list, tuple, etc. and returns a new sequence containing the results. For example:
  - Finding square roots of all numbers in the list and returning a list of these roots.
  - Converting all characters in the list to uppercase and returning the uppercase characters' list.

- A filter operation applies a function to all the elements of a sequence. A sequence of those elements for which the function returns True is returned. For example:
  - Checking whether each element in a list is an alphabet and returning a list of alphabets.
  - Checking whether each element in a list is odd and returning a list of odd numbers.

- A reduce operation performs a rolling computation to sequential pairs of values in a sequence and returns the result. For example:
  - Obtaining product of a list of integers and returning the product.
  - Concatenating all strings in a list and returning the final string.

- Usually, map, filter, reduce operations mentioned above would need a **for** loop and/or **if** statement to control the flow while iterating over elements of sequence types like strings, lists, tuples.

- If we use Python functions **map( )**, **filter( )**, **reduce( )** we do not need a **for** loop or **if** statement to control the flow. This lets the programmer focus on the actual computation rather than on the details of loops, branches, and control flow.

map( ) Function

- Use of **map( )** function:

```
import math
def fun(n) :
    return n * n

lst = [5, 10, 15, 20, 25]
```

```
m1 = map(math.radians, lst)
m2 = map(math.factorial, lst)
m3 = map(fun, lst)
print(list(m1))             # prints list of radians of all values in lst
print(list(m2))             # prints list of factorial of all values in lst
print(list(m3))             # prints list of squares of all values in lst
```

- General form of **map( )** function is
  map(function_to_apply, list_of_inputs)

  map( ) returns a **map** object which can be converted to a list using **list( )** function.

filter( ) Function

- Use of **filter( )** function:

```
def fun(n) :
    if n % 5 == 0 :
        return True
    else :
        return False

lst1 = ['A', 'X', 'Y', '3', 'M', '4', 'D']
f1 = filter(str.isalpha, lst1)
print(list(f1))                     # prints ['A', 'X', 'Y', 'M', 'D']
lst2 = [5, 10, 18, 27, 25]
f2 = filter(fun, lst2)
print(list(f2))                     # prints  [5, 10, 25]
```

- General form of **filter( )** function is:
  filter(function_to_apply, list_of_inputs)

  filter( ) returns a **filter** object which can be converted to a list using **list( )** function.

reduce( ) Function

- Use of **reduce( )** function:

```
import functools

def getsum(x, y) :
    return x + y
```

```
def getprod(x, y) :
    return x * y

lst = [1, 2, 3, 4, 5]
s = functools.reduce(getsum, lst)
p = functools.reduce(getprod, lst)
print(s)                        # prints 15
print(p)                        # prints 120
```

Here the result of the addition of previous two elements is added to the next element, till the end of the list. In our program this translates into operations like ((((1 + 2) + 3) + 4) + 5) and ((((1 * 2) * 3) * 4) * 5).

- General form of **reduce( )** function is:

  reduce(function_to_apply, list_of_inputs)

  The **reduce( )** function operation performs a rolling computation to sequential pairs of values in a sequence and returns the result.

- You can observe that **map( )**, **filter( )** and **reduce( )** abstract away control flow code.

Using Lambda with *map( ), filter( ), reduce( )*

- We can use **map( )**, **filter( )** and **reduce( )** with lambda functions to simplify the implementation of functions that operate over sequence types like, strings, lists and tuples.

- Since **map( )**, **filter( )** and **reduce( )** expect a function to be passed to them, we can also pass lambda functions to them, as shown below.

```
# using lambda with map( )
lst1 = [5, 10, 15, 20, 25]
m = map(lambda n : n * n, lst1)
print(list(m))                  # prints [25, 100, 225, 400, 625]

# using lambda with filter( )
lst2 = [5, 10, 18, 27, 25]
f = filter(lambda n : n % 5 == 0, lst2)
print(list(f))                  # prints [5, 10, 25]

# using lambda with reduce( )
from functools import reduce
lst3 = [1, 2, 3, 4, 5]
```

```
s = reduce(lambda x, y : x + y, lst3)
p = reduce(lambda x, y : x * y, lst3)
print(s, p)        # prints 15  120
```

- If required **map( )**, **filter( )** and **reduce( )** can be used together.

```
def fun(n) :
    return n > 1000

lst = [10, 20, 30, 40, 50]
l = filter(fun, map(lambda x : x * x, lst))
print(list(l))
```

- Here **map( )** and **filter( )** are used together. **map( )** obtains a list of square of all elements in a list. **filter( )** then filters out only those squares which are bigger than 1000.

Where are they Useful?

- Relational databases use the map/filter/reduce paradigm. A typical SQL query to obtain the maximum salary that a skilled worker gets from an Employees table will be:

  SELECT max(salary) FROM Employees WHERE grade = 'Skilled'

  The same query can be written in terms of **map( )**, **filter( )** and **reduce( )** as:

```
reduce(max, map(get_salary, filter(lambda x : x.grade( ) ==
            'Skilled', employees)))
```

  Here **employees** is a sequence, i.e. a list of lists, where each list has the data for one employee. **grade = 'Skilled'** is a filter. **get_salary** is a map which returns the **salary** field from the list and **max** is a reduce.

  In SQL terminology map, filter and reduce are called project, select and aggregate respectively.

- If we can manage our program using map, filter, and reduce, and lambda functions then we can run each operation in separate threads and/or different processors and still get the same results. Multithreading is discussed in detail in Chapter 26.

P</> Programs

Problem 15.1

Define three functions **fun( )**, **disp( )** and **msg( )**, store them in a list and call them one by one in a loop.

Program

```
def fun( ) :
    print('In fun')

def disp( ) :
    print('In disp')

def msg( ) :
    print('In msg')

lst = [fun, disp, msg]
for f in lst :
    f( )
```

Output

```
In fun
In disp
In msg
```

Problem 15.2

Suppose there are two lists, one containing numbers from 1 to 6, and other containing umbers from 6 to 1. Write a program to obtain a list that contains elements obtained by adding corresponding elements of the two lists.

Program

```
lst1 = [1, 2, 3, 4, 5, 6]
lst2 = [6, 5, 4, 3, 2, 1]
result = map(lambda n1, n2: n1 + n2, lst1, lst2)
print(list(result))
```

Output

```
[7, 7, 7, 7, 7, 7]
```

Tips

- lambda function receives two numbers and returns their sum.
- **map( )** function applies lambda function to each pair of elements from **lst1** and **lst2**.
- The **map( )** function returns a **map** object which is then converted into a list using **list( )** before printing.

Problem 15.3

Write a program to create a new list by obtaining square of all numbers in a list.

Program

```
lst1 = [5, 7, 9, -3, 4, 2, 6]
lst2 = list(map(lambda n : n ** 2, lst1))
print(lst2)
```

Output

```
[25, 49, 81, 9, 16, 4, 36]
```

Tips

- lambda function receives a number and returns its square.
- **map( )** function applies lambda function to each element from **lst1**.
- The **map( )** function returns a **map** object which is then converted into a list using **list( )** before printing.

Problem 15.4

Though **map( )** function is available ready-made in Python, can you define one yourself and test it?

Program

```
def my_map(fun, seq) :
    result = [ ]
    for ele in seq :
        result.append(fun(ele))
    return result
lst1 = [5, 7, 9, -3, 4, 2, 6]
lst2 = list(my_map(lambda n : n ** 2, lst1))
print(lst2)
```

Output

```
[25, 49, 81, 9, 16, 4, 36]
```

Tips

- lambda function receives a number and returns its square.
- **my_map( )** function applies lambda function to each element from **lst1**.
- The **my_map( )** function returns a **map** object which is then converted into a list using **list( )** before printing.

Problem 15.5

The following data shows names, ages, and marks of students in a class:

Anil, 21, 80
Sohail, 20, 90
Sunil, 20, 91
Shobha, 18, 93
Anil, 19, 85

Write a program to sort this data based on multiple keys in the order name, age, and marks.

Program

```
import operator
lst = [('Anil', 21, 80), ('Sohail', 20, 90), ('Sunil', 20, 91),
       ('Shobha', 18, 93), ('Anil', 19, 85), ('Shobha', 20, 92)]
```

```
print(sorted(lst, key = operator.itemgetter(0, 1, 2)))
print(sorted(lst, key = lambda tpl : (tpl[0], tpl[1], tpl[2])))
```

Output

```
[('Anil', 19, 85), ('Anil', 21, 80), ('Shobha', 18, 93), ('Shobha', 20, 92),
('Sohail', 20, 90), ('Sunil', 20, 91)]
[('Anil', 19, 85), ('Anil', 21, 80), ('Shobha', 18, 93), ('Shobha', 20, 92),
('Sohail', 20, 90), ('Sunil', 20, 91)]
```

Tips

- Since there are multiple data items about a student, they have been put into a tuple.
- Since there are multiple students, all tuples have been put in a list.
- Two sorting methods have been used. In the first method **itemgetter( )** specifies the sorting order. In the second method a lambda has been used to specify the sorting order.

Problem 15.6

Suppose a dictionary contains key-value pairs, where each key is an alphabet, and each value is a number. Write a program that obtains the maximum and minimum values from the dictionary.

Program

```
d = {'x' : 500, 'y' : 5874, 'z' : 560}
key_max = max(d.keys( ), key = (lambda k: d[k]))
key_min = min(d.keys( ), key = (lambda k: d[k]))
print('Maximum Value: ', d[key_max])
print('Minimum Value: ', d[key_min])
```

Output

```
Maximum Value:  5874
Minimum Value:  500
```

Exercises

[A] State whether the following statements are True or False:

(a) lambda function cannot be used with **reduce( )** function.

(b) lambda, **map( )**, **filter( )**, **reduce( )** can be combined in one single expression.

(c) Though functions can be assigned to variables, they cannot be called using these variables.

(d) Functions can be passed as arguments to function and returned from function.

(e) Functions can be built at execution time, the way lists, tuples, etc. can be.

(f) Lambda functions are always nameless.

[B] Using lambda, map( ), filter( ) and reduce( ) or a combination thereof to perform the following tasks:

(a) Suppose a dictionary contains type of pet (cat, dog, etc.), name of pet and age of pet. Write a program that obtains the sum of all dog's ages.

(b) Consider the following list:

lst = [1.25, 3.22, 4.68, 10.95, 32.55, 12.54]

The numbers in the list represent radii of circles. Write a program to obtain a list of areas of these circles rounded off to two decimal places.

(c) Consider the following lists:

nums = [10, 20, 30, 40, 50, 60, 70, 80]
strs = ['A', 'B', 'C', 'D', 'E', 'F', 'G', 'H']

Write a program to obtain a list of tuples, where each tuple contains a number from one list and a string from another, in the same order in which they appear in the original lists.

(d) Suppose a dictionary contains names of students and marks obtained by them in an examination. Write a program to obtain a list of students who obtained more than 40 marks in the examination.

(e) Consider the following list:

lst = ['Malayalam', 'Drawing', 'madamlamadam', '1234321']

Write a program to print those strings which are palindromes.

(f) A list contains names of employees. Write a program to filter out those names whose length is more than 8 characters.

(g) A dictionary contains following information about 5 employees:
First name
Last name
Age
Grade (Skilled, Semi-skilled, Highly-skilled)

Write a program to obtain a list of employees (first name + last name) who are Highly-skilled.

(h) Consider the following list:

lst = ['Benevolent', 'Dictator', 'For', 'Life']

Write a program to obtain a string 'Benevolent Dictator For Life'.

(i) Consider the following list of students in a class.

lst = ['Rahul', 'Priya', 'Chaaya', 'Narendra', 'Prashant']

Write a program to obtain a list in which all the names are converted to uppercase.

16 Modules and Packages

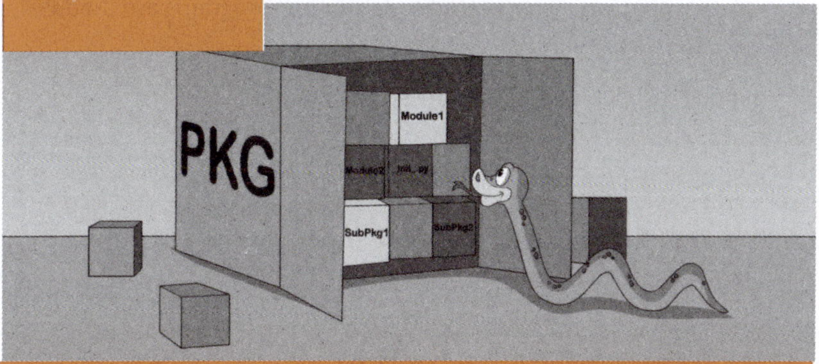

"Organize, and you will be better off..."

Contents

- The Main Module
- Multiple Modules
- Importing a Module
- Variations of *import*
- Search Sequence
- Same Code, Different Interpretation
- Packages
- Third-party Packages
- Programs
- Exercises

KanNotes

The Main Module

- A module is a .py file containing definitions and statements. So, all .py files that we have created so far for our programs are modules.

- When we execute a program its module name is **__main__**. This name is available in the variable **__name__**.

```
def display( ) :
    print('You cannot make History if you use Incognito Mode')

def show( ) :
    print('Pizza is a pie chart of how much pizza is left')

print(__name__)
display( )
show( )
```

On execution of this program, we get the following output:

```
__main__
You cannot make History if you use Incognito Mode
Pizza is a pie chart of how much pizza is left
```

Multiple Modules

- There are two reasons why we may want to create a program that contains multiple modules:

  (a) It makes sense to split a big program into multiple .py files, where each .py file acts as a module.

  Benefit - Ease of development and maintenance.

  (b) We may need a set of handy functions in several programs. In such a case instead of copying these functions in different program files, we may keep them in one file and use them in different programs.

  Benefit - Reuse of existing code.

Importing a Module

- To use the definitions and statements in a module in another module, we need to 'import' it into this module.

```
# functions.py
def display( ) :
    print('Earlier rich owned cars, while poor had horses')

def show( ) :
    print('Now everyone has car, while only rich own horses')
```

```
# usefunctions.py
import functions
functions.display( )
functions.show( )
```

When we execute 'usefunctions.py', it runs as a module with name **__main__**.

import functions makes the definitions in 'functions.py' available in 'usefunctions.py'.

- A module can import multiple modules.

```
import math
import random
import functions            # use function.py of previous program
a = 100
b = 200
print(__name__)
print(math.sin(0.5))
print(math.cos(0.5))
print(random.random( ))
print(random.randint(30, 45))
functions.display( )
functions.show( )
```

Here **__name__** contains **__main__** indicating that we are executing the main module. **random** and **math** are standard modules. **functions** is a user-defined module.

Variations of *import*

- The **import** statement can be used in multiple forms.

```
import math
import random
```

is same as

```
import math, random
```

- If we wish, we can import specific names from a module.

```
from math import sin, cos, tan
from functions import display        # imports only display function
from functions import *              # imports all functions
```

- We can rename a module while importing it. We can then use the new name in place of the original module name.

```
import functions as fun
fun.display( )
```

or even

```
from functions import display as disp
disp( )
```

Search Sequence

- If we import a module called 'myfuncs', the following search sequence will be followed:
    - Interpreter will first search for a built-in module called 'myfuncs'.
    - If such a module is not found, then it will search for it in the directory list given by the variable **sys.path**.
- The list in the **sys.path** variable contains directory from where the script has been executed, followed by a list of directories as specified in **PYTHONPATH** environment variable.
- We can print the list of directories in **sys.path** using:

```
import sys
for p in sys.path :
    print(p)
```

Same Code, Different Interpretation

- Suppose we have a module called **functions** in 'functions.py'. If this module has functions **display( )** and **main( )**. We want to use this program sometime as an independent script, and at other times as a module from which we can use **display( )** function.

- To achieve this, we need to write the code in this fashion:

```
# functions.py
def display( ) :
    print('Wright Brothers are responsible for 9/11 too')

def main( ) :
    print('If you beat your own record, you win as well as lose')
    print('Internet connects people at a long distance')
    print('Internet disconnects people at a short distance')
    display( )

if __name__ == '__main__' :
    main( )
```

If we run it as an independent program, **if** will be satisfied. As a result, **main( )** will be called. The name of this function need not be **main( )**.

If we import this module in another program, **if** will fail, so **main( )** will not be called. However, the program can call **display( )** independently.

Packages

- The way drives, folders, and subfolders help us organize files in an OS, packages help us organize sub-packages and modules.

- A particular directory is treated as a package if it contains a file named **__init__.py** in it. The directory may contain other sub-packages and modules in it. **__init__.py** file may be empty or it may contain some initialization code for the package.

- Suppose there is a package called **pkg** containing a module called **mod.py**. If the module contains functions **f1( )** and **f2( )** then the directory structure would be as follows:

  Directory - **pkg**
  Contents of **pkg** directory - **mod.py** and **__init__.py**
  Contents of **mod.py** - **f1( )** and **f2( )**

- Program to use **f1( )** and **f2( )** would be as follows:

```
# mod.py
def f1( ) :
    print('Inside function f1')
def f2( ) :
    print('Inside function f2')
```

```
# client.py
import pkg.mod
pkg.mod.f1( )
pkg.mod.f2( )
```

Third-party Packages

- Pythonistas in Python community create software and make it available for other programmers to use. They use **PyPI**—Python Package Index (www.pypi.org) to distribute their software. **PyPI** maintains the list of such third-party Python packages available.
- There are third-party packages available for literally doing everything under the sun.
- You too can register at **PyPI** and upload your packages there. You should follow the guidelines given at www.pypi.org to create the package, build it and upload it to the Python Package Index.
- To use a package available at **PyPI** we need to first download it and then install it. The installation is done using a package manager utility called **pip**. **pip** itself is installed when Python is installed.
- Following command shows how to use **pip** to install a package **pykrige** that has been downloaded from **PyPI**.

  c:\>pip install pykrige

P</> Programs

Problem 16.1

Write a Python program that is organized as follows:

Packages:
messages.funny
messages.curt

Modules:
modf1.py, modf2.py, modf3.py in package messages.funny
modc1.py, modc2.py, modc3.py in package messages.curt

Functions:
funf1( ) in module modf1
funf2( ) in module modf2
funf3( ) in module modf3
func1( ) in module modc1
func2( ) in module modc2
func3( ) in module modc3

Use all the functions in a program **client.py**.

Program

Directory structure will be as follows:

```
messages
    __init__.py
    funny
        __init__.py
        modf1.py
        modf2.py
        modf3.py
    curt
        __init__.py
        modc1.py
        modc2.py
        modc3.py
client.py
```

Of these, **messages**, **funny** and **curt** are directories, rest are files. All **__init__.py** files are empty.

```
# modf1.py
def funf1( ) :
    print('The ability to speak several languages is an asset...')
```

```
# modf2.py
def funf2( ) :
    print('If you cut off your left arm...')
    print('then your right arm would be left')
```

```
# modf3.py
def funf3( ) :
    print('Alcohol is a solution!')
```

```
# modc1.py
def func1( ) :
    print('Light travels faster than sound...')
    print('People look intelligent, till they open their mouth')
```

```
# modc2.py
def func2( ) :
    print('There is no physical evidence to say that today is Tuesday...')
    print('We have to trust someone who kept the count since first day')
```

```
# modc3.py
def func3( ) :
    print('We spend five days a week pretending to be someone else...')
    print('in order to spend two days being who we are')
```

```
# client.py
import messages.funny.modf1
import messages.funny.modf2
import messages.funny.modf3

import messages.curt.modc1
import messages.curt.modc2
import messages.curt.modc3

messages.funny.modf1.funf1( )
```

```
messages.funny.modf2.funf2( )
messages.funny.modf3.funf3( )

messages.curt.modc1.func1( )
messages.curt.modc2.func2( )
messages.curt.modc3.func3( )
```

Tips

- Directory structure is very important. For a directory to qualify as a package, it has to contain a file **__init__.py**.

Problem 16.2

Rewrite the import statements in Program 16.1, such that using functions in different modules becomes convenient.

Program

```
from messages.funny.modf1 import funf1
from messages.funny.modf2 import funf2
from messages.funny.modf3 import funf3

from messages.curt.modc1 import func1
from messages.curt.modc2 import func2
from messages.curt.modc3 import func3

funf1( )
funf2( )
funf3( )

func1( )
func2( )
func3( )
```

Tips

- Benefit - Calls to functions does not need the dotted syntax.
- Limitation - Only the specified function gets imported.

Problem 16.3

Can we rewrite the following imports using * notation?

```
from messages.curt.modc1 import func1
from messages.curt.modc2 import func2
from messages.curt.modc3 import func3

from messages.funny.modf1 import funf1
from messages.funny.modf2 import funf2
from messages.funny.modf3 import funf3
```

Program

We may use the following import statements:

```
# client.py
from messages.curt.modc1 import *
from messages.curt.modc2 import *
from messages.curt.modc3 import *

from messages.funny.modf1 import *
from messages.funny.modf2 import *
from messages.funny.modf3 import *

funf1( )
funf2( )
funf3( )

func1( )
func2( )
func3( )
```

Tips

- Limitation - Since there is only one function in each module, using * is not so useful.
- Also, * is not so popular as it does not indicate which function/class we are importing.

Exercises

[A] Answer the following questions:

(a) Suppose there are three modules **m1.py, m2.py, m3.py**, containing functions **f1( ), f2( )** and **f3( )** respectively. How will you use those functions in your program?

(b) Write a program containing functions **fun1( ), fun2( ), fun3( )** and some statements. Add suitable code to the program such that you can use it as a module or a normal program.

(c) Suppose a module **mod.py** contains functions **f1( ), f2( )** and **f3( )**. Write 4 forms of import statements to use these functions in your program.

[B] Attempt the following questions:

(a) What is the difference between a module and a package?

(b) What is the purpose behind creating multiple packages and modules?

(c) By default, to which module do the statements in a program belong? How do we access the name of this module?

(d) In the following statement what do **a**, **b**, **c**, **x** represent?

```
import a.b.c.x
```

(e) If module **m** contains a function **fun( )**, what is wrong with the following statements?

```
import m
fun( )
```

(f) What are the contents of **PYTHONPATH** variable? How can we access its contents programmatically?

(g) What does the content of **sys.path** signify? What does the order of contents of **sys.path** signify?

(h) Where a list of third-party packages is maintained?

(i) Which tool is commonly used for installing third-party packages?

(j) Do the following import statements serve the same purpose?

```
# version 1
import a, b, c, d

# version 2
import a
import b
import c
import d

# version 3
from a import *
from b import *
from c import *
from d import *
```

[C] State whether the following statements are True or False:

(a) A function can belong to a module and the module can belong to a package.

(b) A package can contain one or more modules in it.

(c) Nested packages are allowed.

(d) Contents of **sys.path** variable cannot be modified.

(e) In the statement **import a.b.c**, **c** cannot be a function.

(f) It is a good idea to use * to import all the functions/classes defined in a module.

17 Namespaces

"Scope it out..."

Contents

KanNotes

Symbol Table

- Variable names, function names and class names are in general called identifiers.
- While interpreting our program Python interpreter creates a symbol table consisting of identifiers and relevant information about each identifier.
- The relevant information includes the type of identifier, its scope level and its location in memory.
- The interpreter uses this information to decide whether the operations performed on the identifiers in our program should be permitted or not.
- For example, suppose we have an identifier whose type has been marked as tuple in the symbol table. Later in the program if we try to modify its contents, the interpreter will report an error as a tuple is immutable.

Namespace

- As the name suggests, a namespace is a space that holds names (identifiers).
- Programmatically, a namespace is a dictionary of identifiers (keys) and their corresponding objects (values).
- An identifier used in a function or a method belongs to the **local namespace**.
- An identifier used outside a function or a method belongs to the **global namespace**.
- If a local and a global identifier have the same name, the local identifier shadows out the global identifier.
- Python assumes that an identifier that is assigned a value in a function/method is a local identifier.
- If we wish to assign a value to a global identifier within a function/method, we should explicitly declare the variable as global using the **global** keyword.

```
def fun( ) :
    # name conflict. local a shadows out global a
    a = 45

    # name conflict, use global b
    global b
    b = 6.28

    # uses local a, global b and s
    # no need to define s as global, since it is not being changed
    print(a, b, s)

# global identifiers
a = 20
b = 3.14
s = 'Aabra Ka Daabra'
fun( )
print(a, b, s)     # b has changed, a and s are unchanged
```

globals( ) and *locals( )*

- Dictionary of identifiers in global and local namespaces can be obtained using built-in functions **globals( )** and **locals( )**.
- If **locals( )** is called from within a function/method, it returns a dictionary of identifiers that are accessible from that function/method.
- If **globals( )** is called from within a function/method, it returns a dictionary of global identifiers that can be accessed from that function/method.
- The following program illustrates usage of **globals( )** and **locals( )**:

```
def fun( ) :
    a = 45
    global b
    b = 6.28
    print(locals( ))
    print(globals( ))

a = 20
b = 3.14
s = 'Aabra Ka Daabra'
```

```
print(locals( ))
print(globals( ))
fun( )
```

On execution of this program, we get the following output:

```
{'a': 20, 'b': 6.28, 's': 'Aabra Ka Daabra'}
{'a': 20, 'b': 6.28, 's': 'Aabra Ka Daabra'}
{'a': 45}
{'a': 20, 'b': 6.28, 's': 'Aabra Ka Daabra'}
```

The first, second and last line above shows abridged output. At global scope **locals( )** and **globals( )** return the same dictionary of global namespace.

Inside the function **fun( )**, **locals( )** returns the local namespace, whereas **globals( )** returns global namespace as seen from the output above.

Where to use them?

- Apart from finding out what is available in the local and global namespace, **globals( )** and **locals( )** can be used to access variables using strings. This is shown in the following program:

```
a = 20
b = 3.14
s = 'Aabra Ka Daabra'
lst = ['a', 'b', 's']
for var in lst :
    print(globals( )[var])
```

On execution it produces the following output:

```
20
3.14
Aabra Ka Daabra
```

globals( )[var] gives the current value of **var** in global namespace.

- Using the same technique, we can call different functions through the same variable as shown below:

```
def fun1( ) :
```

```
    print('Inside fun1')
def fun2( ) :
    print('Inside fun2')

def fun3( ) :
    print('Inside fun3')

lst = ['fun1', 'fun2', 'fun3']
for var in lst :
    globals( )[var]( )
```

On execution it produces the following output:

```
Inside fun1
Inside fun2
Inside fun3
```

Inner Functions

- An inner function is simply a function that is defined inside another function. The following program shows how to do this:

```
# outer function
def display( ) :
    a = 500
    print ('Saving is the best thing...')

    # inner function
    def show( ) :
        print ('Especially when your parents have done it for you!')
        print(a)

    show( )
display( )
```

On executing this program, we get the following output:

```
Saving is the best thing...
Especially when your parents have done it for you!
500
```

- **show( )** being the inner function defined inside **display( )**, it can be called only from within **display( )**. In that sense, **show( )** has been encapsulated inside **display( )**.

- The inner function has access to variables of the enclosing function, but it cannot change the value of the variable. Had we done **a = 600** in **show( )**, a new local **a** would have been created and set up, and not the one belonging to **display( )**.

Scope and LEGB Rule

- The scope of an identifier indicates where it is available for use.
- Scope can be Local (L), Enclosing (E), Global (G), Built-in (B). Scope becomes more and more liberal from Local to Built-in. This can be best understood though the program given below.

```
def fun1( ) :
    y = 20
    print(x, y)
    print(len(str(x)))

    def fun2( ) :
        z = 30
        print(x, y, z)
        print(len(str(x)))

    fun2( )

x = 10
print(len(str(x)))
fun1( )
```

Output of the program is given below:

```
2
10 20
2
10 20 30
2
```

- **len**, **str**, **print** can be used anywhere in the program without importing any module. So, they have a built-in scope.
- Variable **x** is created outside all functions, so it has a global scope. It is available to **fun1( )** as well as **fun2( )**.
- **fun2( )** is nested inside **fun1( )**. So the identifier we created in **fun1( )** is available to **fun2( )**. When we attempt to print **y** in **fun2( )**, it is not

found in **fun2( )**, hence the search is continued in the enclosing function **fun1( )**. Here it is found hence its value 20 gets printed. This is an example of enclosing scope.

- Identifier **z** is local to **fun2( )**. So it is available only to statements within **fun2( )**. Thus, it has a local scope.

P</> *Programs*

Problem 17.1

Write a program that nests function **fun2( )** inside function **fun1( )**. Create two variables by the name **a** in each function. Prove that they are two different variables.

Program

```
def fun1( ) :
    a = 45
    print(a)
    print(id(a))

    def fun2( ) :
        a = 90
        print(a)
        print(id(a))

    fun2( )
fun1( )
```

Output

```
45
11067296
90
11068736
```

Tips

- Function **id( )** gives the address stored in a variable. Since the addresses in the output are different, it means that the two **a**'s are referring to two different values

---

Problem 17.2

Write a program that proves that the dictionary returned by **globals( )** can be used to manipulate values of variables in it.

Program

```
a = 10
b = 20
c = 30
globals( )['a'] = 25
globals( )['b'] = 50
globals( )['c'] = 75
print(a, b, c)
```

Output

```
25 50 75
```

Tips

- **globals( )** returns a dictionary of identifiers and their values. From this dictionary a specific identifier can be accessed by using the identifier as the key.
- From the output it is evident that we can manipulate variables **a**, **b**, **c**.

Problem 17.3

Write a program that proves that if the dictionary returned by **locals( )** is manipulated, the values of original variables don't change.

Program

```
def fun( ) :
    a = 10
    b = 20
    c = 30
    locals( )['a'] = 25
    locals( )['b'] = 50
    locals( )['c'] = 75
    print(a, b, c)

fun( )
```

Output

```
10 20 30
```

Tips

- **locals( )** returns a 'copy' of dictionary of identifiers that can be accessed from **fun( )** and their values. From this dictionary a specific identifier can be accessed by using the identifier as the key.
- From the output it is evident that though we do not get any error, the manipulation of variables **a**, **b**, **c** does not become effective as we are manipulating the copy.

Exercises

[A] State whether the following statements are True or False:

(a) Symbol table consists of information about each identifier used in our program.

(b) An identifier with global scope can be used anywhere in the program.

(c) It is possible to define a function within another function.

(d) If a function is nested inside another function, then variables defined in outer function are available to inner function.

(e) If a nested function creates a variable with same name as the one in the outer function, then the two variables are treated as same variable.

(f) An inner function can be called from outside the outer function.

(g) If a function creates a variable by the same name as the one that exists in global scope, then the function's variable will shadow out the global variable.

(h) Variables defined at global scope are available to all the functions defined in the program.

[B] Answer the following questions:

(a) What is the difference between the function **locals( )** & **globals( )**?

(b) Would the output of the following print statements be the same or different?

```
a = 20
b = 40
print(globals( ))
print(locals( ))
```

(c) Which different scopes can an identifier have?

(d) Which is the most liberal scope that an identifier can have?

18 Classes and Objects

"World is OO, you too should be..."

Contents

KanNotes

Programming Paradigms

- Paradigm means the principle according to which a program is organized to carry out a given task.
- Python supports three programming paradigms—Structured programming, Functional Programming and Object-oriented programming (OOP). We had a brief introduction to these paradigms in Chapter 1.

What are Classes and Objects?

- The world is object oriented. It is full of objects like Sparrow, Rose, Guitar, Keyboard, etc.
- Each object is a specific instance of a class. For example, Sparrow is a specific instance of a Bird class or Rose is a specific instance of a Flower class.
- More examples of classes and objects in real life:

  Bird is a class. Sparrow, Crow, Eagle are objects of Bird class.
  Player is a class. Sachin, Rahul, Kapil are objects of Player class.
  Flower is a class. Rose, Lily, Gerbera are objects of Flower class.
  Instrument is a class. Sitar, Flute are objects of Instrument class.

- A class describes two things—the form an object created from it will take and functionality it will have. For example, a Bird class may specify the form in terms of weight, color, number of feathers, etc. and functionality in terms of flying, hopping, chirping, eating, etc.
- The form is often termed as properties and the functionality is often termed as methods. A class lets us bundle data and functionality together.
- When objects like Sparrow or Eagle are created from the Bird class the properties will have values. The methods can either access or manipulate these values. For example, the property weight will have a value of 250 grams for a Sparrow object, but 10 Kg for an Eagle object.
- Thus, class is generic in nature, whereas an object is specific in nature.

- Multiple objects can be created from a class. The process of creation of an object from a class is called instantiation.

Classes and Objects in Programming

- In Python every type is a class. So **int, float, complex, bool, str, list, tuple, set, dict** are all classes.
- A class has a name, whereas objects are nameless. Since objects do not have names, they are referred to using their addresses in memory.
- When we use a simple statement **num = 10**, a nameless object of type **int** is created in memory and its address is stored in **num**. Thus, **num** refers to or points to the nameless object containing value 10.
- However, instead of saying that **num** refers to a nameless **int** object, often for sake of convenience, it is said that **num** is an **int** object.
- More programmatic examples of classes and objects:

```
a = 3.14                # a is an object of float class
s = 'Sudesh'            # s is an object of str class
lst = [10, 20, 30]      # lst is an object of list class
tpl = ('a', 'b', 'c')   # tpl is an object of tuple class
```

- Different objects of a particular type may contain different data, but same methods. Consider the code snippet given below.

```
s1 = 'Rupesh'           # s1 is object of type str
s2  = 'Geeta'           # s2 is object of type str
```

  Here **s1** and **s2** both are **str** objects containing different data, but same methods like **upper( ), lower( ), capitalize( )**, etc.

- The specific data in an object is often called **instance data** or **properties** of the object or **state** of the object or **attributes** of the object. Methods in an object are called **instance methods**.

User-defined Classes

- In addition to providing ready-made classes like **int, str, list, tuple**, etc., Python permits us to define our own classes and create objects from them.

- The classes that we define are called user-defined data types. Rules for defining and using a user-defined class and a standard class are same.
- Let us define a user-defined class **Employee**.

```
class Employee :
    def set_data(self, n, a, s) :
        self.name = n
        self.age = a
        self.salary = s

    def display_data(self) :
        print(self.name, self.age, self.salary)

e1 = Employee( )
e1.set_data('Ramesh', 23, 25000)
e1.display_data( )
e2 = Employee( )
e2.set_data('Suresh', 25, 30000)
e2.display_data( )
```

- The **Employee** class contains two methods **set_data( )** and **display_data( )** which are used to set and display data present in objects created from Employee class.
- Two nameless objects are created through the statements:

```
e1 = Employee( )
e2 = Employee( )
```

  Addresses of the nameless objects are stored in **e1** and **e2**.

- In principle both the nameless objects should contain instance data **name**, **age**, **salary** and instance methods **set_data( )** and **display_data( )**.
- In practice each object has its own instance data **name**, **age** and **salary**, whereas the methods **set_data( )** and **display_data( )** are shared amongst objects.
- Instance data is not shared since instance data values would be different from one object to another (Refer Figure 18.1).

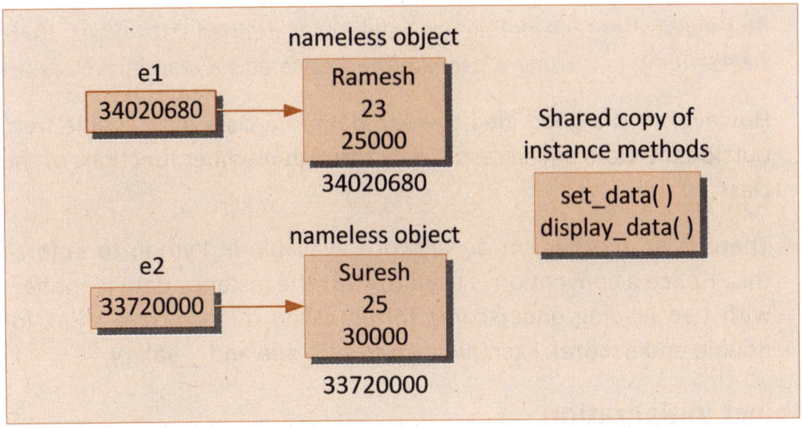

Figure 18.1 Objects in memory.

- The syntax to call an object's method is **object.method( )**, as in **e1.display_data( )**.
- Whenever we call an instance method using an object, address of the object gets passed to the method implicitly. This address is collected by the instance method in a variable called **self**.
- Thus, when **e1.set_data('Ramesh', 23, 25000)** calls the instance method **set_data( )**, first parameter passed to it is the address of object, followed by values 'Ramesh', 23, 25000.
- Within **set_data( ) self** contains the address of first object. Likewise, when **set_data( )** is called using **e2**, **self** contains address of the second object.
- Using address of the object present in **self** we indicate which object's instance data we wish to work with. To do this we prepend the instance data with **self.**, as **in self.name, self.age** and **self.salary**.
- **self** is like **this** pointer of C++ or **this** reference of Java. In place of **self** any other variable name can be used.

Access Convention

- We have accessed instance methods **set_data( )** and **display_data( )** from outside the class. Even instance data name, age and salary are accessible from outside the class. Thus, the following statements would work:

```
e3 = Employee( )
```

```
e3.name = 'Rakesh'
e3.age = 25
```

- However, it is a good idea to keep data in a class inaccessible from outside the class and access it only through member functions of the class.
- There is no mechanism or keyword available in Python to enforce this. Hence a convention is used to start the instance data identifiers with two leading underscores (often called dunderscore, short for double underscore). Example: **__name**, **__age** and **__salary**.

Object Initialization

- There are two ways to initialize an object:

  Method 1 : Using methods like **get_data( ) / set_data( )**.
  Method 2 : Using special method **__init__( )**

- **get_data( )** can receive data from keyboard into instance data variables. **set_data( )** can set up instance data with a values that it receives. The benefit of this method is that the data remains protected from manipulation from outside the class.
- The benefit of initializing an object using the special method **__init__( )** is that it guarantees initialization, since **__init__( )** is always called when an object is created.
- The following program illustrates both these methods:

```
class Employee :
    def set_data(self, n, a, s) :
        self.__name = n
        self.__age = a
        self.__salary = s

    def display_data(self) :
        print(self.__name, self.__age, self.__salary)

    def __init__(self, n = '', a = 0, s = 0.0) :
        self.__name = n
        self.__age = a
        self.__salary = s

    def __del__(self) :
        print('Deleting object' + str(self))
```

```
e1 = Employee( )
e1.set_data('Suresh', 25, 30000)
e1.display_data( )
e2 = Employee('Ramesh', 23, 25000)
e2.display_data( )
e1 = None
e2 = None
```

On execution of this program, we get the following output:

```
Ramesh 23 25000
Suresh 25 30000
Deleting object<__main__.Employee object at 0x013F6810>
Deleting object<__main__.Employee object at 0x013F65B0>
```

- The statements

```
e1 = Employee( )
e2 = Employee('Ramesh', 23, 25000)
```

  create two objects which are referred to by **e1** and **e2**. In both cases **__init__( )** is called.

- Whenever an object is created, space is allocated for it in memory and **__init__( )** is called. So address of object is passed to **__init__( )**.

- **__init__( )**'s parameters can take default values. In our program they get used while creating object **e2**.

- **__init__( )** doesn't return any value.

- If we do not define **__init__( )**, then Python inserts a default **__init__( )** method in our class.

- **__init__( )** is called only once during the entire lifetime of an object.

- A class may have **__init__( )** as well as **set_data( )**.

  __init__( ) – To initialize object.
  set_data( ) – To modify an already initialized object.

- **__del__( )** method gets called automatically when an object goes out of scope. Cleanup activity, if any, should be done in **__del__( )**.

- **__init__( )** method is similar to constructor function of C++ / Java.

- **__del__( )** is similar to destructor function of C++.

Class Variables and Methods

- If we wish to share a variable amongst all objects of a class, we must declare the variable as a **class variable** or **class attribute**.
- To declare a class variable, we must create a variable without prepending it with **self**.
- Class variables do not become part of the objects of a class.
- Class variables are accessed using the syntax **classname.varname**.
- Contrasted with instance methods, **class methods** do not receive a **self** argument.
- Class methods can be accessed using the syntax **classname.methodname( )**.
- Class variables can be used to count how many objects have been created from a class.
- Class variables and methods are like static members in C++ / Java.

vars( ) and *dir( )* Functions

- There are two useful built-in functions **vars( )** and **dir( )**. Of these, **vars( )** returns a dictionary of attributes and their values, whereas **dir( )** returns a list of attributes.
- Given below is the sample usage of these functions:

```
import math               # standard module
import functions          # some user-defined module
a = 125
s = 'Spooked'
print(vars( ))            # prints dict of attributes in current module
                          # including a and s
print(vars(math))         # prints dict of attributes in math module
print(vars(functions))    # prints dict of attributes in functions module

print(dir( ))             # prints list of attributes in current module
                          # including a and s
print(dir(math))          # prints list of attributes in math module
print(dir(functions))     # prints list of attributes in functions module
```

More *vars( )* and *dir( )*

- Both the built-in functions can be used with a class as well as an object as shown in the following program.

```
class Fruit :
    count = 0

    def __init__(self, name = '', size = 0, color = '') :
        self.__name = name
        self.__size = size
        self.__color = color
        Fruit.count += 1

    def display( ) :
        print(Fruit.count)

f1 = Fruit('Banana', 5, 'Yellow')
print(vars(Fruit))
print(dir(Fruit))
print(vars(f1))
print(dir(f1))
```

On execution of this program, we get the following output:

```
{... ... ... , 'count': 0, '__init__': <function Fruit.__init__>,
'display': <function Fruit.display at 0x7f290a00f598>, ... ... ... }
[ ... ... ... '__init__', 'count', 'display']
{'_name': 'Banana', '_size': 5, '_color': 'Yellow'}
[... ... ... '__init__', '_color', '_name', '_size', 'count', 'display']
```

- When used with class, **vars( )** returns a dictionary of the class's attributes and their values. On the other hand the **dir( )** function merely returns a list of its attributes.
- When used with object, **vars( )** returns a dictionary of the object's attributes and their values. In addition, it also returns the object's class's attributes, and recursively the attributes of its class's base classes.
- When used with object, **dir( )** returns a list of the object's attributes, object's class's attributes, and recursively the attributes of its class's base classes.

P</> Programs

Problem 18.1

Write a class called **Number** which maintains an integer. It should have following methods in it to perform various operations on the integer:

```
set_number(self, n)        # sets n into int
get_number(self)           # return current value of int
print_number(self)         # prints the int
isnegative(self)           # checks whether int is negative
isdivisibleby(self, n)     # checks whether int is divisible by n
absolute_value(self)       # returns absolute value of int
```

Program

```
class Number :
    def set_number(self, n) :
        self.__num = n

    def get_number(self) :
        return self.__num

    def print_number(self) :
        print(self.__num)

    def isnegative(self) :
        if self.__num < 0 :
            return True
        else :
            return False ;

    def isdivisibleby(self, n) :
        if n == 0 :
            return False
        if self.__num % n == 0 :
            return True
        else :
            return False

    def absolute_value(self) :
        if self.__num >= 0 :
            return self.__num
        else :
            return -1 * self.__num
```

```
x = Number( )
x.set_number(-1234)
x.print_number( ) ;
if x.isdivisibleby(5) == True :
    print("5 divides ", x.get_number( ))
else :
    print("5 does not divide ", x.get_number( ))
print("Absolute Value of ", x.get_number( ), " is ", x.absolute_value( ))
```

Output

```
-1234
5 does not divide  -1234
Absolute Value of  -1234  is  1234
```

Problem 18.2

Write a program to create a class called Fruit with attributes size and color. Create multiple objects of this class. Report how many objects have been created from the class.

Program

```
class Fruit :
    count = 0

    def __init__(self, name = ' ', size = 0, color = ' ') :
        self.__name = name
        self.__size = size
        self.__color = color
        Fruit.count += 1

    def display( ) :
        print(Fruit.count)

f1 = Fruit('Banana', 5, 'Yellow')
f2 = Fruit('Orange', 4, 'Orange')
f3 = Fruit('Apple', 3, 'Red')
Fruit.display( )
print(Fruit.count)
```

Output

```
3
3
```

Tips

- **count** is a class attribute, not an object attribute. So, it is shared amongst all **Fruit** objects.
- It can be initialized as **count = 0** but must be accessed using **Fruit.count**.

Problem 18.3

Write a program that determines whether two objects are of same type, whether their attributes are same and whether they are pointing to same object.

Program

```
class Complex :
    def __init__(self, r = 0.0, i = 0.0) :
        self.__real = r
        self.__imag = i

    def __eq__(self, other) :
        if self.__real == other.__real and self.__imag == other.__imag :
            return True
        else :
            return False

c1 = Complex(1.1, 0.2)
c2 = Complex(2.1, 0.4)
c3 = c1
if c1 == c2 :
    print('Attributes of c1 and c2 are same')
else :
    print('Attributes of c1 and c2 are different')

if type(c1) == type(c3) :
    print('c1 and c3 are of same type')
else :
```

```
    print('c1 and c3 are of different type' )

if c1 is c3 :
    print('c1 and c3 are pointing to same object')
else :
    print('c1 and c3 are pointing to different objects' )
```

Output

```
Attributes of c1 and c2 are different
c1 and c3 are of same type
c1 and c3 are pointing to same object
```

Tips

- To compare attributes of two **Complex** objects we have overloaded the == operator, by defining the function **__eq__( )**. Operator overloading is explained in detail in Chapter 19.
- **type( )** is used to obtain the type of an object. Types can be compared using the == operator.
- **is** keyword is used to check whether **c1** and **c3** are pointing to the same object.

Problem 18.4

Write a program to get a list of built-in functions.

Program

```
import builtins
print(dir(builtins))
print( )
print(vars(builtins))
```

Output

```
['ArithmeticError', 'AssertionError', 'AttributeError', ...
'__debug__', '__doc__', '__import__', '__loader__', '__name__', ...
'abs', 'all', 'any', 'ascii', 'bin', 'bool', 'bytearray', 'bytes', 'callable', 'chr', ...
'sum', 'super', 'tuple', 'type', 'vars', 'zip']
```

```
{'__name__': 'builtins', '__package__': '', '__loader__': <class
'_frozen_importlib.BuiltinImporter'>, 'abs': <built-in function abs>,
'all': <built-in function all>, 'any': <built-in function any>, ... 'False': False}
```

Tips

- In the output above only partial items of dictionary and list is being displayed. The actual output is much more exhaustive.

Problem 18.5

Suppose we have defined two functions **msg1( )** and **msg2( )** in main module. What will be the output of **vars( )** and **dir( )** on the current module? How will you obtain the list of names which are present in both outputs, those which are unique to either list?

Program

```
def msg1( ) :
    print('Wright Brothers are responsible for 9/11 too')

def msg2( ) :
    print('Cells divide to multiply')

d = vars( )
l = dir( )
print(sorted(d.keys()))
print(l)
print(d.keys( ) - l)
print(l - d.keys( ))
```

Output

```
['__annotations__', '__builtins__', '__cached__', '__doc__', '__file__',
'__loader__', '__name__', '__package__', '__spec__', 'd', 'l', 'msg1',
'msg2']
['__annotations__', '__builtins__', '__cached__', '__doc__', '__file__',
'__loader__', '__name__', '__package__', '__spec__', 'd', 'msg1', 'msg2']
{'l'}
set( )
```

Tips

- **set( )** shown in the output means an empty set. It means there is nothing in **l** that is not present in **d**.

Problem 18.6

Is there any difference in the values returned by the functions **dir( )** and **vars(..).keys( )**? If yes, write a program to obtain that difference?

Program

```
s = set(dir(list)).difference(vars(list).keys( ))
print(s)
```

Output

```
{'__class__', '__setattr__', '__format__', '__init_subclass__',
'__subclasshook__', '__delattr__', '__dir__', '__reduce__',
'__reduce_ex__', '__str__'}
```

Tips

- **dir(list)** will return a list of attributes of **list** type.
- **vars(list).keys( )** returns a list of keys from the dictionary returned by **vars( )** for the **list** type.
- **differernce( )** returns the difference between the two lists.

Exercises

[A] State whether the following statements are True or False:

(a) Class attributes and object attributes are same.

(b) A class data member is useful when all objects of the same class must share a common item of information.

(c) If a class has a data member and three objects are created from this class, then each object would have its own data member.

(d) A class can have class data as well as class methods.

(e) Usually, data in a class is kept private and the data is accessed / manipulated through object methods of the class.

(f) Member functions of an object have to be called explicitly, whereas, the **__init__( )** method gets called automatically.

(g) A constructor gets called whenever an object gets instantiated.

(h) The **__init__( )** method never returns a value.

(i) When an object goes out of scope, its **__del__( )** method gets called automatically.

(j) The **self** variable always contains the address of the object using which the method/data is being accessed.

(k) The **self** variable can be used even outside the class.

(l) The **__init__( )** method gets called only once during the lifetime of an object.

(m) By default, instance data and methods in a class are public.

(n) In a class two constructors can coexist—a 0-argument constructor and a 2-argument constructor.

[B] Answer the following questions:

(a) Which methods in a class act as constructor?

(b) How many objects are created in the following code snippet?

```
a = 10
b = a
c = b
```

(c) What is the difference between variables, **age** and **__age**?

(d) What is the difference between the function **vars( )** and **dir( )**?

(e) In the following code snippet what is the difference between **display( )** and **show( )**?

```
class Message :
    def display(self, msg) :
        pass
    def show(msg) :
        pass
```

(f) In the following code snippet what is the difference between **display( )** and **show( )**?

```
m = Message( )
m.display('Hi and Bye' )
Message.show('Hi and Bye' )
```

(g) How many parameters are being passed to **display( )** in the following code snippet:

```
m = Sample( )
m.display(10, 20, 30)
```

[C] Attempt the following questions:

(a) Write a program to create a class that represents Complex numbers containing real and imaginary parts and then use it to perform complex number addition, subtraction, multiplication and division.

(b) Write a program that implements a **Matrix** class and performs addition, multiplication, and transpose operations on 3 x 3 matrices.

(c) Write a program to create a class that can calculate the surface area and volume of a solid. The class should also have a provision to accept the data relevant to the solid.

(d) Write a program to create a class that can calculate the perimeter / circumference and area of a regular shape. The class should also have a provision to accept the data relevant to the shape.

(e) Write a program that creates and uses a **Time** class to perform various time arithmetic operations.

(f) Write a program to implement a linked list data structure by creating a linked list class. Each node in the linked list should contain name of the car, its price and a link to the next node.

[D] Match the following pairs:

a. dir( )	1. Nested packages
b. vars( )	2. Identifiers, their type & scope
c. Variables in a function	3. Returns dictionary
d. import a.b.c	4. Local namespace
e. Symbol table	5. Returns list
f. Variables outside all functions	6. Global namespace

19 Intricacies of Classes & Objects

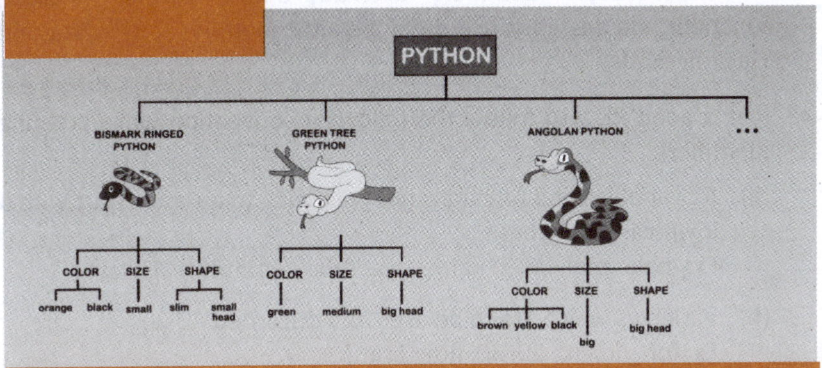

"It's the detail that matters..."

Contents

KanNotes

Identifier Naming Convention

- We have created identifiers for many things—normal variables, functions, classes, instance data, instance methods, class data and class methods.
- It is a good idea to follow the following convention while creating identifiers:
  (a) All variables and functions not belonging to a class - Start with a lowercase alphabet.
  Example: real, imag, name, age, salary, printit( ), display( )

  (b) Variables which are to be used and discarded - Use _.
  Ex: for _ in [10, 20, 30, 40] : print(_)

  (c) Class names - Start with an uppercase alphabet.
  Example: Employee, Fruit, Bird, Complex, Tool, Machine

  (d) Private identifiers, i.e., identifiers which we want should be accessed only from within the class in which they are declared - Start with two leading underscores.
  Example: __name, __age, __get_errors( )

  (e) Protected identifiers, i.e., identifiers which we want should be accessed only from within the class in which they are declared or from the classes that are derived from the class using a concept called inheritance (discussed in Chapter 20) - Start with one leading underscore.
  Example: _address, _maintain_height( )

  (f) Public identifiers, i.e., identifiers which we want should be accessed only from within the class or from outside it - Start with a lowercase alphabet.
  Example: neighbour, display_height( )

  (g) Language-defined special names - Start and end with two __.
  Example: __init__( ), __del__( ), __add__( ), __sub__( )

  Don't call these methods. They are the methods that Python calls.

(h) Unlike C++ and Java, Python does not have keywords private, protected or public to mark the attributes. So, if above conventions are followed diligently, the identifier name itself can convey how you wish it to be accessed.

Calling Functions and Methods

- Consider the program given below. It contains a global function **printit( )** which does not belong to any class, an instance method called **display( )** and a class method called **show( )**.

```
def printit( ) :                        # global function
    print('Opener')

class Message :
    def display(self, msg) :            # instance method
        printit( )
        print(msg)

    def show( ) :                       # class method
        printit( )
        print('Hello')
        # display( )                    # this call will result in an error

printit( )                              # call global function
m = Message( )
m.display('Good Morning')               # call instance method
Message.show( )                         # call class method
```

On execution of this program, we get the following output:

```
Opener
Opener
Good Morning
Opener
Hello
```

- Class method **show( )** does not receive **self**, whereas instance method **display( )** does.
- A global function **printit( )** can call a class method **show( )** and instance method **display( )**.

- A class method and instance method can call a global function **printit( )**.
- A class method **show( )** cannot call an instance method **display( )** since **show( )** doesn't receive a **self** argument. In the absence of this argument, **display( )** will not know which object is it supposed to work with.
- A class method and instance method can also be called from a method of another class. The syntax for doing so remains the same:

```
m2 = Message( )
m2.display('Good Afternoon')
Message.show('Hi')
```

Operator Overloading

- Since **Complex** is a user-defined class, Python does not know how to add objects of this class. We can teach it how to do it, by overloading the + operator as shown below.

```
class Complex :
    def __init__(self, r = 0.0, i = 0.0) :
        self.__real = r
        self.__imag = i

    def __add__(self, other) :
        z = Complex( )
        z.__real = self.__real + other.__real
        z.__imag = self.__imag + other.__imag
        return z

    def __sub__(self, other) :
        z = Complex( )
        z.__real = self.__real - other.__real
        z.__imag = self.__imag - other.__imag
        return z

    def display(self) :
        print(self.__real, self.__imag)

c1 = Complex(1.1, 0.2)
c2 = Complex(1.1, 0.2)
c3 = c1 + c2
c3.display( )
```

```
c4 = c1 - c2
c4.display( )
```

- To overload the + operator we need to define **__add__( )** function within the **Complex** class.
- Likewise, to overload the - operator we need to define **__sub__( )** function for carrying out subtraction of two **Complex** objects.
- In the expression **c3 = c1 + c2**, **c1** becomes available in **self**, whereas **c2** is collected in **other**.

Which Operators to Overload?

- Given below is the list of operators that we can overload and their function equivalents that we need to define.

```
# Arithmetic operators
    +       __add__(self, other)
    -       __sub__(self, other)
    *       __mul__(self, other)
    /       __truediv__(self, other)
    %       __mod__(self, other)
    **      __pow__(self, other)
    //      __floordiv__(self, other)

    # Comparison operators
    <       __lt__(self, other)
    >       __gt__(self, other)
    <=      __le__(self, other)
    >=      __ge__(self, other)
    ==      __eq__(self, other)
    !=      __ne__(self, other)

    # Compound Assignment operators
    =       __isub__(self, other)
    +=      __iadd__(self, other)
    *=      __imul__(self, other)
    /=      __idiv__(self, other)
    //=     __ifloordiv__(self, other)
    %=      __imod__(self, other)
    **=     __ipow__(self, other)
```

- Unlike many other languages like C++, Java, etc., Python does not support function overloading. It means function names in a program, or method names within a class should be unique. If we define two functions or methods by same name, we will not get an error message, but the latest version would prevail.

Everything is an Object

- In python every entity is an object. This includes int, float, bool, complex, string, list, tuple, set, dictionary, function, class, method and module.
- When we say **x = 20**, a nameless object of type **int** is created containing a value 20 and address (location in memory) of the object is stored in **x**. **x** is called a reference to the **int** object.
- The same object can have multiple references.

```
i = 20
j = i         # another reference for same int object referred to by i
k = i         # yet another reference for same object
k = 30
print (k)     # will print 30, as k now points to a new int object
print (i, j)  # will print 20 20 as i, j continue to refer to old object
```

- In the following code snippet **x** and **y** are referring to same object. Changing one does not change the other. The same behavior is shown for **float, complex, bool** and **str** types.

```
x = 20
y = 20        # x and y point to same object
x = 30        # x now points to a new object
```

- In the following code snippet **x** and **y** refer to different objects. Same behavior is shown for list, tuple, set, dictionary, etc.

```
x = Sample(10, 20)
y = Sample(10, 20)
```

- Some objects are mutable, some are not. Also, all objects have some attributes and methods.

- The **type( )** function returns type of the object, whereas **id( )** function returns location of the object in memory.

```
import math
class Message :
    def display(self, msg):
        print(msg)

def fun( ) :
    print('Everything is an object')

i = 45
a = 3.14
c = 3 + 2j
city = 'Nagpur'
lst = [10, 20, 30]
tup = (10, 20, 30, 40)
s = {'a', 'e', 'i', 'o', 'u'}
d = {'Ajay' : 30, 'Vijay' : 35, 'Sujay' : 36}

print(type(i), id(i))
print(type(a), id(a))
print(type(c), id(c))
print(type(city), id(city))
print(type(lst), id(lst))
print(type(tup), id(tup))
print(type(s), id(s))
print(type(d), id(d))
print(type(fun), id(fun))
print(type(Message), id(Message))
print(type(math), id(math))
```

On execution of this program, we get the following output:

```
<class 'int'> 495245808
<class 'float'> 25154336
<class 'complex'> 25083752
<class 'str'> 25343392
<class 'list'> 25360544
<class 'tuple'> 25317808
<class 'set'> 20645208
<class 'dict'> 4969744
```

```
<class 'function'> 3224536
<class 'type'> 25347040
<class 'module'> 25352448
```

Imitating a Structure

- In C if we wish to keep dissimilar but related data together, we create a structure to do so.
- In Python too, we can do this by creating a class that is merely a collection of attributes (and not methods).
- Moreover, unlike C++ and Java, Python permits us to add/delete/ modify these attributes to a class/object dynamically.
- In the following program we have added 4 attributes, modified two attributes and deleted one attribute, all on the fly, i.e., after creation of **Bird** object.

```
class Bird :
    pass

b = Bird( )

# create attributes dynamically
b.name = 'Sparrow'
b.weight = 500
b.color = 'light brown'
b.animaltype = 'Vertebrate'

# modify attributes dynamically
b.weight = 450
b.color = 'brown'

# delete attributes dynamically
del b.animaltype
```

Type Conversion

- There are three types of conversions that we may wish to perform. These are:

  (a) Conversion between different built-in types
  (b) Conversion between different built-in types and container types
  (c) Conversion between built-in and user-defined types

- We are already aware of the first two types of conversions, some examples of which are given below:

```
a = float(25)                # built-in to built-in conversion
b = tuple([10, 20, 30])      # container to container conversion
c = list('Hello')            # built-in to container conversion
d = str([10, 20, 30])        # container to built-in conversion
```

- Conversion between built-in and user-defined types:

  The following program illustrates how a user-defined **String** type can be converted to built-in type **int**. **__int__( )** has been overloaded to carry out conversion from **str** to **int**.

```
class String :
    def __init__(self, s = '') :
        self.__str = s

    def display(self) :
        print(self.__str)

    def __int__(self) :
        return int( self.__str )

s1 = String(123)      # conversion from int to String
s1.display( )
i = int(s1)           # conversion from string to int
print(i)
```

P</> Programs

Problem 19.1

Write a Python program that displays the attributes of integer, float and function objects. Also show how these attributes can be used.

Program

```
def fun( ) :
    print('Everything is an object')

print(dir(55))
print(dir(-5.67))
```

```
print(dir(fun))
print((5).__add__(6))
print((-5.67).__abs__( ))
d = globals( )
d['fun'].__call__( )        # calls fun( )
```

Output

```
['__abs__', '__add__', '__and__', '__bool__', '__ceil__', ...]
['__abs__', '__add__', '__bool__', '__class__', '__delattr__', ...]
['__annotations__', '__call__', '__class__', '__closure__', ... ]
11
5.67
Everything is an object
```

Tips

- Output shows an incomplete list of attributes of **int**, **float** and **function** objects.
- From this list we have used the attributes **__add__( )** to add two integers, **__abs__( )** to get absolute value of float and **__call__( )** to call the function **fun( )**.
- **globals( )** return a dictionary representing the current global symbol table. From this dictionary we have picked the object representing the **fun** function and used it to call **__call__( )**. This results into call to **fun( )**.

Problem 19.2

Create a class **Date** that has a list containing day, month and year attributes. Define an overloaded == operator to compare two **Date** objects.

Program

```
class Date :
    def __init__(self, d, m, y) :
        self.__day, self.__mth, self.__yr = d, m, y

    def __eq__(self, other) :
```

```
        if self.__day == other.__day and self.__mth == other.__mth and
            self.__yr == other.__yr :
            return True
        else :
            return False

d1 = Date(17, 11, 98)
d2 = Date(17, 11, 98)
d3 = Date(19, 10, 92)
print(id(d1))
print(id(d2))
print(d1 == d3)
```

Output

```
44586224
44586256
False
```

Tips

- ids of the two objects referred to by **d1** and **d2** are different. This means that they refer to two different objects.
- To overload the == operator in the **Date** class, we need to define the function **__eq__( )**.

Problem 19.3

Create a class **Weather** that has a list containing weather parameters. Define an overloaded **in** operator that checks whether an item is present in the list.

Program

```
class Weather :
    def __init__(self) :
        self.__params = [ 'Temp', 'Rel Hum', 'Cloud Cover', 'Wind Vel']
    def __contains__(self, p) :
        return True if p in self.__params else False

w = Weather( )
```

```
if 'Rel Hum' in w :
    print('Valid weather parameter')
else :
    print('Invalid weather parameter')
```

Output

```
Valid weather parameter
```

Tips

- To overload the **in** operator we need to define the function **__contains__( )**.

Exercises

[A] State whether the following statements are True or False:

(a) A global function can call a class method as well as an instance method.

(b) In Python a function, class, method and module are treated as objects.

(c) Given an object, it is possible to determine its type and address.

(d) It is possible to delete attributes of an object during execution of the program.

(e) Arithmetic operators, Comparison operators and Compound assignment operators can be overloaded in Python.

(f) The + operator has been overloaded in the classes **str**, **list** and **int**.

[B] Answer the following questions:

(a) Which functions should be defined to overload the +, -, / and // operators?

(b) How many objects are created by **lst = [10, 10, 10, 30]**?

(c) How will you define a structure **Employee** containing the attributes Name, Age, Salary, Address, Hobbies dynamically?

(d) To overload the + operator, which method should be defined in the corresponding class?

(e) To overload the % operator, which method should be defined in the corresponding class?

(f) To overload the //= operator, which method should be defined in the corresponding class?

(g) If a class contains instance methods **__ge__( )** and **__ne__( )**, what do they signify?

(h) What conclusion can be drawn if the following statements work?

```
a = (10, 20) + (30, 40)
b = 'Good' + 'Morning'
c = [10, 20, 30] + [40, 50, 60]
```

(i) What will be the output of the following code snippet?

```
a = (10, 20) - (30, 40)
b = 'Good' - 'Morning'
c = [10, 20, 30] - [40, 50, 60]
```

(j) Will the following statement work? What is your conclusion if it works?

```
print ( 'Hello' * 7)
```

(k) Which out of +, - and * have been overloaded in **str** class?

(l) When would the method **__truediv__( )** defined in the Sample class shown below would get called?

```
class Sample :
    def __truediv__(self, other) :
        pass
```

(m) If **!=** operator has been overloaded in a class then the expression **c1 <= c2** would get converted into which function call?

(n) How will you define the overloaded * operator for the following code snippet?

```
c1 = Complex(1.1, 0.2)
c2 = Complex(1.1, 0.2)
c3 = c1 * c2
```

(o) Implement a **String** class containing the following functions:

- Overloaded += operator function to perform string concatenation.
- Method **toLower( )** to convert upper case letters to lower case.
- Method **toUpper( )** to convert lower case letters to upper case.

[C] Match the following pairs:

a. Can't use as identifier name	1. class name
b. basic_salary	2. class variable
c. CellPhone	3. keyword
d. count	4. local variable in a function
e. self	5. private variable
f. _fuel_used	6. strongly private identifier
g. __draw( )	7. method that Python calls
h. __iter__( )	8. meaningful only in instance func.

20 Containership and Inheritance

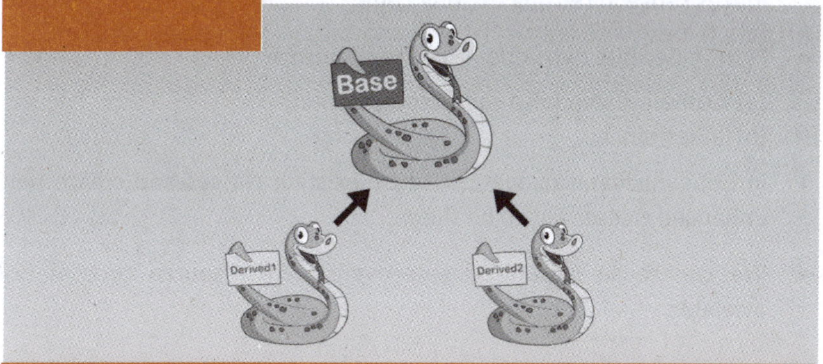

"Reuse, and you will benefit..."

Contents

- Reuse Mechanisms
- Which to use When?
- Containership
- Inheritance
- What is Accessible Where?
- *isinstance( )* and *issubclass( )*
- The *object* Class
- Features of Inheritance
- Types of Inheritance
- Diamond Problem
- Abstract Classes
- Runtime Polymorphism
- Programs
- Exercises

KanNotes

Reuse Mechanisms

- Instead of reinventing the same code that is already available, it makes sense in reusing existing code.
- Python permits two code reuse mechanisms:
  (a) Containership (also called composition)
  (b) Inheritance
- In both mechanisms we can reuse existing classes and create new enhanced classes based on them.
- We can reuse existing classes even if their source code is not available.

Which to use When?

- Containership should be used when the two classes have a 'has a' relationship. For example, a College has Professors. So, **College** class's object can contain one or more **Professor** class's object(s).
- Inheritance should be used when the two classes have a 'like a' relationship. For example, a Button is like a Window. So, **Button** class can inherit features of an existing class called **Window**.

Containership

- A container can contain one or more contained objects apart from other data, thereby reusing contained objects.
- In the following program a **Department** object is contained in an **Employee** object.

```
class Department :
    def set_department(self) :
        self.__id = input('Enter department id: ')
        self.__name = input('Enter department name: ')

    def display_department(self) :
        print('Department ID is: ', self.__id)
        print('Department Name is: ', self.__name)

class Employee :
```

```
    def set_employee(self) :
        self.__eid = input('Enter employee id: ')
        self.__ename = input('Enter employee name: ')
        self.__dobj = Department( )
        self.__dobj.set_department( )

    def display_employee(self) :
        print('Employee ID : ', self.__eid)
        print('Employee Name : ', self.__ename)
        self.__dobj.display_department( )

obj = Employee( )
obj.set_employee( )
obj.display_employee( )
```

Given below is the sample interaction with this program:

```
Enter employee id: 101
Enter employee name: Ramesh
Enter department id: ME
Enter department name: Mechanical Engineering
Employee ID : 101
Employee Name : Ramesh
Department ID is: ME
Department Name is: Mechanical Engineering
```

Inheritance

- In Inheritance a new class called **derived** class can be created to inherit features of an existing class called **base** class.
- Base class is also called **super** class or **parent** class.
- Derived class is also called **sub** class or **child** class.
- In the following program **Index** is the base class and **NewIndex** is the derived class. Note the definition of **NewIndex** class. The mention of **Index** within parentheses indicates that **NewIndex** is being inherited from **Index** class.

```
# base class
class Index :
    def __init__(self) :
        self._count = 0
```

```
    def display(self) :
        print('count = ' + str(self._count))

    def incr(self) :
        self._count += 1

# derived class
class NewIndex(Index) :
    def __init__(self) :
        super( ).__init__( )

    def decr(self) :
        self._count -= 1

i = NewIndex( )
i.incr( )
i.incr( )
i.incr( )
i.display( )
i.decr( )
i.display( )
i.decr( )
i.display( )
```

On execution of this program, we get the following output:

```
count = 3
count = 2
count = 1
```

- Construction of an object should always proceed from base towards derived.
- So when we create the derived class object, base class **__init__( )** followed by derived class **__init__( )** should get called. The syntax used for calling base class constructor is **super( ).__init__( )**.
- Derived class object contains all base class data. So **_count** is available in derived class.
- When **incr( )** is called using derived class object, first it is searched in derived class. Since it is not found here, the search is continued in the base class.

What is Accessible Where?

- Derived class members can access base class members, vice versa is not true.
- There are no keywords in Python to control access of base class members from derived class or from outside the class hierarchy.
- Instead, a convention that suggests the desired access is used while creating variable names or method names. This convention is shown below:

  var - access it from anywhere in the program
  _var - access it only from within the class or its subclass
  __var - access it only within the class

- Using **_var** in the class inheritance hierarchy or using **__var** within the class is only a convention. If we violate it, we will not get errors, but it would be a bad practice to follow.
- The following program shows the usage of the 3 types of variables.

```
class Base :
    def __init__(self) :
        self.i = 10
        self._a = 3.14
        self.__s = 'Hello'
    def display(self) :
        print (self.i, self._a, self.__s)
class Derived(Base) :
    def __init__(self) :
        super( ).__init__( )
        self.i = 100
        self._a = 31.44
        self.__s = 'Good Morning'
        self.j = 20
        self._b = 6.28
        self.__ss = 'Hi'
    def display(self) :
        super( ).display( )
        print (self.i, self._a, self.__s)
        print (self.j, self._b, self.__ss)
```

```
bobj = Base( )
bobj.display( )
print(bobj.i)
print(bobj._a)
print(bobj.__s)          # causes error

dobj = Derived( )
dobj.display( )
print(dobj.i)
print(dobj._a)
print(dobj.__s)          # causes error
```

If we comment out the statements that would cause error, we will get the following output:

```
10 3.14 Hello
10
3.14
100 31.44 Hello
100 31.44 Good Morning
20 6.28 Hi
100
31.44
```

- Why we get error while accessing **__ss** variable? Well, all __var type of variables get name mangled, i.e., in **Base** class **__s** becomes **_Base__s**. Likewise, in **Derived** class **__s** becomes **_Derived__s** and **__ss** becomes **_Derived__ss**.
- When in **Derived** class's **display( )** method we attempt to use **__s**, it is not the data member of **Base** class, but a new data member of **Derived** class that is being used.

isinstance( ) and issubclass( )

- **isinstance( )** and **issubclass( )** are built-in functions.
- **isinstance(o, c)** is used to check whether an object **o** is an instance of a class **c**.
- **issubclass(d, b)** is used to check whether class **d** has been derived from class **b**.

The *object* Class

- All classes in Python are derived from a ready-made base class called **object**. So, methods of this class are available in all classes.
- You can get a list of these methods using:

```
print(dir(object))
print(dir(Index))          # Index is derived from object
print(dir(NewIndex))       # NewIndex is derived from Index
```

Features of Inheritance

- Inheritance facilitates three things:

  (a) Inheritance of existing feature: To implement this just establish inheritance relationship.

  (b) Suppressing an existing feature: To implement this hide base class implementation by defining same method in derived class.

  (c) Extending an existing feature: To implement this call base class method from derived class by using one of the following two forms:

```
super( ).base_class_method( )
Baseclassname.base_class_method(self)
```

Types of Inheritance

- There are 3 types of inheritance:

  (a) Simple Inheritance - Ex. class **NewIndex** derived from class **Index**

  (b) Multi-level Inheritance - Ex. class **HOD** is derived from class **Professor** which is derived from class **Person**.

  (c) Multiple Inheritance - Ex. class **HardwareSales** derived from two base classes—**Product** and **Sales**.

- In multiple inheritance a class is derived from 2 or more than 2 base classes. This is shown in the following program:

```
class Product :
    def __init__(self) :
        self.__title = input ('Enter title: ')
        self.__price = input ('Enter price: ')
```

```
    def display_data(self) :
        print(self.__title, self.__price)

class Sales :
    def __init__(self) :
        self.__sales_figures = [int(x) for x in
            input('Enter sales fig: ').split( )]

    def display_data(self) :
        print(self.__sales_figures)

class HardwareItem(Product, Sales) :
    def __init__(self) :
        Product.__init__(self)
        Sales.__init__(self)
        self.__category = input ('Enter category: ')
        self.__oem = input ('Enter oem: ')

    def display_data(self) :
        Product.display_data(self)
        Sales.display_data(self)
        print(self.__category, self.__oem)

hw1 = HardwareItem( )
hw1.display_data( )
hw2 = HardwareItem( )
hw2.display_data( )
```

Given below is the sample interaction with this program:

```
Enter title: Bolt
Enter price: 12
Enter sales fig: 120 300 433
Enter category: C
Enter oem: Axis Mfg
Bolt 12
[120, 300, 433]
C Axis Mfg
Enter title: Nut
Enter price: 8
```

```
Enter sales fig: 1000 2000 1800
Enter category: C
Enter oem: Simplex Pvt Ltd
Nut 8
[1000, 2000, 1800]
C Simplex Pvt Ltd
```

- Note the syntax for calling **__init__( )** of base classes in the constructor of derived class:

```
Product.__init__(self)
Sales.__init__(self)
```

  Here we cannot use here the syntax **super.__init__( )**.

- Also note how the input for sales figures has been received using list comprehension.

Diamond Problem

- Suppose two classes **Derived1** and **Derived2** are derived from a base class called **Base** using simple inheritance. Also, a new class **Der** is derived from **Derived1** and **Derived2** using multiple inheritance. This is known as diamond relationship.

- If we now construct an object of **Der** it will have one copy of members from the path **Base -> Derived1** and another copy from the path **Base --> Derived2**. This will result in ambiguity.

- To eliminate the ambiguity, Python linearizes the search order in such a way that the left to right order while creating **Der** is honored. In our case it is **Derived1, Derived2**. So, we would get a copy of members from the path **Base --> Derived1**. The following program shows this implementation:

```
class Base :
    def display(self) :
        print('In Base')

class Derived1(Base) :
    def display(self) :
        print('In Derived1')

class Derived2(Base) :
    def display(self) :
```

```
        print('In Derived2')

class Der(Derived1, Derived2) :
    def display(self) :
        super( ).display( )
        Derived1.display(self)
        Derived2.display(self)
        print(Der.__mro__)

d1 = Der( )
d1.display( )
```

On executing the program, we get the following output:

```
In Derived1
In Derived1
In Derived2
(<class '__main__.Der'>, <class '__main__.Derived1'>, <class
'__main__.Derived2'>, <class '__main__.Base'>, <class 'object'>)
```

- **__mro__** gives the method resolution order.

Abstract Classes

- Suppose we have a **Shape** class and from it we have derived **Circle** and **Rectangle** classes. Each contains a method called **draw( )**. However, drawing a shape doesn't make too much sense, hence we do not want **draw( )** of **Shape** to ever get called. This can happen only if we can prevent creation of objects of **Shape** class. This can be done as shown in the following program:

```
from abc import ABC, abstractmethod
class Shape(ABC) :
    @abstractmethod
    def draw(self) :
        pass

class Rectangle(Shape) :
    def draw(self) :
        print('In Rectangle.draw')

class Circle(Shape) :
    def draw(self) :
```

```
        print('In Circle.draw')

s = Shape( )  # will result in error, as Shape is abstract class
c = Circle( )
c.draw( )
```

- A class from which an object cannot be created is called an abstract class.
- **abc** is a module. It stands for abstract base classes. From **abc** we have imported class **ABC** and decorator **abstractmethod**.
- To create an abstract class, we need to derive it from class **ABC**. We also need to mark **draw( )** as an abstract method using the decorator **@abstractmethod**.
- If an abstract class contains only methods marked by the decorator **@abstractmethod**, it is often called an interface.
- Decorators are discussed in Chapter 25.

Runtime Polymorphism

- Polymorphism means one thing existing in several different forms. Runtime polymorphism involves deciding at runtime which function from base class or derived class should get called. This feature is widely used in C++.
- Parallel to Runtime Polymorphism, Java has a Dynamic Dispatch mechanism which works similarly.
- Python is dynamically typed language, where type of any variable is determined at runtime based on its usage. Hence discussion of Runtime Polymorphism or Dynamic Dispatch mechanism is not relevant in Python.

P</> *Programs*

Problem 20.1

Define a class **Shape**. Inherit two classes **Circle** and **Rectangle**. Check programmatically the inheritance relationship between the classes. Create **Shape** and **Circle** objects. Report of which classes are these objects instances of.

Program

```
class Shape :
    pass
class Rectangle(Shape) :
    pass
class Circle(Shape) :
    pass

s = Shape( )
c = Circle( )
print(isinstance(s, Shape))
print(isinstance(s, Rectangle))
print(isinstance(s, Circle))
print(issubclass(Rectangle, Shape))
print(issubclass(Circle, Shape))
```

Output

```
True
False
False
True
True
```

Problem 20.2

Write a program that uses simple inheritance between classes **Base** and **Derived**. If there is a method in **Base** class, how do you prevent it from being overridden in the **Derived** class?

Program

```
class Base :
    def __method(self):
        print('In Base.__method')

    def func(self):
        self.__method( )

class Derived(Base):
```

```
    def __method(self):
        print('In Derived.__method')

b = Base( )
b.func( )
d = Derived( )
d.func( )
```

Output

```
In Base.__method
In Base.__method
```

Tips

- To prevent method from being overridden, prepend it with __.
- When **func( )** is called using **b**, **self** contains address of **Base** class object. When it is called using **d**, **self** contains address of **Derived** class object.
- In **Base** class **__method( )** gets mangled to **_Base__method( )** and in **Derived** class it becomes **_Derived__method( )**.
- When **func( ) calls __method( )** from **Base** class, it is the **_Base__method( )** that gets called. In effect, **__method( )** cannot be overridden. This is true, even when **self** contains address of the **Derived** class object.

Problem 20.3

Write a program that defines an abstract class called **Printer** containing an abstract method **print( )**. Derive from it two classes—**LaserPrinter** and **Inkjetprinter**. Create objects of derived classes and call the **print( )** method using these objects, passing to it the name of the file to be printed. In the **print( )** method simply print the filename and the class name to which **print( )** belongs.

Program

```
from abc import ABC, abstractmethod
class Printer(ABC) :
```

```
    def __init__(self, n) :
        self.__name = n

    @abstractmethod
    def print(self, docName) :
        pass

class LaserPrinter(Printer) :
    def __init__(self, n) :
        super( ).__init__(n)

    def print(self, docName) :
        print('>> LaserPrinter.print')
        print('Trying to print :', docName)

class InkjetPrinter(Printer) :
    def __init__(self, n) :
        super( ).__init__(n)

    def print(self, docName) :
        print('>> InkjetPrinter.print')
        print('Trying to print :', docName)

p = LaserPrinter('LaserJet 1100')
p.print('hello1.pdf')
p = InkjetPrinter('IBM 2140')
p.print('hello2.doc')
```

Output

```
>> LaserPrinter.print
Trying to print :
hello1.pdf
>> InkjetPrinter.print
Trying to print :
hello2.doc
```

Problem 20.4

Define an abstract class called **Character** containing an abstract method **patriotism( )**. Define a class **Actor** containing a method **style( )**. Define a class **Person** derived from **Character** and **Actor**. Implement the method **patriotism( )** in it, and override the method **style( )** in it. Also define a new method **do_acting( )** in it. Create an object of **Person** class and call the three methods in it.

Program

```
from abc import ABC, abstractmethod
class Character(ABC) :
    @abstractmethod
    def patriotism(self) :
        pass

class Actor :
    def style(self) :
        print('>> Actor.Style: ')

class Person(Actor, Character) :
    def do_acting(self) :
        print('>> Person.doActing')

    def style(self) :
        print('>> Person.style')

    def patriotism(self) :
        print('>> Person.patriotism')

p = Person( )
p.patriotism( )
p.style( )
p.do_acting( )
```

Output

```
>> Person.patriotism
>> Person.style
>> Person.doActing
```

Exercises

[A] State whether the following statements are True or False:

(a) Inheritance is the ability of a class to inherit properties and behavior from a parent class by extending it.

(b) Containership is the ability of a class to contain objects of different classes as member data.

(c) We can derive a class from a base class even if the base class's source code is not available.

(d) Multiple inheritance is different from multiple levels of inheritance.

(e) An object of a derived class cannot access members of base class if the member names begin with __.

(f) Creating a derived class from a base class requires fundamental changes to the base class.

(g) If a base class contains a member function **func( )**, and a derived class does not contain a function with this name, an object of the derived class cannot access **func( )**.

(h) If no constructors are specified for a derived class, objects of the derived class will use the constructors in the base class.

(i) If a base class and a derived class each include a member function with the same name, the member function of the derived class will be called by an object of the derived class.

(j) A class **D** can be derived from a class **C**, which is derived from a class **B**, which is derived from a class **A**.

(k) It is illegal to make objects of one class members of another class.

[B] Answer the following questions:

(a) Which module should be imported to create abstract class?

(b) For a class to be abstract from which class should we inherit it?

(c) Suppose there is a base class **B** and a derived class **D** derived from **B**. **B** has two **public** member functions **b1( )** and **b2( )**, whereas **D** has two member functions **d1( )** and **d2( )**. Write these classes for the following different situations:

- **b1( )** should be accessible from main module, **b2( )** should not be.
- Neither **b1( )**, nor **b2( )** should be accessible from main module.
- Both **b1( )** and **b2( )** should be accessible from the main module.

(d) If a class **D** is derived from two base classes **B1** and **B2**, then write these classes each containing a constructor. Ensure that while building an object of type **D**, the constructor of **B2** should get called. Also provide a destructor in each class. In what order would these destructors get called?

(e) Create an abstract class called **Vehicle** containing methods **speed( )**, **maintenance( )** and **value( )** in it. Derive classes **FourWheeler**, **TwoWheeler** and **Airborne** from **Vehicle** class. Check whether you can prevent creation of objects of **Vehicle** class. Call the methods using objects of other classes.

(f) Assume a class **D** that is derived from class **B**. Which of the following can an object of class **D** access?

- members of **D**
- members of **B**

[C] Match the following pairs:

a. __mro__( )	1. 'has a' relationship
b. Inheritance	2. Object creation not allowed
c. __var	3. Super class
d. Abstract class	4. Root class
e. Parent class	5. 'is a' relationship
f. object	6. Name mangling
g. Child class	7. Decides resolution order
h. Containership	8. Sub class

[D] Attempt the following questions:

(a) From which class any abstract class is derived?

(b) At a time, a class can be derived from how many abstract classes?

(c) How do we create an abstract class in Python?

(d) What can an abstract class contain—instance method, class method, abstract method?

(e) How many objects can be created from an abstract class?

(f) What will happen on execution of this code snippet?

```
from abc import ABC, abstractmethod
class Sample(ABC) :
@abstractmethod
def display(self) :
    pass
s = Sample( )
```

(g) Suppose there is a class called **Vehicle**. What should be done to ensure that an object should not be created from **Vehicle** class?

(h) How will you mark an instance method in an abstract class as abstract?

(i) There is something wrong in the following code snippet. How will you rectify it?

```
class Shape(ABC) :
@abstractmethod
def draw(self) :
    pass

class Circle(Shape) :
@abstractmethod
def draw(self) :
    print('In draw')
```

21 Iterators and Generators

"The modern way..."

Contents

KanNotes

Iterables and Iterators

- An object is called iterable if it can return its members one at a time. Basic types like string and containers like list and tuple are iterables.
- Iterator is an object which is used to iterate over an iterable. An iterable provides an iterator object.
- Iterators are implemented in for loops, comprehensions, generators etc.

zip( ) Function

- **zip( )** function typically receives multiple iterable objects and returns an iterator of tuples based on them. This iterator can be used in a **for** loop as shown below.

```
words = ['A', 'coddle', 'called', 'Molly']
numbers = [10, 20, 30, 40]

for ele in zip(words, numbers) :
    print(ele[0], ele[1])

for ele in zip(words, numbers) :
    print(*ele)

for w, n in zip(words, numbers) :
    print(w, n)
```

All three **for** loops will output:

```
A 10
coddle 20
called 30
Molly 40
```

- If two iterables are passed to **zip( )**, one containing 4 and other containing 6 elements, the returned iterator has 4 (shorter iterable) tuples.
- A list/tuple/set can be generated from the iterator of tuples returned by **zip( )**.

```
words = ['A', 'coddle', 'called', 'Molly']
numbers = [10, 20, 30, 40]
it = zip(words, numbers)
lst = list(it)
print(lst)  # prints [('A', 10), ('coddle', 20), ('called', 30), ('Molly', 40)]

it = zip(words, numbers)    # necessary to zip again
tpl = tuple(it)
print(tpl)  # prints (('A', 10), ('coddle', 20), ('called', 30), ('Molly', 40))

it = zip(words, numbers)    # necessary to zip again
s = set(it)
print(s)    # prints {('coddle', 20), ('Molly', 40), ('A', 10), ('called', 30)}
```

- The values can be unzipped from the list into tuples using *.

```
words = ['A', 'coddle', 'called', 'Molly']
numbers = [10, 20, 30, 40]
it = zip(words, numbers)
lst = list(it)
w, n = zip(*lst)
print(w)            # prints ('A', 'coddle', 'called', 'Molly')
print(n)            # print (10, 20, 30, 40)
```

Iterators

- We know that a string and container objects like list, tuple, set, dictionary etc. can be iterated through using a **for** loop as in

```
for ch in 'Good Afternoon' :
    print(ch)

for num in [10, 20, 30, 40, 50] :
    print(num)
```

Both these **for** loops call **__iter__( )** method of **str/list**. This method returns an iterator object. The iterator object has a method **__next__( )** which returns the next item in the **str/list** container.

When all items have been iterated, next call to **__next__( )** raises a **StopIteration** exception which tells the **for** loop to terminate. Exceptions have been discussed in Chapter 22.

- We too can call **__iter__( )** and **__next__( )** and get the same results.

```
lst = [10, 20, 30, 40]
i = lst.__iter__( )
print(i.__next__( ))
print(i.__next__( ))
print(i.__next__( ))
```

- Instead of calling **__iter__( )** and **__next__( )**, we can call the more convenient built-in functions **iter( )** and **next( )**. These functions in turn call **__iter__( )** and **__next__( )** respectively.

  ```
  lst = [10, 20, 30, 40]
  i = iter(lst)
  print(next(i))
  print(next(i))
  print(next(i))
  ```

  Note than once we have iterated a container, if we wish to iterate it again, we need to obtain an iterator object afresh.

- An iterable is an object capable of returning its members one at a time. Programmatically, it is an object that has implemented **__iter__( )** in it.

- An iterator is an object that has implemented both **__iter__( )** and **__next__( )** in it.

- As a proof that an iterable contains **__iter__( )**, whereas an iterator contains both **__iter__( )** and **__next__( )**, we can check it using the **hasattr( )** built-in function.

```
s = 'Hello'
lst = ['Focussed', 'bursts', 'of', 'activity']
print(hasattr(s, '__iter__'))
print(hasattr(s, '__next__'))
print(hasattr(lst, '__iter__'))
print(hasattr(lst, '__next__'))
i = iter(s)
j = iter(lst)
print(hasattr(i, '__iter__'))
print(hasattr(i, '__next__'))
print(hasattr(j, '__iter__'))
print(hasattr(j, '__next__'))
```

On execution of this program, we get the following output:

```
True
False
True
False
True
True
True
True
```

User-defined Iterators

- Suppose we wish our class to behave like an iterator. To do this we need to define **__iter__( )** and **__next__( )** in it.
- Our iterator class **AvgAdj** should maintain a list. When it is iterated upon it should return average of two adjacent numbers in the list.

```
class AvgAdj :
    def __init__(self, data) :
        self.__data = data
        self.__len = len(data)
        self.__first = 0
        self.__sec = 1

    def __iter__(self) :
        return self

    def __next__(self) :
        if self.__sec == self.__len :
            raise StopIteration        # raises exception (runtime error)
        self.__avg = (self.__data[self.__first] +
                        self.__data[self.__sec]) / 2
        self.__first += 1
        self.__sec += 1
        return self.__avg

lst = [10, 20, 30, 40, 50, 60, 70]
coll = AvgAdj(lst)
for val in coll :
    print(val)
```

On execution of this program, we get the following output:

```
15.0
25.0
35.0
45.0
55.0
65.0
```

- **__iter__( )** is supposed to return an object which has implemented **__next__( )** in it. Since we have defined **__next__( )** in **AvgAdj** class, we have returned **self** from **__iter__( )**.
- The length of **lst** is 7, whereas elements in it are indexed from 0 to 6.
- When **self._sec** becomes 7 it means that we have reached the end of list and further iteration is not possible. In this situation we have raised an exception **StopIteration**.

Generators

- Generators are very efficient functions that create iterators. They use **yield** statement instead of **return** whenever they wish to return data from the function.
- Specialty of a generator is that it remembers the state of the function and the last statement it had executed when **yield** was executed.
- So each time **next( )** is called, it resumes where it had left off last time.
- Generators can be used in place of class-based iterator that we saw in the last section.
- Generators are very compact because the **__iter__( )**, **__next__( )** and **StopIteration** code is created automatically for them.
- Given below is an example of a generator that returns the average of next two adjacent numbers in the list every time.

```
def AvgAdj(data) :
    for i in range(0, len(data) - 1) :
        yield (data[i] + data[i + 1]) / 2

lst = [10, 20, 30, 40, 50, 60, 70]
for i in AvgAdj(lst) :
```

```
print(i)
```

On execution of this program, we get the following output:

```
15.0
25.0
35.0
45.0
55.0
65.0
```

Which to use When?

- Suppose from a list of 100 integers we are to return an entity which contains elements which are prime numbers. In this case we will return an 'iterable' which contains a list of prime numbers.

- Suppose we wish to add all prime numbers below three million. In this case, first creating a list of all prime numbers and then adding them will consume a lot of memory. So, we should write an iterator class or a generator function which generates the next prime number on the fly and adds it to the running sum.

Generator Expressions

- Like list/set/dictionary comprehensions, to make the code more compact as well as succinct, we can write compact generator expressions.

- A generator expression creates a generator on the fly without being required to use the **yield** statement.

- Some sample generator expressions are given below.

```
# generate 20 random numbers in the range 10 to 100 and obtain
# maximum out of them
print(max(random.randint(10, 100) for n in range(20)))
# print sum of cubes of all numbers less than 20
print(sum(n * n * n for n in range(20)))
```

- List comprehensions are enclosed within **[ ]**, set/dictionary comprehensions are enclosed within **{ }**, whereas generator expressions are enclosed within **( )**.

- Since a list comprehension returns a list, it consumes more memory than a generator expression. Generator expression takes less memory since it generates the next element on demand, rather than generating all elements upfront.

```
import sys
lst = [i * i for i in range(15)]
gen = (i * i for i in range(15))
print(lst)
print(gen)
print(sys.getsizeof(lst))
print(sys.getsizeof(gen))
```

On execution of this program, we get the following output:

```
[0, 1, 4, 9, 16, 25, 36, 49, 64, 81, 100, 121, 144, 169, 196]
<generator object <genexpr> at 0x003BD570>
100
48
```

- Though useful, generator expressions do not have the same power of a full-fledged generator function.

P</> Programs

Problem 21.1

Write a program that proves that a list is an iterable and not an iterator.

Program

```
lst = [10, 20, 30, 40, 50]
print(dir(lst))
i = iter(lst)
print(dir(i))
```

Output

```
['__add__', '__class__', '__contains__', '__delattr__', '__delitem__',
'__dir__', '__doc__', '__eq__', '__format__', '__ge__', '__getattribute__',
```

```
'__getitem__', '__gt__', '__hash__', '__iadd__', '__imul__', '__init__',
'__init_subclass__', '__iter__', '__le__', '__len__', '__lt__', '__mul__',
'__ne__', '__new__', '__reduce__', '__reduce_ex__', '__repr__',
'__reversed__', '__rmul__', '__setattr__', '__setitem__', '__sizeof__',
'index', 'insert', 'pop', 'remove', 'reverse', 'sort']
['__class__', '__delattr__', '__dir__', '__doc__', '__eq__', '__format__',
'__ge__', '__getattribute__', '__gt__', '__hash__', '__init__',
'__init_subclass__', '__iter__', '__le__', '__length_hint__', '__lt__',
'__ne__', '__new__', '__next__', '__reduce__', '__reduce_ex__',
'__repr__', '__setattr__', '__setstate__', '__sizeof__', '__str__',
'__subclasshook__']
```

Tips

- **lst** is an iterable since **dir(lst)** shows **__iter__** but no **__next__**.
- **iter(lst)** returns an iterator object, which is collected in **i**.
- **dir(i)** shows **__iter__** as well as **__next__**. This shows that it is an iterator object.

Problem 21.2

Write a program that generates prime numbers below 3 million. Print sum of these prime numbers.

Program

```
def generate_primes( ) :
    num = 1
    while True :
        if isprime(num) :
            yield num
        num += 1

def isprime( n ) :
    if n > 1 :
        if n == 2 :
            return True
        if n % 2 == 0 :
            return False
        for i in range(2, n // 2) :
```

```
            if n % i == 0 :
                return False
        else :
            return True
    else :
        return False

total = 0
for next_prime in generate_primes( ) :
    if next_prime < 300000 :
        total += next_prime
    else :
        print(total)
        exit( )
```

Output

```
3709507114
```

Tips

- **exit( )** terminates the execution of the program.

Problem 21.3

Write a program that uses dictionary comprehension to print sin, cos and tan tables for angles ranging from 0 to 360 in steps of 15 degrees. Write generator expressions to find the maximum value of sine and cos.

Program

```
import math
pi = 3.14
sine_table = {ang : math.sin(ang * pi / 180) for ang in range(0, 360, 90)}
cos_table = {ang : math.cos(ang * pi / 180) for ang in range(0, 360, 90)}
tan_table = {ang : math.tan(ang * pi / 180) for ang in range(0, 360, 90)}
print(sine_table)
print(cos_table)
print(tan_table)
maxsin = max((math.sin(ang * pi / 180) for ang in range(0, 360, 90)))
maxcos = max((math.cos(ang * pi / 180) for ang in range(0, 360, 90)))
print(maxsin)
```

```
print(maxcos)
```

Output

```
{0: 0.0, 90: 0.9999996829318346, 180: 0.0015926529164868282, 270: -
0.999997146387718}
{0: 1.0, 90: 0.0007963267107332633, 180: -0.9999987317275395, 270: -
0.0023889781122815386}
{0: 0.0, 90: 1255.7655915007897, 180: -0.0015926549364O7223, 270:
418.58782265388515}
0.9999996829318346
1.0
```

Problem 21.4

Create 3 lists—a list of names, a list of ages and a list of salaries. Generate and print a list of tuples containing name, age and salary from the 3 lists. From this list generate 3 tuples—one containing all names, another containing all ages and third containing all salaries.

Program

```
names = ['Amol', 'Anil', 'Akash']
ages = [25, 23, 27]
salaries= [34555.50, 40000.00, 450000.00]
# create iterator of tuples
it = zip(names, ages, salaries)
# build list by iterating the iterator object
lst = list(it)
print(lst)
# unzip the list into tuples
n, a, s = zip(*lst)
print(n)
print(a)
print(s)
```

Output

```
[('Amol', 25, 34555.5), ('Anil', 23, 40000.0), ('Akash', 27, 450000.0)]
('Amol', 'Anil', 'Akash')
```

```
(25, 23, 27)
(34555.5, 40000.0, 450000.0)
```

Problem 21.5

Write a program to obtain transpose of a 3 x 4 matrix.

Program

```
mat = [[1, 2, 3, 4], [5, 6, 7, 8],  [9, 10, 11, 12]]
ti = zip(*mat)
lst = [[ ] for i in range(4)]
i = 0
for t in ti :
    lst[i] = list(t)
    i += 1
print(lst)
```

Output

```
[[1, 5, 9], [2, 6, 10], [3, 7, 11], [4, 8, 12]]
```

Tips

- **mat** contains a list of lists. These can be accessed using either **mat[0]**, **mat[1]** and **mat[2]** or simply ***mat**.
- **zip(*mat)** receives three lists and returns an iterator of tuples, each tuple containing 3 elements.
- **lst** is initialized as a list of 4 empty lists.
- The iterator returned by **zip( )** is iterated upon and a list is generated using the **list( )** function. Each generated list is inserted in the list of lists at an appropriate index.

Problem 21.6

Write a program to multiply two matrices x(2 x 3) and y(2, 2) using list comprehension.

Program

```
x = [ [1, 2, 3], 4, 5, 6] ]
y = [ [11, 12], [21, 22], [31, 32] ]

l1 = [xrow for xrow in x]
print(l1)
l2 = [(xrow, ycol) for ycol in zip(*y) for xrow in x]
print(l2)
l3 = [[sum(a * b for a, b in zip(xrow,ycol)) for ycol in zip(*y)]for xrow in x]
print(l3)
```

Output

```
[[1, 2, 3], [4, 5, 6]]
[([1, 2, 3], (11, 21, 31)), ([4, 5, 6], (11, 21, 31)), ([1, 2, 3], (12, 22, 32)),
    ([4, 5, 6], (12, 22, 32))]
[[146, 152], [335, 350]]
```

Tips

- To make it easy for you to understand the list comprehension, I have built it in 3 parts. Follow them by checking their output.

Problem 21.7

Suppose we have a list of 5 integers and a tuple of 5 floats. Can we zip them and obtain an iterator? If yes, how?

Program

```
integers = [10, 20, 30, 40, 50]
floats = (1.1, 2.2, 3.3, 4.4, 5.5)
ti = zip(integers, floats)
lst = list(ti)
for i, f in lst :
    print(i, f)
```

Output

```
10 1.1
```

```
20 2.2
30 3.3
40 4.4
50 5.5
```

Tips

- Any type of iterables can be passed to a **zip( )** function.

Problem 21.8

Create two lists' **students** and **marks**. Create a dictionary from these two lists using dictionary comprehension. Use names as keys and marks as values.

Program

```
# lists of keys and values
lstnames = ['Sunil', 'Sachin', 'Rahul', 'Kapil', 'Rohit']
lstmarks = [54, 65, 45, 67, 78]

# dictionary comprehension
d = {k:v for (k, v) in zip(lstnames, lstmarks)}
print(d)
```

Output

```
{'Sunil': 54, 'Sachin': 65, 'Rahul': 45, 'Kapil': 67, 'Rohit': 78}
```

Problem 21.9

Create a dictionary containing names of students and marks obtained by them in three subjects. Write a program to print these names in tabular form with sorted names as columns and marks in three subjects listed below each student name as shown below.

```
Rahul  Rakesh  Sameer
67     59      58
76     70      86
39     81      78
```

Program

```
d = {'Rahul':[67,76,39],'Sameer':[58,86,78],'Rakesh':[59,70,81]}

lst = [(k, *v) for k, v in d.items( )]
print(lst)

lst = [(k, *v) for k, v in sorted(d.items( ))]
print(lst)

for row in zip(*lst) :
    print(row)

for row in zip(*lst) :
    print(*row, sep = '\t')

for row in zip(*((k, *v) for k, v in sorted(d.items( )))):
    print(*row, sep = '\t')
```

Output

```
[('Rahul', 67, 76, 39), ('Sameer', 58, 86, 78), ('Rakesh', 59, 70, 81)]
[('Rahul', 67, 76, 39), ('Rakesh', 59, 70, 81), ('Sameer', 58, 86, 78)]
('Rahul', 'Rakesh', 'Sameer')
(67, 59, 58)
(76, 70, 86)
(39, 81, 78)
Rahul   Rakesh  Sameer
67      59      58
76      70      86
39      81      78
Rahul   Rakesh  Sameer
67      59      58
76      70      86
39      81      78
```

Tips

- Try to understand this program step-by-step:

  lst = [(k, *v) for k, v in d.items( )]

  *v will unpack the marks in v. So, a tuple like ('Rahul', 67, 76, 39) will be created. All such tuples will be collected in the list to create:

[('Rahul', 67, 76, 39), ('Sameer', 58, 86, 78), ('Rakesh', 59, 70, 81)]

- To create a list of tuples sorted by name we have used the **sorted( )** function:

  ```
  lst = [(k, *v) for k, v in sorted(d.items( ))]
  ```

  This will create the list:

  [('Rahul', 67, 76, 39), ('Rakesh', 59, 70, 81), ('Sameer', 58, 86, 78)]

- The sorted list is then unpacked and submitted to the **zip( )** function

  ```
  for row in zip(*lst) :
      print(row)
  ```

  This will print the tuples

  ```
  ('Rahul', 'Rakesh', 'Sameer')
  (67, 59, 58)
  (76, 70, 86)
  (39, 81, 78)
  ```

- We have then unpacked these tuples before printing and added separator '\t' to properly align the values being printed.

  ```
  for row in zip(*lst) :
      print(*row, sep = '\t')
  ```

- Lastly, we have combined all these activities into one loop:

  ```
  for row in zip(*((k, *v) for k, v in sorted(d.items( )))):
      print(*row, sep = '\t')
  ```

Problem 21.10

Write a program that defines a function **pascal_triangle( )** that displays a Pascal Triangle of level received as parameter to the function. A Pascal's Triangle of level 5 is shown below.

```
            1
        1       1
    1       2       1
1       3       3       1
1       4       6       4       1
```

Program

```
def pascal_triangle(n) :
    row = [1]
    z = [0]
    for x in range(n) :
        print(row)
        row = [l + r for l, r in zip(row + z, z + row)]
pascal_triangle(5)
```

Output

```
[1]
[1, 1]
[1, 2, 1]
[1, 3, 3, 1]
[1, 4, 6, 4, 1]
```

Tips

- For **n = 5**, **x** will vary from 0 to 4.
- **row + z** merges two lists.
- For x = 1, row = [1], z = [0], so,

  zip([1, 0], [0, 1]) gives tuples (1, 0), (0, 1)
  l + r gives row = [1, 1]
- For x = 2, row = [1, 1], z = [0], so,

  zip([1, 1, 0], [0, 1, 1]) gives tuples (1, 0), (1, 1), (0, 1)
  l + r gives [1, 2, 1]
- For x = 3, row = [1, 2, 1], z = [0], so,

  zip([1, 2, 1, 0], [0, 1, 2, 1]) gives tuples (1, 0), (2, 1), (1, 2), (0, 1)
  l + r gives [1, 3, 3, 1]
- For x = 4, row = [1, 3, 3, 1], z = [0], so,

  zip([1, 3, 3, 1, 0], [0, 1, 3, 3, 1]) gives (1, 0), (3, 1), (3, 3), (1, 3), (0, 1)
  l + r gives [1, 4, 6, 4, 1]

Problem 21.11

Write a program that defines a class called **Progression** and inherits three classes from it—**AP**, **GP** and **FP**, standing for Arithmetic Progression, Geometric Progression and Fibonacci Progression respectively. **Progression** class should act as a user-defined iterator. By default, it should generate integers starting with 0 and advancing in steps of 1. **AP**, **GP** and **FP** should make use of the iteration facility of **Progression** class. They should appropriately adjust themselves to generate numbers in arithmetic progression, geometric progression or Fibonacci progression.

Program

```
class Progression :
    def __init__(self, start = 0) :
        self._cur = start

    def __iter__(self):
        return self

    def advance(self):
        self._cur += 1

    def __next__(self) :
        if self._cur is None :
            raise StopIteration
        else :
            data = self._cur
            self.advance( )
            return data

    def display(self, n) :
        print(' '.join(str(next(self)) for i in range(n)))

class AP(Progression) :
    def __init__(self, start = 0, step = 1) :
        super( ).__init__(start)
        self.__step = step

    def advance(self) :
        self._cur += self.__step

class GP(Progression) :
    def __init__(self, start = 1, step = 2 ) :
```

```
        super( ).__init__(start)
        self.__step = step

    def advance(self) :
        self._cur *= self.__step

class FP(Progression) :
    def __init__ (self, first = 0, second = 1) :
        super( ).__init__(first)
        self.__prev = second - first

    def advance(self) :
        self.__prev, self._cur = self._cur, self.__prev + self._cur

print('Default progression:')
p = Progression( )
p.display(10)
print('AP with step 5:')
a = AP(5)
a.display(10)
print('AP with start 2 and step 4:')
a = AP(2, 4)
a.display(10)
print('GP with default multiple:')
g = GP( )
g.display(10)
print('GP with start 1 and multiple 3:')
g = GP(1, 3)
g.display(10)
print('FP with default start values:')
f = FP( )
f.display(10)
print('FP with start values 4 and 6:')
f = FP(4, 6)
f.display(10)
```

Output

```
Default progression:
0 1 2 3 4 5 6 7 8 9
AP with step 5:
5 6 7 8 9 10 11 12 13 14
AP with start 2 and step 4:
```

```
2 6 10 14 18 22 26 30 34 38
GP with default multiple:
1 2 4 8 16 32 64 128 256 512
GP with start 1 and multiple 3:
1 3 9 27 81 243 729 2187 6561 19683
FP with default start values:
0 1 1 2 3 5 8 13 21 34
FP with start values 4 and 6:
4 6 10 16 26 42 68 110 178 288
```

Tips

- Since **Progression** is an iterator it has to implement **__iter__( )** and **__next__( )** methods.
- **__next__( )** calls **advance( )** method to suitably adjust the value of **self.cur** (and **self.prev** in case of **FP**).
- Each derived class has an **advance( )** method. Depending on which object's address is present in **self**, that object's **advance( )** method gets called.
- The generation of next data value happens one value at a time, when **display( )** method's **for** loop goes into action.
- There are two ways to create an object and call **display( )**. These are:

  a = AP(5)
  a.display(10)

  or

  AP(5).display(10)

Exercises

[A] Answer the following questions:

(a) Write a program to create a list of 5 odd integers. Replace the third element with a list of 4 even integers. Flatten, sort and print the list.

(b) Write a program to flatten the following list:

mat1 = [[1, 2, 3, 4], [5, 6, 7, 8], [9, 10, 11, 12]]

(c) Write a program to generate a list of numbers in the range 2 to 50 that are divisible by 2 and 4.

(d) Suppose there are two lists, each holding 5 strings. Write a program to generate a list that consists of strings that are concatenated by picking corresponding elements from the two lists.

(e) Suppose a list contains 20 integers generated randomly. Receive a number from the keyboard and report position of all occurrences of this number in the list.

(f) Suppose there are two lists—one contains questions, and another contains lists of 4 possible answers for each question. Write a program to generate a list that contains lists of question and its 4 possible answers.

(g) Suppose a list has 20 numbers. Write a program that removes all duplicates from this list.

(h) Write a program to obtain a median value of a list of numbers, without disturbing the order of the numbers in the list.

(i) A list contains only positive and negative integers. Write a program to obtain the number of negative numbers present in the list.

(j) Write a program to convert a list of tuples

[(10, 20, 30), (150.55, 145.60, 157.65), ('A1', 'B1', 'C1')]

into another list of tuples

[(10, 150.55, 'A1'), (20, 145.60, 'B1'), (30, 157.65, 'C1')]

(k) What will be the output of the following program?

```
x = [[1, 2, 3, 4], [4, 5, 6, 7]]
y = [[1, 1], [2, 2], [3, 3], [4, 4]]
l1 = [xrow for xrow in x]
print(l1)
l2 = [(xrow, ycol) for ycol in zip(*y) for xrow in x]
print(l2)
```

(l) Write a program that uses a generator to create a set of unique words from a line input through the keyboard.

(m) Write a program that uses a generator to find out maximum marks obtained by a student and his name from tuples of multiple students.

(n) Write a program that uses a generator that generates characters from a string in reverse order.

(o) What is the difference between the following statements?

```
sum([x**2 for x in range(20)])
sum(x**2 for x in range(20))
```

(p) Suppose there are two lists, each holding 5 strings. Write a program to generate a list that consists of strings that are concatenated by picking corresponding elements from the two lists.

(q) 36 unique combinations can result from the use of two dice. Create a dictionary which stores these combinations as tuples.

22 Exception Handling

"Expect an exception and prepare for it"

Contents

KanNotes

What may go Wrong?

- While creating and executing a Python program, things may go wrong at two different stages—during compilation and during execution.
- Errors that occur during compilation are called **Syntax Errors**. Errors that occur during execution are called **Exceptions**.
- Sometimes a program may neither contain any syntax errors, nor report any runtime error. But we may still get wrong results. This means that there is something wrong with the logic of the program. Errors that are responsible for creating wrong results are called **Logical Errors** or **Semantic Errors**.
- An easy way to spot the logical errors is to use a debugger as discussed in Appendix B.

Syntax Errors

- If things go wrong during compilation:

  Means - Something in the program is not as per language grammar
  Reported by - Interpreter/Compiler
  Action to be taken - Rectify program
- Examples of syntax errors:

```
print 'Hello'        # ( ) is missing
d = 'Nagpur'
a = b + float(d)     # d is a string, so it cannot be converted to float
a = Math.pow(3)      # pow( ) needs two arguments
```

- Other common syntax errors are:
  - Leaving out a symbol, such as a colon, comma or brackets
  - Misspelling a keyword
  - Incorrect indentation
  - Empty if, else, while, for, function, class, method
  - Missing :
  - Incorrect number of positional arguments
- Suppose we try to compile the following piece of code:

```
basic_salary = int ( input('Enter basic salary') )
if basic_salary < 5000
    print('Does not qualify for Diwali bonus')
```

We get the following syntax error:

```
File 'c:\Users\Kanetkar\Desktop\Phone\src\phone.py', line 2
    if basic_salary < 5000
                         ^
SyntaxError: invalid syntax
```

- ^ indicates the position in the line where an error was detected. It occurred because : is missing after the condition.
- Filename and line number are also displayed to help you locate the erroneous statement easily.

Exceptions

- If things go wrong during execution (runtime):

  Means - Something unforeseen has happened
  Reported by - Python Runtime
  Action to be taken - Tackle it on the fly
- Examples of Runtime errors:

  Memory Related - Stack/Heap overflow, Exceeding bounds
  Arithmetic Related - Divide by zero
  Others - Attempt to use an unassigned reference, File not found
- Even if the program is grammatically correct, things may go wrong during execution causing exceptions.

```
a = int(input('Enter an integer: '))
b = int(input('Enter an integer: '))
c = a / b
```

If during execution of this script we give value of b as 0, then following message gets displayed:

```
Exception has occurred: ZeroDivisionError
division by zero
File    'C:\Users\Kanetkar\Desktop\Phone\src\trial.py',    line    3,    in
<module> c = a / b
```

```
# blah blah... rest of the stack trace showing how we landed here
```

- Another example of exception:

```
a, b = 10, 20
c = a / b * d
```

```
File 'c:\Users\Kanetkar\Desktop\Phone\src\phone.py', line 2, in
<module>    c = a / b * d
NameError: name 'd' is not defined
# blah blah... rest of the stack trace showing how we landed here
```

- The stack trace prints the names of the files, line numbers starting from the first file that got executed, up to the point of exception.
- The stack trace is useful for the programmer to figure out where things went wrong. However, a user is likely to get spooked looking at it, thinking something is very wrong. So, we should try and tackle the exceptions ourselves and provide a graceful exit from the program, instead of printing the stack trace.

How to deal with Exceptions?

- **try** and **except** blocks are used to deal with an exception.
- Statement(s) which you suspect may go wrong at runtime should be enclosed within a **try** block.
- If while executing statement(s) in **try** block, an exceptional condition occurs it can be tackled in two ways:
  (a) Pack exception information in an object and raise an exception.
  (b) Let Python Runtime pack exception information in an object and raise an exception.

  In the examples in previous section Python Runtime raised exceptions **ZeroDivisionError** and **NameError**.

  Raising an exception is same as throwing an exception in C++/Java.
- Two things that can be done when an exception is raised:
  (a) Catch the raised exception object in **except** block.
  (b) Raise the exception further.
- If we catch the exception object, we can either perform a graceful exit or rectify the exceptional situation and continue execution.

- If we raise the exception object further - Default exception handler catches the object, prints stack trace and terminates.
- There are two ways to create exception objects:
  (a) From ready-made exception classes (like **ZeroDivisionError**)
  (b) From user-defined exception classes
- Advantages of tackling exceptions in OO manner:
  - More information can be packed into exception objects.
  - Propagation of exception objects from the point where they are raised to the point where they are tackled is managed by Python Runtime.
- Python facilitates exception handling by providing:
  - Keywords **try**, **except**, **else**, **finally**, **raise**.
  - Readymade exception classes.

How to use *try - except*?

- **try** block - Enclose in it the code that you anticipate will cause an exception.
- **except** block - Catch the raised exception in it. It must immediately follow the **try** block.

```
try :
    a = int(input('Enter an integer: '))
    b = int(input('Enter an integer: '))
    c = a / b
    print('c =', c)
except ZeroDivisionError :
    print('Denominator is 0')
```

Given below is the sample interaction with the program:

```
Enter an integer: 10
Enter an integer: 0
Denominator is 0
```

- If no exception occurs while executing the **try** block, control goes to first line beyond the **except** block.
- If an exception occurs during execution of statements in **try** block, an exception is raised and rest of the **try** block is skipped. Control

now goes to the **except** block. Here, if the type of exception raised matches the exception named after **except** keyword, that **except** block is executed.

- If an exception occurs which does not match the exception named in **except** block, then the default exception handler catches the exception, prints stack trace and terminates execution.
- When exception is raised and **except** block is executed, control goes to the next line after **except** block, unless there is a **return** or **raise** in **except** block.

Nuances of *try* and *except*

- **try** block:
  - Can be nested inside another **try** block.
  - If an exception occurs and if a matching except handler is not found in the **except** block, then the outer **try**'s **except** handlers are inspected for a match.
- **except** block:
  - Multiple **except** blocks for one **try** block are ok.
  - At a time only one **except** block goes to work.
  - If same action is to be taken in case of multiple exceptions, then the except clause can mention these exceptions in a tuple

```
try :
    # some statements
except (NameError, TypeError, ZeroDivisionError) :
    # some other statements
```

  - Order of **except** blocks is important - Derived first, Base last.
  - An empty **except** is like a catchall—catches all exceptions.
  - An exception may be re-raised from any **except** block.
- Given below is a program that puts some of the **try**, **except** nuances to a practical stint:

```
try :
    a = int(input('Enter an integer: '))
    b = int(input('Enter an integer: '))
    c = a / b
    print('c =', c)
```

```
except ZeroDivisionError as zde :
    print('Denominator is 0')
    print(zde.args)
    print(zde)
except ValueError :
    print('Unable to convert string to int')
except :
    print('Some unknown error')
```

Given below is the sample interaction with the program:

```
Enter an integer: 10
Enter an integer: 20
c = 0.5

Enter an integer: 10
Enter an integer: 0
Denominator is 0
('division by zero',)
division by zero

Enter an integer: 10
Enter an integer: abc
Unable to convert string to int
```

- If an exception occurs, the type of exception raised is matched with the exceptions named after **except** keyword. When a match occurs, that **except** block is executed, and then execution continues after the last **except** block.
- If we wish to do something more before doing a graceful exit, we can use the keyword **as** to receive the exception object. We can then access its argument either using its **args** variable, or by simply using the exception object.
- **args** refers to arguments that were used while creating the exception object.

User-defined Exceptions

- Since all exceptional conditions cannot be anticipated, for every exceptional condition there cannot be a class in Python library.

- **In such cases we can define our own exception class as shown in the following program:**

```
class InsufficientBalanceError(Exception) :
    def __init__(self, accno, cb) :
        self.__accno = accno
        self.__curbal = cb

    def get_details(self) :
        return { 'Acc no' : self.__accno,
                'Current Balance' : self.__curbal}

class Customers :
    def __init__(self) :
        self.__dct = { }

    def append(self, accno, n, bal) :
        self.__dct[accno] = { 'Name' : n, 'Balance' : bal }

    def deposit(self, accno, amt) :
        d = self.__dct[accno]
        d['Balance'] = d['Balance'] + amt
        self.__dct[accno] = d

    def display(self) :
        for k, v in self.__dct.items( ) :
            print(k, v)
        print( )

    def withdraw(self, accno, amt) :
        d = self.__dct[accno]
        curbal = d['Balance']
        if curbal - amt < 5000 :
            raise InsufficientBalanceError(accno, curbal)
        else :
            d['Balance'] = d['Balance'] - amt
            self.__dct[accno] = d

c = Customers( )
c.append(123, 'Sanjay', 9000)
c.append(101, 'Sameer', 8000)
c.append(423, 'Ajay', 7000)
c.append(133, 'Sanket', 6000)
c.display( )
```

```
c.deposit(123, 1000)
c.deposit(423, 2000)
c.display( )

try :
    c.withdraw(423, 3000)
    print('Amount withdrawn successfully')
    c.display( )
    c.withdraw(101, 5000)
    print('Amount withdrawn successfully')
    c.display( )
except InsufficientBalanceError as ibe :
    print('Withdrawal denied')
    print('Insufficient balance')
    print(ibe.get_details( ))
```

On execution of this program, we get the following output:

```
123 {'Name': 'Sanjay', 'Balance': 9000}
101 {'Name': 'Sameer', 'Balance': 8000}
423 {'Name': 'Ajay', 'Balance': 7000}
133 {'Name': 'Sanket', 'Balance': 6000}

123 {'Name': 'Sanjay', 'Balance': 10000}
101 {'Name': 'Sameer', 'Balance': 8000}
423 {'Name': 'Ajay', 'Balance': 9000}
133 {'Name': 'Sanket', 'Balance': 6000}

Amount withdrawn successfully
123 {'Name': 'Sanjay', 'Balance': 10000}
101 {'Name': 'Sameer', 'Balance': 8000}
423 {'Name': 'Ajay', 'Balance': 6000}
133 {'Name': 'Sanket', 'Balance': 6000}

Withdrawal denied
Insufficient balance
{'Acc no': 101, 'Current Balance': 8000}
```

- **Each customer in a Bank has data like account number, name and balance amount. This data is maintained in nested dictionaries.**

- If during withdrawal of money from a particular account the balance goes below Rs. 5000, then a user-defined exception called **InsufficientBalanceError** is raised.
- In the matching **except** block, details of the withdrawal transaction that resulted into an exception are fetched by calling **get_details( )** method present in **InsufficientBalanceError** class and displayed.
- **get_details( )** returns the formatted data. If we wish to get raw data, then we can use **ibe.args** variable, or simply **ibe**.

```
print(ibe.args)
print(ibe)
```

else Block

- The **try** .. **except** statement may also have an optional **else** block.
- If it is present, it must occur after all the **except** blocks.
- Control goes to **else** block if no exception occurs during execution of the **try** block.
- The program given below shows how to use the **else** block.

```
try :
    lst = [10, 20, 30, 40, 50]
    for num in lst :
        i = int(num)
        j = i * i
        print(i, j)
except NameError:
    print(NameError.args)
else:
    print('Total numbers processed', len(lst))
    del(lst)
```

We get the following output on executing this program:

```
10 100
20 400
30 900
40 1600
```

```
50 2500
Total numbers processed 5
```

- Control goes to **else** block since no exception occurred while obtaining squares.
- If we replace one of the elements in **lst** to 'abc', then a **NameError** will occur which will be caught by **except** block. In this case **else** block does not go to work.

finally Block

- **finally** block is optional.
- Code in **finally** always runs, no matter what! Even if a **return** or **break** occurs first.
- **finally** block is placed after **except** blocks (if they exist).
- **try** block must have **except** block and/or **finally** block.
- **finally** block is commonly used for releasing external resources like files, network connections or database connections, irrespective of whether the use of the resource was successful or not.

Exception Handling Tips

- Don't catch and ignore an exception.
- Don't catch everything using a catchall **except**, distinguish between types of exceptions.
- Make exception handling optimally elaborate; not too much, not too little.

P</> *Programs*

Problem 22.1

Write a program that infinitely receives positive integer as input and prints its square. If a negative number is entered then raise an exception, display a relevant error message and make a graceful exit.

Program

```
try:
    while True :
        num = int(input('Enter a positive number: '))
        if num >= 0 :
            print(num * num)
        else :
            raise ValueError('Negative number')
except ValueError as ve :
    print(ve.args)
```

Output

```
Enter a positive number: 12
144
Enter a positive number: 34
1156
Enter a positive number: 45
2025
Enter a positive number: -9
('Negative number',)
```

Problem 22.2

Write a program that implements a stack data structure of a specified size. If the stack becomes full and we still try to push an element to it, then an **IndexError** exception should be raised. Similarly, if the stack is empty and we try to pop an element from it then an **IndexError** exception should be raised.

Program

```
class Stack :
    def __init__(self, sz) :
        self.size = sz
        self.arr = [ ]
        self.top = -1

    def push(self, n) :
        if self.top + 1 == self.size :
```

```
                raise IndexError('Stack is full')
            else :
                self.top += 1
                self.arr = self.arr + [n]

    def pop(self) :
        if self.top == -1 :
            raise IndexError('Stack is empty')
        else :
            n = self.arr[self.top]
            self.top -= 1
            return n

    def printall(self) :
        print(self.arr)

s = Stack(5)
try :
    s.push(10)
    n = s.pop( )
    print(n)
    n = s.pop( )
    print(n)
    s.push(20)
    s.push(30)
    s.push(40)
    s.push(50)
    s.push(60)
    s.printall( )
    s.push(70)
except IndexError as ie :
    print(ie.args)
```

Output

```
10
('Stack is empty',)
```

Tips

- **A new element is added to the stack by merging two lists.**

- **IndexError** is a readymade exception class. Here we have used it to raise a stack full or stack empty exception.

Problem 22.3

Write a program that implements a queue data structure of specified size. If the queue becomes full and we still try to add an element to it, then a user-defined **QueueError** exception should be raised. Similarly, if the queue is empty and we try to delete an element from it then a **QueueError** exception should be raised.

Program

```
class QueueError(Exception) :
    def __init__(self, msg, front, rear ) :
        self.errmsg = msg + ' front = ' + str(front) + ' rear = ' + str(rear)

    def get_message(self) :
        return self.errmsg

class Queue :
    def __init__(self, sz) :
        self.size = sz
        self.arr = [ ]
        self.front = self.rear = -1

    def add_queue(self, item) :
        if self.rear == self.size - 1 :
            raise QueueError('Queue is full.', self.front, self.rear)
        else :
            self.rear += 1
            self.arr = self.arr + [item]

            if self.front == -1 :
                self.front = 0

    def delete_queue(self) :
        if self.front == -1 :
            raise QueueError('Queue is empty.', self.front, self.rear)
        else :
            data = self.arr[self.front]
            if ( self.front == self.rear ) :
                self.front = self.rear = -1
```

```
            else :
                self.front += 1
            return data

    def printall(self) :
        print(self.arr)

q = Queue(5)
try :
    q.add_queue(11)
    q.add_queue(12)
    q.add_queue(13)
    q.add_queue(14)
    q.add_queue(15) # oops, queue is full
    q.printall( )
    i = q.delete_queue( )
    print('Item deleted = ', i)
    i = q.delete_queue( )
    print('Item deleted = ', i)
    i = q.delete_queue( )
    print('Item deleted = ', i)
    i = q.delete_queue( )
    print('Item deleted = ', i)
    i = q.delete_queue( )
    print('Item deleted = ', i)
    i = q.delete_queue( ) # oops, queue is empty
    print('Item deleted = ', i)
except QueueError as qe :
    print(qe.get_message( ))
```

Output

```
[11, 12, 13, 14, 15]
Item deleted =  11
Item deleted =  12
Item deleted =  13
Item deleted =  14
Item deleted =  15
Queue is empty. front = -1 rear = -1
```

Problem 22.4

Write a program that receives an integer as input. If a string is entered instead of an integer, then report an error and give another chance to user to enter an integer. Continue this process till correct input is supplied.

Program

```
while True :
    try :
        num = int(input('Enter a number: '))
        break
    except ValueError :
        print('Incorrect Input')

print('You entered: ', num)
```

Output

```
Enter a number: aa
Incorrect Input
Enter a number: abc
Incorrect Input
Enter a number: a
Incorrect Input
Enter a number: 23
You entered:  23
```

Exercises

[A] State whether the following statements are True or False:

(a) The exception handling mechanism is supposed to handle compile time errors.

(b) It is necessary to declare the exception class within the class in which an exception is going to be thrown.

(c) Every exception raised must be caught.

(d) For one **try** block there can be multiple **except** blocks.

(e) When an exception is raised, an exception class's constructor gets called.

(f) **try** blocks cannot be nested.

(g) Proper destruction of an object is guaranteed by exception handling mechanism.

(h) All exceptions occur at runtime.

(i) Exceptions offer an object-oriented way of handling runtime errors.

(j) If an exception occurs, then the program terminates abruptly without getting any chance to recover from the exception.

(k) No matter whether an exception occurs or not, the statements in the **finally** clause (if present) will get executed.

(l) A program can contain multiple **finally** clauses.

(m) **finally** clause is used to perform cleanup operations like closing the network/database connections.

(n) While raising a user-defined exception, multiple values can be set in the exception object.

(o) In one function/method, there can be only one **try** block.

(p) An exception must be caught in the same function/method in which it is raised.

(q) All values set up in the exception object are available in the **except** block that catches the exception.

(r) If our program does not catch an exception, then Python Runtime catches it.

(s) It is possible to create user-defined exceptions.

(t) All types of exceptions can be caught using the **Exception** class.

(u) For every **try** block there must be a corresponding **finally** block.

[B] Answer the following questions:

(a) If we do not catch the exception thrown at runtime then who catches it?

(b) Explain in short the most compelling reasons for using exception handling over conventional error handling approaches.

(c) Is it necessary that all classes that can be used to represent exceptions be derived from base class **Exception**?

(d) What is the use of a **finally** block in Python exception handling mechanism?

(e) How does nested exception handling work in Python?

(f) Write a program that receives 10 integers and stores them and their cubes in a dictionary. If the number entered is less than 3, raise a user-defined exception **NumberTooSmall**, and if the number entered is more than 30, then raise a user-defined exception **NumberTooBig**. Whether an exception occurs or not, at the end print the contents of the dictionary.

(g) What is wrong with the following code snippet?

```
try :
    # some statements
except :
    # report error 1
except ZeroDivisionError :
    # report error 2
```

(h) Which of these keywords is not part of Python's exception handling vocabulary—**try, catch, throw, except, raise, finally, else**?

(i) What will be the output of the following code?

```
def fun( ) :
    try :
        return 10
    finally :
        return 20
k = fun( )
print(k)
```

23 File Input/Output

"Save in file, or perish..."

Contents

KanNotes

I/O System

- Expectations from an I/O System:
  - It should allow us to communicate with multiple sources and destinations.
    Ex. Sources - Keyboard, File, Network
    Ex. Destinations - Screen, File, Network
  - It should allow us to input/output varied entities.
    Ex. Numbers, Strings, Lists, Tuples, Sets, Dictionaries, etc.
  - It should allow us to communicate in multiple ways.
    Ex. Sequential access, Random access
  - It should allow us to deal with the underlying file system.
    Ex. Create, Modify, Rename, Delete files and directories
- Types of data used for I/O:
  Text - '485000' as a sequence of Unicode characters.
  Binary - 485000 as sequence of bytes of its binary equivalent.
- File Types:
  All program files are text files.
  All image, music, video, executable files are binary files.

File I/O

- Sequence of operations in file I/O:
  - Open a file
  - Read/Write data to it
  - Close the file
- Given below is a program that implements this sequence of file I/O operations:

```
# write/read text data
msg1 = 'Pay taxes with a smile...\n'
msg2 = 'I tried, but they wanted money!\n'
msg3 = 'Don\'t feel bad...\n'
msg4 = 'It is alright to have no talent!\n'
f = open('messages', 'w')
f.write(msg1)
f.write(msg2)
```

```
f.write(msg3)
f.write(msg4)
f.close( )
f = open('messages', 'r')
data = f.read( )
print(data)
f.close( )
```

On executing this program, we get the following output:

```
Pay taxes with a smile...
I tried, but they wanted money!
Don't feel bad...
It is alright to have no talent!
```

- Opening a file brings its contents to a buffer in memory. While performing read/write operations, data is read from or written to buffer.

```
f = open(filename, 'r')      # opens file for reading
f = open(filename, 'w')      # opens file for writing
f.close( )                   # closes the file by vacating the buffer
```

Once file is closed read/write operation on it is not feasible.

- **f.write(msg1)** writes **msg1** string to the file.
- **data = f.read( )** reads all the lines present in the file represented by object **f** into **data**.

Read / Write Operations

- There are two functions for writing data to a file:

```
msg = 'Bad officials are elected by good citizens who do not vote.\n'
msgs = ['Humpty\n', 'Dumpty\n', 'Sat\n', 'On\n', 'a\n', 'wall\n']
f.write(msg)
f.writelines(msgs)
```

- To write objects other than strings, we need to convert them to strings before writing:

```
tpl = ('Ajay', 23, 15000)
```

```
lst = {23, 45, 56, 78, 90}
d = {'Name' : 'Dilip', 'Age' : 25}
f.write(str(tpl))
f.write(str(lst))
f.write(str(d))
```

- There are three functions for reading data from a file represented by file object **f**.

```
data = f.read( )       # reads entire file contents and returns as string
data = f.read(n)       # reads n characters, and returns as string
data = f.readline( )   # reads a line, and returns as string
```

If the end of file is reached **f.read( )** returns an empty string.

- There are two ways to read a file line-by-line till the end of file:

```
# first way
while True :
    data = f.readline( )
    if data == '' :
        break
    print(data, end ='')

# second way
for data in f :
    print(data, end ='')
```

- To read all the lines in a file and form a **list** of lines:

```
data = f.readlines( )
```

File Opening Modes

- There are multiple file-opening modes available:

  'r' - Opens file for reading in text mode.
  'w' - Opens file for writing in text mode.
  'a' - Opens file for appending in text mode.
  'r+' - Opens file for reading and writing in text mode.
  'w+' - Opens file for writing and reading in text mode.
  'a+' - Opens file for appending and reading in text mode.

'rb' - Opens file for reading in binary mode.
'wb' - Opens file for writing in binary mode.
'ab' - Opens file for appending in binary mode.
'rb+' - Opens file for reading and writing in binary mode.
'wb+' - Opens file for writing and reading in binary mode.
'ab+' - Opens file for appending and reading in binary mode.

If mode argument is not mentioned while opening a file, then 'r' is assumed.

- While opening a file for writing, if the file already exists, it is overwritten.
- If file is opened for writing in binary mode then a bytes-like object should be passed to **write( )** as shown below:

```
f = open('a.dat', 'wb+')
d = b'\xee\x86\xaa'      # series of 3 bytes, \x indicates hexadecimal
f.write(d)
```

with Keyword

- It is a good idea to close a file once its usage is over, as it will free up system resources.
- If we do not close a file, when the file object is destroyed file will be closed for us by Python's garbage collector program.
- If we use **with** keyword while opening the file, the file gets closed as soon as its usage is over.

```
with open('messages', 'r') as f :
    data = f.read( )
```

- **with** ensures that the file is closed even if an exception occurs while processing it.

Moving within a File

- When we are reading a file or writing a file, the next read or write operation is performed from the next character/byte as compared to the previous read/write operation.
- Thus if we read the first character from a file using **f.read(1)**, next call to **f.read(1)** will automatically read the second character in the file.

- At times we may wish to move to the desired position in a file before reading/writing. This can be done using **f.seek( )** method.
- General form of **seek( )** is given below:

  f.seek(offset, reference)

  reference can take values 0, 1, 2 standing for beginning of file, current position in file and end of file respectively.
- For a file opened in text mode, reference values 0 and 2 alone can be used. Also, using 2, we can only move to the end of file.

```
f.seek(512, 0)   # moves to position 512 from beginning of file
f.seek(0, 2)     # moves to end of file
```

- For file opened in binary mode, reference values 0, 1, 2 can be used.

```
f.seek(0)        # moves to beginning of file
f.seek(12, 0)    # moves to position 12 from beginning of file
f.seek(-15, 2)   # moves 15 positions to left from end of file
f.seek(6, 1)     # moves 6 positions to right from current position
f.seek(-10, 1)   # moves 10 positions to left from current position
```

Serialization and Deserialization

- Compared to strings, reading/writing numbers from/to a file is tedious. This is because **write( )** function writes a string to a file and **read( )** returns a string read from a file. So, we need to do conversions while reading/writing, as shown in the following program:

```
f = open('numberstxt', 'w+')
f.write(str(233)+'\n')
f.write(str(13.45))
f.seek(0)
a = int(f.readline( ))
b = float(f.readline( ))
print(a + a)
print(b + b)
```

- If we are to read/write more complicated data in the form of tuple, dictionaries, etc. from/to file using the above method, it will become more difficult. In such cases a module called **json** should be used.

- **json** module converts Python data into appropriate JSON types before writing data to a file. Likewise, it converts JSON types read from a file into Python data. The first process is called **serialization** and the second is called **deserialization**.

```
# serialize/deserialize a list
import json
f = open('sampledata', 'w+')
lst = [10, 20, 30, 40, 50, 60, 70, 80, 90]
json.dump(lst, f)
f.seek(0)
inlst = json.load(f)
print(inlst)
f.close( )

# serialize/deserialize a tuple
import json
f = open('sampledata', 'w+')
tpl = ('Ajay', 23, 2455.55)
json.dump(tpl, f)
f.seek(0)
intpl = json.load(f)
print(tuple(intpl))
f.close( )

# serialize/deserialize a dictionary
import json
f = open('sampledata', 'w+')
dct = { 'Anil' : 24, 'Ajay' : 23, 'Nisha' : 22}
json.dump(dct, f)
f.seek(0)
indct = json.load(f)
print(indct)
f.close( )
```

- Serialization of a Python type to JSON data is done using a function **dump( )**. It writes the serialized data to a file.

- Deserialization of a JSON type to a Python type is done using a function **load( )**. It reads the data from a file, does the conversion and returns the converted data.

- While deserializing a tuple, **load( )** returns a list and not a tuple. So we need to convert the list to a tuple using **tuple( )** conversion function.

- Instead of writing JSON data to a file, we can write it to a string, and read it back from a string as shown below:

```
import json
lst = [10, 20, 30, 40, 50, 60, 70, 80, 90]
tpl = ('Ajay', 23, 2455.55)
dct = { 'Anil' : 24, 'Ajay' : 23, 'Nisha' : 22}

str1 = json.dumps(lst)
str2 = json.dumps(tpl)
str3 = json.dumps(dct)
l = json.loads(str1)
t = tuple(json.loads(str2))
d = json.loads(str3)
print(l)
print(t)
print(d)
```

- It is possible to serialize/deserialize nested lists and dictionaries as shown below:

```
# serialize/deserialize nested list
import json
lofl = [10, [20, 30, 40], [ 50, 60, 70], 80, 90]
f = open('data', 'w+')
json.dump(lofl, f)
f.seek(0)
inlofl = json.load(f)
print(inlofl)
f.close( )

# serialize/deserialize nested dictionary
import json
contacts = { 'Anil': { 'DOB' : '17/11/98', 'Favorite' : 'Igloo' },
             'Amol': { 'DOB' : '14/10/99', 'Favorite' : 'Tundra' },
             'Ravi': { 'DOB' : '19/11/97', 'Favorite' : 'Artic' } }
f = open('data', 'w+')
json.dump(contacts, f)
f.seek(0)
```

```
incontacts = json.load(f)
print(incontacts)
f.close( )
```

Serialization of User-defined Types

- Standard Python types can be easily converted to JSON and vice versa. However, if we attempt to serialize a user-defined **Complex** type to JSON we get following error:

  TypeError: Object of type 'Complex' is not JSON serializable

- To serialize user-defined types we need to define encoding and decoding functions. This is shown in the following program where we serialize **Complex** type.

```
import json
def encode_complex(x):
    if isinstance(x, Complex) :
        return(x.real, x.imag)
    else :
        raise TypeError('Complex object is not JSON serializable')

def decode_complex(dct):
    if '__Complex__' in dct :
        return Complex(dct['real'], dct['imag'])
    return dct

class Complex :
    def __init__(self, r = 0, i = 0) :
        self.real = r
        self.imag = i

    def print_data(self) :
        print(self.real, self.imag)

c = Complex(1.0, 2.0)
f = open('data', 'w+')
json.dump(c, f, default = encode_complex)
f.seek(0)
inc = json.load(f, object_hook = decode_complex)
print(inc)
```

- To translate a **Complex** object into JSON, we have defined an encoding function called **encode_complex( )**. We have provided this function to **dump( )** method's **default** parameter. **dump( )** method will use **encode_complex( )** function while serializing a **Complex** object.

- In **encode_complex( )** we have checked whether the object received is of the type **Complex**. If it is, then we return the **Complex** object data as a tuple. If not, we raise a **TypeError** exception.

- During deserialization when **load( )** method attempts to parse an object, instead of the default decoder we provide our decoder **decode_complex( )** through the **object_hook** parameter.

Working with CSV Files

- A CSV file is used to store tabular data in a very simple file format, where each line contains one or more field values separated by commas.

- Given below is the typical format of a CSV file containing employee data.

```
Employee code,Name,Age,Salary
A101,Ajay,27,9000.10
A102,Sujay,28,19100.50
A110,Aditya,23,9300.55
A171,Anuj,34,9565.65
A191,Tanmay,33,7800.65
A192,Talleen,27,9155.45
```

- For working with CSV files in Python, there is an inbuilt module called csv.

- Given below is a program that demonstrates how to write employee data in a file 'EmpData.csv' in CSV format.

```
import csv
fields = ['Employee code', 'Name', 'Age', 'Salary']
rows = [['A101', 'Ajay', '27', '9000.10'],
        ['A102', 'Sujay', '28', '19100.50'],
        ['A110', 'Aditya', '23', '9300.55'],
        ['A171', 'Anuj', '34', '9565.65'],
        ['A191', 'Tanmay', '33', '7800.65'],
```

```
        ['A192', 'Talleen', '27', '9155.45']]
csvfile = open('EmpData.csv', 'w', newline = '')
csvwriter = csv.writer(csvfile)
csvwriter.writerow(fields)
csvwriter.writerows(rows)
csvfile.close( )
```

- **fields** is a list containing all field (column) names, whereas **rows** is a list of lists, where each list contains field values of that row.
- The **writer** object returned by **csv.writer( )** contains two methods—**writerow( )** and **writerows( )**.
- **writerow( )** takes as its argument an iterable to write to csv file, whereas **writerows( )** takes an iterable of iterables.
- Once the csv file is created its contents can be read back and printed on the screen as shown in the following program:

```
import csv
fields = [ ]
rows = [ ]

csvfile = open('EmpData.csv', 'r')
csvreader = csv.reader(csvfile)
fields = next(csvreader)
for row in csvreader :
    rows.append(row)

num_of_rows = csvreader.line_num
csvfile.close( )

for fld in fields :
    print(f'{fld:20}', end = '')

for row in rows[:num_of_rows] :
    for col in row :
        print(f'{col:20}', end = '')
```

- **line_num** gives number of lines read by the reader.
- While printing each field and its value is printed in 20 columns.
- The csv module contains classes **DictWriter** and **DictReader** to help writing and reading dictionaries in csv format.

File and Directory Operations

- Python lets us interact with the underlying file system. This lets us perform many file and directory operations.
- File operations include creation, deletion, renaming, copying, checking if an entry is a file, obtaining statistics of a file, etc.
- Directory operations include creation, recursive creation, renaming, changing into, deleting, listing a directory, etc.
- Path operations include obtaining the absolute and relative path, splitting path elements, joining paths, etc.
- '.' represents current directory and '..' represents parent of current directory.
- Given below is a program that demonstrates some file, directory and path operations.

```
import os
import shutil

print(os.name)
print(os.getcwd( ))
print(os.listdir('.'))
print(os.listdir('..'))

if os.path.exists('mydir') :
    print('mydir already exists')
else :
    os.mkdir('mydir')

os.chdir('mydir')
os.makedirs('.\\dir1\\dir2\\dir3')
f = open('myfile', 'w')
f.write('Having one child makes you a parent...')
f.write('Having two you are a referee')
f.close( )
stats = os.stat('myfile')
print('Size = ', stats.st_size)

os.rename('myfile', 'yourfile')
shutil.copyfile('yourfile', 'ourfile')
os.remove('yourfile')
```

```
curpath = os.path.abspath('.')
os.path.join(curpath, 'yourfile')
if os.path.isfile(curpath) :
    print('yourfile file exists')
else :
    print('yourfile file doesn\'t exist')
```

P</> Programs

Problem 23.1

Write a program to read the contents of file 'messages' one character at a time. Print each character that is read.

Program

```
f = open('messages', 'r')
while True :
    data = f.read(1)
    if data == '' :
        break
    print(data, end = '')

f.close( )
```

Output

```
You may not be great when you start, but you need to start to be great.
Work hard until you don't need an introduction.
Work so hard that one day your signature becomes an autograph.
```

Tips

- **f.read(1)** reads 1 character from a file object **f**.
- **read( )** returns an empty string on reaching end of file.
- if **end = ''** is not used in the call to **print( )**, each character read will be printed in a new line.

Problem 23.2

Write a program that writes four integers to a file called 'numbers'. Go to the following positions in the file and report these positions.

10 positions from beginning
2 positions to the right of current position
5 positions to the left of current position
10 positions to the left from end

Program

```
f = open('numbers', 'wb')
f.write(b'231')
f.write(b'431')
f.write(b'2632')
f.write(b'833')
f.close( )
f = open('numbers', 'rb')
f.seek(10, 0)
print(f.tell( ))
f.seek(2, 1)
print(f.tell( ))
f.seek(-5, 1)
print(f.tell( ))
f.seek(-10, 2)
print(f.tell( ))
f.close( )
```

Output

```
10
12
7
1
```

Problem 23.3

Write a Python program that searches for a file, obtains its size and reports the size in bytes/KB/MB/GB/TB as appropriate.

Program

```
import os

def convert(num) :
    for x in ['bytes', 'KB', 'MB', 'GB', 'TB'] :
        if num < 1024.0 :
            return "%3.1f %s" % (num, x)
        num /= 1024.0

def file_size(file_path) :
    if os.path.isfile(file_path) :
        file_info = os.stat(file_path)
        return convert(file_info.st_size)

file_path = r'C:\Windows\System32\mspaint.exe'
print(file_size(file_path))
```

Output

```
6.1 MB
```

Problem 23.4

Write a Python program that reports the time of creation, time of last access and time of last modification for a given file.

Program

```
import os, time

file = 'sampledata'
print(file)

created = os.path.getctime(file)
modified = os.path.getmtime(file)
accessed = os.path.getatime(file)

print('Date created: ' + time.ctime(created))
print('Date modified: ' + time.ctime(modified))
print('Date accessed: ' + time.ctime(accessed))
```

Output

```
sampledata
Date created: Tue May 14 08:51:52 2019
Date modified: Tue May 14 09:11:59 2019
Date accessed: Tue May 14 08:51:52 2019
```

Tips

- Functions **getctime( ), getmtime( )** and **getatime( )** return the creation, modification and access time for the given file. The times are returned as number of seconds since the epoch. The epoch is 1st Jan 1970, 00:00:00.
- **ctime( )** function of **time** module converts the time expressed in seconds since epoch into a string representing local time.

Exercises

[A] State whether the following statements are True or False:

(a) If a file is opened for reading, it is necessary that the file must exist.

(b) If a file opened for writing already exists, its contents would be overwritten.

(c) For opening a file in append mode it is necessary that the file should exist.

[B] Answer the following questions:

(a) What sequence of activities take place on opening a file for reading in text mode?

(b) Is it necessary that a file created in text mode must always be opened in text mode for subsequent operations?

(c) While using the statement,

fp = open('myfile', 'r')

what happens if,

- 'myfile' does not exist on the disk
- 'myfile' exists on the disk

(d) While using the statement,

f = open('myfile', 'wb')

what happens if,

- 'myfile' does not exist on the disk
- 'myfile' exists on the disk

(e) A floating-point list contains percentage marks obtained by students in an examination. To store these marks in a file 'marks.dat', in which mode would you open the file and why?

[C] Attempt the following questions:

(a) Write a program to read a file and display its contents along with line numbers before each line.

(b) Write a program to append the contents of one file at the end of another.

(c) Suppose a file contains student's records with each record containing the name and age of a student. Write a program to read these records and display them in sorted order by name.

(d) Write a program to copy contents of one file to another. While doing so replace all lowercase characters with their equivalent uppercase characters.

(e) Write a program that merges lines alternately from two files and writes the results to a new file. If one file has a smaller number of lines than the other, the remaining lines from the larger file should be simply copied into the target file.

(f) Suppose an **Employee** object contains following details:

employee code, employee name, date of joining, salary

Write a program to serialize and deserialize this data.

(g) A hospital keeps a file of blood donors in which each record has the format:

Name: 20 Columns

Address: 40 Columns
Age: 2 Columns
Blood Type: 1 Column (Type 1, 2, 3 or 4)

Write a program to read the file and print a list of all blood donors whose age is below 25 and whose blood type is 2.

(h) Given a list of names of students in a class, write a program to store the names in a file on disk. Make a provision to display the **n**[th] name in the list, where **n** is read from the keyboard.

(i) Assume that a Master file contains two fields, roll number and name of the student. At the end of the year, a group of students join the class and another set leaves. A Transaction file contains the roll numbers and an appropriate code to add or delete a student.

Write a program to create another file that contains the updated list of names and roll numbers. Assume that the Master file and the Transaction file are arranged in ascending order by roll numbers. The updated file should also be in ascending order by roll numbers.

(j) Given a text file, write a program to create another text file deleting the words “a”, “the”, “an” and replacing each one of them with a blank space.

24 Logging

"Log and be immortal..."

Contents

- Need for Logging
- Log Contents
- Logging Levels
- Logging to a File
- Logging Timestamp
- Logging Variable Data and Exceptions
- Logging in multiple Modules
- Rollover Logs
- What to Log?
- Programs
- Exercises

KanNotes

Need for Logging

- Different events happen when any software runs.
- A few examples of these events could be—a user attempts a login, his login name and password are verified, if they match then he is asked to enter an OTP sent to his registered mobile phone, if his password has become stale, then he is asked to create a new password, for the new password again the OTP procedure is repeated, once he sets a new password, he is made to login again with the new password.
- There is a possibility that any of the above events may not work correctly. To debug where the problem lies, we need to ascertain which events happened successfully and which events failed.
- Since some of these events happen in backend code, checking their occurrence cannot be done merely by using **print( )** statements. So, logging is often done in a persistent storage medium like a log file.
- By examining the logs, the developer can get information about the behavior of the code and would help track down systematically what is wrong with the application.
- Machines on which backend software runs may not have a screen. In such situations logging is almost mission critical.
- The logs can also provide insights into an application's performance and where it needs improvement.

Log Contents

- For logging the occurrence of events, the software developer needs to add logging calls to the code.
- A log can store information about the events that occur during the normal operation of the application, errors within the application, and warnings regarding a specific event.
- A typical log entry contains an importance level of an event (also called severity), a descriptive message and data that is potentially different for each occurrence of the event.

Logging Levels

- Python comes with a built-in logging module, so we do not have to install any package to implement logging in our application.
- Python's built-in logging module provides five logging levels of different severity. These levels indicate the importance of the given log message. They are described below in increasing order of severity:

  Debug (10): It is used to log some diagnostic information about the application.

  Info (20): It is used to record information on a piece of code that works as intended.

  Warning (30): It is used to record events that are likely to cause problems in the application's working in the future.

  Error (40): It is used to record an error when a part of the application did not work as expected, and the code execution failed.

  Critical (50): This is a serious event that needs urgent attention, and failing to fix this may cause the application to stop working.

- Given below is a program that shows how to log events of different severity:

```
import logging
logging.debug('A debug message')
logging.info('An information')
logging.warning('A warning message')
logging.error('An error message')
logging.critical('A message of critical severity')
```

  On executing this program, we get the following output:

```
WARNING:root:A warning message
ERROR:root:An error message
CRITICAL:root:A message of critical severity
```

  Note that the messages for level **debug** and **info** are not logged. This is because, by default, logging begins from the **warning** level.

- The logs are in the format:

<logging-level>:<logger-name>:<message>.

The <logger-name> is by default the root logger, as we have not yet configured custom loggers.

Logging to a File

- Messages can be logged into a file as shown in the following program:

```
import logging
logging.basicConfig(level = logging.INFO,
                    filename = 'mylog.log', filemode = 'w')
logging.debug('A debug message')
logging.info('An information')
logging.warning('A warning message')
logging.error('An error message')
logging.critical('A message of critical severity')
```

On executing this program, the following output gets written to the log file 'mylog.log':

```
INFO:root:An information
WARNING:root:A warning message
ERROR:root:An error message
CRITICAL:root:A message of critical severity
```

- In the call to **basicConfig( )**, we have specified the logging level and the log filename. 'w' indicates that the log file will be opened in write mode. As a result, each time the program is executed the log file is overwritten. Using 'a' in place of 'w' would open the log file in append mode.
- The **filemode** parameter is optional and defaults to 'a'.
- Since we have set the logging level to INFO, except for the debug message, all other messages were written to the file.

Logging Timestamp

- It is a good practice to record the timestamp for each logged message. This makes it easier to figure out what is happening while examining the logs. Following program shows how this can be done:

```
import logging
```

```
logging.basicConfig(level = logging.INFO,
                    filename = 'mylog.log', filemode = 'w',
                    format = '%(asctime)s %(levelname)s %(message)s')
logging.debug('A debug message')
logging.info('An information')
logging.warning('A warning message')
logging.error('An error message')
logging.critical('A message of critical severity')
```

On executing this program, the following output gets written to the log file:

```
2023-04-04 11:19:25,363 INFO An information
2023-04-04 11:19:25,363 WARNING A warning message
2023-04-04 11:19:25,363 ERROR An error message
2023-04-04 11:19:25,363 CRITICAL A message of critical severity
```

- Apart from **asctime**, **levelname** and **message**, there are many other attributes available using which we can customize the log record.
- Since we have not mentioned the logger in the log format, logger-name 'root' is absent in the logs.

Logging Variable Data and Exceptions

- Suppose we wish to perform division on several pairs of numbers. We wish to log the success / failure of different divisions. If an exception occurs during division, we wish to log the exception along with the stack trace. Following program shows how this can be done:

```
import logging
logging.basicConfig(level = logging.INFO, filename = 'mylog.log',
                    filemode = 'w', format = '%(asctime)s %(message)s')

num_vals = [21, 32, 60, 32, 14]
den_vals = [3, 2, 0, 16, 7]

for num, den in zip(num_vals, den_vals) :
    logging.info(f'The values of num and den are {num} and {den}')
    try :
        val = num / den
        logging.info(f'division successful with result: {val}')
    except ZeroDivisionError as err :
```

```
    logging.exception('ZeroDivisionError')
```

On executing this program, the following output gets written to the log file:

```
2023-04-04 11:35:15,126 The values of num and den are 21 and 3
2023-04-04 11:35:15,126 division successful with result: 7.0
2023-04-04 11:35:15,126 The values of num and den are 32 and 2
2023-04-04 11:35:15,126 division successful with result: 16.0
2023-04-04 11:35:15,126 The values of num and den are 60 and 0
2023-04-04 11:35:15,126 ZeroDivisionError
Traceback (most recent call last):
  File "C:/Users/kanet/Desktop/a.py", line 9, in <module>
    val = num / den
          ~~~~^~~~~
ZeroDivisionError: division by zero
2023-04-04 11:35:15,126 The values of num and den are 32 and 16
2023-04-04 11:35:15,126 division successful with result: 2.0
2023-04-04 11:35:15,126 The values of num and den are 14 and 7
2023-04-04 11:35:15,126 division successful with result: 2.0
```

As can be observed from the above log, it contains information of successful as well as unsuccessful events.

Logging in multiple Modules

- If we wish we can direct logs of different modules to different files. This can be done using module-level loggers as shown in the following program:

```
# main.py – Uses the module in functions.py
import logging
import function

# create logger and set logging level
logger1 = logging.getLogger(__name__)
logger1.setLevel(logging.INFO)

# configure handler and formatter
handler1 = logging.FileHandler(f'{__name__}.log', mode = 'w')
formatter1 = logging.Formatter('%(name)s
                %(levelname)s %(message)s')

# add formatter to the handler
```

```
handler1.setFormatter(formatter1)
# add handler to the logger
logger1.addHandler(handler1)

logger1.info(f'Logs for module {__name__}')

num_vals = [21,32,60,32,14]
den_vals = [3,2,0,16,7]

for num, den in zip(num_vals,den_vals) :
    function.division(num, den)
    logger1.info(f'Call division with args {num} and {den}')
```

```
# function.py – module containing division( ) function
import logging

# create logger and set logging level
logger2 = logging.getLogger(__name__)
logger2.setLevel(logging.INFO)

# configure handler and formatter for logger2
handler2 = logging.FileHandler(f'{__name__}.log', mode = 'w')
formatter2 = logging.Formatter('%(name)s
                %(levelname)s %(message)s')

# add formatter to handler
handler2.setFormatter(formatter2)
# add handler to logger
logger2.addHandler(handler2)

logger2.info(f'Logs for module {__name__}')

def division(num, den) :
    try :
        val = num / den
        logger2.info(f'division result: {val}')
    except ZeroDivisionError as err :
        logger2.exception('ZeroDivisionError')
```

- On executing 'main.py' two log files are created—'__main__.log' and 'functions.log'. Their contents are shown below:

```
# contents of __main__.log
__main__ INFO Logs for module __main__
```

```
__main__ INFO Call division with args 21 and 3
__main__ INFO Call division with args 32 and 2
__main__ INFO Call division with args 60 and 0
__main__ INFO Call division with args 32 and 16
__main__ INFO Call division with args 14 and 7
```

```
# contents of function.log
function INFO Logs for module function
function INFO division result: 7.0
function INFO division result: 16.0
function ERROR ZeroDivisionError
Traceback (most recent call last):
  File "C:\Users\kanet\Desktop\functions.py", line 19, in division
    val = num / den
          ~~~~^~~~~
ZeroDivisionError: division by zero
function INFO division result: 2.0
function INFO division result: 2.0
```

- From the logger names '__main__' and 'function' in the respective log records it becomes obvious as to which modules' log records are they.
- Logging is performed by calling methods on instances of the Logger class. The default logger class is **root**. We have named our loggers based on the module names obtained using the statements:

```
logger1 = logging.getLogger(__name__)
logger2 = logging.getLogger(__name__)
```

- It is possible to log messages to different destinations like HTTP GET/POST locations, email via SMTP, etc.
- Handler objects are responsible for dispatching the appropriate log messages (based on the log messages' severity) to the handler's specified destination. In our case, the handler type is **FileHandler**.
- Firstly, we associate a formatter with the handler and then associate the handler with the logger object.

Rollover Logs

- Often, we do not wish to log all messages into one file. Instead, we want new log files on a per day or per hour/minute/second basis. This can be achieved using a **TimedRotatingFileHandler** as shown in the following program.

```
import time
import logging
import logging.handlers
logger = logging.getLogger(__name__)
logger.setLevel(logging.INFO)
handler = logging.handlers.TimedRotatingFileHandler('mylog.log',
            when = 'S', interval = 5, backupCount = 6)
formatter = logging.Formatter('%(asctime)s %(name)s %(levelname)s
                                    %(message)s')
handler.setFormatter(formatter)
logger.addHandler(handler)

try :
   for num in range(500) :
      time.sleep(0.5)
      logger.debug(f'num = {num}')
      logger.info(f'num = {num}')
      logger.warning(f'num = {num}')
      logger.error(f'num = {num}')
      logger.critical(f'num = {num}')
except KeyboardInterrupt :
   # handle Ctrl-C
   logging.warning('Cancelled by user')
except Exception as ex :
   # handle unexpected errors
   logging.exception(f'Unhandled error\n{ex}')
finally :
   # stop logging activity
   logging.shutdown( )
```

- As **num** goes from 0 to 499, messages get logged into the log file. However, here multiple log files are created, one every 5 seconds (as specified by parameters **when** and **interval**).

- Each log file that gets created has an extension of date and time of creation of the log file. For example, mylog.log.2023-04-18_10-43-03.
- Once 6 log files have been created (**backupCount = 6**), the first log file is deleted, and a new one gets created.
- Firstly, we associate a formatter with the handler and then associate the handler with the logger object.
- If the program is interrupted while it is running by pressing Ctrl C, it would be logged as a warning.
- If an unexpected error occurs during program execution it would be logged as an exception.

What to Log?

- The quality of the logs is critical. Logging too much information or too little information are both bad programming practices.
- While logging it is a good idea to log 5Ws and 1 H; i.e., Who, What, Where, When, Why and How.
- 'Who' is used to identify the user or system that made the request. This could be User ID, Name, or IP address.
- 'What' indicates the kind of logging statement is it—DEBUG, INFO, ERROR, WARNING, CRITICAL.
- 'Where' indicates the class (location) where it happened.
- 'When' indicates the timestamp when the event was logged.
- 'Why' generally indicates what you need to find out by reading the logs and inferring from them.
- 'How' like 'why' may not be caught in one log statement and may have to be inferred based on multiple log lines.

Problem 24.1

Write a program to read name, age and salary of 5 persons from keyboard. Log the data into a file 'mylog.log' in the following format, along with any erroneous data entered by the user:

2023-04-17 11:07:24,356 Correct data: Dinesh 23 2345.0

2023-04-17 11:07:25,358 Correct data: Suresh 27 5455.0

Program

```
import logging
logging.basicConfig(level = logging.INFO, filename = 'mylog.log',
                    filemode = 'w', format = '%(asctime)s %(message)s')

for num in range(5) :
    data = input('Enter name, age, salary: ').split( )
    try :
        name = data[0]
        age = int(data[1])
        salary = float(data[2])
        logging.info(f'Correct data: {name} {age} {salary}')
    except ValueError as err :
        logging.exception('ValueError')
```

Output

```
2023-04-17 11:07:24,356 Correct data: Dinesh 23 2345.0
2023-04-17 11:07:29,201 Correct data: Sahil 34 4555.0
2023-04-17 11:07:35,752 Correct data: Sanket 30 4500.0
2023-04-17 11:07:47,510 ValueError
Traceback (most recent call last):
  File "C:/Users/kanet/Desktop/a.py", line 8, in <module>
    age = int(data[1])
          ^^^^^^^^^^^^
ValueError: invalid literal for int() with base 10: 'a23'
2023-04-17 11:07:59,925 Correct data: Sanjay 34 4500.0
```

Tips

- Data read from the keyboard would be treated as string. During conversion of age or salary string into numeric data, a **ValueError** exception may occur.

Problem 24.2

Write a program that has two modules **main** and **function**. The function module should define a function **squareroot_square_cube( )**. This function should receive a number as an argument, obtain its square root, square and cube values and log them. This function should be called from the main module for values in the range 0 to 9 and log these calls into a separate log file.

Program

```
# main.py – Uses the module in functions.py
import logging
import function

# create logger and set logging level
logger1 = logging.getLogger(__name__)
logger1.setLevel(logging.INFO)

# configure handler and formatter
handler1 = logging.FileHandler(f'{__name__}.log', mode = 'w')
formatter1 = logging.Formatter('%(name)s %(levelname)s %(message)s')

# add formatter to the handler
handler1.setFormatter(formatter1)
# add handler to the logger
logger1.addHandler(handler1)

logger1.info(f'Logs for module {__name__}')

for number in range(10) :
    function.squareroot_square_cube(number)
    logger1.info(f'Call squareroot_square_cube with arg {number}')
```

```
# function.py – module with squareroot_square_cube( ) function
import logging
```

```
import math

# create logger and set logging level
logger2 = logging.getLogger(__name__)
logger2.setLevel(logging.INFO)

# configure handler and formatter for logger2
handler2 = logging.FileHandler(f'{__name__}.log', mode = 'w')
formatter2 = logging.Formatter('%(name)s %(levelname)s %(message)s')

# add formatter to handler
handler2.setFormatter(formatter2)
# add handler to logger
logger2.addHandler(handler2)

logger2.info(f'Logs for module {__name__}')

def squareroot_square_cube(num) :
    root = math.sqrt(num)
    sqr = num * num
    cube = num * num * num
    logger2.info(f'Result: {num} {root} {sqr} {cube}')
```

Output

```
# contents of __main__.log
__main__ INFO Logs for module __main__
__main__ INFO Call squareroot_square_cube with arg 0
__main__ INFO Call squareroot_square_cube with arg 1
__main__ INFO Call squareroot_square_cube with arg 2
__main__ INFO Call squareroot_square_cube with arg 3
__main__ INFO Call squareroot_square_cube with arg 4
__main__ INFO Call squareroot_square_cube with arg 5
__main__ INFO Call squareroot_square_cube with arg 6
__main__ INFO Call squareroot_square_cube with arg 7
__main__ INFO Call squareroot_square_cube with arg 8
__main__ INFO Call squareroot_square_cube with arg 9
```

```
# contents of function.log
function INFO Logs for module function
function INFO Result: 0 0.0 0 0
function INFO Result: 1 1.0 1 1
function INFO Result: 2 1.4142135623730951 4 8
```

```
function INFO Result: 3 1.7320508075688772 9 27
function INFO Result: 4 2.0 16 64
function INFO Result: 5 2.23606797749979 25 125
function INFO Result: 6 2.449489742783178 36 216
function INFO Result: 7 2.6457513110645907 49 343
function INFO Result: 8 2.8284271247461903 64 512
function INFO Result: 9 3.0 81 729
```

Problem 24.3

Write a Python program that logs messages to console as well as a file 'myapp.log'. Messages including and above ERROR level should be logged to the console. Messages including and above DEBUG level should be logged to the file.

Program

```
import logging

logger = logging.getLogger(__name__)
logger.setLevel(logging.DEBUG)

# create file handler which logs even debug messages
fh = logging.FileHandler('myapp.log')
fh.setLevel(logging.DEBUG)

# create console handler with a higher log level
ch = logging.StreamHandler()
ch.setLevel(logging.ERROR)

# create formatter and add it to the handlers
formatter = logging.Formatter('%(asctime)s - %(name)s - %(levelname)s -
%(message)s')
ch.setFormatter(formatter)
fh.setFormatter(formatter)

# add the handlers to logger
logger.addHandler(ch)
logger.addHandler(fh)

logger.debug('A debug message')
logger.info('An information')
logger.warning('A warning message')
```

```
logger.error('An error message')
logger.critical('A message of critical severity')
```

Output

```
Console logs:
2023-04-19 10:45:20,838 - __main__ - ERROR - An error message
2023-04-19 10:45:20,838 - __main__ - CRITICAL - A message of critical severity
```

```
Logs in 'myapp.log':
2023-04-19 10:45:20,838 - __main__ - DEBUG - A debug message
2023-04-19 10:45:20,838 - __main__ - INFO - An information
2023-04-19 10:45:20,838 - __main__ - WARNING - A warning message
2023-04-19 10:45:20,838 - __main__ - ERROR - An error message
2023-04-19 10:45:20,838 - __main__ - CRITICAL - A message of critical severity
```

Exercises

[A] State whether the following statements are True or False:

(a) It is a good idea to have multiple print statements in a program instead of a log.

(b) Good logs would contain severity level of events that happen during execution of the program.

(c) It is possible to send the logs to console, file or an email.

(d) Only static data of a program can be logged into log files.

(e) Once the log level has been set, only messages above that level would get logged.

(f) It is possible to employ multiple loggers in the same program.

(g) It is possible to employ different loggers in different modules of the same program.

[B] Answer the following questions:

(a) What is the meaning of each parameter in the following call?

```
logging.basicConfig(level = logging.INFO, filename = 'mylog.log',
filemode = 'w', format = '%(asctime)s %(message)s')
```

(b) What is the meaning of each parameter in the following call?

```
handler = logging.handlers.TimedRotatingFileHandler('mylog.log',
          when = 'M', interval = 4, backupCount = 6)
```

(c) How will you log the values of variables rollno, name, age at INFO level on the console?

[C] Attempt the following questions:

(a) Write a program to calculate factorial values of numbers in the range 10 to 15. Log the results into a file.

(b) Write a program that infinitely generates 500 random numbers, in the range 100 to 200, one every half a second. Log the numbers generated into rollover log files. A rollover should happen every 4 seconds and a maximum of 5 log files should be created. Terminate the program if the user hits Ctrl-C in the middle of random number generation and log that as a warning.

(c) Write a program that logs messages by sending them to an email account. Hint: Use SMTP handler.

25 Miscellany

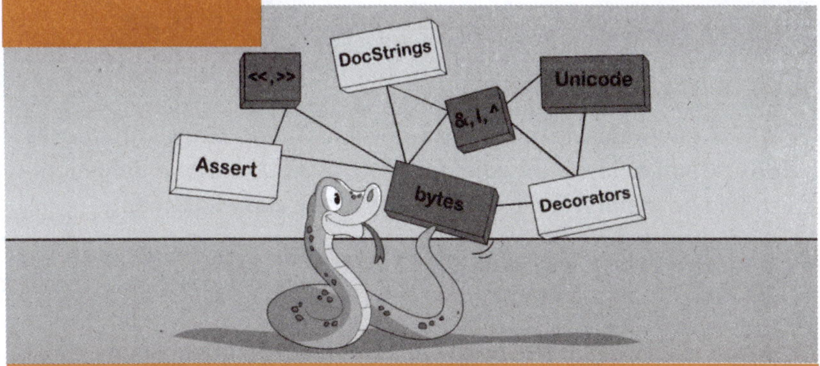

"Efficient is better..."

Contents

- Documentation Strings
- Command-line Arguments
- Parsing of Command-line
- Bitwise Operators
- Assertion
- Decorators
- Decorating Functions with Args
- Unicode
- *bytes* Datatype
- Create Executable File
- Programs
- Exercises

KanNotes

The topics discussed in this chapter are far too removed from the mainstream Python programming for inclusion in the earlier chapters. These topics provide certain useful programming features and could prove to be of immense help in certain programming strategies.

Documentation Strings

- It is a good idea to mention a documentation string (often called doscstring) below a module, function, class or method definition. It should be the first line below the **def** or the **class** statement.
- The docstring is available in the attribute **__doc__** of a module, function, class or method.
- If the docstring is multi-line it should contain a summary line followed by a blank line, followed by a detailed comment.
- Single-line and multi-line docstrings are written within triple quotes.
- Using **help( )** method we can print the functions/class/method documentation systematically.
- In the program given below the function **display( )** displays a message and the function **show(msg1, msg2)** displays **msg1** in lowercase and **msg2** in uppercase. It uses a single line docstring for **display( )** and a multi-line docstring for **show( )**. It displays both the docstrings. Also, it generates help on both the functions.

```
def display( ) :
    """Display a message"""
    print('Hello')
    print(display.__doc__)

def show(msg1 = ' ', msg2 = ' ') :
    """Display 2 messages

    Arguments:
    msg1 -- message to be displayed in lowercase (default ' ')
    msg2 -- message to be displayed in uppercase (default ' ')
    """
    print(msg1.lower( ))
    print(msg2.upper( ))
```

```
    print(show.__doc__)

display( )
show('Cindrella', 'Mozerella')
help(display)
help(show)
```

On execution of the program, it produces the following output:

```
Hello
Display a message.
cindrella
MOZERELLA
Display 2 messages.

        Arguments:
        msg1 -- message to be displayed in lowercase (default ' ')
        msg2 -- message to be displayed in uppercase (default ' ')

Help on function display in module __main__:

display( )
    Display a message.

Help on function show in module __main__:

show(msg1=' ', msg2=' ')
    Display 2 messages.

    Arguments:
    msg1 -- message to be displayed in lowercase (default ' ')
    msg1 -- message to be displayed in uppercase (default ' ')
```

Command-line Arguments

- Arguments passed to a Python script are available in **sys.argv**.

```
# sample.py
import sys
print('Number of arguments received = ', len(sys.argv))
print('Arguments received = ', str(sys.argv))
```

If we execute the script as

C:\>sample.py cat dog parrot

we get the following output:

```
Number of arguments received = 4
Arguments received = sample.py  cat  dog  parrot
```

- If we are to write a program for copying contents of one file to another, we can receive source and target filenames through command-line arguments.

```
# filecopy.py
import sys
import shutil
argc = len(sys.argv)
if argc != 3 :
    print('Incorrect usage')
    print('Correct usage: filecopy source target')
else :
    source = sys.argv[1]
    target = sys.argv[2]
    shutil.copyfile(source, target)
```

Parsing of Command-line

- While using the 'filecopy.py' program discussed above, the first filename is always treated as source and second as target. Instead of this, if we wish to have flexibility in supplying source and target filenames, we can use options at command-line as shown below:

  filecopy.py -s phone -t newphone
  filecopy -t newphone -s phone
  filecopy -h

  Now argument that follows **-s** would be treated as source filename and the one that follows **-t** would be treated as target filename. The option **-h** is for receiving help about the program.

- To permit this flexibility, we should use the **getopt** module to parse the command-line.

```
# filecopy.py
import sys, getopt
```

```
import shutil
if len(sys.argv) == 1 :
    print('Incorrect usage')
    print('Correct usage: filecopy.py -s <source> -t <target>')
    sys.exit(1)

source = ''
target = ''
try :
    options, arguments = getopt.getopt(sys.argv[1:],'hs:t:')
except getopt.GetoptError :
    print('filecopy.py -s <source> -t <target>')
else :
    for opt, arg in options :
        if opt == '-h' :
            print('filecopy.py -s <source> -t <target>')
            sys.exit(2)
        elif opt == '-s' :
            source = arg
        elif opt == '-t' :
            target = arg
    else :
        print('source file: ', source)
        print('target file: ', target)
        if source and target :
            shutil.copyfile(source, target)
```

- **sys.argv[1:]** returns the command-line except the name of the program, i.e. **filecopy.py.**
- Command line and the valid options are passed to **getopt( )**. In our case the valid options are **-s**, **-t** and **-h**. If an option has an argument it is indicated using the **:** after the argument, as in **s:** and **t:**. **-h** option has no argument.
- The **getopt( )** method parses **sys.argv[1:]** and returns two lists—a list of (option, argument) pairs and a list of non-option arguments.
- Some examples of contents of these two lists are given below:

  Example 1:

  filecopy.py -s phone -t newphone

options would be [('-s', 'phone'), ('-t', 'newphone')]
arguments would be [ ]

Example 2:

filecopy.py -h

options would be [('-h', ' ')]
arguments would be [ ]

Example 3:

filecopy.py -s phone -t newphone word1 word2

options would be [('-s', 'phone'), ('-t', 'newphone')]
arguments would be ['word1', 'word2']

- Note that non-option arguments like **word1**, **word2** must always follow option arguments like **-s**, **-t**, **-h**, otherwise they too would be treated as non-option arguments.
- **sys.exit( )** terminates the execution of the program.
- IDLE has no GUI-based provision to provide command-line arguments. So, at command prompt you have to execute program as follows:

  C:\>idle.py -r filecopy.py -s phone -t newphone

  Here **-r** indicates that when IDLE is launched it should run the script following **-r**.
- When we are experimenting with **getopt( )** function, frequently going to command-prompt to execute the script becomes tedious. Instead you can set up **sys.argv[ ]** at the beginning of the program as shown below:

  sys.argv = ['filecopy.py', '-s', 'phone', '-t', 'newphone']

Bitwise Operators

- Bitwise operators permit us to work with individual bits of a byte. There are many bitwise operators available:

  ~ - not (also called complement operator)
  << - left shift, >> - right shift
  & - and, | - or, ^ - xor
- Bitwise operators' usage:

```
ch = 32
dh = ~ch          # toggles 0s to1s and 1s to 0s
eh = ch << 3      # << shifts bits in ch 3 positions to left
fh = ch >> 2      # >> shifts bits in ch 2 positions to right
a = 45 & 32       # and bits of 45 and 32
b = 45 | 32       # or bits of 45 and 32
c = 45 ^ 32       # xor bits of 45 and 32
```

- Remember:

  Anything ANDed with 0 is 0.
  Anything ORed with 1 is 1.
  1 XORed with 1 is 0.
  << - As bits are shifted from left, zeros are pushed from right.
  >> - As bits are shifted from right, left-most bit is copied from left.

- Purpose of each bitwise operator is given below:

  ~ - Convert 0 to 1 and 1 to 0
  << >> - Shift out desired number of bits from left or right
  & - Check whether a bit is on / off. Put off a particular bit
  | - Put on a particular bit
  ^ - Toggle a bit

- Bitwise in-place operators: <<= >>= &= |= ^=

  a = a << 5 is same as **a <<= 5**
  b = b & 2 is same as **b &= 2**

- Except ~ all other bitwise operators are binary operators.

Assertion

- An assertion allows you to express programmatically your assumption about the data at a particular point in execution.

- Assertions perform **run-time checks** of assumptions that you would have otherwise put in code comments.

```
# denominator should be non-zero, i.e., numlist must not be empty
avg = sum(numlist) / len(numlist)
```

Instead of this, a safer way to code will be:

```
assert len(numlist) != 0
```

```
avg = sum(numlist) / len(numlist)
```

If the condition following **assert** is true, the program proceeds to the next instruction. If it turns out to be false, then an **AssertionError** exception occurs.

- Assertion may also be followed by a relevant message, which will be displayed if the condition fails.

```
assert len(numlist) != 0, 'Check denominator, it appears to be 0'
avg = sum(numlist) / len(numlist)
```

- Benefits of Assertions:
    - Over a period of time comments may get out-of-date. Same will not be the case with assert, because if they do, then they will fail for legitimate cases, and you will be forced to update them.
    - Assert statements are very useful while debugging a program as it halts the program at the point where an error occurs. This makes sense as there is no point in continuing the execution if the assumption is no longer true.
    - With assert statements, failures appear earlier and closer to the locations of the errors, which makes it easier to diagnose and fix them.

Decorators

- Functions are 'first-class citizens' of Python. This means like integers, strings, lists, modules, etc. functions too can be created and destroyed dynamically, passed to other functions and returned as values.
- First class citizenship feature is used in developing decorators.
- A decorator function receives a function, adds some functionality (decoration) to it and returns it.
- There are many decorators available in the library. These include the decorator **@abstractmethod** that we used in Chapter 20.
- Other commonly used library decorators are **@classmethod**, **@staticmethod** and **@property**. **@classmethod** and **@staticmethod** decorators are used to define methods inside a class namespace

that are not connected to a particular instance of that class. The **@property** decorator is used to customize getters and setters for class attributes.

- We can also create user-defined decorators, as shown in the following program:

```
def my_decorator(func) :
    def wrapper( ) :
        print('*****************')
        func( )
        print('~~~~~~~~~~~~~~~~~~')
    return wrapper

def display( ) :
    print('I stand decorated')

def show( ) :
    print('Nothing great. Me too!')

display = my_decorator(display)
display( )
show = my_decorator(show)
show( )
```

On executing the program, we get the following output.

```
*****************
I stand decorated
~~~~~~~~~~~~~~~~~~
*****************
Nothing great. Me too!
~~~~~~~~~~~~~~~~~~
```

- Here **display( )** and **show( )** are normal functions. Both these functions have been decorated by a decorator function called **my_decorator( )**. The decorator function has an inner function called **wrapper( )**.

- Name of a function merely contains address of the function object. Hence, in the statement

  display = my_decorator(display)

we are passing address of function **display( )** to **my_decorator( )**. **my_decorator( )** collects it in **func**, and returns address of the inner function **wrapper( )**. We are collecting this address back in **display**.

- When we call **display( )**, in reality **wrapper( )** gets called. Since it is an inner function, it has access to variable **func** of the outer function. It uses the address stored in **func** to call the function **display( )**. It prints a pattern before and after this call.

- Once a decorator has been created, it can be applied to multiple functions. In addition to **display( )**, we have also applied it to **show( )** function.

- The syntax of decorating **display( )** is complex for two reasons. Firstly, we must use the word display thrice. Secondly, the decoration gets hidden away below the definition of the function.

- To solve both the problems, Python permits usage of @ symbol to decorate a function as shown below:

```
def my_decorator(func) :
    def wrapper( ) :
        print('*****************')
        func( )
        print('~~~~~~~~~~~~~~~~~~')
    return wrapper
@my_decorator
def display( ) :
    print('I stand decorated')
@my_decorator
def show( ) :
    print('Nothing great. Me too!')

display( )
show( )
```

Decorating Functions with Arguments

- Suppose we wish to define a decorator that can report the time required for executing any function. We want a common decorator which will work for any function regardless of number and type of arguments that it receives and returns.

```
import time
```

```
def timer(func) :
    def calculate(*args, **kwargs) :
        start_time = time.perf_counter( )
        value = func(*args, **kwargs)
        end_time = time.perf_counter( )
        runtime = end_time - start_time
        print(f'Finished {func.__name__!r} in {runtime:.8f} secs')
        return value
    return calculate

@timer
def product(num) :
    fact = 1
    for i in range(num) :
        fact = fact * i + 1
    return fact

@timer
def product_and_sum(num) :
    p = 1
    for i in range(num) :
        p = p * i + 1
    s = 0
    for i in range(num) :
        s = s + i + 1
    return (p, s)

@timer
def time_pass(num) :
    for i in range(num) :
        i += 1

p = product(10)
print('product of first 10 numbers =', p)
p = product(20)
print('product of first 20 numbers =', p)
fs = product_and_sum(10)
print('product and sum of first 10 numbers =', fs)
fs = product_and_sum(20)
print('product and sum of first 20 numbers =', fs)
time_pass(20)
```

Here is the output of the program...

```
Finished 'product' in 0.00000770 secs
product of first 10 numbers = 986410
Finished 'product' in 0.00001240 secs
product of first 20 numbers = 330665665962404000
Finished 'product_and_sum' in 0.00001583 secs
product and sum of first 10 numbers = (986410, 55)
Finished 'product_and_sum' in 0.00001968 secs
product and sum of first 20 numbers = (330665665962404000, 210)
Finished 'time_pass' in 0.00000813 secs
```

- We have determined the execution time of three functions—**product( )**, **product_and_sum( )** and **time_pass( )**. Each varies in arguments and return type. We are still able to apply the same decorator **@timer** to all of them.
- The arguments passed while calling the three functions are received in ***args** and ****kwargs**. This takes care of any number of positional arguments and any number of keyword arguments that are needed by the function. They are then passed to the suitable functions through the call

  value = func(*args, **kwargs)
- The value(s) returned by the function being called is/are collected in **value** and returned.
- Rather than finding the difference between the start and end time of a function in terms of seconds, a performance counter is used.
- **time.perf_counter( )** returns the value of a performance counter, i.e. a clock in fractional seconds. The difference between two consecutive calls to this function determines the time required for executing a function.
- On similar lines we can define decorators for methods in a class.

Unicode

- Unicode is a standard for representation, encoding, and handling of text expressed in all scripts of the world.
- It is a myth that every character in Unicode is 2 bytes long. Unicode has already gone beyond 65536 characters—the maximum number of characters that can be represented using 2 bytes.

- In Unicode every character is assigned an integer value called code point, which is usually expressed in Hexadecimal.
- Code points for A, B, C, D, E are 0041, 0042, 0043, 0044, 0045. Code points for characters **अ आ इ ई उ** of Devanagari script are 0905, 0906, 0907, 0908, 0909.
- Computers understand only bytes. So, we need a way to represent Unicode code points as bytes to store or transmit them. Unicode standard defines several ways to represent code points as bytes. These are called encodings.
- There are different encoding schemes like UTF-8, UTF-16, ASCII, 8859-1, Windows 1252, etc. UTF-8 is perhaps the most popular encoding scheme.
- The same Unicode code point will be interpreted differently by different encoding schemes.
- Code point 0041 maps to byte value 41 in UTF-8, whereas it maps to byte values ff fe 00 in UTF-16. Similarly, code point 0905 maps to byte values e0 a4 85 and ff fe 05 \t in UTF-8 and UTF-16 respectively. You may refer table available at https://en.wikipedia.org/wiki/UTF-8 for one-to-one mapping of code points to byte values.
- UTF-8 uses a variable number of bytes for each code point. Higher the code point value, more the bytes it needs in UTF-8.

bytes Datatype

- In Python text is always represented as Unicode characters and is represented by **str** type, whereas binary data is represented by **bytes** type. You can create a **bytes** literal with a prefix **b**.

```
s = 'Hi'
print(type(s))
print(type('Hello'))

by = b'\xe0\xa4\x85'
print(type(by))
print(type(b'\xee\x84\x65'))
```

will output

```
<class 'str'>
```

```
<class 'str'>
<class 'bytes'>
<class 'bytes'>
```

- We cannot mix **str** and **bytes** in concatenation, in checking whether one is embedded inside another, or while passing one to a function that expects the other.
- Strings can be encoded to bytes, and bytes can be decoded back to strings as shown below:

```
eng = 'A B C D'
dev = 'अ आ  इ ई'
print(type(eng))
print(type(dev))
print(eng)
print(dev)
print (eng.encode('utf-8') )
print (eng.encode('utf-16') )
print (dev.encode('utf-8') )
print (dev.encode('utf-16') )
print(b'A B C D'.decode('utf-8'))
print(b'\xff\xfeA\x00 \x00B\x00 \x00C\x00 \x00D\x00'
    .decode('utf-16'))
print(b'\xe0\xa4\x85 \xe0\xa4\x86 \xe0\xa4\x87\xe0\xa4\x88'
    .decode('utf-8'))
print(b'\xff\xfe\x05\t \x00\x06\t \x00\x07\t \x00\x08\t'
    .decode('utf-16'))
```

Execution of this program produces the following output:

```
<class 'str'>
<class 'str'>
अ आ  इ ई
A B C D
b'A B C D'
b'\xff\xfeA\x00 \x00B\x00 \x00C\x00 \x00D\x00'
b'\xe0\xa4\x85 \xe0\xa4\x86 \xe0\xa4\x87 \xe0\xa4\x88'
b'\xff\xfe\x05\t \x00\x06\t \x00\x07\t \x00\x08\t'
A B C D
```

```
A B C D
अ आ  इ ई
अ आ  इ ई
```

- How these Unicode code points will be interpreted by your machine or your software depends upon the encoding scheme used. If we do not specify the encoding scheme, then the default encoding scheme set on your machine will be used.

- We can find out the default encoding scheme by printing the value present in **sys.stdin.encoding**. On my machine it is set to UTF-8.

- So, when we print **eng** or **dev** strings, the code points present in the strings are mapped to UTF-8 byte values and characters corresponding to these byte values are printed.

Create Executable File

- If we are developing a program for a client, rather than giving the source code of our program, we would prefer to given an executable version of it. The steps involved in creating the executable file are given below:

- Step 1: Install the Pyinstaller Package

  In the Windows Command Prompt, type the following command to install the pyinstaller package (and then press Enter):

  C:\Users\Kanetkar>pip install pyinstaller

- Step 2: Go to folder where the Python script is stored.

  C:\Users\Kanetkar>CD Programs

- Step 3: Create the Executable using Pyinstaller

  C:\Users\Kanetkar\Programs>pyinstaller --onefile ScriptName.py

- Step 4: Executable file pythonScriptName.exe will be created in 'dist' folder. Double-click the EXE file to execute it.

P</> Programs

Problem 25.1

Write a program that displays all files in the current directory. It can receive options **-h** or **-l** or **-w** from command-line. If **-h** is received display help about the program. If **-l** is received, display files one line at a time. If **-w** is received, display files separated by tab character.

Program

```
# mydir.py
import os, sys, getopt

if len(sys.argv) == 1 :
    print(os.listdir('.'))
    sys.exit(1)

try :
    options, arguments = getopt.getopt(sys.argv[1:],'hlw')
    print(options)
    print(arguments)
    for opt, arg in options :
        print(opt)
        if opt == '-h':
            print('mydir.py -h -l -w')
            sys.exit(2)
        elif opt == '-l' :
            lst = os.listdir('.')
            print(*lst, sep = '\n')
        elif opt == '-w' :
            lst = os.listdir('.')
            print(*lst, sep = '\t')
except getopt.GetoptError :
    print('mydir.py -h -l -w')
```

Output

```
C:\>mydir -l
data
messages
```

```
mydir
nbproject
numbers
numbersbin
numberstxt
sampledata
src
```

Problem 25.2

Define a function **show_bits( )** which displays the binary equivalent of the integer passed to it. Call it to display binary equivalent of 45.

Program

```
def show_bits(n) :
    for i in range(32, -1, -1) :
        andmask = 1 << i
        k = n & andmask
        print('0', end = '') if k == 0 else print('1', end = '')

show_bits(45)
print( )
print(bin(45))
```

Output

```
000000000000000000000000000101101
0b101101
```

Tips

- **show_bits( )** performs a bitwise and operation with individual bits of 45, and prints a 1 or 0 based on the value of the individual bit.

Problem 25.3

Windows stores the date of creation of a file as a 2-byte number with the following bit distribution:

left-most 7 bits: year - 1980

middle 4 bits - month
right-most 5 bits - day

Write a program that converts 9766 into a date 6/1/1999.

Program

```
dt = 9766
y = (dt >> 9) + 1980
m = (dt & 0b111100000) >> 5
d = (dt & 0b11111)
print(str(d) + '/' + str(m) + '/' + str(y))
```

Output

```
6/1/1999
```

Tips

- Number preceded by 0b is treated as a binary number.

Problem 25.4

Windows stores the time of creation of a file as a 2-byte number. Distribution of different bits which account for hours, minutes and seconds is as follows:

left-most 5 bits - hours
middle 6 bits - minutes
right-most 5 bits - seconds / 2

Write a program to convert the time represented by a number 26031 into 12:45:30.

Program

```
tm = 26031
hr = tm >> 11
min = (tm & 0b11111100000) >> 5
sec = (tm & 0b11111) * 2
print(str(hr) + ':' + str(min) + ':' + str(sec))
```

Output

```
12:45:30
```

Problem 25.5

Write assert statements for the following with suitable messages:

- Salary multiplier **sm** must be non-zero
- Both **p** and **q** are of same type
- Value present in **num** is part of the list **lst**
- Length of combined string is 45 characters
- Gross salary is in the range 30,000 to 45,000

Program

```
# Salary multiplier m must be non-zero
sm = 45
assert sm != 0, 'Oops, salary multiplier is 0'

# Both p and q are of type Sample
class Sample :
    pass

class NewSample :
    pass

p = Sample( )
q = NewSample( )
assert type(p) == type(q), 'Type mismatch'

# Value present in num is part of the list lst
num = 45
lst = [10, 20, 30, 40, 50]
assert num in lst, 'num is missing from lst'

# Length of combined string is less than 45 characters
s1 = 'A successful marriage requires falling in love many times...'
s2 = 'Always with the same person!'
s = s1 + s2
assert len(s) <= 45, 'String s is too long'
```

```
# Gross salary is in the range 30,000 to 45,000
gs = 30000 + 20000 * 15 / 100 + 20000 * 12 / 100
assert gs >= 30000 and gs <= 45000, 'Gross salary out of range'
```

Problem 25.6

Define a decorator that will decorate any function such that it prepends a call with a message indicating that the function is being called and follows the call with a message indicating that the function has been called. Also, report the name of the function being called, its arguments and its return value. A sample output is given below:

Calling sum_num ((10, 20), { })
Called sum_num ((10, 20), { }) got return value: 30

Program

```
def calldecorator(func) :
    def _decorated(*arg, **kwargs) :
        print(f'Calling {func.__name__} ({arg},  {kwargs})')
        ret = func(*arg, **kwargs)
        print(f'Called {func.__name__} ({arg}, {kwargs}) got ret val: {ret}')
        return ret

    return _decorated

@calldecorator
def sum_num(arg1,arg2) :
    return arg1 + arg2

@calldecorator
def prod_num(arg1,arg2) :
    return arg1 * arg2
@calldecorator
def message(msg) :
    pass

sum_num(10, 20)
prod_num(10, 20)
message('Errors should never pass silently')
```

Output

```
Calling sum_num ((10, 20), { })
Called sum_num ((10, 20), { }) got return value: 30
Calling prod_num ((10, 20), { })
Called prod_num ((10, 20), { }) got return value: 200
Calling message (('Errors should never pass silently',), { })
Called message (('Errors should never pass silently',), { }) got return value: None
```

Exercises

[A] State whether the following statements are True or False:

(a) We can send arguments at command-line to any Python program.

(b) The zeroth element of **sys.argv** is always the name of the file being executed.

(c) In Python a function is treated as an object.

(d) A function can be passed to a function and can be returned from a function.

(e) A decorator adds some features to an existing function.

(f) Once a decorator has been created, it can be applied to only one function within the program.

(g) It is mandatory that the function being decorated should not receive any arguments.

(h) It is mandatory that the function being decorated should not return any value.

(i) Type of 'Good!' is bytes.

(j) Type of **msg** in the statement **msg = 'Good!'** is **str**.

[B] Answer the following questions:

(a) Is it necessary to mention the docstring for a function immediately below the **def** statement?

(b) Write a program using command-line arguments to search for a word in a file and replace it with the specified word. The usage of the program is shown below.

C:\> change -o oldword -n newword -f filename

(c) Write a program that can be used at command prompt as a calculating utility. The usage of the program is shown below.

C:\> calc <switch> <n> <m>

Where, **n** and **m** are two integer operands. **switch** can be any arithmetic operator. The output should be the result of the operation.

(d) Rewrite the following expressions using bitwise in-place operators:

```
a = a | 3       a = a & 0x48       b = b ^ 0x22
c = c << 2      d = d >> 4
```

(e) Consider an unsigned integer in which the rightmost bit is numbered as 0. Write a function **checkbits(x, p, n)** which returns True if all 'n' bits starting from position 'p' are on, False otherwise. For example, **checkbits(x, 4, 3)** will return true if bits 4, 3 and 2 are 1 in number **x**.

(f) Write a program to receive a number as input and check whether its 3rd, 6th and 7th bit is on.

(g) Write a program to receive an 8-bit number into a variable and then exchange its higher 4 bits with lower 4 bits.

(h) Write a program to receive an 8-bit number into a variable and then set its odd bits to 1.

26 Concurrency and Parallelism

"Efficient is better..."

Contents

KanNotes

Concurrency and Parallelism

- A task is an activity that we carry out. For example, driving a car, watering a plant, cooking food, etc. are all tasks.
- Though the words concurrency and parallelism indicate the happening of two or more tasks at the same time, they are not the same.
- When we perform multiple tasks *intermittently,* we are doing them *concurrently*. At any given moment only one task is being done.
- When we perform tasks *simultaneously,* we are doing them *parallelly*. At any given moment all tasks are being done.
- Example 1 of concurrency: We watch TV, read a newspaper, check the mobile phone intermittently. At any given moment we are doing only one task.
- Example 2 of concurrency: If we are editing two documents in Notepad and Excel then we are doing the two tasks intermittently.
- Example 1 of parallelism: While driving a car we carry out several activities in parallel—we listen to music, we drive the car, and we talk to the co-passengers.
- Example 2 of parallelism: If we are loading 5 pages in different tabs of a browser, all the pages are fetched from the web server in parallel.

What are Threads?

- A program may have several logical units (parts). Each unit of execution is called a thread.
- Example 1 of multiple threads: One unit of execution may carry out copying of files, whereas another unit may display a progress bar.
- Example 2 of multiple threads: One unit of execution may download images, whereas another unit may display text.
- Example 3 of multiple threads: One unit may let you edit a document, second unit may check spellings, third unit may check grammar, and fourth unit may do printing.

- Example 4 of multiple threads: One unit may scan disk for viruses, second unit may scan memory for viruses and third unit may let you interact with the program's user-interface to stop/pause the scanning of viruses by first two units.

Concurrency and Parallelism in Programming

- **Concurrency** is when multiple threads of a program start, run, and complete in *overlapping* time periods.
- Once the program execution begins, one thread may run for some time, then it may stop, and the second thread may start running. After some time, the second thread may stop and the third may start running.
- Threads may get executed in a round-robin fashion or based on priority of each thread. At any given instance only one thread is running.
- **Parallelism** is when multiple threads of a program literally run *at the same time*. So, at any given instance multiple threads are running.
- In concurrency multiple units of a program can run on a single-core processor, whereas, in parallelism multiple units can run on multiple cores of a multi-core processor.
- Figure 25.1 shows working how threads t1, t2 and t3 in a program may run concurrently or in parallel over a period of time.

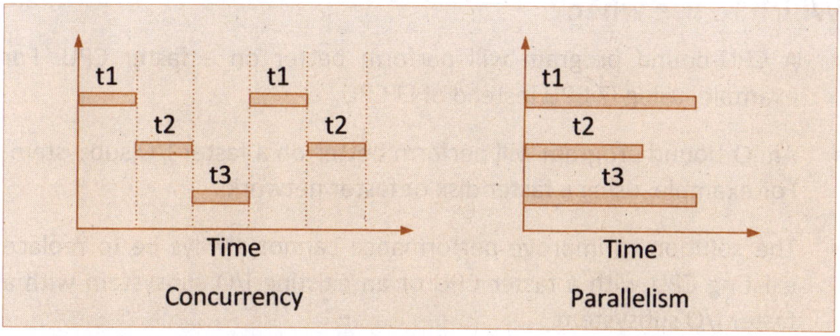

Figure 25.1. Concurrency and Parallelism.

- Advantages of Concurrency:
    - Improves application's speed, by making CPU do other things instead of waiting for slow I/O operations to finish.

  - Simplifies program design. For example, the logic that copies files and logic that displays the progress bar can be kept separate.

- Advantage of Parallelism:
  - The capability of multi-core processors can be exploited by running different processes in each processor simultaneously.

CPU-bound and I/O-bound Programs

- A program typically performs two types of operations:
  - Operations involving CPU for calculations, comparisons, etc.
  - Operations that perform input or output

- Usually, CPU operations run several times faster than I/O operations.

- A program that predominantly performs CPU operations is called CPU-bound program. A program that predominantly performs I/O operations is called I/O-bound program.

- Example of CPU-bound program: A program that performs multiplication of matrices, or a program that finds sum of first 200 prime numbers.

- Example of I/O-bound program: A program that processes files on the disk, or a program that does database queries or sends a lot of data over a network.

Which to use when?

- A CPU-bound program will perform better on a faster CPU. For example, using i7 CPU instead of i3 CPU.

- An IO-bound program will perform better on a faster I/O subsystem. For example, using a faster disk or faster network.

- The solution to improve performance cannot always be to replace existing CPU with a faster CPU or an existing I/O subsystem with a faster I/O subsystem.

- Instead, we should organize our program to use concurrency or parallelism to improve performance.

- Performance of I/O-bound program can improve if different units of the program are executed intermittently.

- Performance of CPU-bound program can improve if different units of the program are executed in parallel on multiple cores of a processor.
- It is quite easy to imagine how performance of a CPU-bound program can improve with parallelism. Performance improvement of an I/O-bound program using concurrency is discussed in the next section.

Concurrency for Improving Performance

- Suppose we wish to write a program that finds squares and cubes of first 5000 natural numbers and prints them on the screen.
- We can write this program in two ways:
  - A single-threaded program - calculation of squares, calculation of cubes and printing are done in same thread.
  - A multi-threaded program - calculation of squares is done in one thread, calculation of cubes in second thread and printing in third thread.
- In the single-threaded program the CPU has to frequently wait for printing of square/cube (I/O operation) to get over before it can proceed to calculate square or cube of the next number. So, CPU remains under-utilized. This scenario is shown in Figure 25.2.

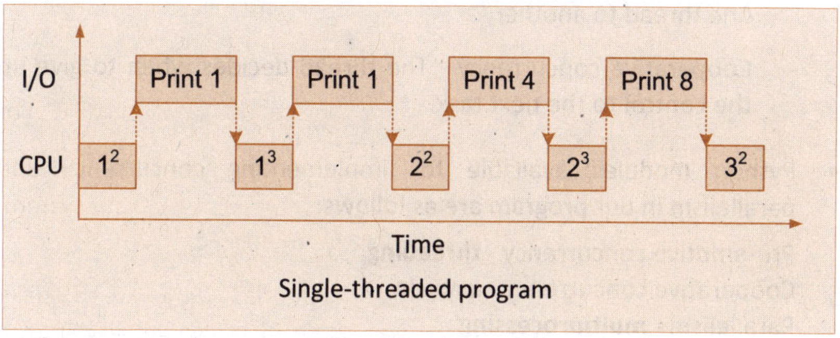

Figure 25.2 Working of Single-threaded program.

- In the multi-threaded program, the CPU can proceed with the next calculation (square or cube) and need not wait for the square or cube to get printed on the screen. This scenario is shown in Figure 25.3.

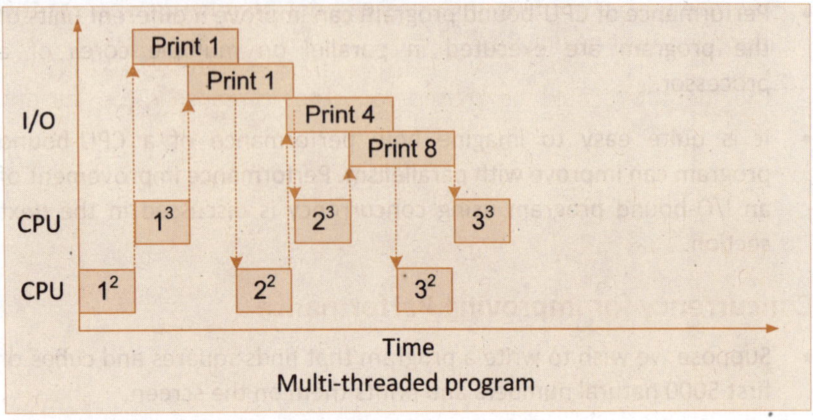

Figure 25.3. Working of Multi-threaded program.

Types of Concurrencies

- In a multi-threaded program one thread runs for some time, then it stops, and the second thread starts running. After some time, the second thread stops, and the third thread starts running. This is true even if the program is being executed on a multi-core processor.

- When context would switch from one thread to another depends on the type of concurrency that we use in our program.

- Concurrencies are of two types:
    - Pre-emptive concurrency - The OS decides when to switch from one thread to another.
    - Cooperative concurrency - The thread decides when to give up the control to the next task.

- Python modules available for implementing concurrency and parallelism in our program are as follows:

  Pre-emptive concurrency - **threading**
  Cooperative concurrency - **asyncio**
  Parallelism - **multiprocessing**

  This book discusses the technique for pre-emptive concurrency alone.

Thread Properties

- Every running thread has a name a number called thread identifier associated with it.

- The name of all running threads need not be unique, whereas the identifier must be unique.

- The identifier could be reused for other threads, if the current thread ends.

```
import threading
t = threading.current_thread( )   # returns current Thread object
print("Current thread:", t)  # prints thread name, identifier & status
print("Thread name:", t.name)
print("Thread identifier:", t.ident)
print("Is thread alive:", t.is_alive( ))
t.name = 'MyThread'
print("After name change:", t.name)
```

Here, **current_thread( )** is a function defined in **threading** module and **name** and **ident** are attributes of **Thread** object.

Launching Threads

- There are two ways to launch a new thread:
  - By passing the name of the function that should run as a separate thread, to the constructor of the **Thread** class.
  - By overriding **__init__( )** and **run( )** methods in a subclass of **Thread** class.

- Method 1 - thread creation

```
th1 = threading.Thread(name = 'My first thread', target = func1)
th2 = threading.Thread(target = func2)      # use default name
th1.start( )
th2.start( )
```

- Method 2 - thread creation

```
class SquareGeneratorThread(threading.Thread) :
    def __init__(self) :
        threading.Thread.__init__(self)

    def run(self) :
        print('Launching...')

th = SquareGeneratorThread( )
```

```
th.start( )
```

- Once a thread object is created, its activity must be started by calling the thread's **start( )** method. This method in turn invokes the **run( )** method.

- **start( )** method will raise an exception **RuntimeError** if called more than once on the same thread object.

Passing Parameters to a Thread

- Sometimes we may wish to pass some parameters to the target function of a thread object.

```
th1 = threading.Thread(target = squares, args = (a, b))
th2 = threading.Thread(target = cubes, args = (a,))
```

  Arguments being passed to the constructor of **Thread** class will ultimately be passed to the target function. Arguments must be in the form of a tuple.

- Once threads have been launched, we have no control over the order in which they are executed. It is controlled by the thread scheduler of the Python runtime environment.

- Sometimes we may wish to pass some parameters to the **run( )** method in the **thread** class. For this pass the parameters to the constructor while creating the thread object. The constructor should store them in object's variables. Once stored, **run( )** will be able to access them.

```
th = SquareGeneratorThread(a, b, c)
```

P</> Programs

Problem 26.1

Write a program that launches three threads, assigns new names to two of them. Suspend each thread for 1 second after it has been launched.

Program

```
import threading
```

```
import time

def fun1( ):
    t = threading.current_thread( )
    print('Starting', t.name)
    time.sleep(1)
    print('Exiting', t.name)

def fun2( ):
    t = threading.current_thread( )
    print('Starting', t.name)
    time.sleep(1)
    print('Exiting', t.name)

def fun3( ):
    t = threading.current_thread( )
    print('Starting', t.name)
    time.sleep(1)
    print('Exiting', t.name)

t1 = threading.Thread(target=fun1)  # use default name
t2 = threading.Thread(name = 'My second thread', target = fun2)
t3 = threading.Thread(name = 'My third thread', target = fun3)
t1.start( )
t2.start( )
t3.start( )
```

Output

```
Starting Thread-1
Starting My second thread
Starting My third thread
Exiting Thread-1
Exiting My third thread
Exiting My second thread
```

Tips

- **sleep( )** function of **time** module suspends execution of the calling thread for the number of seconds passed to it.

Problem 26.2

Write a program that calculates the squares and cubes of first 6 odd numbers through functions that are executed sequentially. Incorporate a delay of 0.5 seconds after calculation of each square/cube value. Report the time required for execution of the program.

Program

```
import time
import threading

def squares(nos) :
    print('Calculating squares...')
    for n in nos :
        time.sleep(0.5)
        print('n = ', n, ' square =', n * n)

def cubes(nos) :
    print('Calculating cubes...')
    for n in nos :
        time.sleep(0.5)
        print('n = ', n, ' cube =', n * n * n)

arr = [1, 3, 5, 7, 9, 11]
startTime = time.time( )
squares(arr)
cubes(arr)
endTime = time.time( )
print('Time required = ', endTime - startTime, 'sec')
```

Output

```
Calculating squares...
n = 1 square = 1
n = 3 square = 9
n = 5 square = 25
n = 7 square = 49
n = 9 square = 81
n = 11 square = 121
Calculating cubes...
n = 1 cube = 1
```

```
n =  3  cube = 27
n =  5  cube = 125
n =  7  cube = 343
n =  9  cube = 729
n =  11  cube = 1331
Time required =  6.000343322753906 sec
```

Tips

- The functions **squares( )** and **cubes( )** are running in the same thread.
- **time( )** function returns the time in seconds since the epoch (Jan 1, 1970, 00:00:00) as a floating point number.

Problem 26.3

Write a program that calculates squares and cubes of first 6 odd numbers through functions that are executed in two independent threads. Incorporate a delay of 0.5 seconds after calculation of each square/cube value. Report the time required for execution of the program.

Program

```
import time
import threading

def squares(nos) :
    print('Calculating squares...')
    for n in nos :
        time.sleep(0.5)
        print('n = ', n, ' square =', n * n)

def cubes(nos) :
    print('Calculating cubes...')
    for n in nos :
        time.sleep(0.5)
        print('n = ', n, ' cube =', n * n * n)

arr = [1, 3, 5, 7, 9, 11]
startTime = time.time( )
```

```
th1 = threading.Thread(target = squares, args = (arr,))
th2 = threading.Thread(target = cubes, args = (arr,))
th1.start( )
th2.start( )
th1.join( )
th2.join( )
endTime = time.time( )
print('Time required = ', endTime - startTime, 'sec')
```

Output

```
Calculating squares...
Calculating cubes...
n =  1  square = 1
n =  1  cube = 1
n =  3  square = 9
n =  3  cube = 27
n =  5  square = 25
n =  5  cube = 125
n =  7  square = 49
n =  7  cube = 343
n =  9  square = 81
n =  9  cube = 729
n =  11  square = 121
n =  11  cube = 1331
Time required =  3.001171588897705 sec
```

Tips

- **squares( )** and **cubes( )** are being launched in separate threads.
- Since **squares( )** and **cubes( )** need **arr**, it is passed to the constructor while launching the threads.
- Arguments meant for target functions must be passed as a tuple.
- **join( )** waits until the thread on which it is called terminates.
- If this program is executed on a single processor machine it will still work faster than the one in Problem 25.2. This is because when one thread is performing I/O, i.e., printing value of square/cube, the other thread can proceed with the calculation of cube/square.

- The output shows values of squares and cubes mixed. How to take care of it has been shown in Chapter 27.

Problem 26.4

Write a program that reads the contents of 3 files a.txt, b.txt and c.txt sequentially and reports the number of lines present in it as well as the total reading time. These files should be added to the project and filled with some text. The program should receive the file names as command-line arguments. Suspend the program for 0.5 seconds after reading a line from any file.

Program

```
import time, sys

startTime = time.time( )
lst = sys.argv
lst = lst[1:]

for file in lst:
    f = open(file, 'r')
    count = 0
    while True :
        data = f.readline( )
        time.sleep(0.5)
        if data == '' :
            break
        count = count + 1

    print('File:', file, 'Lines:', count)

endTime = time.time( )
print('Time required =', endTime - startTime, 'sec')
```

Output

```
File: a.txt Lines: 5
File: b.txt Lines: 24
File: c.txt Lines: 6
Time required = 19.009087324142456 sec
```

Tips

- If you are using IDLE then create three files a.txt, b.txt and c.txt these files in the same folder as the source file.
- If you are using NetBeans add files a.txt, b.txt and c.txt to the project as 'Empty' files by right-clicking the project in Project window in NetBeans. Once created, add some lines to each of these files.
- If you are using IDLE then provide command-line arguments as follows:

  c:\>idle -r SingleThreading.py a.txt b.txt c.txt

  Ensure that the path of idle batch file given below is added to PATH environment variable through Control Panel:

  C:\Users\Kanetkar\AppData\Local\Programs\Python\Python36-32\Lib\idlelib
- If you are using NetBeans, to provide a.txt, b.txt and c.txt as command-line arguments, right-click the project in Project window in NetBeans and select 'Properties' followed by 'Run'. Add 'a.txt b.txt c.txt' as 'Application Arguments'.
- Application arguments become available through **sys.argv** as a list. This list also includes application name as the 0th element in the list. So we have sliced the list to eliminate it.
- File is opened for reading using **open( )** and file is read line by line in a loop using **readline( )**.

Problem 26.5

Write a program that reads the contents of 3 files a.txt, b.txt and c.txt in different threads and reports the number of lines present in it as well as the total reading time. These files should be added to the project and filled with some text. The program should receive the file names as command-line arguments. Suspend the program for 0.5 seconds after reading a line from any file.

Program

```
import time
```

```
import sys
import threading

def readFile(inputFile):
    f = open(inputFile, 'r')
    count = 0
    while True :
        data = f.readline( )
        time.sleep(0.5)
        if data == '' :
            break
        count = count + 1

    print('File:', inputFile, 'Lines:', count)

startTime = time.time( )
lst = sys.argv
lst = lst[1:]

tharr = [ ]
for file in lst:
    th = threading.Thread(target = readFile, args = (file,))
    th.start( )
    tharr.append(th)

for th in tharr:
    th.join( )

endTime = time.time( )
print('Time required = ', endTime - startTime, 'sec')
```

Output

```
File: a.txt Lines: 5
File: c.txt Lines: 6
File: b.txt Lines: 24
Time required = 12.504715204238892 sec
```

Tips

- For details of adding files to the project, making them available to application as command-line arguments and slicing the command-line argument list refer tips in Problem 25.4.

- As each thread is launched, the thread object is added to the thread array through **tharr.append( )**. This is necessary, so that we can later call **join( )** on each thread.
- This program performs better than the one in Problem 25.4 because as one thread is busy printing the file statistics, the other thread can continue reading a file.

Exercises

[A] State whether the following statements are True or False:

(a) Multi-threading improves the speed of execution of the program.

(b) A running task may have several threads running in it.

(c) Multi-processing is the same as multi-threading.

(d) If we create a class that inherits from the **Thread** class, we can still inherit our class from some other class.

(e) It is possible to change the name of the running thread.

(f) To launch a thread, we must explicitly call the function that is supposed to run in a separate thread.

(g) To launch a thread we must explicitly call the **run( )** method defined in a class that extends the **Thread** class.

(h) Though we do not explicitly call the function that is supposed to run in a separate thread, it is possible to pass arguments to the function.

(i) We cannot control the priority of multiple threads that we may launch in a program.

[B] Answer the following questions:

(a) What is the difference between multi-processing and multi-threading?

(b) What is the difference between preemptive multi-threading and cooperative multi-threading?

(c) Which are the two methods available for launching threads in a Python program?

(d) If **Ex** class extends the **Thread** class, then can we launch multiple threads for objects of **Ex** class? If yes, how?

(e) What do different elements of the following statement signify?

th1 = threading.Thread(target = quads, args = (a, b))

(f) Write a multithreaded program that copies contents of one folder into another. The source and target folder paths should be input through keyboard.

(g) Write a program that reads the contents of 3 files a.txt, b.txt and c.txt sequentially and converts their contents into uppercase and writes them into files aa.txt, bb.txt and cc.txt respectively. The program should report the time required in carrying out this conversion. The files a.txt, b.txt and c.txt should be added to the project and filled with some text. The program should receive the file names as command-line arguments. Suspend the program for 0.5 seconds after reading a line from any file.

(h) Write a program that accomplishes the same task mentioned in Exercise [B](g) above by launching the conversion operations in 3 different threads.

[C] Match the following pairs:

a. Multiprocessing	1. use multiprocessing module
b. Pre-emptive multi-threading	2. use multi-threading
c. Cooperative multi-threading	3. use threading module
d. CPU-bound programs	4. use multi-processing
e. I/O-bound programs	5. use asyncio module

27 Synchronization

"Well-oiled threads run smoother..."

Contents

KanNotes

Synchronization

- In a multithreaded application we may need to coordinate (synchronize) the activities of the threads running in it.
- The need to coordinate activities of threads will arise in two situations:
  (a) When data or other resources are to be shared amongst threads.
  (b) When we need to carry out communication between threads.

Examples of Sharing Resources

- **Example 1**: Suppose a function has a statement **n = n + 1**. Here value of **n** is read, 1 is added to it and the result is written back. If multiple threads call this function, then **n** will be shared amongst these threads. In such a case, if one thread has read **n** and before it is able to update **n**, another thread may read and update **n**. Such overlapping accesses and modifications from multiple threads may not increment **n** systematically.
- **Solution to Example 1**: To ensure proper incrementation of **n**, we should ensure that whichever thread gets the timeslot first should complete its working with **n**. In the meanwhile, if another thread that wishes to work with **n** gets the timeslot, it should be made to wait. Only when the first thread is done, the other thread should be able to access **n**.
- **Example 2**: Suppose there are two threads in an application. One thread reads a list of numbers and prints its squares and another thread reads the list and prints cubes of numbers in it. So, both threads are going to share the list. When the two threads print the squares and cubes, the output is likely to get mixed up.
- **Solution to Example 2**: To avoid mixing output we should ensure that whichever thread gets the timeslot first should complete working with the list. In the meanwhile, if other thread gets the timeslot, it should be made to wait. Only when the first thread is done, the other thread should be able to access the list.

Example of Communication between Threads

- Suppose one thread is generating numbers in an infinite loop and another thread is calculating squares of generated numbers. Unless the new number is generated its square cannot be calculated. So, if the squaring thread gets the time slot earlier than the generating thread, the squaring thread must be made to wait. Also, when square is being generated, new numbers should not get generated. This is necessary, otherwise the squaring thread may miss some numbers.

- This is a typical producer-consumer problem, where the number generating thread is the producer and the squaring thread is the consumer.

- Here communication between two threads would be required. When producer thread completes generation of number, it should communicate to the squaring thread that it is done with production. When consumer thread completes squaring, it should communicate to the producer thread that it is done, and then producer thread can produce the next number.

Mechanisms for Sharing Resources

- Python's **threading** module provides three mechanisms for sharing resources between threads:

  (a) Lock
  (b) RLock
  (c) Semaphore

- They should be used in the following situations:
  - For synchronized access to shared resources - use lock.
  - For nested access to shared resources - use re-entrant lock.
  - For permitting limited number of accesses to a resource - use semaphore.

Lock

- Locks are used to synchronize access to a shared resource. We should first create a **Lock** object. When we need to access the resource we should call **acquire( )**, then use the resource and once done, call **release( )** as shown below:

```
lck = threading.Lock( )
```

```
lck.acquire( )
# use the resource
lck.release( )
```

- A lock can be in two states—'Locked' or 'Unlocked'.
- A **Lock** object has two methods—**acquire( )** and **release( )**. **acquire( )** puts the lock in 'Locked' state, whereas, **release( )** puts it in 'Unlocked' state. When the **Lock** object is created the lock is in 'Unlocked' state.
- Suppose two threads are trying to access a resource (a resource is variable, file, anything else). Both threads follow the sequence acquire – use – release. While launching the two threads the same **Lock** object **lck** is used by them.

```
lck = threading.Lock( )
th1 = threading.Thread(target = fun1)
th2 = threading.Thread(target = fun2)
```

- If first thread calls **acquire( )** it puts the lock in 'Locked' state since it is currently in 'Unlocked' state and returns. So, the first thread can work with the shared resource. If in the meanwhile the second thread gets a time-slot, it will call **acquire( )**, and would be blocked—means control would not return from **acquire( )**.
- When the first thread is done with usage of the resource and calls **release( )**, it would put the lock in 'Unlocked' state. When the second thread which is currently blocked gets a timeslot it finds that the lock stands unlocked. So it will put the lock in 'Locked' state and return from **acquire( )** and start working with the shared resource. Once done, it will call **release( )** and put the lock in 'Unlocked' state.
- If one thread tries to calls **acquire( )** twice, the second call will block.

RLock

- Sometimes a recursive function may be invoked through multiple threads. In such cases, if we use **Lock** to provide synchronized access to shared variables it would lead to a problem—thread will be blocked when it attempts to acquire the same lock second time.
- This problem can be overcome by using a re-entrant Lock or **RLock.** A re-entrant lock only blocks if another thread currently holds the

lock. If the current thread tries to acquire a lock that it is already holding, execution continues as usual.

- A lock/rlock acquired by one thread can be released either by same thread or by another thread.
- **release( )** should be called as many times as **acquire( )** is called.
- Following code snippet shows working of normal lock and re-entrant lock.

```
lck = threading.Lock( )
lck.acquire( )
lck.acquire( )          # this will block

rlck = threading.RLock( )
rlck.acquire( )
rlck.acquire( )         # this won't block
```

- A lock/rlock is also known as mutex as it permits mutual exclusive access to a resource.

Semaphore

- If we wish to permit access to a resource like network connection or a database server to a limited number of threads, we can do so using a semaphore object.
- A semaphore object uses a counter rather than a lock flag. The counter can be set to indicate the number of threads that can acquire the semaphore before blocking occurs.
- Once the counter is set, the counter decreases per **acquire( )** call, and increases per **release( )** call. Blocking occurs only if more than the set number of threads attempt to acquire the semaphore.
- We have to only initialize the counter to the maximum number while creating the semaphore object, and the semaphore implementation takes care of the rest.

Mechanisms for Inter-thread Communication (ITC)

- Python's **threading** module provides two mechanisms for inter-thread communication:

  (a) Event

(b) Condition

Event

- An **Event** object is used to communicate between threads. It has an internal flag which threads can set or clear through methods **set( )** and **clear( )**.
- Typical working: If thread 1 calls the **wait( )** method, it will wait (block) if internal flag has not yet been set. Thread 2 will set the flag. Since the flag now stands set, Thread 1 will come out its wait state, perform its work and then clear the flag. This scenario is shown in the following program:

```
def fun1( ) :
    while True :
        # wait for the flag to be set
        ev.wait( )
        # once flag is set by thread 2, do the work in this thread
        ev.clear( ) # clear the flag

def fun2( ) :
    while True :
        # perform some work
        # set the flag
        ev.set( )

ev = Event( )
th1 = threading.Thread(target = fun1)
th2 = threading.Thread(target = fun2)
```

Condition

- A **Condition** object is an advanced version of the **Event** object. It too is used to communicate between threads. It has methods **acquire( )**, **release( )**, **wait( )**, **notify( )** and **notifyAll( )**.
- A **Condition** object internally uses a lock that can be acquired or released using **acquire( )** and **release( )** functions respectively. **acquire( )** blocks if the lock is already in locked state.
- **Condition** object can notify other threads using **notify( )/notifyAll( )** about a change in the state of the program.

- The **wait( )** method releases the lock, and then blocks until it is awakened by a **notify( )** or **notifyAll( )** call for the same **Condition** object in another thread. Once awakened, it re-acquires the lock and returns.
- A thread should release a **Condition** object once it has completed the related actions, so that other threads can acquire the **Condition** object for their purposes.
- Producer-Consumer algorithm is a technique for generating requests and processing the pending requests. Producer produces requests, Consumer consumes generated requests. Both Producer and Consumer work as independent threads.
- **Condition** object can be used to implement a Producer-Consumer algorithm as shown below:

```
# Producer thread
cond.acquire( )
# code here to produce one item
cond.notify( )
cond.release( )

# Consumer thread
cond.acquire( )
while item_is_not_available( ) :
    cond.wait( )
# code here to consume the item
cond.release( )
```

- Working of Producer-Consumer problem:
  - Consumer waits while Producer is producing.
  - Once Producer has produced it sends a signal to Consumer.
  - Producer waits while Consumer is consuming.
  - Once Consumer has consumed it sends a signal to Producer.

P</> Programs

Problem 27.1

Write a program through which you can prove that in this programming situation synchronization is really required. Then write a program to demonstrate how synchronization can solve the problem.

Program

```
import time
import threading

def fun1( ) :
    print('Entering fun1')
    global g
    g += 1
    #time.sleep(10)
    g -= 1
    print('In fun1 g =', g)
    print('Exiting fun1')

def fun2( ) :
    print('Entering fun2')
    global g
    g += 2
    g -= 2
    print('In fun2 g =', g)
    print('Exiting fun2')

g = 10
th1 = threading.Thread(target = fun1)
th2 = threading.Thread(target = fun2)
th1.start( )
th2.start( )
th1.join( )
th2.join( )
```

Output

```
Entering fun1
In fun1 g = 10
Exiting fun1
Entering fun2
In fun2 g = 10
Exiting fun2
```

If you uncomment the call to **time.sleep( )**, the output changes to:

```
Entering fun1
```

```
Entering fun2
In fun2 g = 11
Exiting fun2
In fun1 g = 10
Exiting fun1
```

Tips

- We are using the global variable **g** in **fun1( )** and **fun2( )** which are running in two different threads. As expected, both print the value of **g** as 10, as both increment and decrement it by 1 and 2 respectively.
- If you uncomment the call to **sleep( )** the output becomes inconsistent. **fun1( )** increments the value of **g** to 11, but before it can decrement the incremented value, **fun2( )** gets the time-slot, which increments **g** to 13, decrements it to 11 and prints it. The time-slot again goes to **fun1( )**, which decrements **g** to 10 and prints it.
- The solution to avoid this mismatch is given in the program shown below.

Program

```
import time
import threading

def fun1( ) :
    print('Entering fun1')
    global g
    lck.acquire( )
    g += 1
    g -= 1
    lck.release( )
    print('In fun1 g =', g)
    print('Exiting fun1')

def fun2( ) :
    print('Entering fun2')
    global g
    lck.acquire( )
    g += 2
```

```
    g -= 2
    lck.release( )
    print('In fun2 g =', g)
    print('Exiting fun2')

g = 10
lck = threading.Lock( )
th1 = threading.Thread(target = fun1)
th2 = threading.Thread(target = fun2)
th1.start( )
th2.start( )
th1.join( )
th2.join( )
```

Tips

- In the main thread we have created a **Lock** object through the call **threading.Lock( )**.
- If **fun1** thread gets the first time-slot, it calls **acquire( )**. This call puts the lock in 'Locked' state and returns. So **fun1** thread can work with **g**. If midway through, its time-slot expires and **fun2** thread gets it, it will also call **acquire( )**, but it will be blocked (control will not return from it) since lock is in 'Locked' state. In the next time-slot **fun1** thread finishes its work and releases the lock (puts the lock in 'Unlocked' state) by calling **release( )**. As a result, **fun2** thread can now work with **g** when it gets time-slot.

Problem 27.2

Write a program that calculates the squares and cubes of first 6 odd numbers through functions that are executed in two independent threads. Incorporate a delay of 0.5 seconds after calculation of each square/cube value. Report the time required for execution of the program. Make sure that the output of **squares( )** and **cubes( )** doesn't get mixed up.

Program

```
import time
import threading

def squares(nos, lck) :
```

```
    lck.acquire( )
    print('Calculating squares...')
    for n in nos :
        time.sleep(0.5)
        print('n = ', n, ' square =', n * n)
    lck.release( )

def cubes(nos, lck) :
    lck.acquire( )
    print('Calculating cubes...')
    for n in nos :
        time.sleep(0.5)
        print('n = ', n, ' cube =', n * n * n)
    lck.release( )

arr = [1, 3, 5, 7, 9, 11]
startTime = time.time( )
lck = threading.Lock( )

th1 = threading.Thread(target = squares, args = (arr, lck))
th2 = threading.Thread(target = cubes, args = (arr, lck))
th1.start( )
th2.start( )
th1.join( )
th2.join( )

endTime = time.time( )
print('Time required = ', endTime - startTime, 'sec')
```

Output

```
Calculating squares...
n =  1  square = 1
n =  3  square = 9
n =  5  square = 25
n =  7  square = 49
n =  9  square = 81
n =  11  square = 121
Calculating cubes...
n =  1  cube = 1
n =  3  cube = 27
n =  5  cube = 125
n =  7  cube = 343
```

```
n = 9 cube = 729
n = 11 cube = 1331
Time required = 6.001343250274658 sec
```

Tips

- To ensure that the output of **squares( )** doesn't get mixed up with output of **cubes( )** we should ensure that when one is working another should be put on hold.
- In main thread we have created a **Lock** object through the call **threading.Lock( )**. Along with the list, this **Lock** object is shared between **squares( )** and **cubes( )**.
- If **squares** thread gets the first time-slot, it calls **acquire( )**. This call puts the lock in the 'Locked' state and returns. So, **squares** thread can start generating and printing squares. If midway through its time-slot expires and **cubes** thread gets it, it will also call **acquire( )**, but it will be blocked (control will not return from it) since lock is in 'Locked' state. In the next time-slot **squares** thread finishes its work and releases the lock (puts the lock in 'Unlocked' state) by calling **release( )**. The **cubes** thread can now calculate and print cubes of numbers in the array.
- Similar reasoning would hold good if **cubes** thread gets the first timeslot.
- Suppose there were three threads **squares**, **cubes** and **quadruples** and **squares** thread acquires the lock. When it releases the lock which of the two waiting threads will proceed is not defined and may vary across Python implementations.

Problem 27.3

Write a program that prints the following 3 messages through 3 different threads:

[What is this life...]
[We have no time...]
[To stand and stare!]

Each thread should be passed the relevant message and should print '[', message and ']' through three different **print( )** calls.

Program

```
import time
import threading

def printMsg(msg, lck):
    lck.acquire( )
    print('[', end = '')
    print(msg, end = '')
    time.sleep(0.5)
    print(']')
    lck.release( )

lck = threading.Lock( )
th1 = threading.Thread(target = printMsg,
          args = ('What is this life...', lck))
th1.start( )
th2 = threading.Thread(target = printMsg,
          args = ('We have no time...', lck))
th2.start( )
th3 = threading.Thread(target = printMsg,
          args = ('To stand and stare!', lck))
th3.start( )

th1.join( )
th2.join( )
th3.join( )
```

Tips

- Three threads are created. In each thread the **printMsg( )** function is executed, but a different message is passed to it in each thread.
- To ensure that '[', message and ']' are printed in the same order in each thread, the activity of the threads is synchronized.
- When one thread acquires a lock, others are blocked until the thread that acquired the lock releases it.

Problem 27.4

Write a program that runs a recursive **print_num( )** function in 2 threads. This function should receive an integer and print all numbers from that number up to 1.

Program

```
import threading

def print_num(n) :
    rlck.acquire( )
    if n != 0 :
        t = threading.current_thread( )
        print(t.name, ':', n)
        n -= 1
        print_num(n)
    rlck.release( )

rlck = threading.RLock( )
th1 = threading.Thread(target = print_num, args = (8,))
th1.start( )
th2 = threading.Thread(target = print_num, args = (5,))
th2.start( )
th1.join( )
th2.join( )
```

Output

```
Thread-1 : 8
Thread-1 : 7
Thread-1 : 6
Thread-1 : 5
Thread-1 : 4
Thread-1 : 3
Thread-1 : 2
Thread-1 : 1
Thread-2 : 5
Thread-2 : 4
Thread-2 : 3
Thread-2 : 2
Thread-2 : 1
```

Tips

- Since we are sharing resources in a recursive function, we have used **RLock** instead of **Lock**.
- The lock gets acquired only when control lands into the function **print_num( )** for the first time. Since we are using **RLock,** the second and subsequent calls to **acquire( )** do not block. The lock gets released when control returns from **print_num( )** last time after completing all recursive calls.
- We have printed name of each thread along with the current value of **n** so that we get an idea of which thread are we working in.
- If we replace **RLock** with **Lock** we will get output from one thread only. This is because one thread will acquire the lock and do some printing. When it's time-slot expires and another thread gets it, it will also call **acquire( )** and would get blocked.
- If you do not use any lock, the output from the two threads will get mixed up.

Problem 27.5

Write a program that runs a recursive **factorial( )** function in 2 threads.

Program

```
import threading

def factorial(n):
    lck.acquire( )
    p = 0
    if n != 0 :
        t = threading.current_thread( )
        p = n * factorial(n - 1)
        print(t.name, ": ", n, '! = ', p)
    else:
        p = 1
    lck.release( )
    return p

lck = threading.RLock( )
th1 = threading.Thread(target=factorial, args = (4,))
```

```
th2 = threading.Thread(target=factorial, args = (6,))
th1.start( )
th2.start( )
th1.join( )
th2.join( )
```

Output

```
Thread-1 :  1! = 1
Thread-1 :  2! = 2
Thread-1 :  3! = 6
Thread-1 :  4! = 24
Thread-2 :  1! = 1
Thread-2 :  2! = 2
Thread-2 :  3! = 6
Thread-2 :  4! = 24
Thread-2 :  5! = 120
Thread-2 :  6! = 720
```

Tips

- Since we are sharing resources in a recursive function, we have used **RLock** instead of **Lock**.
- The lock gets acquired only when control lands into the function **factorial( )** for the first time. Since we are using **RLock,** the second and subsequent calls to **acquire( )** do not block. The lock gets released when control returns from **factorial( )** last time after completing all recursive calls.
- If we replace **RLock** with **Lock** we will get output from one thread only. This is because one thread will acquire the lock and do some calculation and printing. When its' time-slot expires and other thread gets it, it will also call **acquire( )** and would get blocked.
- If we do not use any lock, the output from the two threads will get mixed up.

Problem 27.6

Write a program that defines a function **fun( )** that prints a message that it receives infinite times. Limit the number of threads that can invoke **fun( )** to 3. If the 4th thread tries to invoke **fun( )**, it should not get invoked.

Program

```
import threading

def fun(msg) :
    s.acquire( )
    t = threading.current_thread( )
    while True :
        print(t.name, ':', msg)
    s.release( )

s = threading.BoundedSemaphore(3)
th1 = threading.Thread(target = fun, args = ('Hello',))
th2 = threading.Thread(target = fun, args = ('Hi',))
th3 = threading.Thread(target = fun, args = ('Welcome',))
th4 = threading.Thread(target = fun, args = ('ByeBye',))
th1.start( )
th2.start( )
th3.start( )
th4.start( )
th1.join( )
th2.join( )
th3.join( )
th4.join( )
```

Output

```
Thread-2 : Hi
Thread-1 : Hello
Thread-2 : Hi
Thread-1 : Hello
Thread-2 : Hi
Thread-3 : Welcome
Thread-1 : Hello
Thread-2 : Hi
Thread-3 : Welcome
```

```
Thread-3 : Welcome
Thread-3 : Welcome
...
```

Tips

- From the output it is evident that the 4th thread could not invoke **fun( )**.

Problem 27.7

Write a program that runs functions **fun1( )** and **fun2( )** in two different threads. Using an **event** object, function **fun1( )** should wait for **fun2( )** to signal it at random intervals that its wait is over. On receiving the signal, **fun1( )** should report the time and clear the event flag.

Program

```
import threading
import random
import time

def fun1(ev, n) :
    for i in range(n) :
        print(i + 1, 'Waiting for the flag to be set...')
        ev.wait( )
        print('Wait complete at:', time.ctime( ))
        ev.clear( )
        print( )

def fun2(ev, n):
    for i in range(n):
        time.sleep(random.randrange(2, 5))
        ev.set( )

ev = threading.Event( )
th = [ ]
num = random.randrange(4, 8)
th.append(threading.Thread(target = fun1, args = (ev, num)))
th[-1].start( )
th.append(threading.Thread(target = fun2, args = (ev, num)))
th[-1].start( )
for t in th :
```

```
    t.join( )
print('All done!!')
```

Output

```
1 Waiting for the flag to be set...
Wait complete at: Wed Apr 28 11:03:43 2021

2 Waiting for the flag to be set...
Wait complete at: Wed Apr 28 11:03:45 2021

3 Waiting for the flag to be set...
Wait complete at: Wed Apr 28 11:03:48 2021

4 Waiting for the flag to be set...
Wait complete at: Wed Apr 28 11:03:52 2021

5 Waiting for the flag to be set...
Wait complete at: Wed Apr 28 11:03:54 2021

All done!!
```

Tips

- Note how the thread array is maintained using the index value '-1' to refer to the last thread added to the array.

Problem 27.8

Write a program that implements a Producer - Consumer algorithm. The producer thread should generate random numbers in the range 10 to 20. The consumer thread should print the square of the random number produced by the producer thread.

Program

```
import threading
import random
import queue
import time

def producer( ) :
    for i in range(5) :
        time.sleep(random.randrange(2, 5))
```

```
        cond.acquire( )
        num = random.randrange(10, 20)
        print('Generated number =', num)
        q.append(num)
        cond.notify( )
        cond.release( )

def consumer( ) :
    for i in range(5) :
        cond.acquire( )
        while True:
            if len(q) :
                num = q.pop( )
                break
            cond.wait( )

        print('Its square =', num * num)
        cond.release( )

cond = threading.Condition( )
q = [ ]
th1 = threading.Thread(target = producer)
th2 = threading.Thread(target = consumer)
th1.start( )
th2.start( )
th1.join( )
th2.join( )
print('All done!!')
```

Output

```
Generated number = 14
Its square = 196
Generated number = 10
Its square = 100
Generated number = 13
Its square = 169
Generated number = 15
Its square = 225
Generated number = 10
Its square = 100
All done!!
```

Tips

- Examine the program for the following possibilities and satisfy yourself that it works as per expectation in all situations:

- Producer gets a timeslot before Consumer
- Producer gets timeslot when Consumer is consuming
- Producer finishes producing before its timeslot expires
- Consumer gets a timeslot after Producer
- Consumer finishes before its timeslot expires
- Consumer gets a timeslot before Producer
- Consumer gets timeslot when Producer is busy

Exercises

[A] State whether the following statements are True or False:

(a) All multi-threaded applications should use synchronization.

(b) If 3 threads are going to read from a shared list it is necessary to synchronize their activities.

(c) A **Lock** acquired by one thread can be released by either the same thread or any other thread running in the application.

(d) If **Lock** is used in reentrant code, then the thread is likely to get blocked during the second call.

(e) Lock and **RLock** work like a Mutex.

(f) A thread will wait on an **Event** object unless its internal flag is cleared.

(g) A **Condition** object internally uses a lock.

(h) While using **RLock** we must ensure that we call **release( )** as many times as the number of calls to **acquire( )**.

(i) Using **Lock**, we can control the maximum number of threads that can access a resource.

(j) There is no difference between the synchronization objects **Event** and **Condition**.

(k) If in a Python program one thread reads a document and another thread writes to the same document, then the two threads should be synchronized.

(l) If in a Python program one thread copies a document and another thread displays progress bar, then the two threads should be synchronized.

(m) If in a Python program one thread lets you type a document, and another thread performs spellcheck on the same document then the two threads should be synchronized.

(n) If in a Python program one thread can scan a document for viruses and another thread can pause or stop the scan, then the two threads should be synchronized.

[B] Answer the following questions:

(a) Which synchronization mechanisms are used for sharing resources amongst multiple threads?

(b) Which synchronization objects are used for inter-thread communication in a multi-threaded application?

(c) What is the difference between a **Lock** and **RLock**?

(d) What is the purpose of the **Semaphore** synchronization primitive?

(e) Write a program that has three threads in it. The first thread should produce random numbers in the range 1 to 20, the second thread should display the square of the number generated by the first thread on the screen, and the third thread should write cube of number generated by first thread into a file.

(f) Suppose one thread is producing numbers from **1** to **n** and another thread is printing the produced numbers. Comment on the output that we are likely to get.

(g) What will happen if thread **t1** waits for thread **t2** to finish and thread **t2** waits for **t1** to finish?

[C] Match the following pairs:

a. RLock	1. limits no. of threads accessing a resource
b. Event	2. useful in sharing resource in reentrant code
c. Semaphore	3. useful for inter-thread communication
d. Condition	4. signals waiting threads on change in state
e. Lock	5. useful in sharing resource among threads

28 Numpy Library

"Arrays of a mature kind..."

Contents

KanNotes

Numpy stands for Numerical Python. It is a popular library used for solving problems in science and engineering. It provides a high-performance multidimensional array object, and methods for fast operations on arrays. These operations include mathematical, logical, shape manipulation, sorting, selecting, I/O, statistical operations, etc.

Creation of Array

- To use Numpy library, it must be downloaded and installed as shown below:

  C:\Users\Kanetkar>pip install numpy

- Though Numpy array looks like Python lists, it is optimized to run faster than lists.
- Unlike lists, all elements of a Numpy array are of the same type.
- To create a Numpy array we have to use the **np.array( )** function and pass a list of numbers to it as shown below:

```
import numpy as np
intarr = np.array([1, 2, 3, 4])             # creates array of ints
floatarr = np.array([1.1, 2.2, 3.3, 4.4])   # creates array of floats
```

- If we mix ints and floats, Numpy defaults to an array of floats.
- While creating an array if we do not specify the type of elements in it, then from the values Numpy guesses the type. If we wish we can also specify the type.

```
intarr = np.array([1, 2, 3, 4], int)
floatarr = np.array([1.1, 2.2, 3.3, 4.4], float)
```

- 2D array (matrix) is a collection of several 1D arrays and 3D array is a collection of several 2D arrays. They can be created as shown below:

```
a1 = np.array([[1, 2, 3], [4, 5, 6]])                # 2 rows x 3 col
a2 = np.array([[[1, 2], [4, 5]], [[6, 7], [8, 9]]])  # 2, 2 x 2 arrays
```

- An array of complex numbers can also be created:

```
c = np.array( [[1, 2], [3, 4]], complex)
```

Creation of Filler Arrays

- We can create Numpy arrays which contain initial placeholder values, which can be replaced later.
- For example, we can create arrays which are filled with all 0s, all 1s or a fixed value. We can even create empty arrays which are filled with garbage values.

```
import numpy as np
a1 = np.empty((3, 4))         # creates 2D array with garbage values
a2 = np.zeros((3, 4))         # creates 2D array of zeros
a3 = np.ones((3, 4))          # create 2D array of ones
a4 = np.full((2, 2), 7)       # creates 2D array with all values set to 7
```

  Note that tuples need to be passed to these functions. The tuples (3, 4) and (2, 2) indicate the shape of the array that we wish to create.

- We can create arrays with random values or with evenly space values.

```
import numpy as np
a1 = np.random.random((4))    # creates array with 4 random val
a2 = np.arange(5)             # creates [0  1  2  3  4]
a2 = np.arange(0, 20, 5)      # creates [ 0  5  10  15]
a3 = np.linspace(0, 2, 5)     # creates [0.0  0.5  1.0  1.5  2.0]
```

- The first two parameters of **arange( )** and **linspace( )** indicate the starting an ending values. The third parameter of **arange( )** indicates the step value, whereas that of **linspace( )** indicates number of values that we wish to create.
- Numpy allows us to create an identity matrix, a matrix in which all elements in the principal diagonal are ones, and all other elements are zeros.

```
import numpy as np
a1 = np.eye(3)
a2 = np.identity(3)
```

- Since identity matrix is a square matrix we are required to pass only 1 dimension to **eye( )** and **identity( )**.

Array Attributes

- A Numpy array has several attributes that indicate the element type, element size, shape of array, size of array, etc.
- We can obtain the type of elements present in a Numpy array, their sizes, their location in memory, etc.

```
import numpy as np
a1 = np.array([1, 2, 3, 4])
a2 = np.array([1.1, 2.2, 3.3, 4.4])
print(a1.dtype)          # prints int32
print(a2.dtype)          # prints float64
print(a1.itemsize)       # prints 4
print(a2.itemsize)       # prints 8
print(a1.nbytes)         # prints 16
print(a2.nbytes)         # prints 32
print(a1.data)           # prints <memory at 0x024BEE08>
print(a1.strides)        # prints (4,)
print(a2.data)           # prints <memory at 0x0291EE08>
print(a2.strides)        # prints (8,)
```

- Here **dtype** specifies the type of elements contained in the array. Number of bytes occupied by individual array element and by entire array are available through attributes **itemsize** and **nbytes**, respectively.
- **data** gives the address in memory where the array begins (often called base address) and **strides** indicates the number of bytes that should be added to base address to reach the next array element.
- The attributes **ndim**, **shape** and **size** yield the number of dimensions in the array the shape of the array and the number of elements in it.

```
import numpy as np
a1 = np.array([1, 2, 3, 4])
a2 = np.array([[1, 2, 3, 4],[5, 6, 7, 8]])
print(a1.ndim)           # prints 1
print(a2.ndim)           # prints 2
print(a1.shape)          # prints tuple (4,)
print(a2.shape)          # prints tuple (2, 4)
print(a1.size)           # prints 4
print(a2.size)           # prints 8
```

Array Operations

- Many operations can be performed on Numpy arrays. These operations are compact and fast. The speed is achieved through the already precompiled routines present in the library.
- The different array operations include the following:
  (a) Arithmetic operations
  (b) Statistical operations
  (c) Linear algebra operations
  (d) Bitwise operations
  (e) Copying, sorting
  (f) Comparison operations

Arithmetic Operations

- You can perform many operations like +, -, *, /, % on two arrays. When we use these operators, the operations are performed on corresponding elements of the two arrays. Instead of using these operators, you may also use methods like **add( )**, **subtract( )**, **multiply( )**, **divide( )** and **remainder( )**. These operations are often known as vector operations.

```
import numpy as np
a1 = np.array([[10, 2, 3, 4],[5, 6, 7, 8]])
a2 = np.array([[1, 1, 1, 1],[2, 2, 2, 2]])
a3 = a1 + a2          # same as a3 = np.add( a1, a2)
a4 = a1 - a2
a5 = a1 * a2
a6 = a1 / a2
a7 = a1 % a2
a8 = a1 ** 2          # raises every element to a power of 2
```

- We can perform scalar arithmetic operations on array elements.

```
import numpy as np
a1 = np.array([[10, 2, 3, 4],[5, 6, 7, 8]])
a2 = a1 + 2           # adds 2 to every element
a3 = a1 ** 2          # raises every element to a power of 2
```

- In place operators +=, -=, *=, /=, %= modify an existing array, instead of creating a new one.

```
a1 += a2          # is same as a1 = a1 + a2
```

```
a3 += 5            # is same as a3 = a3 + 5
```

- Other operations that can be done on array elements include **exp( )**, **sqrt( )**, **sin( )**, **cos( )**, **log( )**.

```
a1 = np.array([[10, 2, 3, 4],[5, 6, 7, 8]])
a2 = 25 * np.sin(a1)
```

Statistical Operations

- Numpy can perform following operations either on all elements of the array or on the elements of the specified axis. Note that axis means dimension, so a 1D array has 1 axis, a 2D array has 2 axes and so on.

```
import numpy as np
a = np.array([[1, 2, 3], [4, 5, 6]])
print(a.sum( ))
print(a.min( ))                   # finds minimum in array
print(a.max(axis = 0))            # finds maximum in each column
print(a.max(axis = 1))            # finds maximum in each row
print(a.sum(axis = 1))            # sum along axis 1
print(a.cumsum(axis = 1))         # cumulative sum
print(np.mean(a))
print(np.median(a))
print(np.corrcoef(a))
print(np.std(a)
```

It is important to understand the use of axis in calls to **max( )**. Our array is a 2D array of dimensions 2 x 3. When we use axis = 0, don't think about this as 'max along columns' or 'max along rows'. Instead, think that when we use axis = 0, Numpy finds maximum by condensing (or collapsing) size 2. So, the result is an array containing 3 elements [4, 5, 6]. Similarly, when we use axis = 1, Numpy condenses size 3, resulting in an array containing elements [3, 6].

Linear Algebra Operations

- Note the difference between the two multiplication operations:

```
a3 = a1 * a2        # multiplies corresponding elements of a1 and a2
a3 = a1 @ a2        # performs matrix multiplication
a4 = a1.dot (a2)    # performs matrix multiplication
```

- Transpose of a matrix can also be obtained:

```
a1 = np.array([[1, 2, 3, 4],[5, 6, 7, 8]])
a2 = np.transpose(a1)
```

- Trace of a matrix is the sum of its diagonal elements. It can be obtained as shown below.

```
a = np.array([[1, 2, 3], [4, 5, 6], [7, 8, 9]])
s = np.trace(a)        # stores 1 + 5 + 9 = 15
```

- Inverse of a matrix is a matrix which when multiplied with the original matrix results in an identity matrix.

```
a = np.array([[1, 2], [3, 4]])
b = np.linalg.inv(a)
```

- We can also obtain a solution to linear simultaneous equations. For example, the solution to a system of equations 3x + y = 9 and x = 2y = 8 can be obtained as shown below.

```
a = np.array([[3, 1], [1, 2]])
b = np.array([9, 8])
x = np.linalg.solve(a, b)
print(x)
```

Bitwise Operations

- Bitwise operations can also be performed on array elements as shown below:

```
a1 = np.array([[10, 2, 3, 4],[5, 6, 7, 8]])
a2 = np.array([[1, 1, 1, 1],[2, 2, 2, 2]])
a3 = biwise_and(a1, a2)
a4 = biwise_or(a1, a2)
a5 = biwise_xor(a1, a2)
a6 = invert(a1)
a7 = left_shift(a1, 3)        # shifts each element 3 bits to left
a8 = right_shift(a1, 2)       # shifts each element 2 bits to right
```

Copying and Sorting

- There are 3 possible copy operations—no copy, shallow copy operation and deep copy.

- In no copy, neither the object nor its data gets copied. Only address of array is assigned to a variable. In shallow copy a new array object is created but it points to the same data as the old array object. In deep copy a new array object and copies old object's attributes and data in it.

```
import numpy as np
a = np.array([[3, 3, 7], [1, 5, 2]])
b = a                  # no copy
print(b is a)          # prints True, a and b are referring to same array
b[0][0] = 100          # changes a[0][0]

c = a.view( )
print(c is a)          # prints False, a and c are referring to diff objects
c[0][0] = 50           # changes a[0][0]
                       # changing shape of c does not change shape of a

d = np.copy(a)         # deep copy
print(d)               # prints [[3  3  7] [1  5  2]]
print(d is a)          # prints False. d, a are referring to diff objects
d[0][0] = 150          # doesn't change a[0][0]

a = np.array([[3, 7, 6], [1, 5, 2]])
b = np.array([[3, 7, 6], [1, 5, 2]])
a.sort( )
b.sort(axis = 0)       # sort elements in each column
```

Comparison

- Three types of comparisons are common with arrays:
  (a) Compare all elements of an array with one value and return a Boolean array of the result.

  (b) Compare the corresponding elements of two arrays and return an array of Booleans.

  (c) Compare shape and elements of two array, return True if equal, False otherwise.

- Comparison of all array elements with one value:

```
import numpy as np
a = np.array([[3, 7, 6], [1, 5, 2]])
```

```
print(a < 5)          # prints [[True  False  False][True  False  True]]
```

- Comparison of corresponding array elements:

```
import numpy as np
a = np.array([[3, 7, 6], [1, 5, 2]])
b = np.array([[3, 1, 2], [1, 7, 2]])
print(a < b)          # prints [[False  False  False][False  True  False]]
```

- Comparison of two arrays:

```
import numpy as np
a = np.array([[3, 7, 6], [1, 5, 2]])
b = np.array([[3, 7, 6], [1, 5, 2]])
c = np.array([[3, 7], [6, 1], [5, 2]])
print(np.array_equal(a, b))          # True, shape & elements match
print(np.array_equal(a, c))          # False, different shapes
```

Indexing and Slicing

- As with lists, single element indexing is 0-based and accepts negative indices for indexing from the end of the array.

```
a = np.array([3, 7, 6, 1, 5, 2])
print(a[0], a[-1])                   # prints 3 2
```

- Individual elements of a multi-dimensional array are accessed using multiple indices.

```
a = np.array([[3, 7, 6], [1, 5, 9]])
print(a[1][2], a[1, 2])        # prints 9 9
```

  Note that in **a[1][2]**, a new temporary array is created after first index (i.e. [1, 5, 9]) and then its second element is fetched.

- Slicing works the same as lists except that it can be applied to multiple dimensions.

```
import numpy as np
a = np.array([8, 2, 4, 1, 5, 9])
b = np.array([[3, 7, 6, 9, 8], [1, 5, 9, 2, 4], [0, 0, 3, 1, 5]])
print(a[2:5])                  # prints [4  1  5]
print(a[:-4])                  # prints [8  2]
```

```
print(b[1:3, 2:4])          # prints [[9  2][3  1]]
print(b[1:3][2:4])          # prints [ ]
```

Note that in **b[1:3][2:4]** firstly array [[1, 5, 9, 2, 4][0, 0, 3, 1, 5]] is created and then elements 2 to 3 are fetched from it. Since this new array has only two elements, it returns [ ].

Array Manipulation

- Once an array is created we can change its shape using the method **reshape( )**. This method returns an array containing same data, but a new shape.

```
import numpy as np
a = np.array([[3, 7, 6, 9], [1, 5, 2, 4], [0, 3, 1, 5]])
b = a.reshape(2, 6)
print(b)                # prints [[3 7 6 9 1 5][2 4 0 3 1 5]]
c = a.reshape(4, -1)
print(c)                # prints [[3 7 6][9 1 5][2 4 0][3 1 5]]
d = np.arange(12).reshape(2, 6)
print(d)                # prints [[ 0  1  2  3  4  5] [ 6  7  8  9 10 11]]
```

- We can flatten a multi-dimensional array.

```
import numpy as np
a = np.array([[3, 7, 6, 9], [1, 5, 2, 4], [0, 3, 1, 5]])
b = a.ravel( )
print(b)                # prints [3 7 6 9 1 5 2 4 0 3 1 5]
```

- We can append values at the end of an existing array.

```
import numpy as np
a = np.array([[3, 7, 6, 9], [1, 5, 2, 4]])
b = np.array([[0, 3, 1, 5], [1, 1, 1, 1]])
c = np.append(a, b, axis = 0)
d = np.append(a, b, axis = 1)
print(c)                # prints [[3 7 6 9][1 5 2 4][0 3 1 5][1 1 1 1]]
print(d)                # prints [[3 7 6 9 0 3 1 5][1 5 2 4 1 1 1 1]]
```

Note that the values are appended to a copy of existing array. The values being appended must be of same shape as existing array. If *axis* is not specified, *values* can be any shape and will be flattened before use.

- There exist functions that let you insert elements, delete elements, split array etc. You are advised to explore them on your own.

P</> *Programs*

Problem 28.1

Write a program that constructs a 3D array of dimensions 4 x 2 x 3. Initialize the array to some values. Find the maximum along each axis.

Program

```
import numpy as np
a = np.array([[[3, 7, 6], [1, 5, 2]],
              [[1, 2, 4], [7, 2, 9]],
              [[1, 0, 0], [5, 4, 3]],
              [[8, 1, 4], [2, 7, 8]]])
print('Maximum along axis 0')
print(np.max(a, axis = 0))
print('Maximum along axis 1')
print(np.max(a, axis = 1))
print('Maximum along axis 2')
print(np.max(a, axis = 2))
```

Output

```
Maximum along axis 0
 [[8 7 6]
 [7 7 9]]
Maximum along axis 1
[[3 7 6]
 [7 2 9]
 [5 4 3]
 [8 7 8]]
Maximum along axis 2
[[7 5]
 [4 9]
 [1 5]
 [8 8]]
```

Problem 28.2

Write a program to create an array of shape 5 x 4 containing elements 1 to 20. Find the sum of entire array as well as sums along each row and column.

Program

```
import numpy as np
a = np.arange(20).reshape((5, 4))
print(a)
print(np.sum(a))
print(np.sum(a, axis = 0))
print(np.sum(a, axis = 1))
```

Output

```
[[ 0  1  2  3]
 [ 4  5  6  7]
 [ 8  9 10 11]
 [12 13 14 15]
 [16 17 18 19]]
190
[40 45 50 55]
[ 6 22 38 54 70]
```

Problem 28.3

Write a program to achieve the following tasks:

- Create an array **a** of size 10 with each element of it set to a value 3.
- Find the memory size of this array and its individual element.
- Create an array **b** of size 10 with values ranging from 0 to 90 evenly spaced.
- Reverse elements of array **b**.
- Add arrays **a** and **b** and store the result in array **c**.

Program

```
import numpy as np
a = np.full(10, 3)
```

```
print(a)
print(a.nbytes)
print(a.itemsize)
b = np.linspace(0, 90, 10)
print(b)
b = b[::-1]
print(b)
c = a + b
print(c)
```

Output

```
[3 3 3 3 3 3 3 3 3 3]
40
4
[ 0. 10. 20. 30. 40. 50. 60. 70. 80. 90.]
[90. 80. 70. 60. 50. 40. 30. 20. 10.  0.]
[93. 83. 73. 63. 53. 43. 33. 23. 13.  3.]
```

Problem 28.4

Write a program to achieve the following tasks:

- Create a 2d array of size 5 x 5 with elements on border set to 1, and all inner elements set to
- a value 3.
- Multiply a 4 x 3 matrix containing all 1s with a 3 x 5 matrix containing all 2s.
- Given a 1D array, negate all elements which are between 2 and 8, in place.

Program

```
import numpy as np
a = np.ones((5,5))
a[1:-1,1:-1] = 3
print(a)
b = np.ones((4,3))
c = np.full((3,5), 2)
d = b @ c
print(d)
```

```
e = np.arange(11)
print(e)
e[(2 < e) & (e < 8)] *= -1
print(e)
```

Output

```
[[1. 1. 1. 1. 1.]
 [1. 3. 3. 3. 1.]
 [1. 3. 3. 3. 1.]
 [1. 3. 3. 3. 1.]
 [1. 1. 1. 1. 1.]]
[[6. 6. 6. 6. 6.]
 [6. 6. 6. 6. 6.]
 [6. 6. 6. 6. 6.]
 [6. 6. 6. 6. 6.]]
[ 0  1  2  3  4  5  6  7  8  9 10]
[ 0  1  2 -3 -4 -5 -6 -7  8  9 10]
```

Problem 28.5

Write a program to achieve the following tasks:

- Find indices of non-zero elements from [11, 22, 0, 0, 40, 50, 0].
- Create a 5 x 5 identity matrix.
- Create a 5 x 6 array with random values and find the minimum and maximum values.
- Create an 8 x 8 array and fill it with a chess board pattern.

Program

```
import numpy as np
a = np.array([11, 22, 0, 0, 40, 50, 0])
print(np.nonzero(a))
b = np.eye(5)
print(b)
c = np.random.random((4, 4))
print(c)
mn = c.min( )
mx = c.max( )
print(mn, mx)
```

```
d = np.zeros((8,8), int)
d[1::2,::2] = 1
d[::2,1::2] = 1
print(d)
```

Output

```
(array([0, 1, 4, 5], dtype=int32),)
[[1. 0. 0. 0. 0.]
 [0. 1. 0. 0. 0.]
 [0. 0. 1. 0. 0.]
 [0. 0. 0. 1. 0.]
 [0. 0. 0. 0. 1.]]
[[0.05935627 0.85188925 0.17574069 0.3803101 ]
 [0.33995412 0.46862198 0.46498014 0.85957442]
 [0.04520398 0.2855793  0.60825711 0.50541311]
 [0.29781956 0.30728004 0.82198384 0.76704277]]
0.04520397811365395 0.859574415767098
[[0 1 0 1 0 1 0 1]
 [1 0 1 0 1 0 1 0]
 [0 1 0 1 0 1 0 1]
 [1 0 1 0 1 0 1 0]
 [0 1 0 1 0 1 0 1]
 [1 0 1 0 1 0 1 0]
 [0 1 0 1 0 1 0 1]
 [1 0 1 0 1 0 1 0]]
```

Exercises

[A] State whether the following statements are True or False:

(a) Numpy library gets installed when we install Python.

(b) Numpy arrays work faster than lists.

(c) Numpy array elements can be of different types.

(d) Once created, a Numpy arrays size and shape can be changed dynamically.

(e) **np.array_equal(a, b))** would return **True** if shape and elements of **a** and **b** match.

[B] Answer the following questions:

(a) How will you create a Numpy array of the first 10 natural numbers?

(b) Can we create an array of complex numbers using Numpy?

(c) How would you create 5 arrays each of size 3 x 4 x 5 and fill them with values 0, 1, 5, random and garbage values respectively?

(d) How would you create a 50-element array and fill it with odd numbers starting from 1?

(e) How will you obtain the type of elements, number of elements, base address and number of bytes occupied by the following Numpy array?

(f) How will you obtain dimensions and shape of a Numpy array created by **a1 = np.array([[1, 2, 3, 4], [5, 6, 7, 8]])**?

(g) Given two 3 x 4 matrices how would you add, subtract, multiply and divide corresponding elements of these matrices?

(h) Which of the following are the scalar arithmetic operations on Numpy array?

```
a1 = np.array([[10, 2, 3, 4],[5, 6, 7, 8]])
a2 = np.array([[1, 1, 1, 1],[2, 2, 2, 2]])
a3 = a1 + a2
a4 = a1 - a2
a5 = a1 * a2
a6 = a1 / a2
a7 = a1 % a2
a8 = a1 ** 2
a9 += a1
a10 += 5
a11 = a1 + 2
a12 = a1 ** 2
```

[C] Match the following pairs:

a. s = np.trace(a)	1. Statistical operation
b. s = a.cumsum(axis = 1))	2. Linear algebra operation
c. a2 = np.copy(a1)	3. Deep copy operation
d. print(a1 < 2)	4. Corresponding ele. comparison
e. print(a1 > a2)	5. Comparison with one value
f. print(a[1:3[3:6])	6. Bitwise operation
g. a2 = invert(a1)	7. Slicing operation

29 Matplotlib

"Picture is worth a thousand words..."

Contents

KanNotes

Brief Introduction

- While analyzing any data, instead of looking at raw data in the form of numbers, we get a much better understanding of it, if it is represented in the form of a graph.
- Matplotlib is a very popular open-source graph plotting library that is popularly used to visualize data.
- Matplotlib can be used to draw different types of graphs including Line graph, Scatter graph, Bar chart, Histogram, Pie chart, Violin chart, Box chart, Contour chart, etc.
- Matplotlib can also be used to work with images and perform different operations on them.
- Graphs drawn using Matplotlib can either be saved and then included in presentation or reports, or they can be embedded into applications using GUI toolkits like Tkinter, Qt and GTK.
- It is possible to create static, animated, and interactive data visualizations using Matplotlib library. It is possible to zoom, pan or update the interactive figures created by Matplotlib.
- Matplotlib library was created by John D. Hunter in 2003. It is written in Python.

Installation and Usage

- You can install Matplotlib and check its version as follows:

```
C:\> pip install matplotlib
```

- Matplotlib has multiple versions. Your installed version can be checked as follows:

```
import matplotlib
print(matplotlib.__version__)        # printed 3.5.2 in my case
```

- Instead of importing the exhaustive 'matplotlib' module, for plotting purposes 'matplotlib.pyplot' module is imported. Since plotting functions in Matplotlib library expect the input data in the form of numpy arrays, most Matplotlib programs begin with following import statements:

```
import matplotlib.pyplot as plt
import numpy as np
```

First Graph Using Matplotlib

- The following program shows how to use Matplotlib to draw a simple graph.

```
import matplotlib.pyplot as plt
import numpy as np
xvalues = np.linspace(0, 2, 100)
yvalues = np.linspace(0, 2, 100)
plt.plot(xvalues, yvalues)
plt.title("Simple Plot")
plt.xlabel("x values")
plt.ylabel("y values")
plt.show( )
```

On execution, the program produces output shown in Figure 29.1.

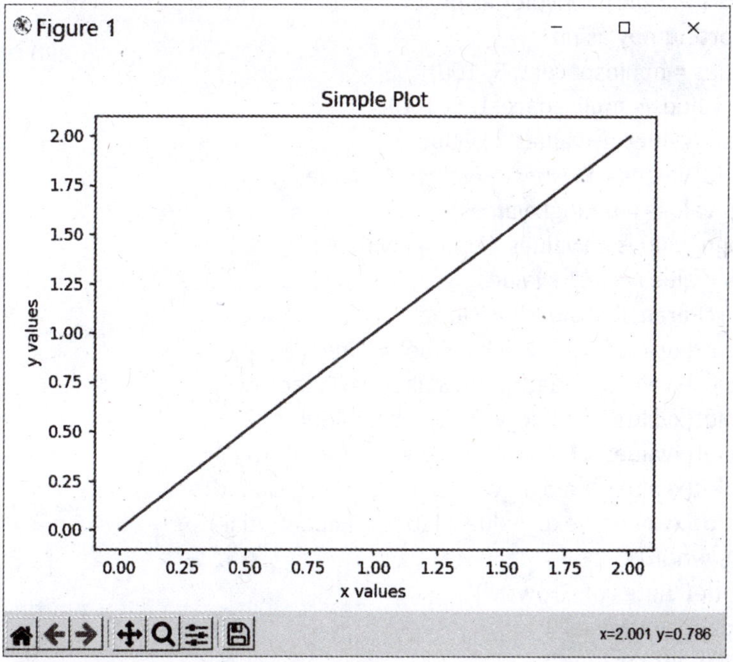

Figure 29.1

- The call to **linspace( )** creates 100 values in the range 0 to 2. Since we wanted to draw a linear graph, we kept xvalues and yvalues same.
- **plot( )** function is responsible for plotting the values in **xvalues** and **yvalues** arrays and **title( )**, **xlabel( )** and **ylabel( )** display the title of the graph, x-axis label and y-axis label respectively.
- **show( )** function manages to display the plot.
- Note that once the graph is displayed, as we move the cursor within the graph, its current position is displayed in the bottom right corner of the figure.
- The other buttons in the toolbar at the bottom of the figure let you zoom or pan the figure or even save it to the disk.

Plotting Multiple Graphs

- The following program shows how to plot different growth-rates along with legend for each.

```
import matplotlib as mpl
import matplotlib.pyplot as plt
import numpy as np
xvalues = np.linspace(1, 5, 100)
ylin_values = np.linspace(1, 5, 100)
yquad_values = xvalues * xvalues
ycubic_values = xvalues * xvalues * xvalues
ylog_values = np.log(xvalues)
ynlogn_values = xvalues * np.log(xvalues)
yexp_values = 2 ** xvalues
mpl.rcParams['toolbar'] = 'None'
plt.plot(xvalues, ylin_values, label = 'Linear')
plt.plot(xvalues, yquad_values, label = 'Quadratic')
plt.plot(xvalues, ycubic_values, label = 'Cubic')
plt.plot(xvalues, ylog_values, label = 'Logarithmic')
plt.plot(xvalues, ynlogn_values, label = 'Log Linear')
plt.plot(xvalues, yexp_values, label = 'Exponential')
plt.legend( )
plt.title("Rates of Growth")
plt.xlabel("x values")
plt.ylabel("y values")
plt.show( )
```

On execution, the program produces output shown in Figure 29.2.

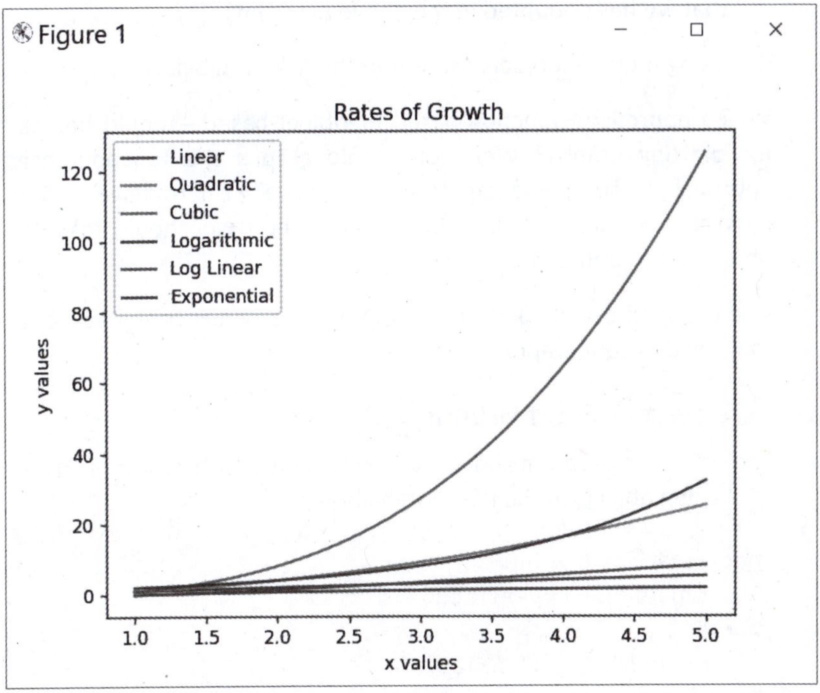

Figure 29.2

- Multiple graphs are drawn here for different growth rates of y values for x values present in the array **xvalues**.
- The **legend** keyword argument of **plot( )** function is used to specify the legend for each graph drawn. They get displayed when the **legend( )** function is called.
- Note that we do not have the toolbar at the bottom of the plot. This has been achieved through the statement

```
import matplotlib as mpl
mpl.rcParams['toolbar'] = 'None'
```

- Note that this statement should be executed before any plotting activity begins.

Two Ways to use Matplotlib

- There are 2 ways to use the Matplotlib library:

(a) Using functions in **matplotlib.pyplot** module. This is the method that we have adopted in the above programs.

(b) Using multiple objects present in the Matplotlib library.

- Which approach—function-based or object-based—should be used for plotting graphs? Well, for simple graphs the function-based approach is good enough. However, if we wish to have a finer control over each element of a graph, then we should take the object-based approach.

- In the rest of the chapter, we would use the object-based approach to draw different graphs.

Using Objects to Plot Graphs

- The following program shows how to draw the plots shown in Figure 29.2 using objects in the Matplotlib library:

```
import matplotlib as mpl
import matplotlib.pyplot as plt
import numpy as np
xvalues = np.linspace(1, 5, 100)
ylin_values = np.linspace(1, 5, 100)
yquad_values = xvalues * xvalues
ycubic_values = xvalues * xvalues * xvalues
ylog_values = np.log(xvalues)
ynlogn_values = xvalues * np.log(xvalues)
yexp_values = 2 ** xvalues
mpl.rcParams['toolbar'] = 'None'
(fig, ax) = plt.subplots( )              # returns a tuple
ax.plot(xvalues, ylin_values, label='Linear')
ax.plot(xvalues, yquad_values, label='Quadratic')
ax.plot(xvalues, ycubic_values, label='Cubic')
ax.plot(xvalues, ylog_values, label='Logarithmic')
ax.plot(xvalues, ynlogn_values, label='Log Linear')
ax.plot(xvalues, yexp_values, label='Exponential')
ax.legend( )
ax.set_title("Rates of Growth")
ax.set_xlabel("x values")
ax.set_ylabel("y values")
fig.show( )
```

- Here, we should first understand the concept of **Figure** and **Axes**.
- **Figure** is an object that represents the whole figure, including the graph, title, labels and legend.
- **Axes** represents the plotting area. So, Axes are contained with a Figure. Usually, they are created together through the statement **(fig, ax) = plt.subplots( )**. It creates a **Figure** with one **Axes**.
- If we wish, we can first create a **Figure** and then add **Axes** later as shown below:

```
fig = plt.figure( )          # create an empty figure with no Axes
ax = fig.subplots( )         # add a single Axes to the Figure
```

- Note that Axes represents multiple sub-plots in a figure and is not a plural of Axis that represents X-axis and Y-axis.

Multiple Plots

- We can create multiple Axes in a Figure if we wish to plot each growth-rate graph separately as shown in the following program:

```
import matplotlib as mpl
import matplotlib.pyplot as plt
import numpy as np
xvalues = np.linspace(1, 5, 100)
ylin_values = np.linspace(1, 5, 100)
yquad_values = xvalues * xvalues
ycubic_values = xvalues * xvalues * xvalues
ylog_values = np.log(xvalues)
mpl.rcParams['toolbar'] = 'None'
(fig, ax) = plt.subplots(2, 2)
ax[0,0].plot(xvalues, ylin_values, 'r', label = 'Linear')
ax[0,1].plot(xvalues, yquad_values, 'g', label = 'Quadratic')
ax[1,0].plot(xvalues, ycubic_values, 'b', label = 'Cubic')
ax[1,1].plot(xvalues, ylog_values, 'k', label = 'Logarithmic')
ax[0,0].legend( )
ax[0,1].legend( )
ax[1,0].legend( )
ax[1,1].legend( )
fig.show( )
```

- **(fig, ax) = plt.subplots(2, 2)** returns a tuple of a **Figure** object and a 2D array of **Axes** objects.
- 'r', 'g', 'b', 'k' indicate the color (Red, Green, Blue, Black) to be used for drawing each graph as shown in Figure 29.3.

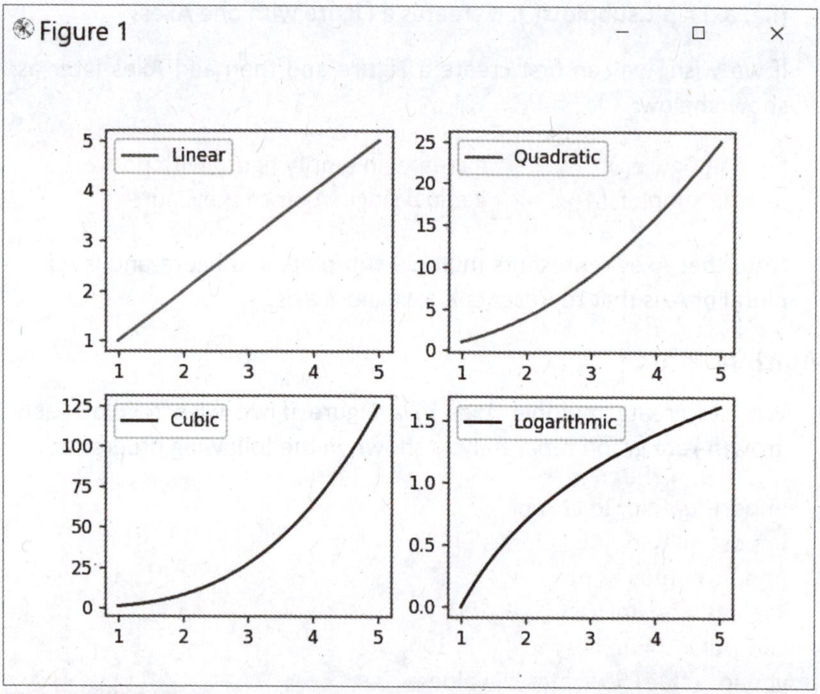

Figure 29.3

Data Visualization

- Data science and data modeling lets us identify and explore relationships that exist within our data by firstly analyzing it and then visualizing that data.
- Data analysis is done using Descriptive statistics and Inferential statistics. Data visualization is done using the Matplotlib library.
- Descriptive statistics lets you describe the characteristics of a data set. In descriptive statistics, there is no uncertainty; the statistical measures (like say, mean) precisely describe the data.

- Inferential statistics lets you use the sample data to make a prediction (called hypothesis) about the whole population and then test the prediction using different statistical tests.
- Under descriptive statistics, based on the nature of the data it can be described using univariate, bivariate, and multivariate analysis.
- Univariate analysis should be done when you are dealing with a single variable; bivariate when you are dealing with the relationships that exist between two variables; and multivariate when you are dealing with the relationships that exist among multiple variables.
- Examples:

  Univariate: Heights of students in a class
  Bivariate: How heights of students are related to parents' income
  Multivariate: How heights are related to weights, how weights are related with parents' income

Analysis of Univariate Data

- In univariate analysis, data is described using measures of frequency, measures of central tendency and measures of dispersion (variation).
- Measures of frequency include frequency tables and histograms. In frequency tables you tabulate how often a particular value appears in your dataset. In histograms you group continuous data and see how many data points fall within a certain group.
- In statistics, a central tendency is a central or a typical value that represents the data. For univariate analysis measures of central tendency are mean, median and mode.
- Mean is the average of all data points, median is the data point at the 50th percentile (i.e., 50% of values are below it and 50% above it), and mode is the most commonly occurring value in data.
- An outlier is a data point that differs significantly from other data values.
- The mean of your data as a measure of central tendency is sensitive to the presence of outliers. Median and mode changes little due to outliers and may be used if you expect outliers to be present in your data.

- Measures of dispersion try to capture how your data points jump around. Common measures of dispersion are range, inter-quartile range, variance, and standard deviation.
- Range is the difference between the maximum and minimum values of the variable. Range completely ignores the mean and is swayed by outliers present in your data. So, if the data has one extremely large or a small value, it will directly affect the range. Since range is very sensitive to the presence of outliers in the data, it is often not used to measure variation.
- The inter-quartile range is the difference between the 75th percentile data point and the 25th percentile data point. Thus, it is that range within your data where the middle 50% of your points lie. This measure of dispersion is not very sensitive to the presence of outliers in your data.
- Variance is the squared mean deviation of all the data points from mean. The mean deviation is the mean value subtracted from all your data points.
- The standard deviation is simply the square root of the variance. It tells you how far a particular data point lies from the mean.

Analysis of Bivariate and Multivariate Data

- While working with bivariate data, we wish to measure the strength of the relationship that exists between these two variables. This is done using correlation and covariance.
- Covariance is a measure of the relationship between two variables. It checks whether greater values of one variable correspond to greater values in the other variable.
- Positive covariance between X and Y indicates that the deviation around the means of the two data series is in-sync. The two variables are said to have negative covariance if the deviations around the means of the two series are out-of-sync.
- The correlation between two variables is something that is derived from the covariance; it measures whether greater values of one variable correspond to greater values in the other.
- The correlation between two variables is expressed in terms of a correlation coefficient, which is scaled to always lie between +1 and

-1. +1 indicates a positive linear relationship; -1 a negative linear relationship. If the variables are independent, that is, changes in the value of 1 variable, are not associated with changes in the value of the other variable, they will exhibit zero correlation, they are set to be independent variables.

- Independent variables have zero covariance and zero correlation.
- When you apply descriptive statistics to summarize multivariate data, you set up correlation matrices or covariance matrices. This will give you the correlation and covariance values for each pair of variables in your data.

Visualizing Relationships – Example 1

- Many different types of plots can be drawn for given data using Matplotlib library. Which of these different types of plots should be drawn depends primarily upon the information that we wish to get out of the graph.
- For example, if we have the following univariate data about the age of persons sitting in a restaurant on a Sunday evening:

  2, 5, 22, 34, 6, 65, 26, 22, 19, 17, 4, 43, 29, 18, 21, 65, 58, 8, 41, 7, 5, 15, 17, 19

  We wish to get answers to the following questions:

  (a) Are there more kids (1-12), or teenagers (13-19) or young persons (20-29) or middle-aged persons (30-50) in the restaurant?

  (b) What is the minimum and maximum age of the persons in the restaurant.

  (c) How many teenagers are present in the restaurant?

  (d) What is the median age of persons in the restaurant?

- We can draw a Dot plot, a Histogram and a Box plot for this data. A Dot plot merely plots a dot for each person's age. A Histogram plots the age groups (instead of individual ages) on X-axis and frequency of persons belonging to each age group on Y-axis.
- A Box plot depicts five values—minimum value, the first quartile, the median, the third quartile, and the maximum value. A box is drawn around the first quartile, median, and third quartile and two lines

are drawn from the box's edges to the minimum and maximum values.

- The program given below draws the Dot plot, Histogram and Box plot.

```
import matplotlib as mpl
import matplotlib.pyplot as plt
import numpy as np
data = np.array([12, 15, 22, 34, 16, 45, 26, 22, 39, 37, 4, 43, 29, 18,
21, 45, 28, 8, 41, 7, 5, 35, 47, 19])
mpl.rcParams['toolbar'] = 'None'
fig = plt.figure(constrained_layout = True)
ax = fig.subplots(1,3)
bins = np.arange(50)
freq, ages = np.histogram(data, bins = bins)
ages = ages[:-1]
ages_list = [ ]
freq_list = [ ]
for x in ages :
    count = 0
    while count < freq[x] :
        count = count + 1
        ages_list.append(x)
        freq_list.append(count)

ax[0].plot(ages_list, freq_list, 'bo')
ax[0].set_ylim(0, 5)
ax[0].set_title('Dot Plot')
ax[0].set_xlabel('Age')
ax[0].set_ylabel('No. of persons')

bins = np.array([1, 13, 20, 30, 51])
ax[1].hist(data, bins, edgecolor = "black", color = "purple")
ax[1].set_title('Histogram')
ax[1].set_xlabel('Age')
ax[1].set_ylabel('No. of persons')

lbls = ["Persons"]
ax[2].boxplot(data, notch = True, patch_artist = True, labels = lbls)
ax[2].set_title('Box Plot')
ax[2].set_ylabel("Ages")
ax[2].yaxis.grid(True)
```

```
plt.show( )
```

- The output of the program is shown in Figure 29.4.

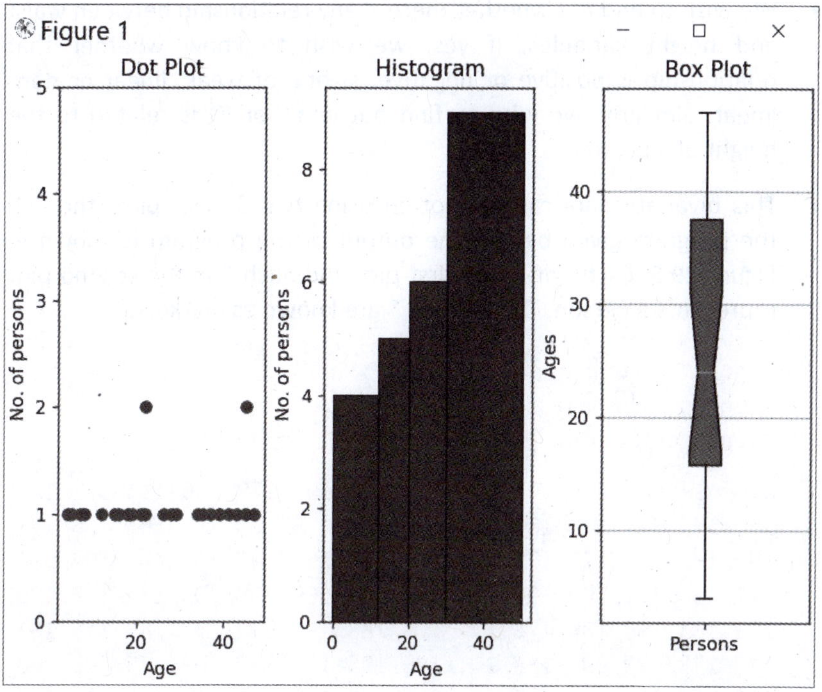

Figure 29.4

- In our data there are two persons aged 22. So, for them two dots should appear in the Dot plot, with coordinates (22, 1) and (22, 2). The loops used in the code generate these coordinates.
- From Figure 29.4, it is obvious that Dot plot can answer only question (b), Histogram can answer (a), (b) and (c), whereas a Box plot can answer (b) and (d). This emphasizes the fact that the plot chosen depends on the question that we wish to get an answer to.
- If there are multiple data sets—say ages of persons in 3 different restaurants in a hotel, then instead of 3 side-by-side Histograms, it makes more sense in drawing Box plots as they are less detailed and take less space.

Visualizing Relationships – Example 2

- Suppose we have data about waists (stomach girth in inches), heights (in cms) and IQ of obese persons staying in a city.
- We wish to find out whether there is any relationship between waist and height variables. If yes, we wish to know whether that relationship is positive or negative, strong or weak, linear or non-linear. Similarly, we wish to find out whether IQ is related to the height of a person.
- This bivariate data can be plotted using two Scatter plots through the program given below. The output of the program is shown in Figure 29.5. Each dot in the first plot and each * in the second plot represents a person. The dot and * are known as markers.

```
import matplotlib as mpl
import matplotlib.pyplot as plt
import numpy as np

heights = np.array([197, 164, 189, 174, 191, 179, 186, 191, 173, 186,
180, 179, 175, 178, 187, 189, 172, 192, 179, 160, 183, 184, 166, 188,
190, 173, 182, 177, 178, 178, 195, 188, 192, 177, 191, 185, 194, 191,
191, 184, 171, 201, 194, 188, 196, 169, 169, 193, 205, 174, 198, 192,
179, 183, 186, 184, 178, 191, 173, 188, 191, 203, 172, 185, 176, 181,
179, 178, 179, 194, 188, 201, 185, 195, 178, 177, 199, 175, 175, 168,
176, 186, 183, 195, 185, 166, 193, 181, 178, 182, 173, 183, 168, 190,
183, 176, 179, 189, 164, 179, 189, 174, 188, 196, 180, 202, 189, 179,
197, 183, 179, 192, 179, 179, 186, 194, 177, 175, 177, 178, 194, 194,
189, 178, 188, 193, 192, 179, 180, 171, 184, 191, 185, 198, 183, 189,
192, 174, 196, 187, 176, 168, 177, 187, 169, 186, 189, 190, 170, 187,
172, 175, 180, 179, 189, 190, 177, 170, 182, 177, 171, 207, 165, 182,
184, 187, 187, 195, 182, 170, 189, 170, 164, 164, 183, 183, 180, 171,
193, 190, 173, 160, 182, 186, 205, 173, 192, 185, 176, 187, 181, 174,
182, 179, 190, 200, 193, 172, 188, 187])

girth = np.array([73, 59, 68, 62, 68, 67, 67, 70, 60, 64, 64, 64, 65, 67,
69, 72, 64, 68, 65, 58, 70, 65, 60, 67, 71, 64, 66, 66, 65, 63, 69, 68,
69, 64, 71, 67, 69, 70, 69, 65, 63, 74, 70, 69, 70, 61, 64, 71, 75, 62,
69, 68, 64, 67, 67, 67, 66, 72, 62, 70, 70, 74, 61, 67, 64, 65, 66, 68,
63, 71, 70, 74, 65, 72, 64, 64, 71, 64, 63, 62, 65, 68, 66, 69, 67, 59,
69, 65, 65, 65, 65, 66, 62, 69, 65, 63, 61, 68, 60, 66, 69, 63, 67, 73,
65, 76, 69, 67, 71, 65, 64, 70, 65, 64, 67, 70, 64, 65, 65, 61, 71, 70,
71, 67, 68, 70, 70, 64, 65, 62, 68, 70, 70, 71, 68, 67, 68, 67, 71, 69,
```

```
65, 60, 64, 71, 63, 66, 70, 69, 62, 66, 64, 64, 65, 66, 68, 72, 65, 66,
64, 65, 59, 77, 59, 67, 67, 68, 67, 71, 64, 62, 67, 63, 61, 59, 64, 70,
63, 65, 72, 68, 61, 60, 64, 67, 75, 63, 69, 65, 66, 68, 68, 64, 65, 65,
70, 75, 69, 63, 68, 67])

iq = np.array([66, 77, 77, 53, 43, 85, 75, 91, 42, 62, 67, 71, 72, 77, 59,
80, 87, 12, 89, 62, 80, 52, 84, 89, 86, 54, 59, 64, 65, 64, 73, 79, 76,
72, 95, 83, 86, 54, 55, 64, 40, 53, 37, 91, 87, 86, 49, 31, 42, 57, 53,
45, 31, 32, 71, 76, 72, 46, 88, 32, 40, 42, 61, 67, 48, 77, 89, 68, 44,
43, 65, 63, 68, 64, 45, 48, 61, 69, 74, 75, 54, 82, 77, 72, 79, 76, 59,
52, 58, 75, 47, 42, 42, 88, 64, 57, 37, 55, 62, 62, 68, 69, 45, 73, 83,
59, 49, 73, 51, 56, 57, 59, 81, 57, 52, 54, 37, 35, 58, 51, 54, 84, 84,
81, 82, 49, 57, 64, 73, 72, 54, 73, 76, 58, 84, 52, 85, 77, 66, 63, 65,
82, 77, 84, 82, 65, 71, 76, 73, 53, 83, 85, 87, 72, 73, 74, 85, 62, 67,
88, 72, 76, 80, 88, 83, 81, 45, 43, 41, 48, 42, 68, 65, 76, 88, 88, 65,
67, 62, 47, 48, 55, 72, 76, 41, 47, 73, 82, 76, 72, 83, 55, 65, 52, 75,
52, 87, 76, 77, 88])

mpl.rcParams['toolbar'] = 'None'

fig = plt.figure(constrained_layout = True)
ax = fig.subplots(1, 2)

ax[0].set_title('Height & Waist Distribution')
ax[0].scatter(heights, girth, color = "red", alpha = 0.4)
ax[0].set_xlabel("Height (cm)")
ax[0].set_ylabel("Waist (inches)")

ax[1].set_title('Height & IQ distribution')
ax[1].scatter(heights, iq, color = "blue", alpha=0.4, marker = "*")
ax[1].set_xlabel("Height (cm)")
ax[1].set_ylabel("IQ")

plt.show( )
```

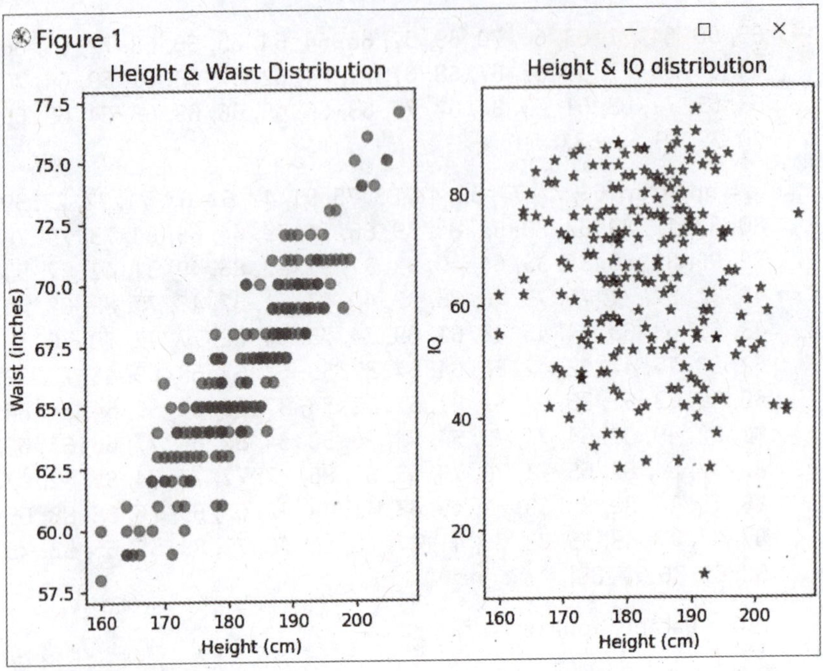

Figure 29.5

- From the first Scatter plot, we can see there is a tight positive correlation between a person's waist and his height. We can also observe an outlier point, a person whose girth is much larger than the others.
- On the other hand, the second Scatter plot suggests that the height and IQ are unrelated.
- Thus, the dots in a Scatter plot not only report the values of individual data points, but also patterns when the data are taken as a whole.
- A word of caution—simply because we observe a relationship between two variables in a Scatter plot, it does not mean that changes in one variable are responsible for changes in the other. It is possible that the observed relationship is driven by some third variable, say age of person, that affects both plotted variables. In statistics this is often called as 'correlation does not imply causation'.

Programs

Problem 29.1

Write a program that plots a sine and a cosine curve in two different sub-plots. Each curve should be drawn using 100 x co-ordinates between 1 and 5.

Program

```
import matplotlib.pyplot as plt
import numpy as np
xvalues = np.linspace(1, 5, 100)
sinvalues = np.sin(xvalues)
cosvalues = np.cos(xvalues)
(fig, ax) = plt.subplots(2, 1)
ax[0].plot(xvalues, sinvalues, 'r', label = 'Sin Curve')
ax[1].plot(xvalues, cosvalues, 'g', label = 'Cos Curve')
ax[0].legend( )
ax[1].legend( )
ax[0].grid( )
ax[1].grid(linestyle='dotted')
fig.show( )
```

Output

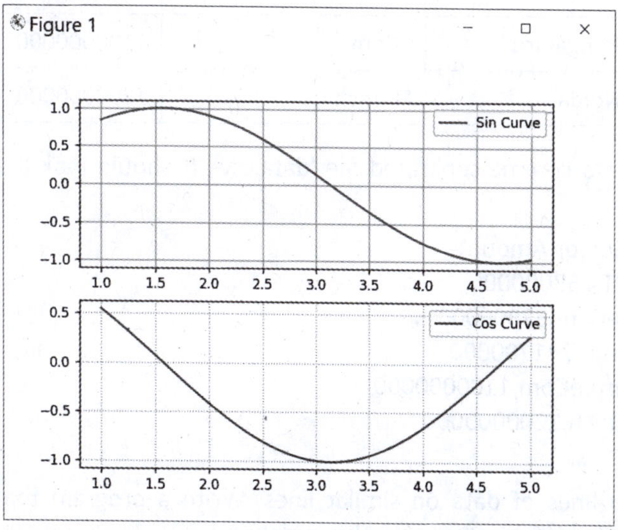

Figure 29.6

Tips

- **linspace( )** function is used to generate 100 x co-ordinates in the range 1 to 5. Y co-ordinates for each curve are generated using the Numpy **sin( )** and **cos( )** functions.
- **plot( )** function is used to draw the curves.
- **grid( )** function is used to draw gridlines, whose style is controlled using the **linestyle** parameter.
- Apart from the elements of the graph shown in Figure 29.6, many other elements can be controlled using functions available in Matplotlib. These include graph title, x-axis label, y-axis label, major/minor tick locator, major/minor tick label, etc. It is left to the reader to experiment with these elements to get their hang.

Problem 29.2

The following table shows partial data about startups.

Name	Location	Sector	Amount
Dyte	Bengaluru	IT	15300000
Kirana	Gurgaon	eCom	32800000
FirstCry	Pune	eCom	741700000
Meesho	Bengaluru	eCom	1100000000
Paytm	Noida	Fintech	1200000000

Store this data in a comma-separated file 'data.csv'. It should look like this:

```
Name,Location,Sector,Amount
Dyte,Bengaluru,IT,15300000
Kirana,Gurgaon,eCom,32800000
FirstCry,Pune,eCom,741700000
Meesho,Bengaluru,eCom,1100000000
Paytm,Noida,Fintech,1200000000
... ... ... ... ... ... ... ... ...
```

Add a few more lines of data on similar lines. Write a program that depicts the following information using bar graphs:

(a) City-wise funding

(b) Number of companies that were funded in each sector and the total funding that those companies have received.

Program

```
import matplotlib as mpl
import matplotlib.pyplot as plt
import numpy as np

data = np.genfromtxt('Data.csv', delimiter = ',', skip_header = 1,
   dtype = 'str')
unq_cty, inv_cty = np.unique(data[:, 1], return_inverse = True)
unq_sec, inv_sec, sec_counts = np.unique(data[:, 2],
   return_inverse = True, return_counts = True)

sum_by_cty = np.zeros(len(unq_cty), dtype="f8")
sum_by_sec = np.zeros(len(unq_sec), dtype="f8")

for i in range(len(inv_cty)) :
   sum_by_cty[inv_cty[i]] = sum_by_cty[inv_cty[i]] + float(data[i][3])
for i in range(len(inv_sec)):
   sum_by_sec[inv_sec[i]] = sum_by_sec[inv_sec[i]] + float(data[i][3])
for i in range(len(sum_by_cty)):
   sum_by_cty[i] = sum_by_cty[i] / pow(10, 9)
for i in range(len(sum_by_sec)):
   sum_by_sec[i] = sum_by_sec[i] / pow(10, 9)

mpl.rcParams['toolbar'] = 'None'
fig = plt.figure(constrained_layout = True)
ax = fig.subplots(2, 1)
width = 0.35
bar_cont = ax[0].bar(unq_cty, sum_by_cty, width,
   label = 'Total Funding', color = 'r')
ax[0].bar_label(bar_cont, padding = 3)
ax[0].set_ylabel('Dollars (* 10^9)')
ax[0].set_title('Startups Funded in every City')
ax[0].legend( )
coord = np.arange(len(unq_sec))
count_bar_cont = ax[1].bar(coord - width / 2, sec_counts,
   width, label = "Count")
fund_bar_cont = ax[1].bar(coord + width / 2, sum_by_sec,
   width, label = "Funding")
```

```
ax[1].set_xticks(coord, unq_sec)
ax[1].bar_label(count_bar_cont, padding = 3)
ax[1].bar_label(fund_bar_cont, padding = 3)
ax[1].set_title('Startup count and funding (* 10^9) in every Sector')
ax[1].legend( )

plt.show( )
```

Output

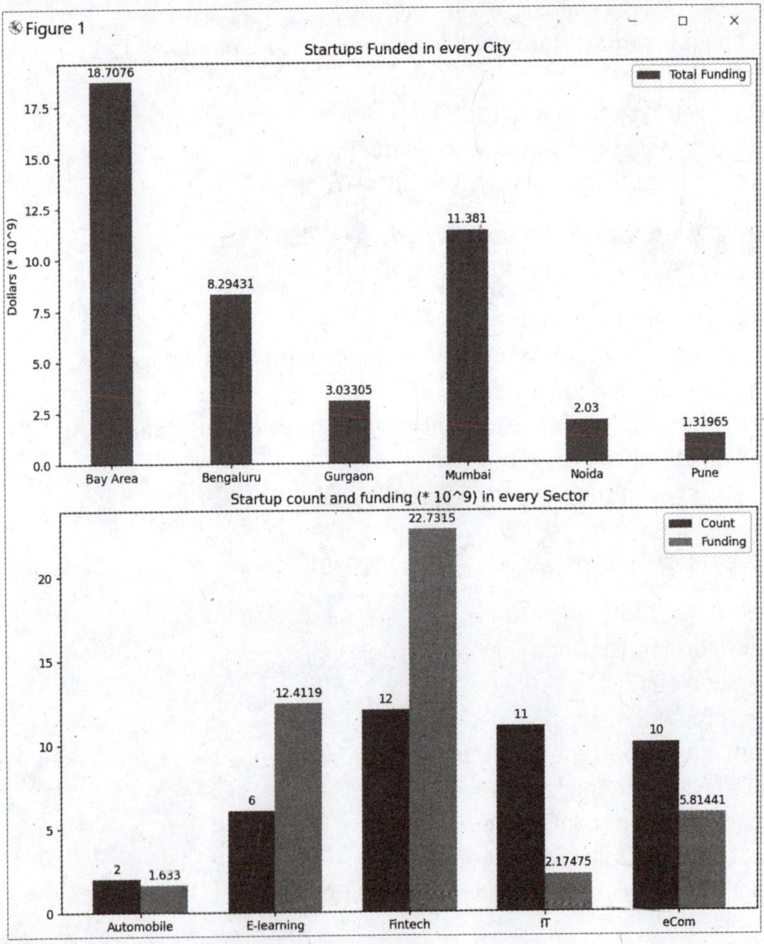

Figure 29.7

Tips

- **genfromtxt( )** function is used to read from the comma-separated values into a 2D numpy array **data**.

- Since there are many rows for each city, to obtain a list of unique city names, **unique( )** function is used. **data[:, 1]** picks names of cities from **data** array. **return_inverse = True** ensures that **inv_city** is filled with list of values which contain the index of each city. This means if 'Bay Area' occurs in rows 3, 7, 12 and 15 in **data** array, then **inv_city** list is filled with 0 in positions 3, 7, 12 and 15. If 'Bengaluru' occurs in rows 2, 5 then positions 2 and 5 are filled with 1, and so on.

- While filtering sector data, in addition to unique sector names, and their positions, count of each sector is also obtained.

- The **for** loops are used to aggregate funding city-wise and sector-wise.

- **bar( )** function returns an object of type BarContainer. Using this object, labels for each bar are set up.

- For drawing the second barchart showing number of companies and their aggregate funding, the **bar( )** function is called twice.

Problem 29.3

For the same data in 'data.csv' mentioned in Problem 29.2, draw a Pie chart showing percentage of startups in each sector.

Program

```
import matplotlib as mpl
import matplotlib.pyplot as plt
import numpy as np

data = np.genfromtxt('Data.csv', delimiter = ',', skip_header = 1,
   dtype = 'str')
unq_sectors, sector_counts = np.unique(data[:, 2],
   return_counts = True)
mpl.rcParams['toolbar'] = 'None'
(fig, ax) = plt.subplots( )
ax.set_title('Startup % in every Sector')
ax.pie(sector_counts, labels = unq_sectors, startangle = 90,
   autopct = '%1.1f%%')
ax.axis("equal")
plt.show( )
```

Output

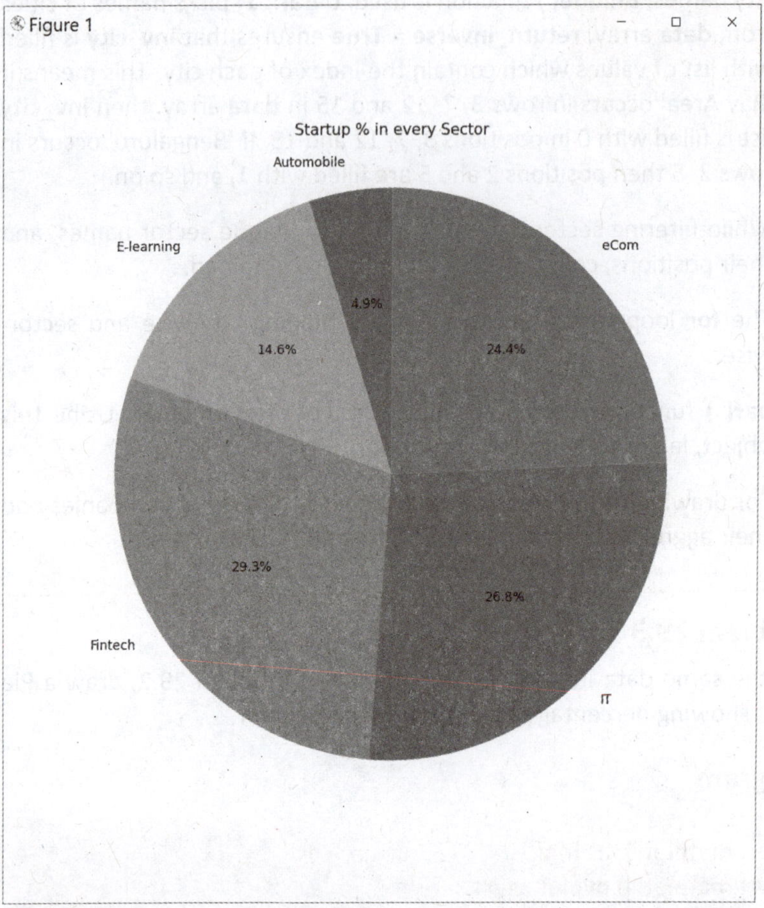

Figure 29.8

Tips

- **genfromtxt( )** function is used to read from the comma-separted values into a 2D numpy array **data**.
- From the **data** array unique sector names and count of companies working in each sector are obtained using the function **unique( )**.
- **pie( )** function is used to draw the Pie chart, ensuring that first sector begins at an angle of 90 degrees.

30 Pandas Library

"The Data Science potion..."

Contents

KanNotes

What is Pandas?

- Pandas is a powerful Python library that helps us to streamline data analysis workflows for various data science and machine learning tasks.
- It simplifies data loading, cleaning, manipulation, analysis and visualization of data.
- It is built on top of the NumPy library and is particularly well-suited for working with tabular data, such as spreadsheets or SQL tables.
- In data science applications, Pandas library is often used in conjunction with other libraries like Matplotlib, SciPy, and Scikit-learn.
- To use Pandas library, it must be downloaded and installed as shown below:

  C:\Users\Kanetkar>pip install pandas

  C:\Users\Kanetkar>pip install openpyxl

Pandas Data Structures

- Pandas library provides two data structures for manipulating and analyzing data. They are **Series** and **DataFrame.**
- Series is a one-dimensional labeled array capable of holding data of any type (integer, string, float, python objects, etc.). So, a series has indices and values.
- DataFrame is a two-dimensional data structure with labeled axes (rows and columns).
- Pandas Series and DataFrame can be built from data in memory or data read from a CSV, TSV, Excel, JSON or SQL files.

Creating Series

- A Series can be created as shown below:

```
import pandas as pd
import numpy as np
```

```
ser1 = pd.Series( )                                # empty series
print(ser1)

data = np.array(['a', 'e', 'i', 'o', 'u'])         # simple series
ser2 = pd.Series(data)
print(ser2)
```

- A Series can also be created from a list, tuple, or dictionary.

```
import pandas as pd

lst = ['Sam', 'Prash', 'Raj', 'Kulki', 'Adi']
ser1 = pd.Series(lst)
print(ser1)

tpl = ('Sam', 'Prash', 'Raj', 'Kulki', 'Adi')
ser2 = pd.Series(tpl)
print(ser2)

dct = {'Sam' : 23, 'Prash' : 25, 'Raj' : 22, 'Kulki' : 21, 'Adi' : 29}
ser3 = pd.Series(dct)
print(ser3)
```

- Pandas is optimized for homogeneous data types, meaning that for efficiency and performance, it works best when all elements of a Series are of the same data type (like all integers, all floats, or all strings).
- A Series can hold mixed data types, such as a combination of integers, floats, strings, and other objects. However, when mixed types are present, Pandas will typically upcast them to a more general data type, such as object, which is a catch-all type for Python objects.

```
ser = pd.Series([1, 'two', 3.0, True])  # each element is of object type
```

Properties of Series

- Pandas Series object has many useful properties to help you gain insights into the structure and content of your data. These are listed below.

  shape - Returns the number of elements in the Series as a tuple
  size - Returns the total number of elements in the Series
  ndim - Returns the dimension of Series (always 1)

dtype - Returns the data type of the elements in the Series
index - Returns the index (row labels) of the Series
values - Returns the data in the Series as a NumPy array
empty - Returns True if the Series is empty, otherwise False

- The following program shows the usage of these properties:

```
import pandas as pd
import numpy as np
data = np.array(['a', 'e', 'i', 'o', 'u'])
ser = pd.Series(data )
print("shape:", ser.shape)        # shape: (5,)
print("size:", ser.size)          # size: 5
print("ndim:", ser.ndim)          # ndim: 1
print("dtype:", ser.dtype)        # dtype: object
print("index:", ser.index)        # RangeIndex(start=0, stop=5, step=1)
print("values:", ser.values)      # values: ['a' 'e' 'i' 'o' 'u']
print("empty:", ser.empty)        # empty: False
```

Accessing Series Data

- A Series contains index and values. We can give custom labels to indices of a series. The contents of the Series can then be accessed using these custom labels and **at[ ]**, **iat[ ]**, **loc[ ]** and **iloc[ ]** methods.

```
import pandas as pd
data = [100, 200, 300, 400]
ndx = ['Apple', 'Kiwi', 'Orange', 'Grapes']   # custom index labels
ser = pd.Series(data, index=ndx)

# access individual values
print(ser.at['Kiwi'], ser.at['Grapes'])        # prints 200 400
print(ser.iat[1], ser.iat[3])                  # prints 200 400

# access range of values
print(ser.loc['Kiwi':'Grapes'])                # prints Kiwi      200
                                               # prints Orange  300
                                               # prints Grapes  400

print(ser.iloc[1:])                            # output same as above
```

at[ ] and **iat[ ]** are used to access a single value by label and by position respectively. **loc[ ]** and **iloc[ ]** permits access to a range of values by labels and position respectively.

Note that **loc[ ]** uses custom labels, supports label slicing, and the slice is inclusive of both start and end labels. As against this, **iloc[ ]** uses integer positions (starting with 0), supports slicing by positions, but the slice follows Python slicing rules, where the end index is exclusive.

Series Methods

- Pandas Series objects provide a wide variety of functions for data manipulation, analysis, and transformation. Here's a categorized overview of commonly used functions and methods available in a Series object:

- **1. Basic Information and Descriptive Statistics**

  head(n): Returns the first **n** rows
  tail(n): Returns the last **n** rows
  describe( ): Generates statistics such as count, mean, std, etc.
  count( ): Returns the number of non-null elements
  unique( ): Returns unique values
  nunique( ): Returns the number of unique values
  value_counts( ): Returns a Series of counts of unique values
  mean( ), median( ), mode( ): Return mean, median, and mode values
  std( ), var( ): Return standard deviation and variance
  min( ), max( ): Return minimum, and maximum
  sum( ), cumsum( ): Returns the sum and cumulative sum of values
  prod( ), cumprod( ): Returns the product and cumulative product
  quantile(q): Returns the value at the given quantile **q**

- **2. Indexing, Selecting and Slicing**

  loc[ ]: Access a group of rows/columns by labels
  iloc[ ]: Access a group of rows/columns by index position
  at[ ]: Access a single value by label
  iat[ ]: Access a single value by position

- **3. Data Cleaning & Handling Missing Values**

  isnull( ) / notnull( ): Detect missing values
  dropna( ): Remove missing values
  fillna(val): Fill NA/NaN values with **val**
  replace(to_replace, val): Replace **to_replace** with **val**

- **4. Element-wise Operations**

  apply(func): Apply a function **func** to each element

map(func): Map values of the Series using an input correspondence (a function, dict, or Series)
round(n): Round each value to **n** number of places
abs( ): Return the absolute value of each element

- **5. Sorting & Ranking**

  sort_values(ascending = True): Sort by values
  sort_index(ascending = True): Sort by index
  rank(method = 'average'): Rank the values, with different methods like 'min', 'max', 'first', etc

- **6. String Operations (for Series with string data)**

  str.upper( ), str.lower( ): Convert strings to uppercase or lowercase
  str.contains(pattern): Check if each string contains the **pattern**
  str.replace(old, new): Replace occurrences of a string
  str.split(sep): Split strings by the separator **sep**
  str.strip( ): Remove leading and trailing whitespace

- **7. Mathematical Functions**

  add( ), sub( ), mul( ), div( ), pow( ): Element-wise operations
  mod( ): Element-wise modulus operation
  corr( ): Compute the correlation with another Series
  cov( ): Compute the covariance with another Series

- **8. Handling Duplicates**

  duplicated( ): Return boolean Series denoting duplicate values
  drop_duplicates( ): Remove duplicate values from Series

- **9. Aggregation Functions**

  sum( ): Sum of the values
  prod( ): Product of the values
  min( ), max( ): Minimum and maximum values
  mean( ): Mean of the values
  median( ): Median of the values
  std( ): Standard deviation of the values

- **10. Miscellaneous**

  astype(dt): Convert the Series to the data type **dt**
  copy( ): Return a copy of the Series
  append( ): Append another Series to this one
  between(left, right): Check if values are between two values
  idxmax( ) / idxmin( ): Return the index of the max or min value
  memory_usage( ): Return the memory usage of the Series

Creating DataFrame

- Since a DataFrame is a 2D structure, they are usually created from a 2D NumPy array or a Dictionary.

```
import pandas as pd
import numpy as np

df1 = pd.DataFrame( )                               # empty dataframe
print(df1)

data = np.array([[1, 2, 3], [4, 5, 6]])             # 2 rows x 3 cols
df2 = pd.DataFrame(data)
print(df2)

data = {'Name': ['Raju', 'Sam'], 'Age': [25, 30], 'Sal': [5000, 6000]}
df3 = pd.DataFrame(data)
print(df3)
```

Creating DataFrame from File

- In the above examples we have created DataFrame from data in memory. However, typically a DataFrame is constructed by reading data from CSV or Excel files.
- Suppose a comma-separated values (CSV) file contains following people data:

```
Name,Age,City
Rohan,30,Mumbai
Shreya,25,Bangalore
Radhika,35,Hyderabad
```

  This data can be read into a Pandas DataFrame using the **read_csv( )** method.

```
import pandas as pd
df = pd.read_csv('sample.csv')
print(df)
```

- Pandas allows reading contents of an Excel file into a DataFrame. Either all sheets in the file can be read together or specific sheets data can be read based on the **sheet_name** parameter. If the

sheet_name parameter is not passed, it reads the contents of the first sheet present in the Excel file.

```
import pandas as pd

# read default sheet
df1 = pd.read_excel('ppl.xlsx')
print(df1)

# read second sheet
df2 = pd.read_excel('ppl.xlsx', sheet_name='Sheet2')
print(df2)

# read all sheets
df3 = pd.read_excel('ppl.xlsx', sheet_name=None)
print(df3)
```

Properties of A DataFrame

- Properties of a DataFrame object are listed below.

  shape - Returns the rows and columns in the DataFrame as a tuple
  size - Returns number of elements (rows x cols) in the DataFrame
  ndim - Returns the dimension of DataFrame (always 2)
  dtype - Returns the data types of each column
  index - Returns the index (row labels) of the DataFrame
  columns - Returns the column labels of the DataFrame
  axes - Returns a list of row and column labels of the DataFrame
  values - Returns the data in the DataFrame as a NumPy array
  empty - Returns True if the DataFrame is empty, otherwise False.
  Transpose - Returns the transpose of the DataFrame.

- The usage of these properties is shown in the following program:

```
import pandas as pd
import numpy as np
data = {'Name': ['Raju', 'Sam'], 'Age': [25, 30], 'Salary': [5000, 6000]}
df = pd.DataFrame(data)
print("shape:", df.shape)          # shape: (2, 3)
print("size:", df.size)            # size: 6
print("ndim:", df.ndim)            # ndim: 2
print("dtypes:", df.dtypes)        # Name object, Age int64, Salary int64
print("index:", df.index)          # RangeIndex(start=0, stop=2, step=1)
print("columns:", df.columns)      # Index(['Name', 'Age', 'Salary'])
print("axes:", df.axes)            # RangeIndex(start=0, stop=2, step=1)
```

```
                              # Index(['Name', 'Age', 'Salary'])
print("values:", df.values)   # [['Raju' 25 5000] ['Sam' 30 6000]...]
print("empty:", df.empty)     # False
```

Accessing DataFrame Data

- Custom labels can be set for rows and columns of a DataFrame. **at[ ]**, **iat[ ]**, **loc[ ]** and **iloc[ ]** can then be used to access specific values or a range of values from the DataFrame.

```
data = [['A101', 90, 78], ['A102', 92, 81], ['A103', 85, 89]] data = [['A101', 90, 78], ['A102', 92, 81], ['A103', 85, 89]]
cols = ['Roll No', 'Science', 'English']   # custom column labels
rows = ['Ajay', 'Amol', 'Anuj']            # custom index labels
df = pd.DataFrame(data, columns=cols, index=rows)

print(df.at['Ajay','Roll No'])             # prints A101
print(df.iat[0,0])                         # prints A101

print(df.loc['Ajay':'Anuj','Science'])     # Ajay 90  Amol 92 Anuj 85
print(df.iloc[0:3,1])                      # Ajay 90  Amol 92 Anuj 85
```

DataFrame Methods

- Given below is a list of properly categorized methods available in DataFrame objects along with the purpose of each. Pandas library is very exhaustive and the following list is a subset of commonly used methods.

- **1. Data Inspection and Summarization**

  head( ) - Returns the first n rows of the DataFrame
  tail( ) - Returns the last n rows of the DataFrame
  info( ) - Prints a summary of the DataFrame, like column data types, non-null counts, etc.
  describe( ) - Generates descriptive statistics for numerical columns

- **2. Data Selection and Indexing**

  loc[ ]: Access rows and columns by labels
  iloc[ ]: Access rows and columns by index position
  at[ ]: Access a single value by label
  iat[ ]: Access a single value by position
  get( ) - Access a single column or row
  filter( ) - Subset the DataFrame rows or columns based on criteria

- **3. Data Manipulation**

  assign( ) - Adds new columns or modifies existing ones
  drop( ) - Removes specified labels from rows or columns
  sort_values( ) - Sorts by the values along either axis
  sort_index( ) - Sorts by row or column index
  set_index( ) - Sets one or more columns as the index
  reset_index( ) - Resets the index, moving the current index to a column
  apply( ) - Applies a function along an axis of the DataFrame
  applymap( ) - Applies a function elementwise to the entire DataFrame
  agg( ) - Performs aggregation on DataFrame columns
  replace( ) - Replaces specified values with others

- **4. Handling Missing Data**

  isna( ) or isnull( ) - Detect missing values
  fillna( ) - Fill missing data with a specified value or method
  dropna( ) - Remove missing data
  notna( ) or notnull( ) - Detect non-missing values

- **5. Data Merging and Reshaping**

  merge( ) - Merge two DataFrames on common columns or indices (like SQL joins)
  concat( ) - Concatenate DataFrames along a particular axis
  join( ) - Combine two DataFrames on their indices
  pivot( ) - Reshape data using column values as new rows/columns
  pivot_table( ) - Creates a pivot table for summarizing data
  melt( ) - Unpivot a DataFrame from wide to long format

- **6. Group By and Aggregation**

  groupby( ) - Group the DataFrame using a mapper or by columns
  aggregate( ) or agg( ) - Perform multiple operations on grouped data
  transform( ) - Apply a function to each group independently and combine the results
  size( ) - Returns the size of each group

- **7. File I/O**

  to_csv( ) - Write DataFrame to a CSV file
  to_excel( ) - Write DataFrame to an Excel file
  to_json( ) - Write DataFrame to a JSON string or file
  read_csv( ) - Read a CSV file into a DataFrame
  read_excel( ) - Read an Excel file into a DataFrame

- **8. Plotting**

  plot( ) - Plot data from the DataFrame

- **9. Mathematical Operations**

  mean( ) - Compute the mean of each column or row
  sum( ) - Compute the sum of each column or row
  std( ) - Compute the standard deviation
  cumsum( ) - Compute the cumulative sum of values
  min( ) - Returns the minimum value
  max( ) - Returns the maximum value
  corr( ) - Compute pairwise correlation of columns

- **10. Miscellaneous**

  sample( ) - Return a random sample of rows
  memory_usage( ) - Return the memory usage of each column
  duplicated( ) - Detect duplicate rows
  nunique( ) - Count the number of unique values in each column

Pandas Library Capabilities

- Pandas library shines when used for Data Science or AI applications. While doing so it is more likely that you will perform operations on data read from one or more CSV files present in a dataset.

- To be able to learn the capabilities of Pandas library, for all the programs in the 'Programs' section we would use data read from CSV files. There are many ready-made CSV files available in datasets hosted at https://www.kaggle.com. From here, you can download the 'IPL Complete Dataset (2008-2024)'. It contains two CSV files—'matches.csv' and 'deliveries.csv'.

- As their names suggest, 'matches.csv' contains data of all IPL matches played, whereas 'deliveries.csv' contains data of all the deliveries bowled in all matches played. Thus, one row in 'matches.csv' represents one match, whereas one row in 'deliveries.csv' is one delivery bowled.

Programs

Problem 30.1

Write a program that reads the 'matches.csv' file and prints the following:

- First 5 rows and last 4 rows

- Number of rows and columns
- Column names and type of each
- Count of non-null values in each column
- Statistical information like mean, standard deviation, min max values, 25%, 50% and 75% centile values of numeric columns

Program

```
import pandas as pd
data = pd.read_csv('matches.csv')
print(data.head(5))
print(data.tail(5))
print(data.info( ))
print(data.describe( ))
```

Output

```
// Each row has many columns hence not shown here
RangeIndex: 1095 entries, 0 to 1094
Data columns (total 20 columns):
 #  Column        Non-Null Count        Dtype
--- ----------    --------------------  --------
 0  id            1095 non-null         int64
 1  season        1095 non-null         object
 2  city          1044 non-null         object
...

// output of describe( )
                 id   result_margin   target_runs   target_overs
count  1.095000e+03     1076.000000   1092.000000    1092.000000
mean   9.048283e+05       17.259294    165.684066      19.759341
std    3.677402e+05       21.787444     33.427048       1.581108
min    3.359820e+05        1.000000     43.000000       5.000000
25%    5.483315e+05        6.000000    146.000000      20.000000
50%    9.809610e+05        8.000000    166.000000      20.000000
75%    1.254062e+06       20.000000    187.000000      20.000000
max    1.426312e+06      146.000000    288.000000      20.000000
```

Problem 30.2

Write a program that reads the 'matches.csv' file and prints the names of the winning teams (from 'winner' column) and the number of matches they have won across different IPL seasons in ascending order of number of wins.

Program

```
import pandas as pd
data = pd.read_csv('matches.csv')
print(data.columns)
print(data['winner'].value_counts( ).sort_values(ascending = True))
```

Output

```
Rising Pune Supergiants           5
Kochi Tuskers Kerala              6
Royal Challengers Bengaluru       7
Rising Pune Supergiant           10
....                            ...
Chennai Super Kings             138
Mumbai Indians                  144
```

Problem 30.3

Data of all matches played across all IPL seasons is available in the file 'matches.csv' file. Define a function that receives a team name and returns the number of matches won by that team across seasons. Also define a function that receives a team name and the season (year) and returns the number of matches won by that team in that season.

Program

```
def wins(team) :
    filter = data['winner'] == team
    number_of_wins = data[filter].shape[0]
    return(number_of_wins)

def wins_in_season(team, year) :
    filter1 = data['winner'] == team
```

```
    filter2 = data['season'] == year
    wins = data[(filter1) & (filter2)].shape[0]
    return(wins)

import pandas as pd
data = pd.read_csv('matches.csv')
w = wins('Punjab Kings')
print('No. of Punjab Kings wins =', w )
w = wins('Mumbai Indians')
print('No. of Mumbai Indian wins =', w )

w = wins_in_season('Rajasthan Royals', '2022')
print('No. of Rajasthan Royals wins in 2010 =', w )
w = wins_in_season('Mumbai Indians', '2023')
print('No. of Punjab Kings wins in 2018 =', w )
```

Output

```
No. of Punjab Kings wins = 24
No. of Mumbai Indian wins = 144
No. of Rajasthan Royals wins in 2010 = 10
No. of Punjab Kings wins in 2018 = 9
```

Problem 30.4

Data of all matches played across all IPL seasons is available in the file 'matches.csv' file. Write a program to print the following:

- A list of winner and margin of runs by which the match was won if winning margin is more than 100 runs.
- A list of winners and number of wickets by which the match was won if winning margin is more than 5 wickets.

Program

```
import pandas as pd
data = pd.read_csv('matches.csv')
df = data[['winner', 'result', 'result_margin']]

mask = (df['result'] == 'runs') & (df['result_margin'] > 100)
filtered_df = df[mask]
print(filtered_df)
```

```
mask = (df['result'] == 'wickets') & (df['result_margin'] > 5)
filtered_df = df[mask]
print(filtered_df)
```

Output

```
                    winner     result   result_margin
0    Kolkata Knight Riders       runs           140.0
55       Rajasthan Royals        runs           105.0
236       Kings XI Punjab        runs           111.0
...                   ...         ...             ...

                    winner     result   result_margin
2         Delhi Daredevils    wickets             9.0
5         Rajasthan Royals    wickets             6.0
11     Chennai Super Kings    wickets             9.0
...                   ...         ...             ...
```

Problem 30.5

Data of all matches played across all IPL seasons is available in the file 'matches.csv' file. Columns 'team1' and 'team2' contain names of team participating in a match. Write a program to print a list of all teams who played across seasons along with abbreviation of team name containing only first letter of each word in the team-name.

Program

```
# function to get the abbreviation
def get_abbreviation(team_name):
  return ''.join(word[0] for word in team_name.split())

import pandas as pd
df = pd.read_csv('matches.csv')
teams = df['team1'].unique( )
# apply the function to each team and create a list of tuples
team_data = [(team, get_abbreviation(team)) for team in teams]
print(team_data)
```

Output

```
[('Royal Challengers Bangalore', 'RCB'), ('Kings XI Punjab', 'KXP'), ('Delhi Daredevils', 'DD'), ('Mumbai Indians', 'MI'), ('Kolkata Knight Riders', 'KKR'), ('Rajasthan Royals', 'RR'), ('Deccan Chargers', 'DC'), ('Chennai Super Kings', 'CSK'), ('Kochi Tuskers Kerala', 'KTK'), ('Pune Warriors', 'PW'), ('Sunrisers Hyderabad', 'SH'), ('Gujarat Lions', 'GL'), ('Rising Pune Supergiants', 'RPS'), ('Rising Pune Supergiant', 'RPS'), ('Delhi Capitals', 'DC'), ('Punjab Kings', 'PK'), ('Lucknow Super Giants', 'LSG'), ('Gujarat Titans', 'GT'), ('Royal Challengers Bengaluru', 'RCB')]
```

Problem 30.6

Data of all matches played, and all deliveries bowled across all IPL seasons is available in files 'matches.csv' and 'deliveries.csv' respectively. Write a program to obtain the following information from the data:

- Number of matches played at each stadium
- Number of matches played in each season
- Number of teams in each season
- Number of super overs played in each season
- Total number of matches played (in two ways)
- Percentage of matches won by toss winner

Program

```
import pandas as pd
df1 = pd.read_csv('matches.csv')
df2 = pd.read_csv('deliveries.csv')

# number of matches played at each stadium
stads = df1['venue'].value_counts( ).sort_values(ascending = True)
print(stads)

# number of matches played in each season
num = df1['season'].value_counts().sort_values(ascending = True)
print(num)

# number of teams in each season
num =  df1[['season', 'winner']].drop_duplicates( ).groupby('season')
            .count( )
print(num)
```

```
# number of super overs played in each season
mask = df1['super_over'] == 'Y'
df_super_over = df1[mask]
season_counts = df_super_over['season'].value_counts( )
print(season_counts.reset_index( ))

# total number of matches – first method
print('Number of matches played = ', df1.shape[0])

# total number of matches – second method
num = len(df2['match_id'].drop_duplicates( ))
print('Number of matches played = ', num)

# percentage of matches won by toss winner
matches_played = len(df1)
mask = df1['toss_winner'] == df1['winner']
matches_won_by_toss_winner = len(df1[mask])
per_won = matches_won_by_toss_winner / matches_played * 100
print('% matches won by toss winner = ', per_won)
```

Output

```
stadium
Dr. YSR Reddy ACA-VDCA Cricket Stadium, Visakhapatnam     2
OUTsurance Oval                                           2
Buffalo Park                                              3
... ...                                                   ..

season
2009       57
2007/08    58
2015       59
...        ..

season
2007/08    8
2009       8
2009/10    8
...        ..
    season  count
0  2020/21      4
1     2013      2
2     2019      2
```

```
..    ...         ..

Number of matches played =  1095
Number of matches played =  1095
% matches won by toss winner =  50.593607305936075
```

Problem 30.7

Data of all matches played across all IPL seasons is available in the file 'matches.csv'. Write a program to plot a Bar Chart of number of wins scored by 'Mumbai Indians' team in different IPL seasons.

Program

```
import pandas as pd
data = pd.read_csv('matches.csv')
filter = data['winner'] == 'Mumbai Indians'
mi_wins = data[filter]
# group by 'season' and count the number of wins in each season
mi_wins_per_season = mi_wins.groupby('season').size( )
mi_wins_per_season.plot(kind = 'bar')
```

Output

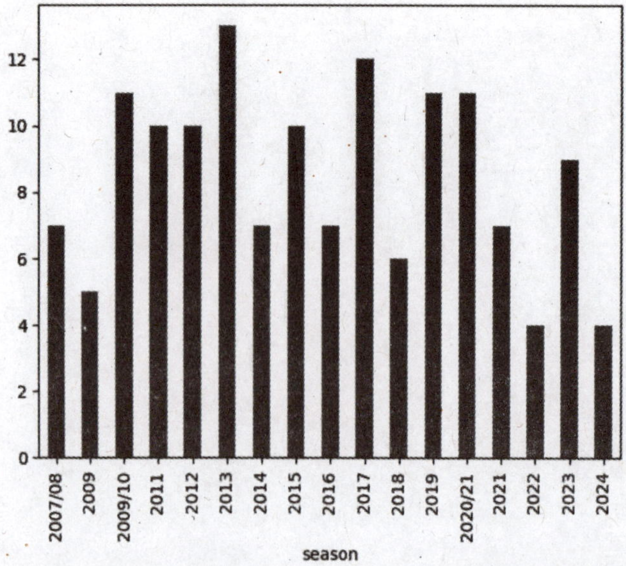

Exercises

[A] State which Pandas function will you use to perform the following operations:

(a) Read data from a .csv file.

(b) Combine data frow two DataFrames.

(c) Count the number of rows that meet a particular criterion.

(d) Organize the data in a DataFrame into different categories based on a particular criterion.

(e) Pick only the first row from a set of rows.

(f) Access a range of values from a Series.

(g) Access a range of values from using positions of values.

[B] Answer the following questions:

(a) Data of all deliveries bowled across all IPL seasons is available in the file 'deliveries.csv'. Write a program to obtain the following information:

- Total runs scored
- Total wickets fallen
- Batting strike rate
- Bowling strike rate

(b) Data of all deliveries bowled across all IPL seasons is available in the file 'deliveries.csv', and data of all matches in all IPL seasons is present in 'matches.csv'. Write a program to obtain the following information:

- Total runs scored per IPL season
- Batting strike rate per season

(c) Data of all deliveries bowled across all IPL seasons is available in the file 'deliveries.csv' and data of all matches in all IPL seasons is present in 'matches.csv'. Write a program to obtain the following information:

- Find Orange Cap holder of each season (batter who scores maximum runs in a season)
- Find Purple Cap holder of each season (bowler who takes maximum wickets in a season)

(d) Data of all deliveries bowled across all IPL seasons is available in the file 'deliveries.csv' and data of all matches in all IPL seasons is present in 'matches.csv'. Write a program to obtain the following information:
 - Top 5 batters who have scored maximum runs across all seasons
 - Top 3 bowlers who have taken maximum wickets across all seasons

(e) Using data from 'matches.csv' and 'deliveries.csv' define a function that receives the name of a batter and returns the name of the team against which the batter has scored maximum number of runs.

(f) Using data from 'matches.csv' and 'deliveries.csv' define a function that receives the name of a bowler and returns the name of the team against which the bowler has taken maximum number of wickets.

(g) Using data from 'matches.csv' and 'deliveries.csv' define a function that receives the name of a batter and returns the name of the team against which the batter has hit maximum number of fours and sixes.

(h) Write a program to create a DataFrame containing names of animals and their approximate weights. Export the data in this DataFrame to a file 'sample.csv'. The file should contain headers 'Name' and 'Weight' in its first row.

31 Security Programming

"Unlock the power of Security..."

Contents

KanNotes

Understanding security programming in Python will equip you with tools to protect your applications and data from threats. With this knowledge, you'll be able to implement SHA256 checksums, verify authenticity, encrypt and decrypt data using AES, and ensure non-repudiation through digital signing. This chapter guides you through these crucial security techniques.

Daily Tryst with Security

- Security is an integral part of our daily digital interactions, ensuring the safety and integrity of our sensitive information.
- A few examples where we encounter security in our digital interactions:
  (a) When making payments using a credit card, encryption protocols like SSL/TLS protect our card details from unauthorized access.

  (b) While doing online banking through a bank's website, multi-factor authentication and secure sessions are used to prevent fraud and keep our financial transactions confidential.

  (c) Online trading of stocks necessitates secure platforms to protect not only our investments but also our personal data from cyber threats.

  (d) Filing Income Tax returns involves submitting sensitive financial information, which is safeguarded by encryption and secure authentication methods to prevent identity theft and data breaches.

  (e) Connecting remotely to an office machine utilizes VPNs and secure login methods to protect corporate data and maintain the confidentiality of our work activities.

Importance of Security

Security has become very important due to several key reasons:

(a) **Connectivity**: With the ubiquity of internet access, our devices are constantly connected, making them susceptible to various cyber threats. Ensuring secure connectivity is essential to protect our personal and professional information from unauthorized access.

(b) **Distributed Computing**: Modern computing relies heavily on distributed systems, where data and processing are spread across multiple locations. This increases the complexity of securing data as it moves across different networks and systems, making robust security measures critical to maintain data integrity and confidentiality.

(c) **Digital Data**: In today's world, digital data is one of the most valuable assets. From personal information and financial records to corporate secrets and intellectual property, protecting this data from breaches and cyber-attacks is essential to maintain trust, privacy, and the overall functioning of our digital economy.

- These factors underscore the importance of implementing comprehensive security strategies to safeguard our digital lives.

Four Aspects of Security

- From the examples of security given above, four critical aspects of security can be identified. They are as follows:

    (a) **Integrity:** Integrity in security programming ensures that data has not been altered, corrupted or tampered with during storage or transmission.

    (b) **Authenticity:** Authenticity verifies the identity of users or systems, ensuring that data originates from a trusted source.

    (c) **Confidentiality:** Confidentiality protects sensitive information from unauthorized **access**, ensuring that only intended recipients can access the data.

    (d) **Non-repudiation: Non**-repudiation provides proof of the origin and integrity of data, ensuring that a party cannot deny sending a message or performing a transaction.

Data Integrity

- Data integrity can be achieved using algorithms known as hashing algorithms.

- Examples of these algorithms include MD5 (Message Digest version 5), SHA256 (Secure Hash Algorithm that generates hash value of 256 bits), SHA384 (384 bits), and SHA512 (512 bits).
- These algorithms compute a unique hash value for a given input data, which is often referred to as a message digest, fingerprint or checksum.
- The process of generating this hash value is known as hashing. One of the key properties of hashing is that two distinct inputs will always produce different hash values, ensuring the uniqueness of the hash.
- Hashing process is also known as one-way transformation or one-way hash, as it is computationally infeasible to reverse the hash value back to the original input data.

Computing SHA256

- Given below is a program that computes the SHA-256 hash of a string "How green was my valley" using Python's **cryptography** module and outputs it as a hexadecimal string.

```
from cryptography.hazmat.primitives import hashes
from cryptography.hazmat.backends import default_backend

def get_sha256(input_string):
    # create a SHA256 hash object
    digest = hashes.Hash(hashes.SHA256( ),
                backend = default_backend( ))

    # update the hash object with the bytes of the input string
    digest.update(input_string.encode('utf-8'))

    # finalize the hash and get the result
    return digest.finalize( ).hex( )

str = "How green was my valley!"
chksum = get_sha256(str)
print( "String:", str )
print( "Checksum:", chksum)
```

- In the beginning of this program, we have imported two modules here—**hashes** and **default_backend**.

- The **hashes** module allows us to use cryptographic hash functions, such as SHA-256, SHA-1, SHA-512, and others.
- The **default_backend** module provides an interface between the high-level Python code and the lower-level cryptographic implementations, such as OpenSSL, CommonCrypto, etc.
- Computing a message digest involves three key steps: initialization, updating, and finalization.
- During the initialization step, a hash object called **digest** is created using the **Hash( )** function. This object allows us to feed data (in chunks or all at once) and compute its cryptographic hash.
- The **digest** object is initialized with a specific hash algorithm (**hashes.SHA256( )**) and a cryptographic backend (**backend = default_backend( )**) to process the hash.
- The function **default_backend( )** returns the default backend available on our system. Typically, this backend is OpenSSL, which is one of the most widely used cryptographic libraries, though it can vary depending on the platform.
- In the updating phase, the input data is fed to the **digest** object. This step may involve multiple updates if data is long. The utf-8 encoded bytes of the input string are now processed by the SHA-256 hash function.
- In the finalization step, the computation of the message digest is completed, resulting in a 32-byte hash value whose hexadecimal form is returned.
- Before executing the program install the cryptography module using the command:

  C:> pip install cryptography

SHA256 of A File

- It is possible to compute the SHA256 checksum of a file containing text or binary data. The following program illustrates how this can be done for a file "humor.txt" containing some data.

```
from cryptography.hazmat.primitives import hashes
from cryptography.hazmat.backends import default_backend
```

```
def sha256_of_file(source):
    # create a SHA-256 hash object
    digest = hashes.Hash(hashes.SHA256( ),
                backend=default_backend( ))
    # open file, read it in chunks and update digest object
    f = open(source, "rb")
    chunk_size = 4096
    while 1 :
        chunk = f.read(chunk_size)
        if not chunk :
            break
        digest.update(chunk)

    f.close( )
    # finalize the hash and return the digest in hexadecimal form
    return digest.finalize( ).hex( )

file_path = "humor.txt"
chksum = sha256_of_file(file_path)
print("SHA-256 Hash:", chksum)
```

- Most of the working of this function is same as what we learnt in **get_sha256( )** in previous section.
- The only piece of code that is different is opening of the file and the **while** loop.
- Once the specified file (**source**) is opened in read mode ("r"), the **while** loop reads chunks of data from the file and updates the **digest** object with each chunk of data. Thus, through the loop we can process large files to obtain their SHA256 checksum.
- Often along with the files that are made available for downloading from server, their SHA256 checksum is also published. So, once we download a file, we can compute its checksum (using the above program) and then compare this checksum with the checksum published on the server. If they match in all 32 bytes, we can be sure that the downloaded file is an exact replica of the file on the server. If not, it means that the two files are different and hence data integrity has been violated.

Authenticity

- We can use the SHA256 checksum to check whether the user of an application/website is an authentic user or not. For this, specific tasks are carried out during the 'sign up' and sign-in' processes.
- During 'sign-up' when the user enters his login name and password, the server stores the login name and SHA256 checksum of password in a database on server.
- During 'sign-in' when the user enters the login name and password, the SHA256 checksum stored against the login name is retrieved from the server database. Next, the SHA256 checksum of the entered password is computed. Then the retrieved checksum is compared with the computed checksum. If there is an exact match then the user is an authentic user, otherwise not.
- We can implement this authentication scheme with some simplification. Instead of storing the login name and SHA256 checksum of password in a database on server, we will store it in a text file locally. During 'sign-in' we will read this SHA256 checksum from the local file. Both these programs are given below.

```
# Program 1 - Create user during 'sign-up'
from cryptography.hazmat.backends import default_backend
from cryptography.hazmat.primitives import hashes

def get_sha256(password):
    digest = hashes.Hash(hashes.SHA256( ),
                         backend=default_backend( ))
    digest.update(password.encode('utf-8'))
    return digest.finalize( ).hex( )

username = input("Loginname: ")
password = input("Password: ")

# generate SHA-256 hash of the password
sha256_of_password = get_sha256(password)

# write username and SHA-256 of password to a file
f = open("userData.txt", "w")
f.write(f"{username}:{sha256_of_password}\n")
f.close( )
```

```
# Program 2: Validate user during 'sign-in'
from cryptography.hazmat.backends import default_backend
from cryptography.hazmat.primitives import hashes

def get_sha256(password) :
    digest = hashes.Hash(hashes.SHA256( ),
                    backend=default_backend( ))
    digest.update(password.encode('utf-8'))
    return digest.finalize( ).hex( )
uname = input("Loginname: ")
pw = input("Password: ")

sha256_input_pw = get_sha256(pw)

# read the stored username and SHA-256 password from file
f = open("userData.txt", "r")
stored_data = f.readline().strip( )
stored_uname, sha256_stored_pw = stored_data.split(':')

if uname == stored_uname and
      sha256_input_pw == sha256_stored_pw :
    print("Legal user")
else:
    print("Illegal user")
```

- Today in practise instead of Basic Authentication demonstrated above, Two-factor Authentication (2FA) is used. In this scheme after validating the login name and password, authenticity is checked using one of the following methods:

  (a) One-time password (OTP)
  (b) Fingerprint recognition
  (c) Face recognition
  (d) Pattern recognition
  (e) Security question

  Implementation of these schemes is quite involved and beyond the scope of this book.

- In the above schemes authenticity of user is being checked by the server. For user to feel assured, the user should also be able to check the authenticity of the server. For instance, while carrying out financial transactions on a bank's web site, the user should be able to find out whether he is transacting with a legitimate financial institution or not. This is done using Digital Certificates.

Confidentiality

- Confidentiality is about keeping data private and inaccessible to unauthorized parties. Confidentiality is crucial in scenarios like credit card transactions, where personal and financial information must be safeguarded against eavesdropping.

- Confidentiality is achieved through encryption algorithms like AES (Advanced Encryption Standard), which encrypt the data into an unreadable format for unauthorized users. AES is a virtually impenetrable algorithm, extremely secure and widely used worldwide.

- AES is a symmetric encryption technique to secure data. Here "symmetric" means that for encryption and decryption same key is used. In addition to key, AES also uses an Initialization Vector (IV) for encryption and decryption. The primary purpose of the IV is to ensure that even if the same plaintext is encrypted multiple times, the ciphertext will be different each time. This prevents attackers from inferring patterns based on repeated ciphertexts. This makes the encryption process unique and unpredictable.

- Let us now see how a file "humor.txt" can be encrypted using a key and IV. The program for this is given below.

```
from cryptography.hazmat.primitives.ciphers import Cipher,
        algorithms, modes
from cryptography.hazmat.backends import default_backend
from cryptography.hazmat.primitives import padding
from cryptography.hazmat.primitives import hashes
from cryptography.hazmat.primitives.kdf.pbkdf2
        import PBKDF2HMAC
import os

# function to encrypt a file using AES-256-CBC
def encrypt_file(input_file, output_file, key, iv) :
  # initialize the cipher (AES-256 in CBC mode)
  cipher = Cipher(algorithms.AES(key), modes.CBC(iv),
            backend=default_backend( ))
  encryptor = cipher.encryptor( )
```

```
    # pad the data to ensure it's a multiple of the block size (16 bytes)
    padder = padding.PKCS7(algorithms.AES.block_size).padder( )

    with open(input_file, 'rb') as f_in, open(output_file, 'wb') as f_out :
        # read and encrypt the file in chunks
        while True :
            chunk = f_in.read(1024)
            if len(chunk) == 0 :
                break
            padded_data = padder.update(chunk)
            f_out.write(encryptor.update(padded_data))

        # write the final padded block and finalize encryption
        f_out.write(encryptor.update(padder.finalize( )))
        f_out.write(encryptor.finalize( ))
# generate a 256-bit (32 bytes) AES key and a 128-bit (16 bytes) IV
key = os.urandom(32)  # AES-256 requires a 32-byte key
iv = os.urandom(16)    # AES CBC mode uses a 16-byte IV

# save the key and IV to binary files
with open('key.bin', 'wb') as key_out :
    key_out.write(key)

with open('iv.bin', 'wb') as iv_out :
    iv_out.write(iv)

# encrypt the file 'humor.txt' and save output to 'encrypted.bin'
encrypt_file('humor.txt', 'encrypted.bin', key, iv)

print("File encrypted successfully!")
```

- The working of this program and the various operations being carried out in it are discussed below.

- Imports: **cryptography.hazmat.primitives.ciphers**: Provides the Cipher, algorithms.AES, and modes.CBC needed for encryption. **cryptography.hazmat.backends.default_backend()**: Ensures we use the appropriate cryptographic backend (usually OpenSSL).

- AES-256-CBC: We are using AES-256, which requires a 32-byte key and a 16-byte initialization vector (IV). CBC (Cipher Block Chaining) mode requires that the input data size be a multiple of the block size (16 bytes). If not, we need to pad the data.

- Padding: **PKCS7** padding is used to pad the input data to a multiple of the AES block size (16 bytes). This is handled by **padding.PKCS7( )**.
- File Encryption: The **encrypt_file( )** function reads the input file in chunks of 1024 bytes, applies padding, and encrypts it. The final block is padded and written to the output file. The input file "humor.txt" is read, encrypted, and saved as "encrypted.bin".
- Random Key and IV**: os.urandom(32)** generates a secure random 32-byte key for AES-256. **os.urandom(16)** generates a secure random 16-byte IV for CBC mode. Both the key and IV are saved to binary files (key.bin and iv.bin).
- Let us now do the reverse process, i.e. decrypt the "encrypted.bin" file by reading the key and IV from "key.bin" and "iv.bin". Here is the program...

```
from cryptography.hazmat.primitives.ciphers import Cipher,
    algorithms, modes
from cryptography.hazmat.backends import default_backend
from cryptography.hazmat.primitives import padding
import os

# function to decrypt a file using AES-256-CBC
def decrypt_file(input_file, output_file, key, iv) :
  # initialize the cipher (AES-256 in CBC mode)
  cipher = Cipher(algorithms.AES(key), modes.CBC(iv),
           backend=default_backend( ))
  decryptor = cipher.decryptor( )

  # unpad the data after decryption
  unpadder = padding.PKCS7(algorithms.AES.block_size).unpadder()

  with open(input_file, 'rb') as f_in, open(output_file, 'wb') as f_out :
    while True :
      chunk = f_in.read(1024 + algorithms.AES.block_size)
      if len(chunk) == 0:
        break
      decrypted_data = decryptor.update(chunk)
      f_out.write(unpadder.update(decrypted_data))

    # finalize the decryption and write the final block
    f_out.write(unpadder.update(decryptor.finalize()))
    f_out.write(unpadder.finalize( ))
```

```
# read the AES key and IV from their respective binary files
with open('key.bin', 'rb') as key_in :
    key = key_in.read(32)  # AES-256 requires a 32-byte key
with open('iv.bin', 'rb') as iv_in :
    iv = iv_in.read(16)    # AES-CBC requires a 16-byte IV

# decrypt the file 'encrypted.bin' and save the output to 'decrypted_humor.txt'
decrypt_file('encrypted.bin', 'decrypted_humor.txt', key, iv)

print("File decrypted successfully!")
```

- The working of this program and the various operations being carried out in it are discussed below.
- The program decrypts the file "encrypted.bin" using the key and IV, writing the decrypted data to "decrypted_humor.txt".
- Reading Key and IV: The AES-256 key (32 bytes) and IV (16 bytes) are read from the binary files ("key.bin" and "iv.bin") that were generated during encryption.
- Decryption Process: The **decrypt_file( )** function sets up the AES-256 cipher in **CBC mode** using the key and IV read from the binary files (key.bin and iv.bin). It reads the encrypted file ("encrypted.bin") in chunks, decrypts it, and writes the result to the output file ("decrypted_humor.txt"). After decryption, the **PKCS7 unpadding** is applied to remove padding added during encryption.

Non-repudiation

- Non-repudiation prevents individuals from denying their actions. This section demonstrates how to use digital signatures to provide undeniable proof of the origin and integrity of a document. To achieve this, we need a pair of keys—a public key and a private key.
- As their names suggest, the public key can be shared openly with anyone, whereas its corresponding private key must be kept secret.
- The idea of key pairs was conceived by Rivest-Shamir-Adleman (RSA) and is widely used for two purposes: Encryption and Non-repudiation.
- Encryption: A symmetric key encrypted using a public key can be decrypted only using its corresponding private key. Since the key

used for encryption is different than the one used for decryption, this process is called asymmetric encryption. Contrast this with the method discussed in "Confidentiality" section above which used symmetric encryption (same key used for encryption and decryption). Note that RSA is being used for encryption / decryption of symmetric key and not for data (file) encryption and decryption.

- Note that symmetric encryption is faster than asymmetric encryption. So, symmetric encryption is used for file encryption/decryption, whereas asymmetric encryption is used for sharing the key used for symmetric encryption.
- Non-repudiation: Data signed using a private key can be verified by anyone using the corresponding public key.
- In this section we will concentrate on non-repudiation and not on symmetric key encryption/decryption.
- The private and public keys are usually stored in Privacy-Enhanced Mail (.PEM) files. These files are Base64 encoded, and the key is usually encapsulated between "-----BEGIN" and "-----END" lines.
- The following OpenSSL commands can be used to generate private and public keys.

```
# Generate a private key, store it in private_key.pem file
$ openssl genpkey -algorithm RSA -out private_key.pem

# Extract the public key, store it in public_key.pem file
$ openssl rsa -pubout -in private_key.pem -out public_key.pem
```

- The key generation relies on the mathematical properties of large prime numbers. The size of private and public keys is 2048 bits (256 bytes) by default. However, if you open the two PEM files you will observe that the private key appears to be bigger than the public key. This is because the private key file contains all the information needed to generate the public key.
- Let us now develop two programs. The first one will sign a file "humor.txt" using a private key stored in "private_key.pem" and the second one will verify the signature using the corresponding public key stored in "public_key.pem". This mechanism ensures that the signer cannot deny having signed the document, providing a robust non-repudiation solution. Here is the first program.

```
from cryptography.hazmat.primitives import hashes
from cryptography.hazmat.primitives.asymmetric import padding
from cryptography.hazmat.primitives.serialization import
        load_pem_private_key
from cryptography.hazmat.backends import default_backend
import os

def sign_file(input_file, output_file, private_key_file) :
    # read the contents of the input file (humor.txt)
    with open(input_file, "rb") as f :
        file_data = f.read( )

    # load the private key from private_key.pem
    with open(private_key_file, "rb") as key_file :
        private_key = load_pem_private_key(key_file.read( ),
            password=None, backend=default_backend( ))

    # compute the SHA256 hash of the file content
    digest = hashes.Hash(hashes.SHA256( ),
                backend=default_backend( ))
    digest.update(file_data)
    file_hash = digest.finalize( )

    pkcs1v15_padding = padding.PKCS1v15( )
    hash_algorithm = hashes.SHA256( )

    # perform the signing operation using the private key, padding,
    # and hash algorithm
    signature = private_key.sign(file_hash, pss_padding,
                    hash_algorithm)

    # write the signature to the output file (signature.bin)
    with open(output_file, "wb") as sig_file :
        sig_file.write(signature)

sign_file("humor.txt", "signature.bin", "private_key.pem")
print("File signed successfully!")
```

- The program reads the contents of "humor.txt", computes the SHA256 checksum of the content, and then signs this digest using the private key stored in "private_key.pem". The generated signature is then written to "signature.bin". The signing process involves encrypting the hash with the private key. Thus, the signature stored in "signature.bin" is essentially an encrypted version of the hash and is unique to both the file content and the private key.

- The working of this program and the various operations being carried out in it are discussed below.
- Imports: **hashes** is used for computing the SHA-256 hash. **Asymmetric c**ontains cryptographic padding and key handling for signing. **serialization** is used for loading the private key from a PEM file. **default_backend** provides the backend to handle cryptographic operations.
- **sign_file( ):** This function reads file contents from "humor.txt" and private key from "private_key.pem". Then the SHA-256 hash of file's contents is computed. The private key is used to sign the computed SHA-256 hash using the PSS padding scheme. The generated signature is written to "signature.bin" file.
- **Padding and Signature**: PKCS1v15, a deterministic padding scheme is used for padding, and the SHA-256 hash algorithm is used for both the hash and padding.
- Let us now go to the next step, i.e. verifying the signature. This can be done using the program given below:

```
from cryptography.hazmat.primitives import hashes
from cryptography.hazmat.primitives.asymmetric import padding
from cryptography.hazmat.primitives.serialization import
    load_pem_public_key
from cryptography.hazmat.backends import default_backend

def verify_file(input_file, signature_file, public_key_file) :
    # read the contents of the input file (humor.txt)
    with open(input_file, "rb") as f :
        file_data = f.read( )

    # load the public key from public_key.pem
    with open(public_key_file, "rb") as key_file :
        public_key = load_pem_public_key(key_file.read( ),
                            backend=default_backend( ))

    # compute the SHA256 hash of the file content
    digest = hashes.Hash(hashes.SHA256( ),
                    backend=default_backend( ))
    digest.update(file_data)
```

```
    file_hash = digest.finalize( )

    # read the signature from the signature.bin file
    with open(signature_file, "rb") as sig_file :
        signature = sig_file.read( )

    # verify the signature using the public key and PKCS1v15 padding
    try:
        public_key.verify( signature, file_hash, padding.PKCS1v15( ),
                hashes.SHA256( ))
        print("Signature verified successfully!")
        return True
    except Exception as e :
        print("Signature verification failed:", str(e))
        return False

result = verify_file("humor.txt", "signature.bin", "public_key.pem")
```

- The working of this program and the various operations being carried out in it are discussed below.
- Imports: **hashes** is used for computing the SHA-256 hash. **asymmetric.padding** contains the PKCS1v15 padding scheme for RSA signatures. s**erialization** is used for loading the public key from a PEM file. **default_backend** provides the backend to handle cryptographic operations.
- **verify_file( )**: This function reads the contents of "**humor.txt"** and loads the **public key** from "public_key.pem". Then the SHA-256 hash of file contents is computed. Next, the digital signature stored in the "signature.bin" file is read.
- **public_key.verify( )**: This method verifies that the signature matches the file's hash. This method takes the signature, the computed hash, PKCS1v15 padding, and the SHA-256 hash algorithm as parameters.
- Error Handling: If the signature verification fails, an exception is raised, and the message "Signature verification failed" is printed along with the error details.

Digital Signing in Practice

- There are multiple options available for signing a document using a digital signature. These are as follows:
- USB Dongle: It stores the digital certificate and private key securely.

Usage: The dongle is attached to a USB drive and the software that comes with the dongle is used to sign a document digitally.

- Smart card: It stores the digital certificate and private key securely.

  Usage: Insert the smart card into the reader and use it to sign documents digitally.

- Software-Based Digital Signature: Obtain a digital certificate from a trusted Certificate Authority (CA) and store it on your computer.

  Usage: Use software such as Adobe Acrobat, Microsoft Word, or specialized digital signature applications to apply digital signature.

- Hardware Security Module (HSM): These are dedicated hardware devices that manage digital keys and perform cryptographic operations.

  Usage: Often used by organizations to centrally manage and secure digital keys for signing documents and transactions.

- Cloud-Based Digital Signatures: Services like DocuSign, Adobe Sign, and HelloSign offer cloud-based digital signing solutions.

  Usage: Users can sign documents from any device with internet access. The service handles key management and applies digital signatures.

- Mobile-Based Signing Solutions: Apps like SignEasy, Adobe Fill & Sign, and others allow users to sign documents directly from their mobile devices.

  Usage: These apps may use biometrics (fingerprint, facial recognition) to secure the signing process.

- Public Key Infrastructure (PKI) Solutions: Organizations can implement their own PKI solutions to issue and manage digital certificates internally.

  Usage: Users can sign documents using the digital certificates issued by the organization's PKI.

- Browser-Based Digital Signatures: Browser extensions like CertifyID use the browser's built-in security features.

  Usage: Users can sign documents directly within their web browser using their digital certificates.

- Each of these digital signing solutions has its own advantages and is suited for different use cases. USB dongles and smart cards offer high security, while cloud-based and software-based solutions provide flexibility and convenience. The choice of method depends on the specific security requirements, convenience needs, and the technological infrastructure of the user or organization.

- When signing a document digitally using any of the above methods, the process involves the following steps:

  Hashing: The document's content is hashed using a secure hash algorithm like SHA256.

  Encryption: The hash is encrypted using the signer's private key, creating a digital signature.

  Attachment: The digital signature is attached to the document.

- On receiving the document, the following steps are performed:

  Hashing: The document's content is hashed again using the same hash algorithm.

  Decryption: The attached digital signature is decrypted using the signer's public key.

  Comparison: The decrypted hash is compared to the newly computed hash. If they match, the signature is verified, ensuring the document's integrity and authenticity.

Exercises

[A] Match the pairs:

(a) Integrity	(1) Signing, Verification
(b) Authenticity	(2) Encryption / Decryption
(c) Confidentiality	(3) SHA256
(d) Non-repudiation	(4) MD5

[B] Pick the correct choice:

(a) Which of the following techniques will you use if you wish to transmit a file ensuring its confidentiality.

(1) Use asymmetric encryption for encryption/decryption

(2) Use symmetric encryption for encryption/decryption
(3) Use asymmetric encryption for sharing symmetric key, use symmetric encryption/decryption for file
(4) Use symmetric encryption for sharing symmetric key, use asymmetric encryption/decryption for file

(b) We wish to download a file from the server and check whether it has been downloaded correctly or not. Which technique would you employ to achieve this?

(1) Download the file, compute its SHA256 checksum
(2) Download the file, compute its SHA256 checksum, compare this checksum with checksum of file reported on server
(3) Download the file using RSA
(4) Use symmetric encryption while downloading the file

[C] Answer the following questions:

(a) Which are the four aspects of security? Does every secure application need to implement them?

(b) Obtain MD5 checksum of the following strings and check whether they are same:

"Six slippery snails slid slowly seaward."
"Six silppery snails slid slowly seaward."

(c) Obtain SHA256 checksum of any executable file.

32 Interaction With ChatGPT

"AI... The programmer's magic lamp"

Contents

- AI Terminology
- What is ChatGPT?
- Ways to Use ChatGPT
- The First ChatGPT Program
- Speech to Text Conversion
- Text to Image Conversion
- ChatGPT Endpoints
- Exercises

KanNotes

Artificial Intelligence (AI) has become the rage of the day. Multiple AI tools are available that let us write programs, translate text, produce images, create videos etc. The most popular amongst these tools is ChatGPT, created by a company named OpenAI. In this chapter we will see how to interact with ChatGPT through Python programs. Before we get down to that, let us understand some terminology commonly used with AI.

AI Terminology

- AI refers to the simulation of human intelligence in machines, enabling them to perform tasks that typically require human cognition, such as understanding language, recognizing patterns, and making decisions. Some commonly used terms in relation to AI are given below:
- **Machine Learning**: It is a subset of artificial intelligence that focuses on building algorithms that enable computers to learn from and make decisions based on data without being explicitly programmed.
- **Deep Learning**: It is a specialized branch of machine learning that uses neural networks with many layers to automatically learn and extract complex patterns from large datasets. Deep learning is inspired by the working of the human brain and is particularly effective in handling complex tasks like image recognition, speech synthesis, and natural language processing, where they can uncover intricate relationships within large datasets.
- **Natural Language Processing (NLP)**: It is a field of artificial intelligence that focuses on the interaction between computers and humans through natural language. It involves the development of algorithms and models that enable machines to understand, interpret, and generate human language, facilitating tasks such as translation, sentiment analysis, and conversation.

What is ChatGPT?

- The name "ChatGPT" breaks down as follows:

  Chat: This refers to the conversational aspect of the model. The model is designed to engage in dialogue or "chat" with users, answering questions, providing information, or engaging in conversation on various topics.

G: Stands for Generative. This signifies that the model is a generative model, meaning it generates text based on the input it receives. It doesn't simply retrieve information but creates responses dynamically.

P: Stands for Pre-trained. This indicates that the model has undergone extensive training on a large dataset before it is fine-tuned or used in specific applications. The pre-training phase allows the model to learn language patterns, grammar, facts, and some reasoning abilities.

T: Stands for Transformer. The transformer is a type of deep learning model architecture that is particularly effective for natural language processing tasks. The "T" refers to the underlying architecture that powers the GPT model.

- So, "ChatGPT" essentially means a Generative Pre-trained Transformer model that is used for chat or conversational purposes.
- The core of ChatGPT is built upon the Transformer architecture, a deep learning model that has revolutionized the way computers understand and generate human language. Trained on vast amounts of text data, ChatGPT aims to achieve seamless and intuitive interactions, enabling users to obtain information, solve problems, and engage in creative tasks with a level of fluency and coherence that closely mirrors natural human communication. Whether it's answering questions, providing recommendations, or assisting in technical tasks, ChatGPT's goal is to enhance human capabilities by providing an accessible, intelligent, and responsive virtual assistant.

Ways to Use ChatGPT

- There are two main ways to use ChatGPT: interactively and programmatically.
- **Interactively**: We can use ChatGPT by visiting the OpenAI website at https://chatgpt.com. Here, you can engage in a conversational interface where you type your questions or prompts, and ChatGPT responds in real-time. This method is user-friendly and requires no technical setup, making it ideal for casual use or quick queries.

- **Programmatically**: For more advanced users, ChatGPT can be accessed programmatically via the ChatGPT API. This approach allows developers to integrate ChatGPT's capabilities into their own applications, automating interactions and customizing the model's behaviour according to specific needs.

  By sending HTTP requests to the API endpoint with the necessary parameters and receiving responses in a structured format, developers can leverage ChatGPT to power chatbots, virtual assistants, or any application that requires natural language understanding and generation.

- Interactive usage of ChatGPT is free, whereas when we use ChatGPT programmatically, we get a free credit of 18$, beyond which it is a paid service. There is a catch here - 18$ is a combination of your interactive use and programmatic use. If your quota of free usage exceeds 18$ credit, you may either subscribe to paid service or open a completely new account at OpenAI with a fresh email address and mobile number.

The First ChatGPT Program

- Let us now write our first Python program that interacts with ChatGPT. For this we need to make API calls using the HTTPS protocol. This is facilitated by a module called **requests**.

- The 'requests' module provides a flexible and efficient way to interact with web servers and other online resources programmatically. We need to install it using the following command:

  ```
  C:\> pip install requests
  ```

- Another thing that you need to do before writing the program is to get an API key from OpenAI. The OpenAI API uses an API key for authentication when we make calls to the API. It can be obtained by visiting

  https://platform.openai.com/api-keys

- You need to copy the generated API key and paste it in your program. A sample API key is given below:

  sk-proj-AndnR8ixP_icm9CPw7KYFeB3Ah2x4Sh5PJNApwDg1jCzsKGBB

GLz9x3jjsT3BlbkFJ8e5PvPljb1w7wswpX7l4eg6rdfvls7V72hE9ShSSFw4afu7ky3XmY5oB

- Let us now write a program that asks ChatGPT "What is Pythagoras theorem?"

```
import requests
import json

api_key = "INSERT YOUR API KEY HERE"
url = "https://api.openai.com/v1/chat/completions"

# set up the headers with your API key
hdrs = { "Authorization": f"Bearer {api_key}",
         "Content-Type": "application/json" }

# define the payload
data = {
        "model": "gpt-3.5-turbo",
        "messages": [{"role": "user",
                      "content": "What is Pythogoras theorem"}]
    }

# make the API request
response = requests.post(url, headers=hdrs, data=json.dumps(data))

# check for a successful response
if response.status_code == 200 :
    res = response.json( )
    print(res)
else :
    print("Request failed")
```

- Before executing the program remember to replace "INSERT YOUR API KEY HERE" with your API key.

- There are different types of HTTP requests that can be made using 'request' module. While interacting with ChatGPT we need to make a POST request to a URL. When we make a POST request to ChatGPT, it returns a response. To make the HTTP POST request we need to perform the following steps:

Set the URL for POST request
Set the necessary custom headers
Set the POST data

Make the POST request
Collect the POST response

- While setting the header we have specified "Content-Type" as application/json. This informs the server that the body of the HTTP request contains data in JSON (JavaScript Object Notation) format. When the server receives this request, it knows to parse and handle the body content as JSON.

- The **data** variable contains the payload to be transferred during the POST request. This payload is organized in JSON format of key-value pairs. The JSON data in our program is shown below.

```
data = {
        "model": "gpt-3.5-turbo",
        "messages": [{"role": "user",
                      "content": "What is Pythogoras theorem"}]
    }
```

- Once all settings have been done, to perform the HTTP request, **requests.post( )** is called and ChatGPT's response is collected in a **response** object.

- On executing the program, the **response** object would contain the following data in JSON format:


```
Response: {
 "id": "chatcmpl-A0iWEIjAva4Q4leshpkIQiLR3kUGG",
 "object": "chat.completion",
 "created": 1724734494,
 "model": "gpt-3.5-turbo-0125",
 "choices": [
  {
   "index": 0,
   "message": {
    "role": "assistant",
    "content": "Pythagoras theorem is a fundamental principle in geometry that states that in a right-angled triangle, the square of the length of the hypotenuse is equal to the sum of the squares of the lengths of the other two sides. This theorem is named after the ancient Greek mathematician Pythagoras, who is credited with
```

```
discovering the relationship between the sides of a right-angled
triangle.",
        "refusal": null
      },
      "logprobs": null,
      "finish_reason": "stop"
    }
  ],
  "usage": {
    "prompt_tokens": 14,
    "completion_tokens": 142,
    "total_tokens": 156
  },
  "system_fingerprint": null
}
```


- In this response the value of "content" key explains ChatGPT's understanding of Pythagoras Theorem.
- If we wish to eliminate other parts of the response and print only the value against the key "contents", we can do so by modifying the **print( )** statement as follows:

```
print(res['choices'][0]['message']['content'])
```

Speech to Text Conversion

- ChatGPT has an ability to convert Speech into text. So, if an audio file "WebService.wav" is submitted to OpenAI API, it can transcribe the audio into text and send the transcribed text as a response.
- To achieve this, our program should perform the following steps:
  (a) Configure the necessary HTTP headers.
  (b) Prepare the MIME-formatted form data, including the audio file and model selection.
  (c) Send the form data to the API.
  (d) Capture and process the response from the API using a callback function.
- In the context of using the OpenAI API for speech-to-text conversion, the "form" refers to the structured set of data sent in an HTTP POST request. The form includes various parts, such as the audio file ("WebService.wav") being uploaded, the AI speech recognition

model to be used ("Whisper-1") for transcribing and other parameters needed by the API. The "whisper-1" model for transcribing audio into text is known for its accuracy and robustness in handling diverse audio inputs.

- Let us now look at the program that performs the transcription of the audio file "WebService.wav".

```
import requests

api_key = "INSERT YOUR API KEY HERE"
url = "https://api.openai.com/v1/audio/transcriptions"
audio_file = "WebService.wav"  # replace with your audio file

# set the headers
hdrs = { "Authorization": f"Bearer {api_key}" }

# prepare the data and files for the POST request
files = {
            "file": (audio_file, open(audio_file, "rb")),
            "model": (None, "whisper-1")
      }

# send the POST request to the OpenAI API
response = requests.post(url, headers=hdrs, files=files)

# check if the request was successful
if response.status_code == 200 :
    # print the transcription response
    print("Transcription Response:", response.json( ))
else :
    # print the error if something went wrong
    print(f"Failed: {response.text}")
```

- In this program the procedure for performing the request and obtaining the response is exactly same as the previous program.
- The transcribed text returned as a response is shown below.

```
Transcription Response: {
 "text": "now to make use of the web service that we have created which is able to implement the subscription feature we need to create a client which can make use of this web service. For that I will
```

```
open firstly the visual studio projects folder from where I would locate currency service 2 and open the current web service"
}
```

Text to Image Conversion

- OpenAI has developed an innovative AI model called DALL·E that generates images from textual descriptions.
- The word DALL·E is inspired by the surrealist art of Salvador Dalí and the imaginative nature of the animated robot WALL·E.
- By simply describing a scene, object, or concept in words, users can harness DALL·E to produce unique images that reflect their input, making it an invaluable tool for artists, designers, and content creators.
- Given below is a program that generates an image for the text prompt "Draw a picture of a monkey sitting on a crocodile's back".

```
import requests
import json

api_key = "INSERT YOUR API KEY HERE"
url = "https://api.openai.com/v1/images/generations"
prompt = "Draw a picture of a monkey sitting on a crocodile's back"

# set up the headers with the API key
hdrs = {
        "Authorization": f"Bearer {api_key}",
        "Content-Type": "application/json"
    }

# set up the data to send in the POST request
data = {
        "prompt": prompt,
        "n": 1, # number of images to generate
        "size": "1024x1024"  # size of the image
    }

# send the POST request to the API
response = requests.post(url, headers=hdrs, data=json.dumps(data))

# check if the request was successful
if response.status_code == 200 :
```

```
    response_data = response.json( )
    # extract the image URL from the response
    image_url = response_data['data'][0]['url']
    print("Generated Image URL:")
    print(image_url)
else :
    print("Failed to generate image")
    print(response.text)
```

- Except for the API endpoint and the POST data being sent in the HTTP request, the rest of the program is same as the first program in this chapter.
- Let us dissect the POST data set up in the variable **data.**

```
data = {
        "prompt": prompt,
        "n": 1,                  # number of images to generate
        "size": "1024x1024"      # size of the image
    }
```

- The **data** variable essentially instructs the API about what image to generate, how many images to create (**"n": 1)**, and the desired size (**"size": "1024x1024"**) of the output image. These values are specified in JSON format of key:value pairs.
- On executing this program, it produces the following output:

```
Generated Image URL:
https://oaidalleapiprodscus.blob.core.windows.net/private/org-
DXVRyJfL4rz5iWtSnZUTknx9/user-
tPfz0FfLPbZWrmHnYwDSzGJ0/img-
WkOnVjdif1f6fyChzs57lVVq.png?st=2024-09-
23T03%3A13%3A57Z&se=2024-09-
23T05%3A13%3A57Z&sp=r&sv=2024-08-
04&sr=b&rscd=inline&rsct=image/png&skoid=d505667d-d6c1-4a0a-
bac7-5c84a87759f8&sktid=a48cca56-e6da-484e-a814-
9c849652bcb3&skt=2024-09-22T23%3A13%3A47Z&ske=2024-09-
23T23%3A13%3A47Z&sks=b&skv=2024-08-
04&sig=tCDNwibr6uNsab9yOHhM5/Ht%2BQ6SH5EcNJ6j6QANsxl%3
D
```

- From this output copy the URL "https://oaidalleapiprodscus....xl%3D" and paste it in a browser. On doing this you should get the following image. Make sure that you grab this image within an hour, since OpenAI preserves your image only for an hour.

- The quality and the details of the image can be improved by using a more descriptive prompt. The better you describe the image, better will be the output.

ChatGPT Endpoints

- To engage in a conversation with ChatGPT we made a POST request to the URL https://api.openai.com/v1/chat/completions. Similarly, to transcript a wav file we made a POST request to the URL https://api.openai.com/v1/audio/transcriptions. These URLs are often referred to as ChatGPT API endpoints.
- Thus, an endpoint is a specific URL path provided by the OpenAI API that allows developers to interact with different features of ChatGPT.
- By making requests to these endpoints, developers can perform tasks such as generating text, creating images, converting speech to text, or moderating content, all by communicating with ChatGPT's underlying models.

- Each endpoint is designed for a particular function, making it easier to integrate AI capabilities into various applications.
- Given below is a list of some of the primary endpoints and their purposes:

  /v1/completions - Generates text based on a given prompt
  /v1/chat/completions - Engages in a conversation with ChatGPT
  /v1/edits - Edits a given text based on user instructions
  /v1/images/generations - Creates images from text descriptions
  /v1/embeddings - Generates vector representations of text for tasks like similarity or clustering
  /v1/audio/transcriptions - Converts audio files into text
  /v1/audio/translations - Translates audio files into English
- While making a POST request to an URL there are some 'required' and some 'optional' parameters that we must pass in the request body. Details of these parameters are available in ChatGPT API documentation available at https://platform.openai.com/docs/api-reference.

Exercises

[A] Answer the following questions:

(a) Arrange the following steps involved in making a HTTP request in correct sequence:

(1) Set the response variable
(2) Set the POST method
(3) Set the URL for POST request
(4) Set the POST data
(5) Set the necessary custom headers

(b) How does ChatGPT API authenticate a user request made through a HTTP call?

(c) Which are the ways to interact with ChatGPT?

[B] Attempt the following questions:

(a) Write a program to convert a given text into an audio file. Use the following information to make the HTTP request.

Endpoint - https://api.openai.com/v1/audio/speech

model - string containing Text to Speech model name tts-1 or tts-1-hd

input - string containing the text to generate audio for (maximum length is 4096 characters)

voice - string containing the voice to use when generating the audio. Supported voices are alloy, echo, fable, onyx, nova, and shimmer

(b) Write a program to generate 4 images of birds flying in the sky with a computer's mouse in their beak. Use the following information to make the HTTP request.

Endpoint - https://api.openai.com/v1/images/generations

prompt - string describing the image to be drawn by the model

input - string containing the text to generate audio for (maximum length is 4096 characters)

n - Number of images to be drawn

size - Size of the image

(c) Write a program to analyse a given sentence with a view to detect the mood of the sentence. For example, the mode of the sentence "I am so impressed by your performance" is "admiration and appreciation". Use the following information to make the HTTP request.

Endpoint - https://api.openai.com/v1/chat/completions

model - string containing the model name gpt-3.5-turbo

messages - A list of messages comprising the conversation

A Precedence Table

"Preferential treatments..."

Description	Operator	Associativity
Grouping	( )	Left to Right
Function call	function( )	Left to Right
Slicing	[start:end:step]	Left to Right
Exponentiation	**	Right to Left
Bitwise NOT	~	Right to Left
Unary plus / minus	+ -	Left to Right
Multiplication	*	Left to Right
Division	/	Left to Right
Modular Divsion	%	Left to Right
Addition	+	Left to Right
Subtraction	-	Left to Right
Bitwise left shift	<<	Left to Right
Bitwise right shift	>>	Left to Right
Bitwise AND	&	Left to Right
Bitwise XOR	^	Left to Right
Bitwise OR	|	Left to Right
Membership	In not in	Left to Right
Identity	is is not	Left to Right
Relational	< > <= >=	Left to Right
Equality	==	Left to Right
Inequality	!= <>	Left to Right
Logical NOT	not	Left to Right
Logical AND	and	Left to Right
Logical OR	or	Left to Right
Assignment	= += -= *= /= %= //= **= &= |= ^= >>= <<=	Right to Left

B Debugging in Python

"Don't bug others, debug instead..."

KanNotes

Debugging

- Two types of errors occur while creating programs—Syntax errors and Logical errors.
- Syntax errors are grammatical errors and are reported by Python interpreter. It is easy to rectify these errors as the interpreter tells us exactly which statement in the program is incorrect and why is it so.
- Logical errors are difficult to locate because we do not get any hint as to where things are wrong in our program and why we are not getting the desired results.
- Bug means an error. Debugging means the process of removal of errors. Debugger is a special program that can help us detect Logical errors in our program.
- There are many debuggers available for debugging Python programs. No matter which debugger we use, the steps for debugging remain the same. These steps are given below:

  (a) Start the debugger
  (b) Set breakpoints
  (c) Step through the source code one line at a time
  (d) Inspect the values of variables as they change
  (e) Make corrections to the source code
  (f) Rerun the program to make sure the fixes are correct

  Given below is a detailed explanation of these steps for IDLE debugger.

Start Debugger

- Start IDLE and type any program in it or open an already typed source file.
- In the Shell window, click on the 'Debug' menu option at the top and then choose 'Debugger' from the pop-up menu. A new window shown in Figure B.1 and titled 'Debug Control' will appear on the screen.

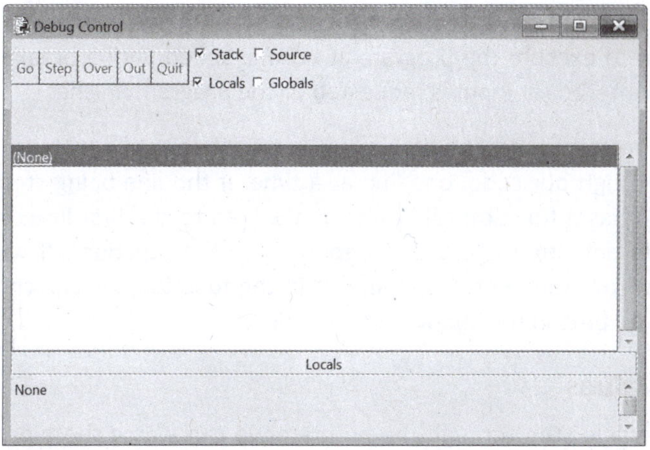

Figure B.1

- The Shell window will show:

  >>>
  [DEBUG ON]
  >>>

Set Breakpoints

- A breakpoint is a marker in our code that tells the debugger that execution should proceed at normal speed up to the breakpoint and stop there. Execution will not proceed beyond it unless we do so through manual intervention.

- Break points can be set in a program wherever we suspect something may go wrong. We can have many of them at different statements in one program.

- To set up a break point right click on a line of the source and choose 'Set breakpoint' from the menu.

- On setting a breakpoint the background color of the line turns yellow to show that a breakpoint has been set at that line.

Single Step through Program

- Execute the program using F5.

- The Debug Control window will now show in blue color the first line from where our program execution is to start. This means that line is ready to be executed.

- From this point we can click the 'Go' button in the Debug Control window to execute the program at normal speed until a breakpoint is encountered (or input is requested or the program finishes).
- Once control reaches the breakpoint, we can use the 'Step' button to step through our code, one line at a time. If the line being stepped through has a function call, execution will go to the first line of the function definition (we are "stepping into" the function). If we do not wish to examine the statements in the function, we can choose the 'Over' button to step over the function.

Inspect Values

- As we single step through the program we can watch the type and value of local and global variables used in our program at the bottom of the Debug Control window.
- As different steps of our program get executed and the values of the variables change, the changed values are displayed in the Debug Control window.

Correct and Run Again

- By watching the values of the variables if we get a clue as to what is wrong with our program, we can stop the execution using the 'Quit' button. We can then rectify the program and debug it again using the same steps.
- While single stepping if we reach inside a function and we wish to finish execution of the function at normal speed and return from the function, we can do so using the 'Out' button.

Try your Hand...

- Given below are three programs—first one finds the greatest common divisor for two numbers input through the keyboard. The second program determines whether a given year is a leap year or not and the third program finds sum of digits of a given number recursively. All three programs work correctly for some input and do not for some other input. Using the IDLE debugger fix the logical errors in the three programs.

```
# Program 1
# Program works correctly for input 5, 15
```

```
# Program does not work correctly for input 7, 5

def find_gcd(num1, num2) :
   min_num = min(num1, num2)
   for i in range(min_num, 1, -1) :
      if (num1 % i == 0) and (num2 % i == 0) :
         gcd = i
   return gcd

n1 = int(input('Enter first number: '))
n2 = int(input('Enter second number: '))
print(find_gcd(n1, n2))
```

```
# Program 2
# Program works correctly for input 1998
# Program works correctly for input 2000
# Program does not work correctly for input 1900

def isLeap(y) :
   return year % 100 == 0 or year % 4 == 0 or year % 400 == 0

year = int(input('Enter any year: '))
result = 'Leap' if isLeap(year) else 'Not Leap'
print(result)
```

```
# Program 3
# Program works correctly for input 0
# Program does not work correctly for input 12345
# Program does not work correctly for input 54321

def rsum(num) :
     if num != 0 :
          digit = num % 10
          num = int(num / 10)
          sum = digit + rsum(num)
     else :
          return 0

n = int(input('Enter number: '))
rs = rsum(n)
```

```
print('Sum of digits = ', rs)
```

pdb

- A Python debugger module called pdb comes built-in as part of Python standard library. This module can be used at command-line.
- It is popularly used for debugging Python code on remote servers where we do not have the privilege of an IDLE-like GUI-based debugger.

C Chasing the Bugs

"Wading through the choppy waters..."

KanNotes

How can we chase away the bugs in a Python program? No sure-shot way for that. So, I thought if I make a list of more common programming mistakes, it might be of help. I have presented them below. They are not arranged in any particular order, but I think they would be a good help!

Bug 1

Mixing tabs with spaces in indentation.

Consider the code snippet given below:

```
if a < b :
    a = 10
    b = 20
```

Here the first statement in if block has been indented using tab, whereas the second has been indented using spaces. So, on the screen the snippet looks alright, but Python interpreter will flag an error. Such errors are difficult to spot, so always use 4 spaces for indentation.

Bug 2

Missing : after if, loop, function, class.

Since other languages do not need a : those who migrate to Python from other languages tend to forget to use :.

Bug 3

Using ++ or --.

Don't increment/decrement using ++ or --. There are only two ways to increment/decrement a variable:

```
i = i + 1
i += 1
```

Bug 4

No static types for variables.

Unlike other languages, we do not have to define the type of variable. Type of the variable is determined dynamically at the time of execution based on the usage of the variable. So, in the following code snippet **a** is integer to begin with, but when the context changes its type changes to str.

```
a = 25
print(type(a))        # prints <class 'int'>
a = 'Hi'
print(type(a))        # prints <class 'str'>
```

Bug 5

Deleting an item from a list while iterating it.

```
lst = [n for n in range(10)]
for i in range(len(lst)) :
if i % 2 == 0 :
    del lst[i]
```

The correct way to do this is to use list comprehension as shown below:

```
lst = [n for n in range(10)]
lst = [n for n in lst if n % 2 != 0]
print(lst)
```

Bug 6

Improper interpretation of **range( )** function.

Remember the following for loop will generate numbers from 0 to 9 and not from 1 to 10.

```
for i in range(10) :
    print(i)
```

Bug 7

Using = in place of ==.

When performing a comparison between two objects or value, you just use the equality operator (==), not the assignment operator (=). The assignment operator places an object or value within a variable and doesn't compare anything.

Bug 8

Difference in built-in and other types while referring to objects.

```
i = 10
j = 10
a = 'Hi'
b = 'Hi'
x = [10]
y = [10]
print(id(i), id(j), id(a), id(b), id(x), id(y))
```

id( ) returns the address stored in its argument. Since **i** and **j** are referring to same int, they contain same address. Since **a** and **b** are referring to the same string, they contain same address. However, addresses stored in **x** and **y** are different as two objects each containing [10] are created.

Bug 9

Using improper case in logical values.

All keywords and operator (like **and**, **or**, **not**, **in**, **is**) are in small case, but logical values are **True** and **False** (not true and false).

Bug 10

Improper order of function calls.

While creating complex Python statements we may place function calls in wrong order producing unexpected results. For example, in the following code snippet if we change the order of the function calls, we get different results.

```
s = "  Hi  "
print(s.strip().center(21, "!"))          # prints !!!!!!!!!!Hi!!!!!!!!!
print(s.center(21, "!").strip( ))         # prints !!!!!!!!  Hi  !!!!!!!
```

Remember that Python always executes functions from left to right.

Bug 11

Improperly initializing a mutable default value for a function argument.

Consider the following code snippet:

```
def fun(lst = [ ]) :
    lst.append('Hi')
    print(lst)

fun( )        # prints ['Hi']
fun( )        # prints ['Hi', 'Hi']
```

It may appear that during each call to fun 'Hi' would be printed. However, this does not happen since the default value for a function argument is only evaluated once, at the time that the function is defined. The correct way to write this code would be:

```
def fun(lst = None) :
  if lst is None :
    lst = [ ]
  lst.append('Hi')
  print(lst)

fun( )
fun( )
```

Bug 12

Common exceptions.

The following is a list of common exceptions that occur at runtime and the reasons that cause them:

AssertionError - It is raised when the **assert** statement fails.

```
age = int(input('Enter your age: '))
assert age >= 0, 'Negative age'
```

AttributeError - It is raised when we try to use an attribute that doesn't exist.

```
s = 'Hi'
s.convert( )# str doesn't have convert( ) method
```

EOFError - It is raised when the **input( )** function hits the end-of-file condition.

ImportError - It is raised when the imported module is not found.

IndexError - It is raised when the index of a sequence is out of range.

```
lst = [10, 20, 30]
print(lst[3])
```

KeyError - It is raised when a key is not found in a dictionary.

KeyboardInterrupt - It is raised when the user hits Ctrl+c.

MemoryError - It is raised when an operation runs out of memory.

NameError - It is raised when a variable is not found in the local or global scope.

RuntimeError - It is raised when an error does not fall under any other category.

StopIteration - It is raised by the **next( )** function to indicate that there is no further item to be returned by the iterator.

TypeError - It is raised when a function or operation is applied to an object of an incorrect type.

D

Periodic Tests

"When confident, get tested..."

Periodic Test I
(Based on Chapters 1 to 6)

Time: 90 Minutes | Maximum Marks: 40

[A] Fill in the blanks: [5 Marks, 1 Mark each]

(1) In Python every entity is treated as ________.

(2) Python has ____ keywords.

(3) The function used to obtain address of an object is _________.

(4) The function used to find out whether a variable is of int type is _________.

(5) The three varieties of types in Python are ________, _______ and _________.

[B] State True or False: [5 Marks, 1 Mark each]

(1) In Python there is no need to define type of a variable.

(2) In Python an int can have any arbitrary value.

(3) A single line comment in Python language starts with # sign.

(4) Effect of switch statement can be obtained using if - elif -else.

(5) There is no do-while loop in Python.

[C] What would be the output of the following programs: [5 Marks, 1 Mark each]

(1) print(6 // 2)

(2) print(b = 3 % -2)

(3) print(c = -2 % -4)

(4) print(17 / 4)

(5) print(-5 // -3)

[D] Point out the error, if any, in the following programs: [5 Marks, 1 Mark each]

(1)
```
import math
x = 2
print(math.sqrt(x))
```

(2)
```
msg = 'C:\\newfolder\\newfile'
print('msg')
```

(3)
```
a = 4
b = 2
if a = b :
    print('Equal')
else :
    print('Unequal')
```

(4)
```
lst = ['00', '01', '02', '03']
i = 0
while i < len(lst) :
    print(i, lst[i])
    i += 1
```

(5)
```
lst = ['Lion', 'Tiger', 'Wolf', 'Cheetah']
for i, ele in enum(lst) :
    print(i, ele)
```

[E] Attempt the following questions: [20 Marks, 5 Marks each]

(1) Write a program to enter the numbers till the user wants and at the end it should display the count of positive, negative and zeros entered.

(2) Write a program to find the range of a set of numbers that are input through the keyboard. Range is the difference between the smallest and biggest numbers in the list.

(3) If three integers are entered through the keyboard, write a program to determine whether they form a Pythagorean triplet or not.

(4) Write a program to calculate the sum of the first 10 terms of the following series:

1! 2! + 2! 3! + 3! 4! + 4! 5! + ... + 9! 10!

Periodic Test II
(Based on Chapters 7 to 11)

Time: 90 Minutes Maximum Marks: 40

[A] Answer the following questions: [5 Marks, 1 Mark each]

(1) How will you create an empty list, empty tuple, empty set and empty dictionary?

(2) What is the difference between a set and a frozenset?

(3) What is wrong with the set s = {[10, 20, 30], (10, 20, 30)}?

(4) How will you convert the list [10, 20, 30, 40, 10, 30] into a list [40, 10, 20, 30] without using del( ) or remove( ) method?

(5) How will you print a float centrally justified in 10 columns, with 3 places beyond decimal point?

[B] State True or False: [5 Marks, 1 Mark each]

(1) Similar elements are usually stored in a set.

(2) Dissimilar elements are usually stored in a list.

(3) Key - value pairs are usually stored in a tuple.

(4) Unique elements are usually stored in a dictionary.

(5) Raw strings are used to format the output in a print( ) function.

[C] Match the following: [5 Marks, 1 Mark each]

a) Dictionary	1) a = set( )
b) Tuple	2) x = { }
c) Set	3) b = 'msg'
d) List	4) d = (10, 20, 30)
e) String	5) f = [10, 20, 30]

[D] Point out the error, if any, in the following programs: [5 Marks, 1 Mark each]

(1)
```
l, b, h = input('Enter length, breadth & height: ')
print(l, b, h)
```

(2)
```
lst = [11, 10, 5, 77, 24]
lst.add(45)
print(lst)
```

(3)
```
tpl = ((1, 5), (2, 3), (4, 5))
for x, y in tpl :
    print(x, y)
```

(4)
```
s = {77, 41, 22}
s.del(41)
print(s)
```

(5)
```
dct = { 'Lion' : 4, 'Tiger' : 2, 'Wolf' : 9, 'Cheetah' : 1 }
for k, v in dct.keys( ) :
    print(k, v)
```

[E] Attempt the following questions: [20 Marks, 5 Marks each]

(1) Write a program to receive the value of radius of a circle and calculate and print its area and circumference. Make sure that both values are printed in 15 columns each with 2 places beyond decimal point.

(2) A dictionary contains roll number as key and first name, middle name and last name as values. Write a program to print the dictionary items in alphabetical order by first name.

(3) A tuple contains tuples of book title and author. Write a program to print the titles and author names with first letter of each in capital and rest in small case.

(4) A list contains numbers. One of these numbers occurs only once, all others occur twice. Write a program to identify the number which occurs only once.

Periodic Test III
(Based on Chapters 12 to 17)

Time: 90 Minutes Maximum Marks: 40

[A] State True or False: [5 Marks, 1 Mark each]

(1) We cannot create a tuple using comprehension.

(2) A Python function can receive Positional arguments, Keyword arguments, Variable-length positional arguments and Variable-length keyword arguments.

(3) When we execute a program its module name is __module__ and it is available in the variable __name__.

(4) Functions show( ) and display( ) defined in a module functions can be used by importing them using the statement:

import show, display

(5) For a directory to be treated as a package it must contain a file named __init__.py in it.

[B] Answer the following questions: [10 Marks, 1 Mark each]

(1) How will you receive 4 numbers as input from keyboard using list comprehension?

(2) How will you generate 20 random numbers in the range 10 to 100 using list comprehension?

(3) How will you generate the following list using comprehension?

[[25, 125], [36, 216], [49, 343], [64, 512], [81, 729], [100, 1000]]

(4) How will you create a set of even numbers in the range 10 to 30 using comprehension?

(5) How will you delete all numbers having a value between 20 and 50 from the following list using comprehension?

lst = [10, 3, 4, 5, 15, 20, 21, 23, 46, 50]

(6) Using dictionary comprehension how will you convert

d = {'AMOL': 20, 'ANIL': 12, 'SUNIL': 13, 'RAMESH': 10}

into

{'Amol': 400, 'Anil': 144, 'Sunil': 169, 'Ramesh': 100}

(7) Consider the following code snippet:

```
def print_it(a, b, c, d, e) :
    print(a, b, c, d, e)

tpl = ('A', 'B', 'C', 'D', 'E')
```

How will you pass all elements of a tuple t to a function print_it( )?

(8) Consider the following code snippet:

```
def print_it(i, j, *args, x, y, **kwargs) :
    pass

print_it(10, 20, 100, 200, x = 30, y = 40)
```

What gets passed to args and kwargs?

(9) If a function cal_sum( ) receives 3 integers and returns their sum, which of the following calls to a function cal_sum( ) are acceptable?

i. sum = cal_sum(a, b, c)
ii. print(cal_sum(a, b, c))
iii. sum = cal_sum(a, calSum(25, 10, 4), b)

(10) Consider the following code snippet:

```
def print_it(**kwargs) :
    pass

dct = {'Student' : 'Ajay', 'Age' : 23}
```

Which is the CORRECT way to pass dct to print_it( )?

[C] Attempt the following questions: **[25 Marks, 5 Marks each]**

(1) Write a program that converts list of temperature in Celsius degrees to equivalent Fahrenheit using list comprehension.

(2) Write a recursive function to obtain sum of first 25 natural numbers.

(3) A string is entered through the keyboard. Write a recursive function that counts the number of capital letters in this string.

(4) Write a program (using functional programming) to prepend a string 'Hi ' to every element in a list of strings.

(5) Suppose a dictionary contains names of students and marks obtained by them in an examination. Write a program (using functional programming) to obtain a list of students who obtained less than 40 marks in the examination.

Periodic Test IV
(Based on Chapters 18 to 21)

Time: 90 Minutes Maximum Marks: 40

[A] Fill in the blanks: [4 Marks, 1 Mark each]

(1) Every class is derived from an ________ class.

(2) ________ and ________ reuse mechanisms are provided in Python.

(3) When we are using containership, we are doing ______ code level reuse.

(4) Generator functions create ________.

[B] State True or False: [12 Marks, 1 Mark each]

(1) Construction of an object always proceeds from derived towards base.

(2) From an abstract class an object cannot be created.

(3) On calling an instance method of an object, address of the object always gets passed to it.

(4) Iterable(s) cannot be passed to a zip( ) function.

(5) In containership an object is nested inside another object.

(6) +, - and * operators have been overloaded in str class.

(7) The + operator has been overloaded in str, list and int classes.

(8) It is possible to call a global function, another class method and instance method from a class method.

(9) The size of the object is influenced by instance data, class data, global data and local variables.

(10) Class methods can access class data and global data.

(11) If NewSample class is derived from Sample class and an object of NewSample is created then __init__( ) of Sample class followed by __init__( ) of NewSample class will be called.

(12) A generator expression generates the next element on demand, rather than generating all elements upfront.

[C] Answer the following: **[14 Marks, 5 Marks each]**

(1) Separate the following into classes and objects:

Bird, Player, Crow, Raj, Eagle, Flower, Rose, Lily, Flute, Instrument

(2) How will you create an object of a Trial class?

(3) Which of the following can be done with regards to a class?

i. A class can be inherited from another class
ii. A class can be defined inside another class

(4) What does the following code do?

```
e = Sample( )
```

(5) What happens when control returns from fun( )?

```
def func( ) :
    t = new Tiral( )
```

(6) How many arguments will be passed to the __init__( ) in the following statement?

```
t = Trial(10, 3.14, 'Hello')
```

(7) How many times does the __init__( ) of Student class get called on execution of the following code snippet?

```
lst = [ ]
lst.append(Sample('Raju', 25))
lst.append(Sample('Anand', 34))
```

(8) How should show( ) be defined in Example class?

```
e = Example( )
e.show('A', '3.14, 10, 20, 30)
```

(9) To overload the % operator, which method should be defined in the corresponding class?

(10) To overload the //= operator, which method should be defined in the corresponding class?

(11) How will you prevent a new class from getting inherited from an existing class Employee?

(12) Suppose a base class contains two instance variables x, y and one class variable z. A class derived from it contains an instance variable a, and two class variables b and c. What will the derived class object contain?

(13) What does an __iter__( ) function of list or str return?

(14) What will be the output of the following code snippet?

```
lst = ['A', 20, 'C', 4.50]
item = lst.__iter__( )
print(item.__next__( ))
```

[D] Attempt the following: **[10 Marks, 5 Marks each]**

(1) Write a program that implements a Person class containing name, and age. Derive a class Student from Person class and maintain roll number and marks in 3 subjects in it. Create a list of 5 Student objects and fill them with suitable values through the class constructors. Define a class method display( ) to print the list contents on the screen.

(2) Create two lists, one containing names of fruits and another containing their corresponding weights. Write a program to take the two lists as input and create a dictionary containing name of fruit as the key and weight as value.

Periodic Test V
(Based on Chapters 22 to 26)

Time: 90 Minutes Maximum Marks: 40

[A] Fill in the blanks: [5 Marks, 1 Mark each]

(1) A Python decorator begins with ____.

(2) Arguments passed to a Python script are available in variable ________.

(3) The command-line arguments passed to a script can be parsed using ________ function.

(4) In Unicode every character is assigned an integer value called _________ which are usually expressed in hexadecimal.

(5) Communication between threads can be done using ________ or _________ object.

[B] State True or False: [10 Marks, 1 Mark each]

(1) In Parallelism multiple threads are running at the same time.

(2) In Concurrency, at any given time only one thread is running.

(3) Performance of I/O-bound program can improve if different units of the program are executed in overlapping times.

(4) It is quite easy to imagine how performance of a CPU-bound program can improve with parallelism.

(5) A 100-meter race is a good example of concurrency.

(6) Order of except blocks matters.

(7) Assertion performs run-time checks of assumptions.

(8) Serialization means writing objects to a file.

(9) 'r+' and 'w+' modes are same since both permit reading from and writing to a file.

(10) When with keyword is used for opening a file, the file gets closed as soon as its usage is over.

[C] Answer the following questions: [10 Marks, 1 Mark each]

(1) Which out of syntax error, logical error and exception occurs at the time of execution?

(2) How will you apply a decorator @yk_decorator to a function fun( )?

(3) Consider the following code snippet:

```
def yk_decorator(func) :
    def wrapper( ) :
        print('###############')
        func( )
        print('###############')
```

which statement will you add at the end of this code snippet to make the decorator work?

(4) If we execute a script as

C:\>sample.py cat dog parrot

How will you access 'C:\>sample.py'?

(5) If a script is executed as

C:\>filecopy.py -s sourcefilename -t targetfilename

then how will you parse the arguments using getopt( ) function?

(6) What will be the output of the following code snippet?

```
import sys, getopt
sys.argv =['C:\\a.py', '-h', 'word1', 'word2']
options, arguments = getopt.getopt(sys.argv[1:],'s:t:h')
print(options)
print(arguments)
```

(7) How will you launch a function fun( ) in a thread and pass arguments a, b, c to it?

(8) How will you check whether 5th and 7th bit in num are on or off?

(9) How will you store a hexadecimal value E0A485 in a bytes data type?

(10) How many except blocks will you write if the same action is to be taken in case of 3 exceptions?

[D] Attempt the following questions: [15 Marks, 5 Marks each]

(1) Write a program that defines a function to calculate the value of c using following formula. Perform proper exception handling.

c = ((a + b) / (a - b))

(2) A file 'sent.txt' contains multiple lines, each containing multiple words. Write a program to find the longest words in the file.

(3) Define a decorator function @timer which calculates the time required to execute any function. Use this decorator to time the function factorial( ) while calculating factorial values of 7, 10 and 25.

I

Index

"Random access begins here..."

A

B

C

D

E

T

U

V

W

X

Y

Z